Twin Star Exorcists

ONMYOJI

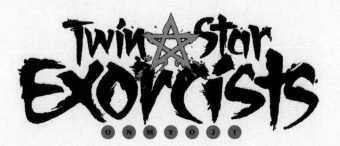

Twin Star Exorcists

ONMYOJI

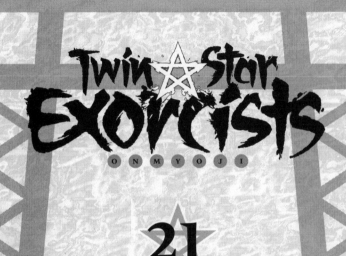

21

STORY & ART

YOSHIAKI SUKENO

Character Introduction

Arimori Tsuchimikado

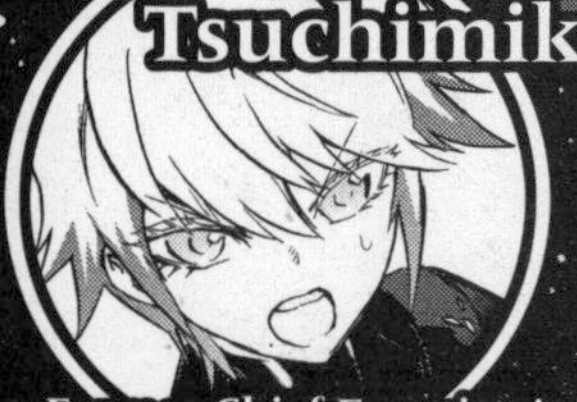

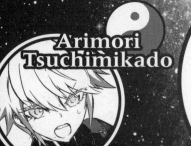

Former Chief Exorcist Arima's son. He used to be a member of the Enmado Clan but returned to the Tsuchimikado Family to assume the position of family head after the death of his father.

Mayura Otomi

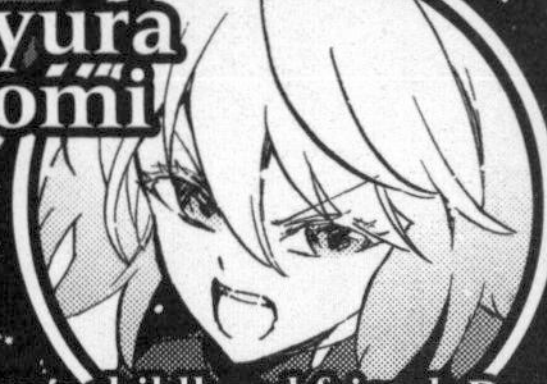

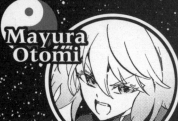

Rokuro's childhood friend. During a fierce battle in Magano, her commitment to protecting others earned her the guardian White Tiger. She has become the new head of the Amawaka Family.

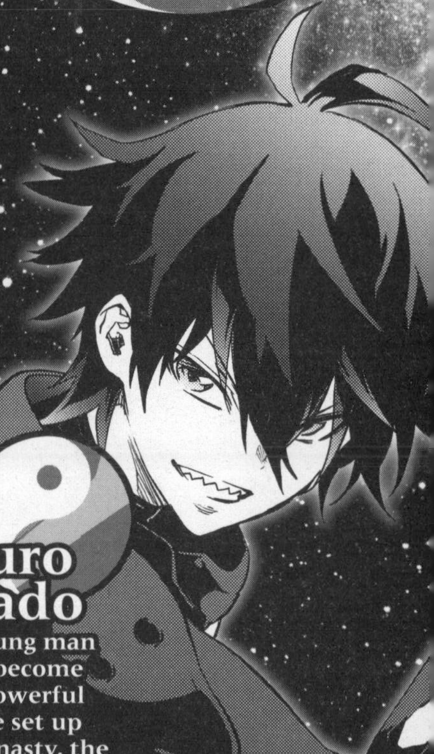

Rokuro Enmado

A brave young man striving to become the most powerful exorcist. He set up his own dynasty, the Enmado Family, on Tsuchimikado Island to settle his score with his archenemy Yuto. He defeated Yuto after receiving a new power from Arima Tsuchimikado and with the aid of Benio.

Story Thus Far...

Kegare are creatures from Magano, the underworld, and it is the duty of an exorcist to hunt, exorcise and purify them. Rokuro and Benio are the Twin Star Exorcists, fated to bear the Prophesied Child who will defeat the Kegare. Their goal in their early teens is to go to the exorcist's headquarters on Tsuchimikado Island to train and defeat Yuto, Benio's twin brother and the murderer of Rokuro's childhood friends.

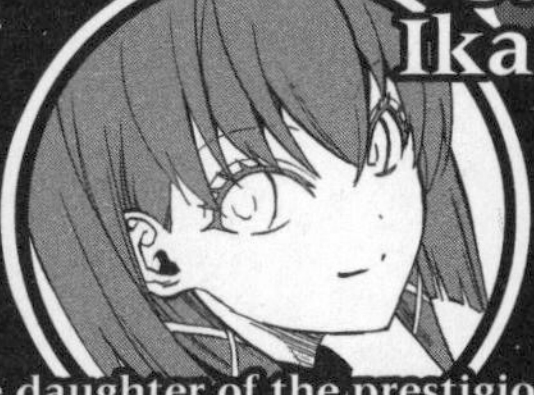

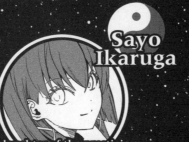

Sayo Ikaruga

The daughter of the prestigious Ikaruga Family of Tsuchimikado Island. She and Shimon grew up like siblings. Her Spiritual Guardian is Kuzu no Ha, the mother of Abeno Seimei. She has a crush on Rokuro.

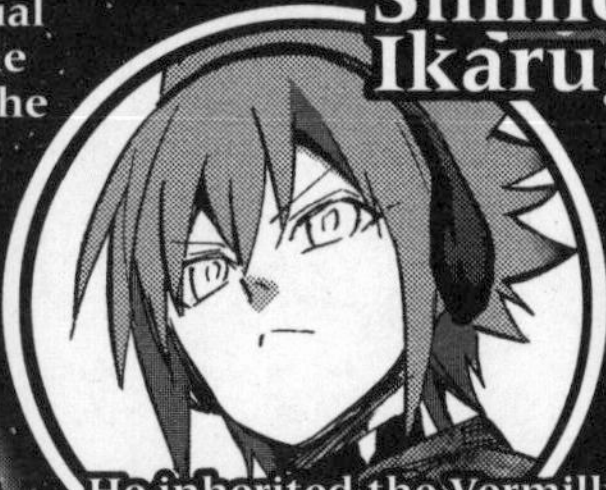

Shimon Ikaruga

He inherited the Vermillion Bird guardian when he was just 14. At the Imperial Tournament, Tenma went out of control and cut off Shimon's right leg, but fitted out with a new prosthetic leg, he joined the battle against Yuto.

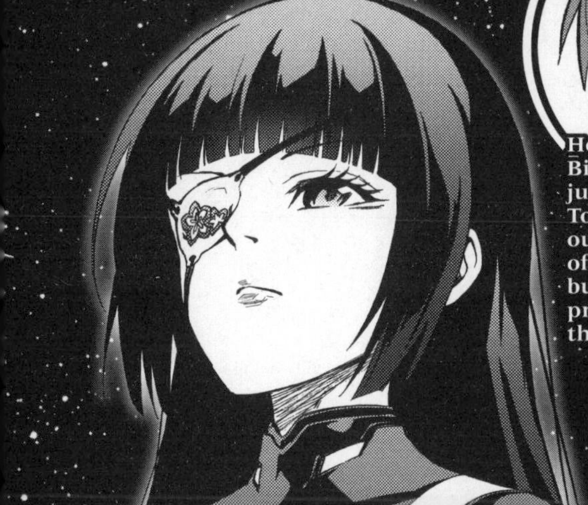

Benio Adashino

The daughter of a once-prestigious family of exorcists who dreams of a world free of Kegare. She went to meet the Basara Chinu, in order to retrieve her spiritual power and discovered that she was the Great Yin. She went missing in battle with the warped Basara Kaguya, but reappeared in the nick of time...

But before they depart, Benio loses her spiritual power in battle, and Rokuro must go alone. As older teens, while Rokuro trains with the other exorcists, Benio journeys into Magano to regain her powers and learns the chilling truth about the origins of the Kegare. Then, when Yuto and an army of Basara launch an all-out attack, many exorcists, including Chief Exorcist Arima, are killed. Finally, Yuto and Rokuro face off. In the nick of time, a newly powerful Benio returns, and together the reunited Twin Star Exorcists finally defeat their archenemy! After the battle, Benio reveals to Rokuro that she has been transformed into a Kegare known as the Great Yin. Rokuro is unfazed, and the two confess their feelings for each other. Four years later, Rokuro and Benio are 20 years old and ready for a new chapter in their lives...

Twin Star Exorcists

ONMYOJI

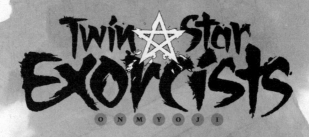

EXORCISMS

21

ONMYOJI have worked for the Imperial Court since the Heian era. In addition to exorcising evil spirits, as civil servants they performed a variety of roles, including advising nobles by foretelling the future, creating the calendar, observing the movements of the stars, measuring time...

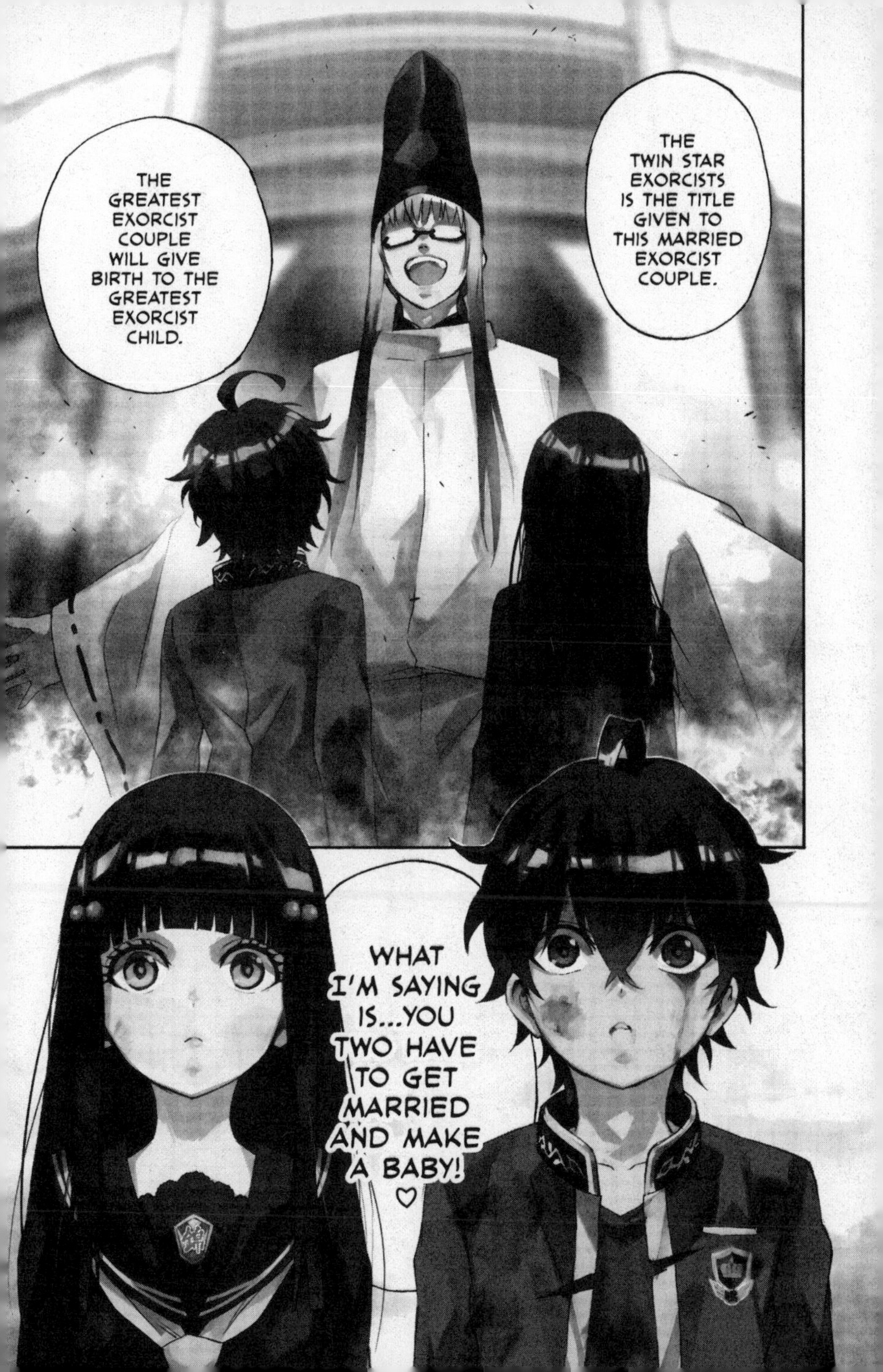
THE TWIN STAR EXORCISTS IS THE TITLE GIVEN TO THIS MARRIED EXORCIST COUPLE.
THE GREATEST EXORCIST COUPLE WILL GIVE BIRTH TO THE GREATEST EXORCIST CHILD.
WHAT I'M SAYING IS...YOU TWO HAVE TO GET MARRIED AND MAKE A BABY! ♡

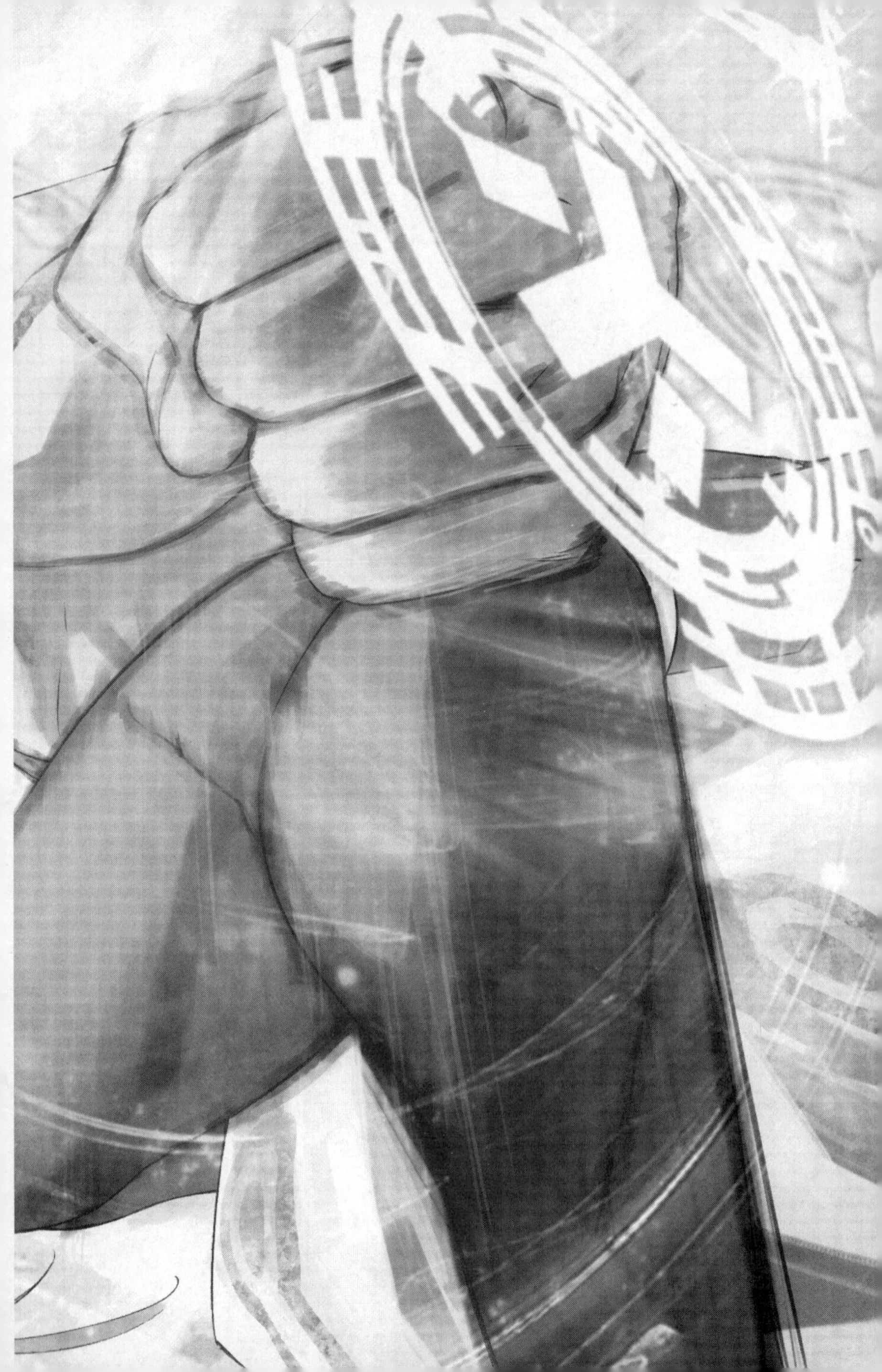

#77 The Grown-Up Twin Stars

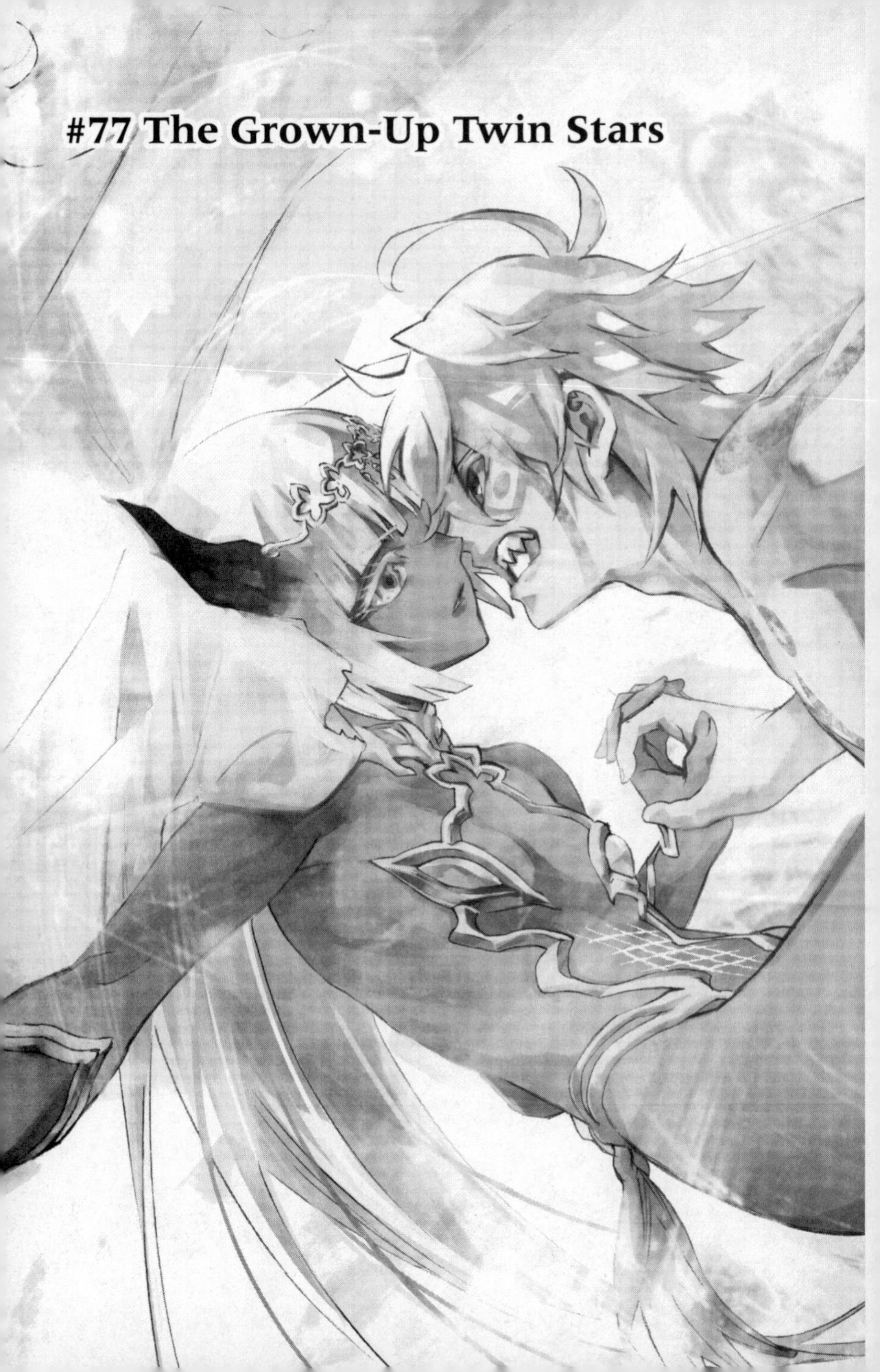

Twin Star Exorcists

ONMYOJI

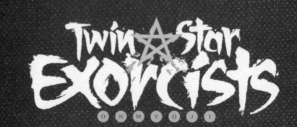

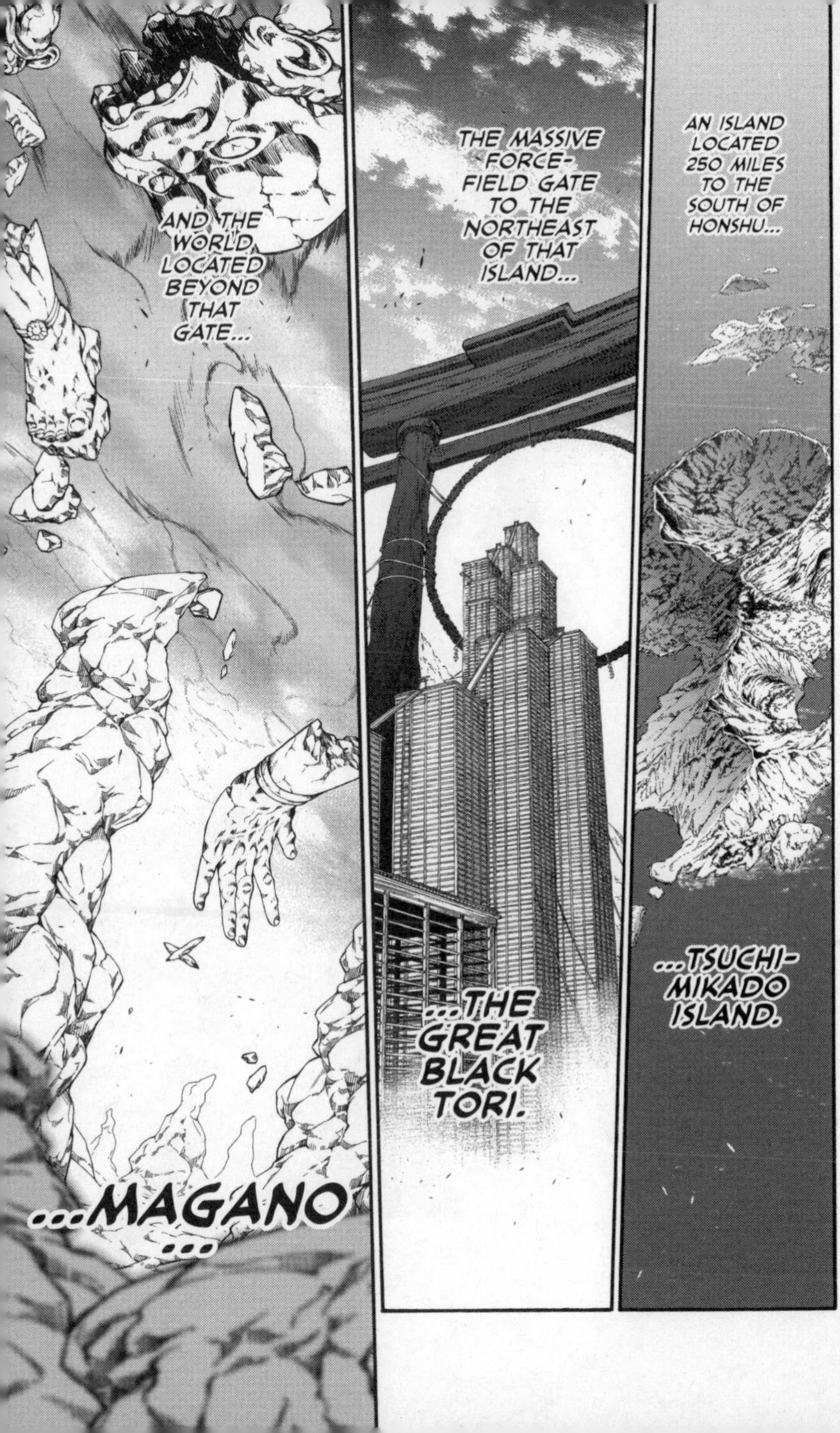
AN ISLAND LOCATED 250 MILES TO THE SOUTH OF HONSHU...
...TSUCHI-MIKADO ISLAND.
THE MASSIVE FORCE-FIELD GATE TO THE NORTHEAST OF THAT ISLAND...
...THE GREAT BLACK TORI.
AND THE WORLD LOCATED BEYOND THAT GATE...
...MAGANO...

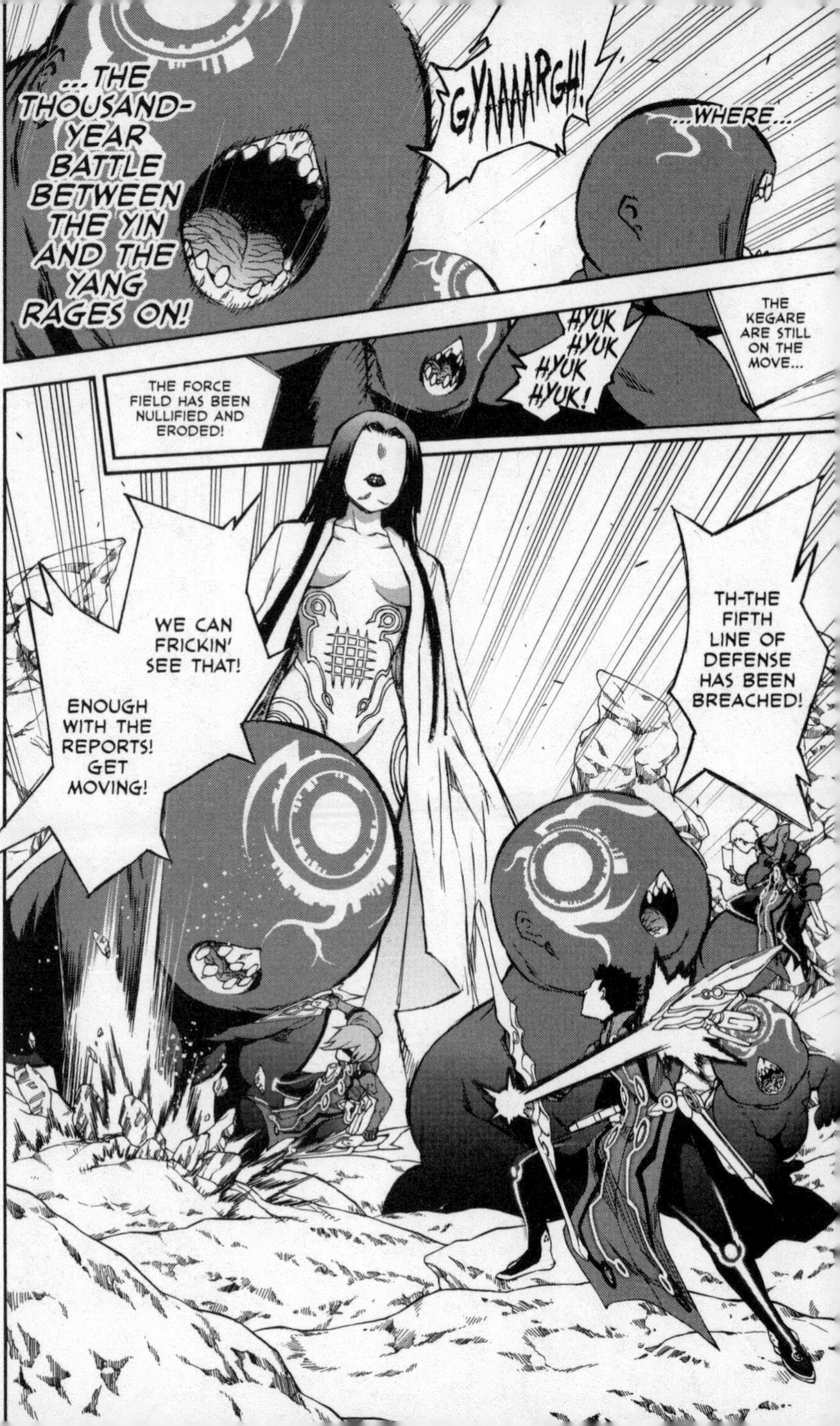
...WHERE...
GYAAAARGH!
...THE THOUSAND-YEAR BATTLE BETWEEN THE YIN AND THE YANG RAGES ON!
THE KEGARE ARE STILL ON THE MOVE...
HYUK HYUK HYUK HYUK!
THE FORCE FIELD HAS BEEN NULLIFIED AND ERODED!
TH-THE FIFTH LINE OF DEFENSE HAS BEEN BREACHED!
WE CAN FRICKIN' SEE THAT!
ENOUGH WITH THE REPORTS! GET MOVING!

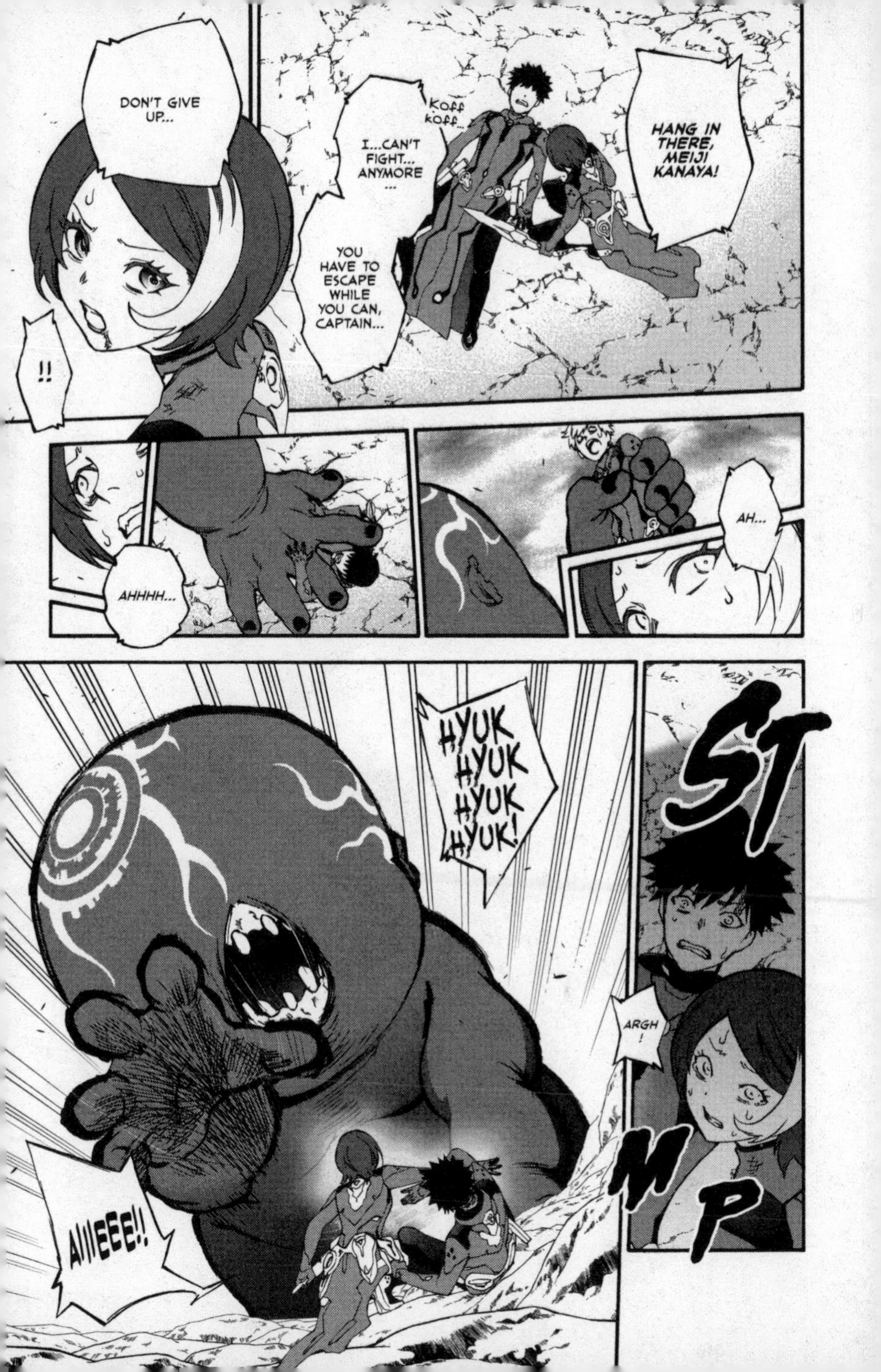
HANG IN THERE, MEIJI KANAYA!
Koff koff...
I...CAN'T FIGHT... ANYMORE...
YOU HAVE TO ESCAPE WHILE YOU CAN, CAPTAIN...
DON'T GIVE UP...
!!
AH...
AHHHH...
ST M P
ARGH!
HYUK HYUK HYUK HYUK!
AIIIEEE!!

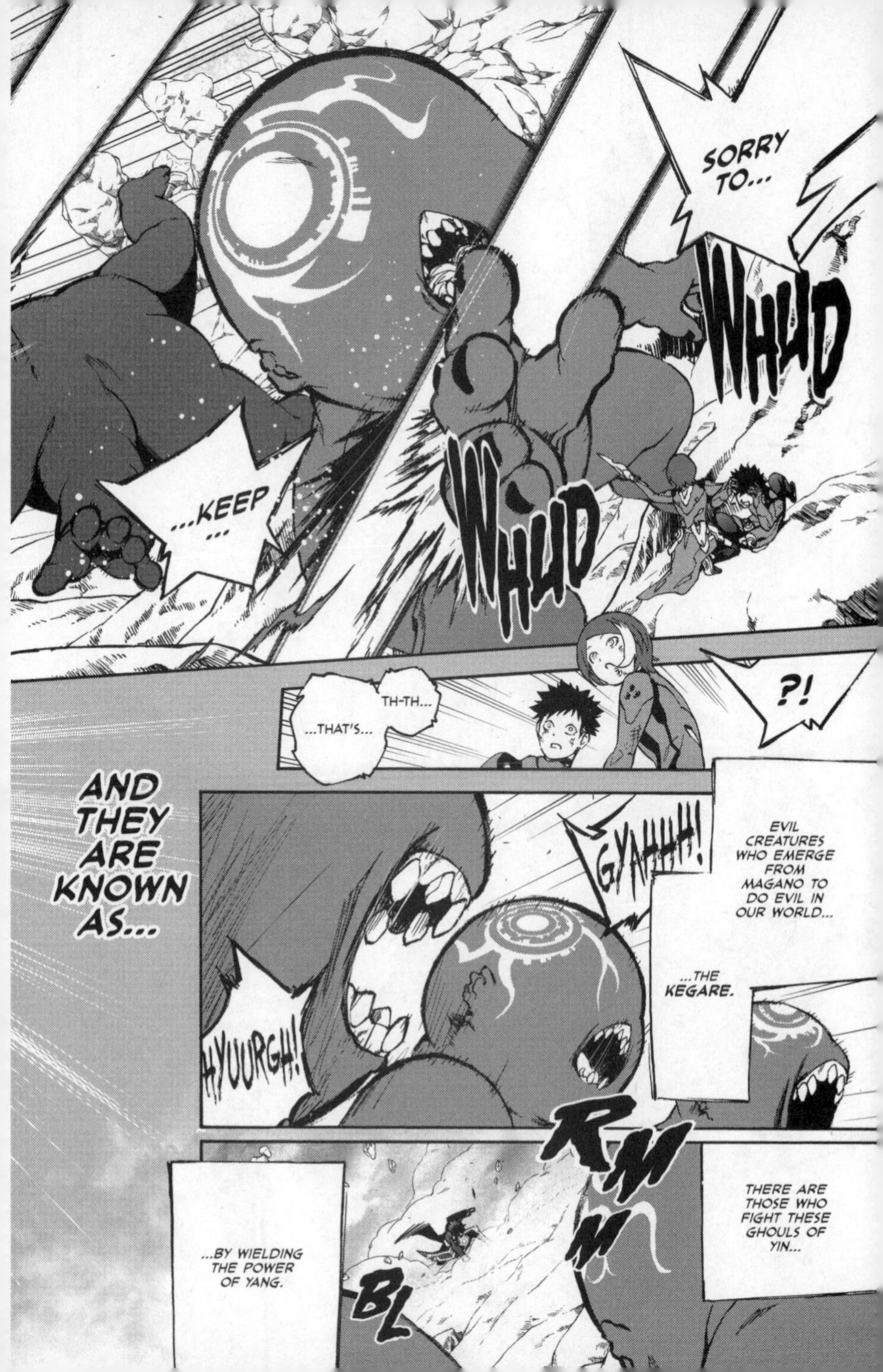
SORRY TO...
WHUD
WHUD
...KEEP...
?!
TH-TH...
...THAT'S...
EVIL CREATURES WHO EMERGE FROM MAGANO TO DO EVIL IN OUR WORLD...
AND THEY ARE KNOWN AS...
...THE KEGARE.
GYAHHH!
HYUURGH!
THERE ARE THOSE WHO FIGHT THESE GHOULS OF YIN...
RMM
BL
...BY WIELDING THE POWER OF YANG.

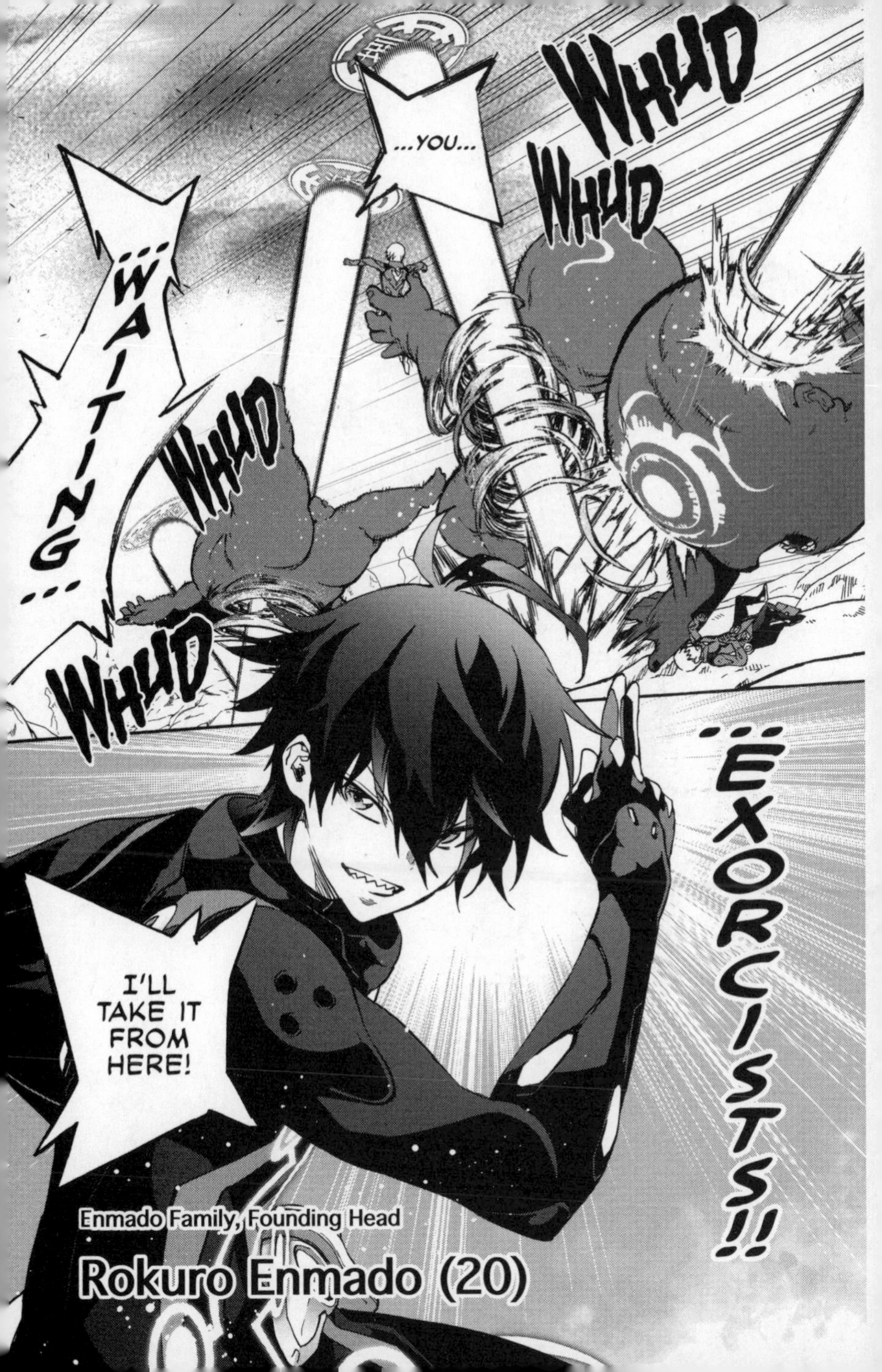
WHUD
WHUD
...YOU...
...WAITING...
WHUD
WHUD
...EXORCISTS!!
I'LL TAKE IT FROM HERE!
Enmado Family, Founding Head
Rokuro Enmado (20)

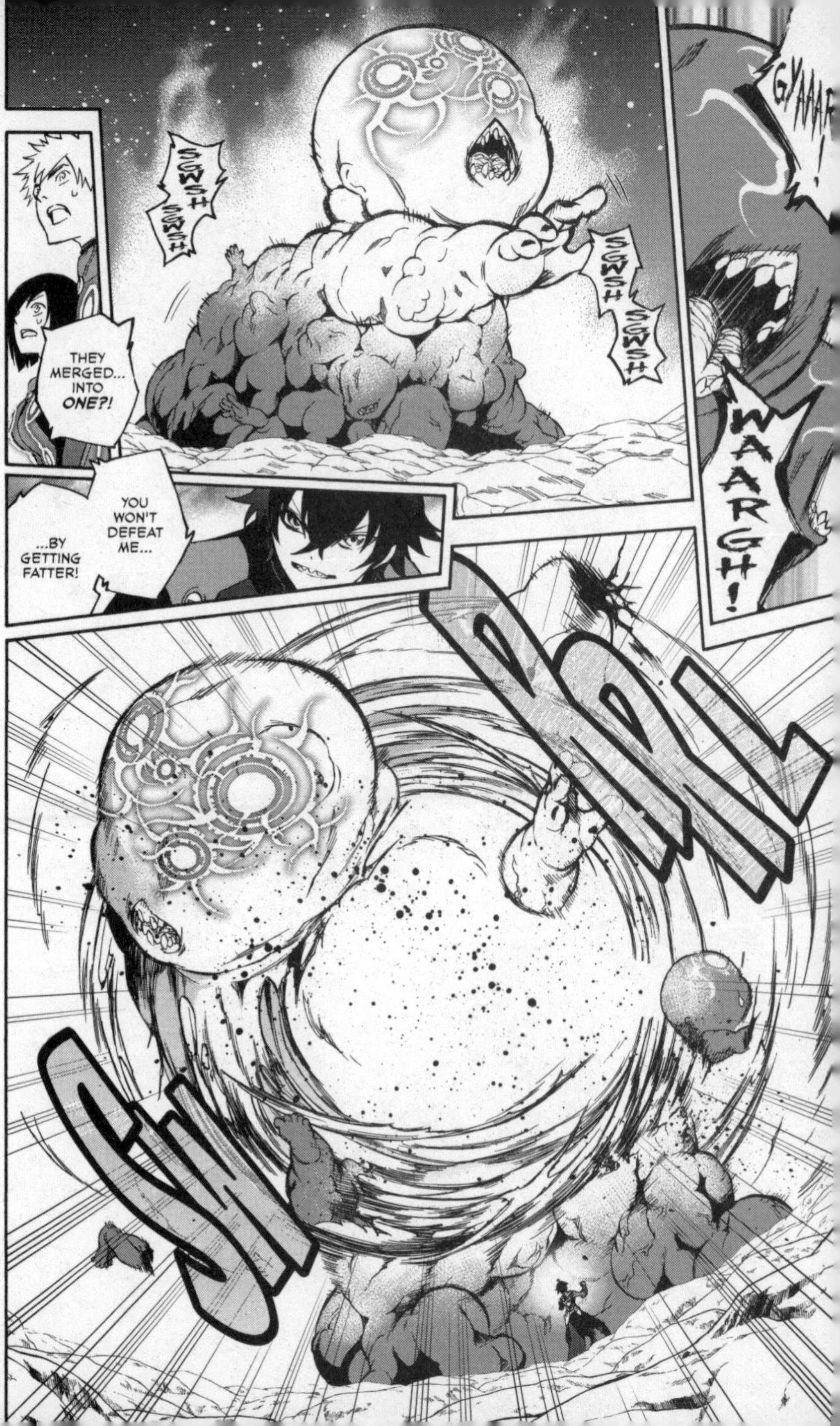
GYAAAR!
WAARGH!
SGWSH SGWSH
SGWSH SGWSH
THEY MERGED... INTO ONE?!
YOU WON'T DEFEAT ME...
...BY GETTING FATTER!

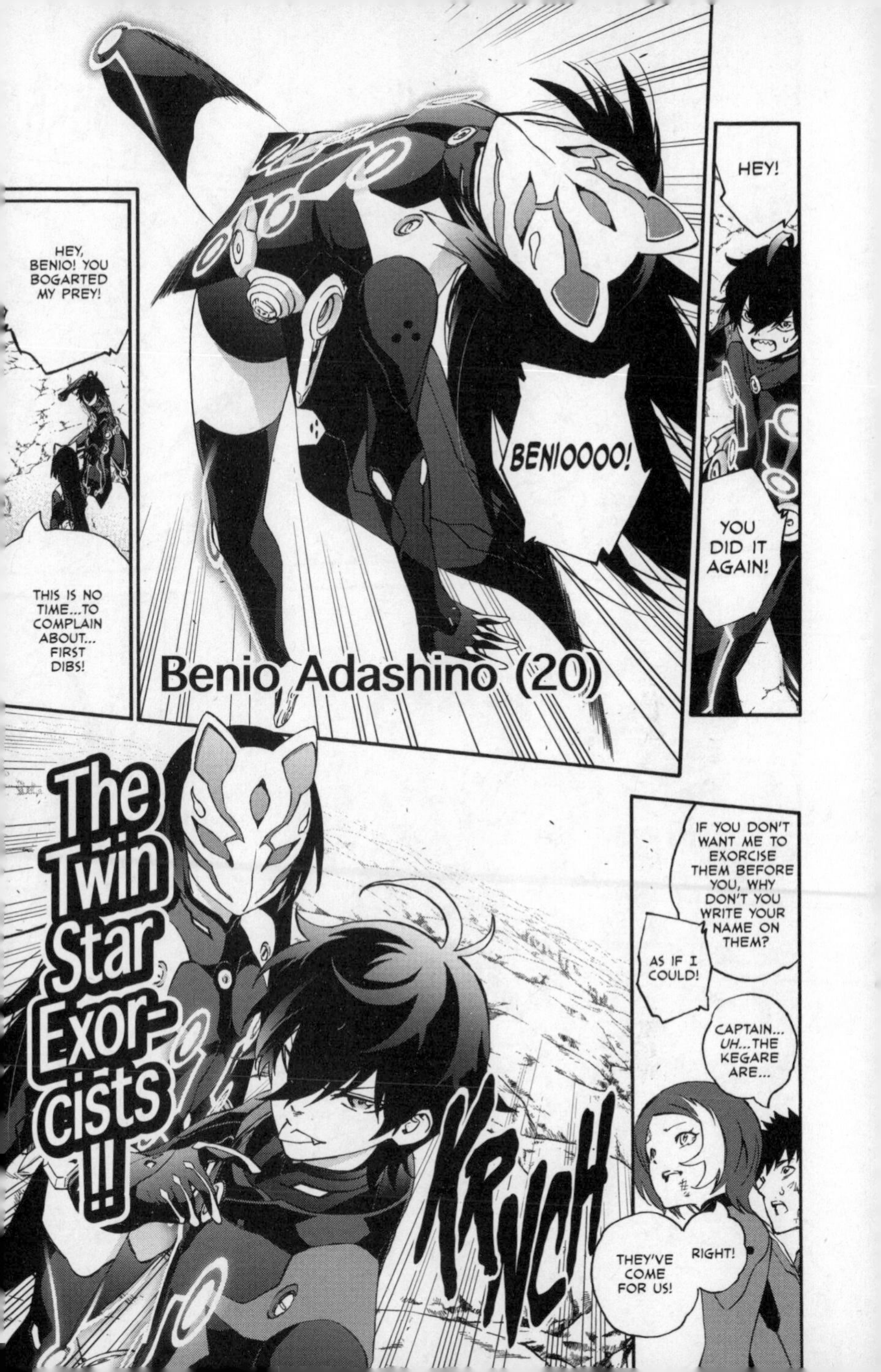
HEY!
YOU DID IT AGAIN!
BENIOOOO!
Benio Adashino (20)
HEY, BENIO! YOU BOGARTED MY PREY!
THIS IS NO TIME...TO COMPLAIN ABOUT... FIRST DIBS!
IF YOU DON'T WANT ME TO EXORCISE THEM BEFORE YOU, WHY DON'T YOU WRITE YOUR NAME ON THEM?
AS IF I COULD!
CAPTAIN... *UH*...THE KEGARE ARE...
RIGHT!
THEY'VE COME FOR US!
KRUNCH
The Twin Star Exor-cists!!

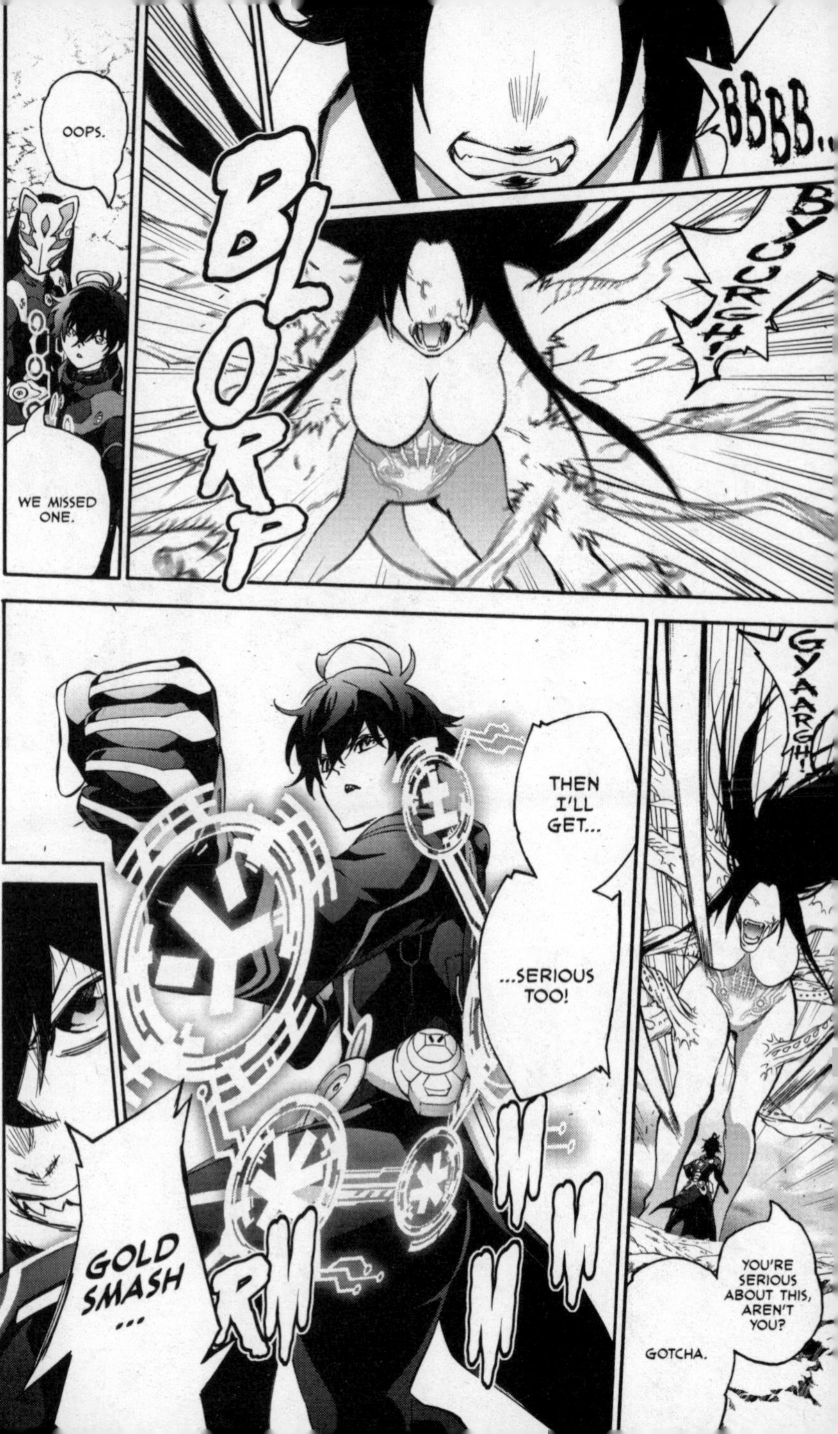
BBBB...
BYUURGH!
BLORP
OOPS.
WE MISSED ONE.
GYAARGH!
YOU'RE SERIOUS ABOUT THIS, AREN'T YOU?
GOTCHA.
THEN I'LL GET...
...SERIOUS TOO!
RMMMM
GOLD SMASH...

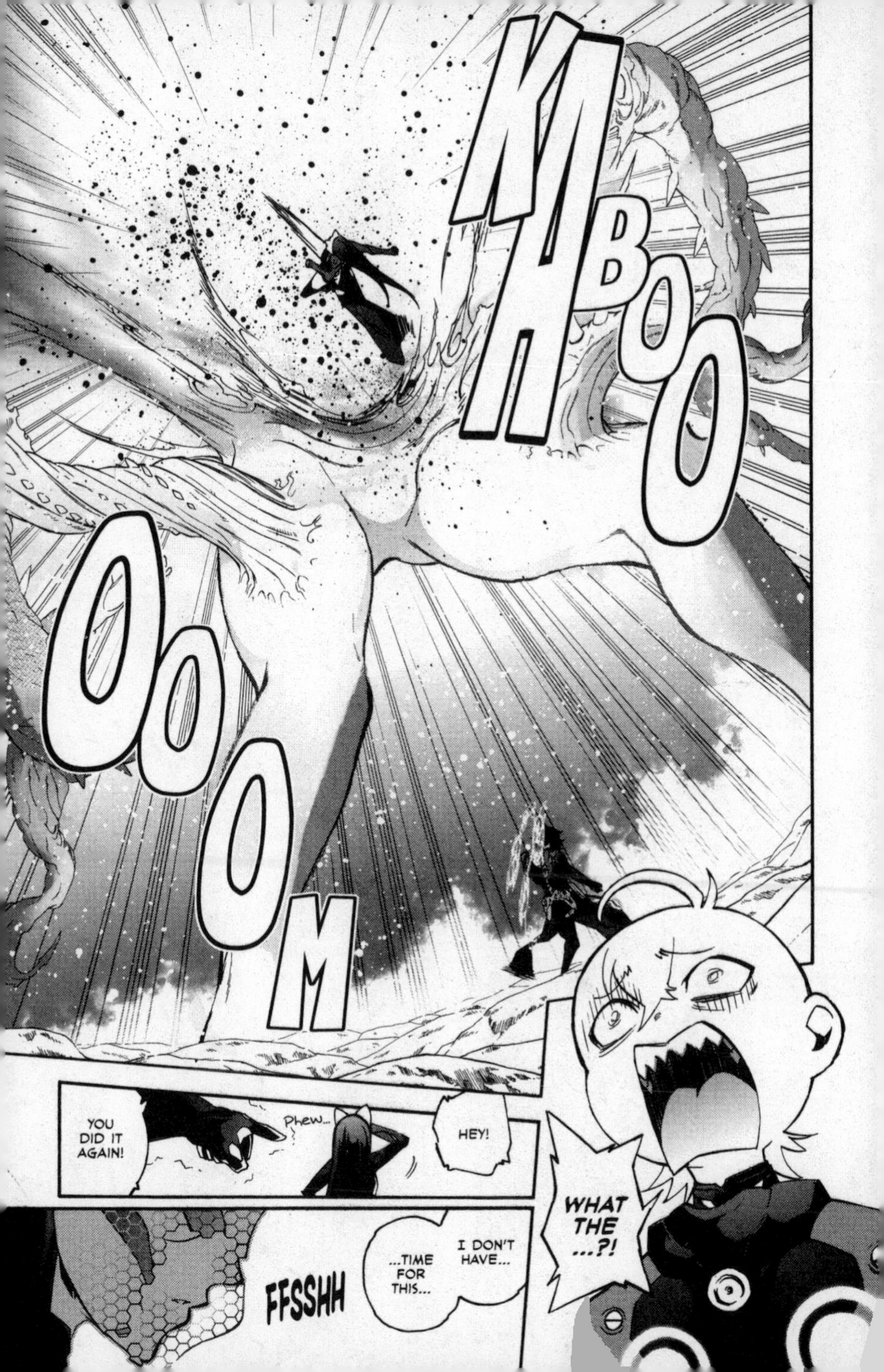
KABOOOOOOM
WHAT THE ...?!
HEY!
Phew...
YOU DID IT AGAIN!
I DON'T HAVE...
...TIME FOR THIS...
FFSSHH

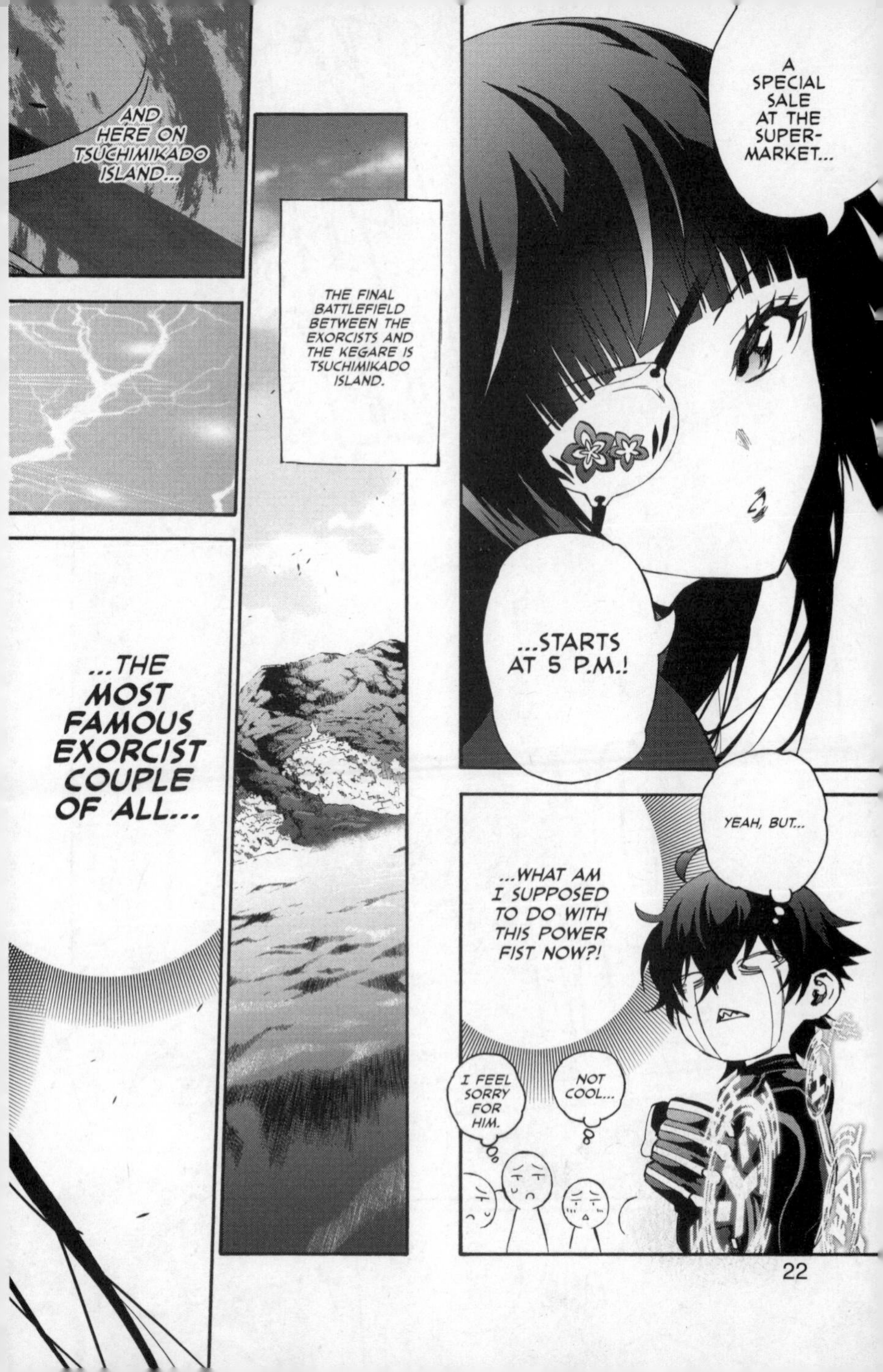
A SPECIAL SALE AT THE SUPER-MARKET...
...STARTS AT 5 P.M.!
YEAH, BUT...
...WHAT AM I SUPPOSED TO DO WITH THIS POWER FIST NOW?!
NOT COOL...
I FEEL SORRY FOR HIM.
THE FINAL BATTLEFIELD BETWEEN THE EXORCISTS AND THE KEGARE IS TSUCHIMIKADO ISLAND.
AND HERE ON TSUCHIMIKADO ISLAND...
...THE MOST FAMOUS EXORCIST COUPLE OF ALL...

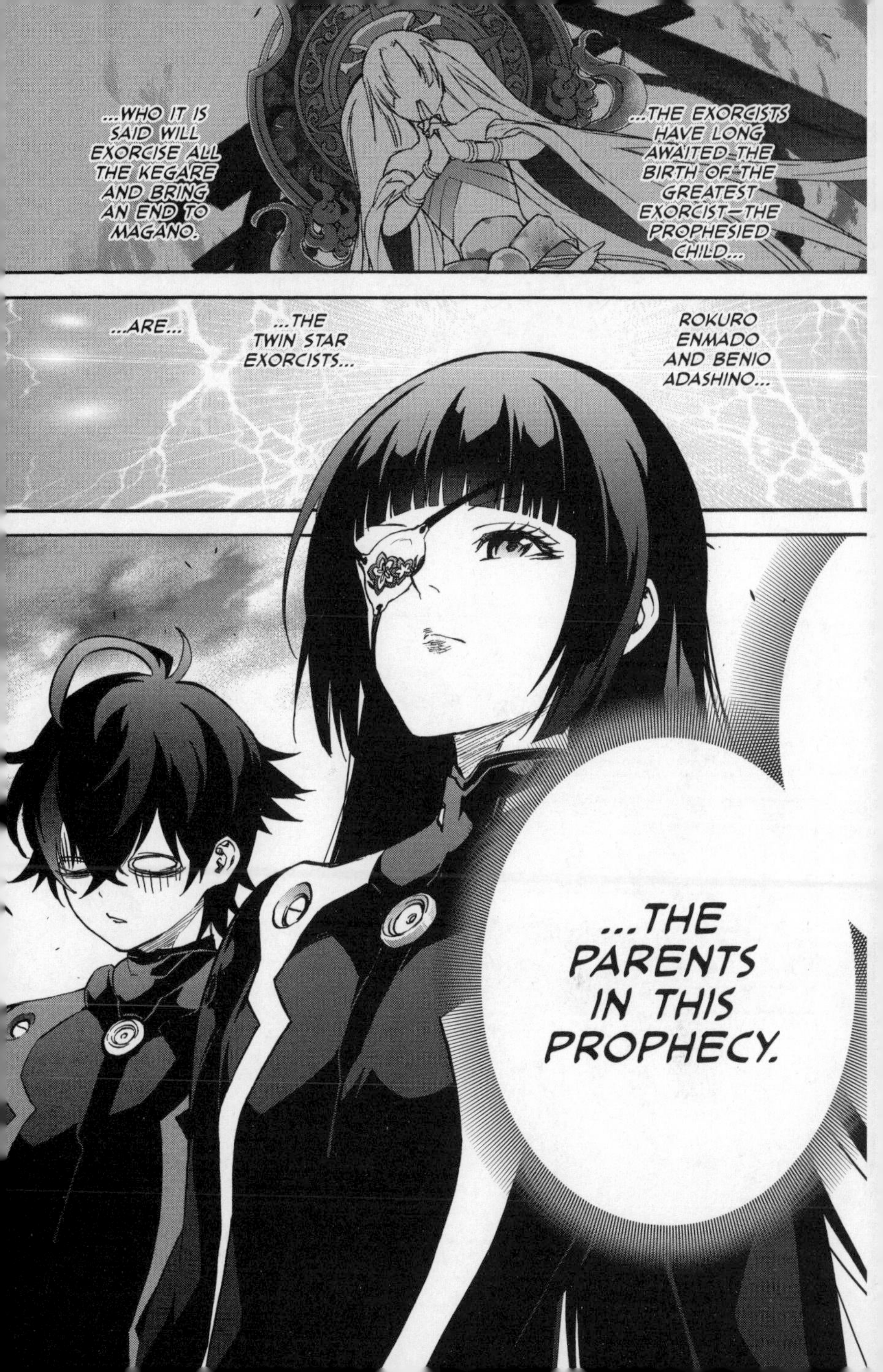
...THE EXORCISTS HAVE LONG AWAITED THE BIRTH OF THE GREATEST EXORCIST—THE PROPHESIED CHILD...
...WHO IT IS SAID WILL EXORCISE ALL THE KEGARE AND BRING AN END TO MAGANO.
ROKURO ENMADO AND BENIO ADASHINO...
...THE TWIN STAR EXORCISTS...
...ARE...
...THE PARENTS IN THIS PROPHECY.

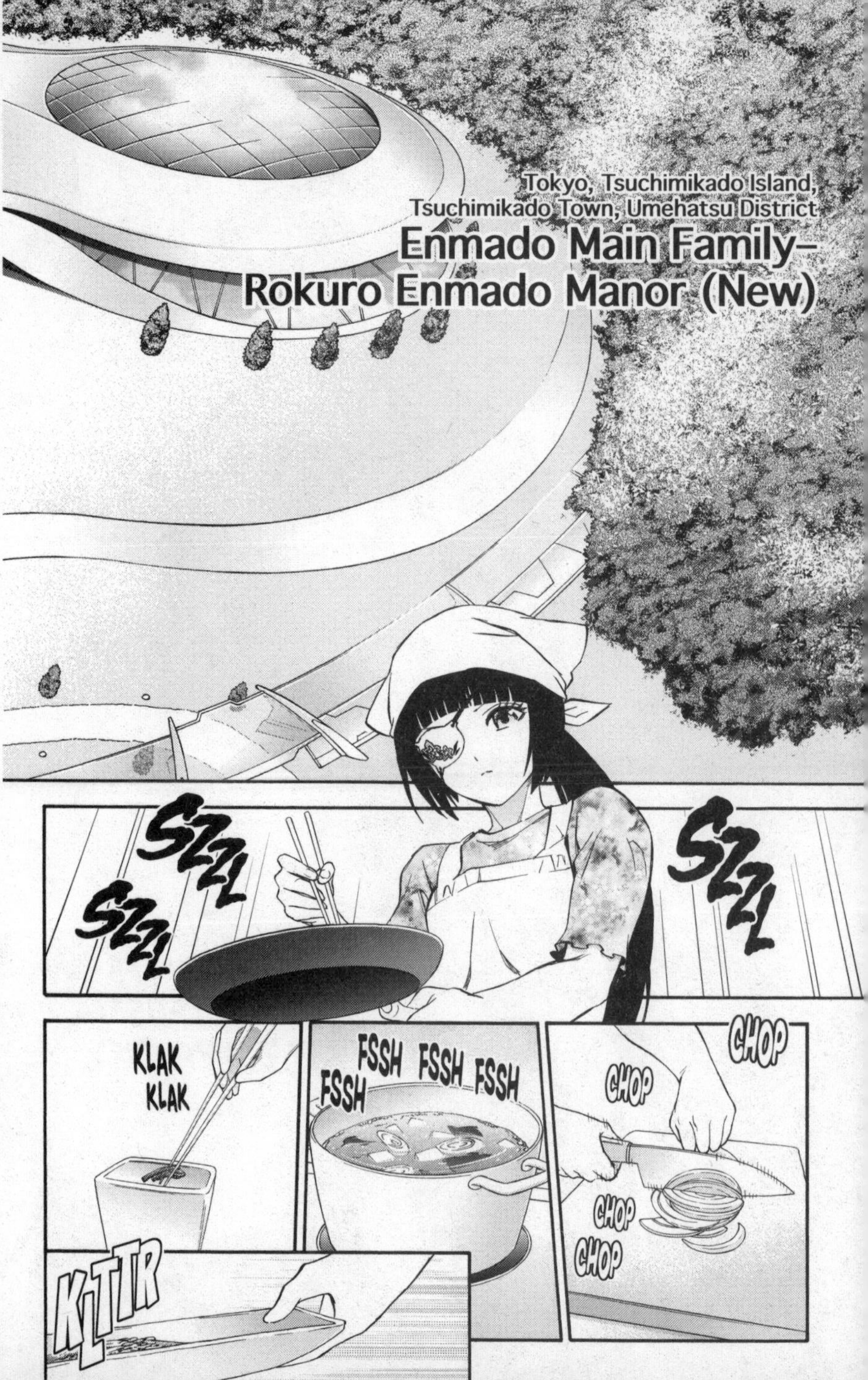
Tokyo, Tsuchimikado Island,
Tsuchimikado Town, Umehatsu District
Enmado Main Family–
Rokuro Enmado Manor (New)
SZZZL
SZZZL
SZZZL
CHOP
CHOP
CHOP
CHOP
FSSH FSSH FSSH
FSSH
KLAK
KLAK
KLTTR

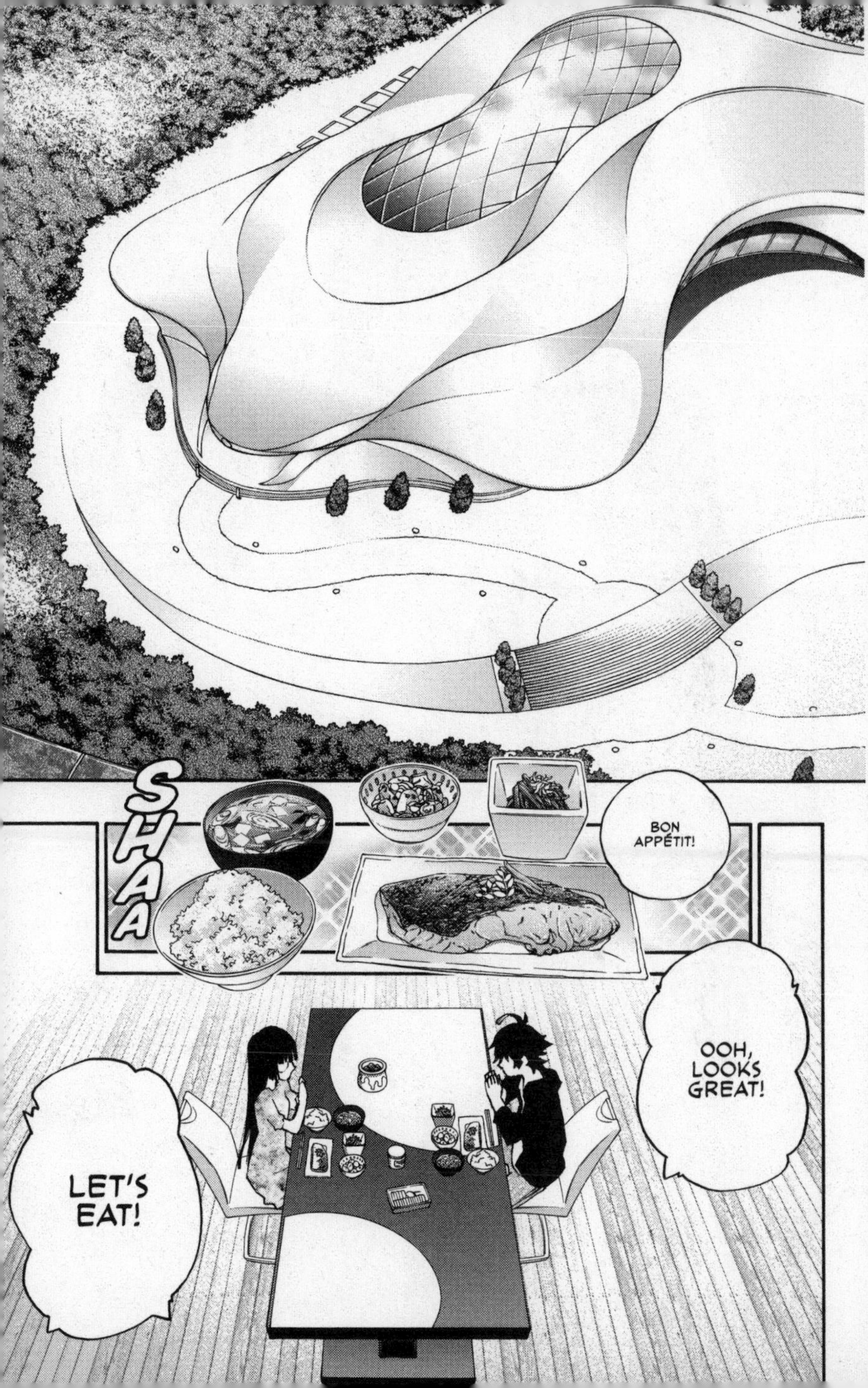
BON APPÉTIT!
SHAA
OOH, LOOKS GREAT!
LET'S EAT!

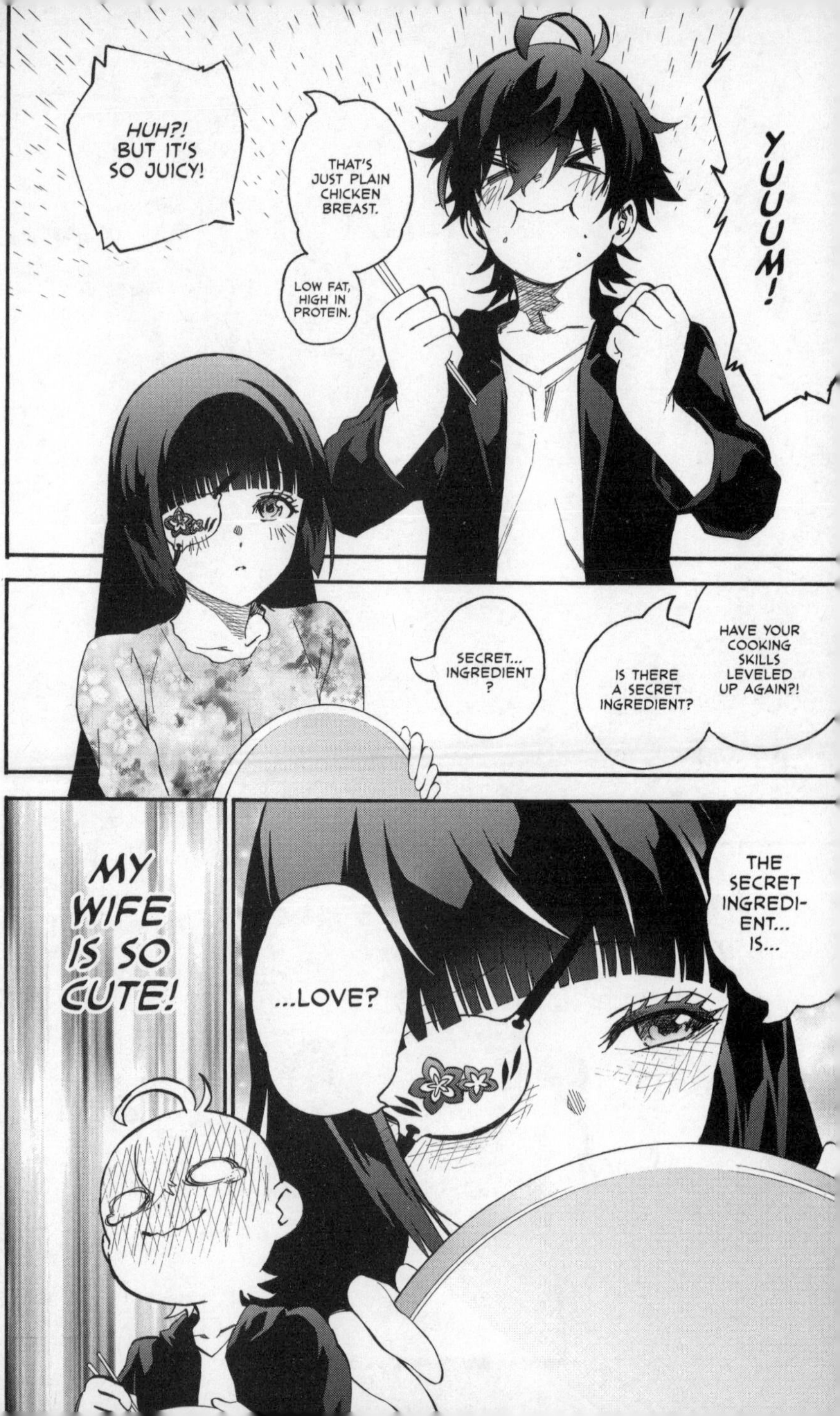
YUUUM!
THAT'S JUST PLAIN CHICKEN BREAST.
LOW FAT, HIGH IN PROTEIN.
HUH?! BUT IT'S SO JUICY!
HAVE YOUR COOKING SKILLS LEVELED UP AGAIN?!
IS THERE A SECRET INGREDIENT?
SECRET... INGREDIENT?
THE SECRET INGREDI-ENT... IS...
...LOVE?
MY WIFE IS SO CUTE!

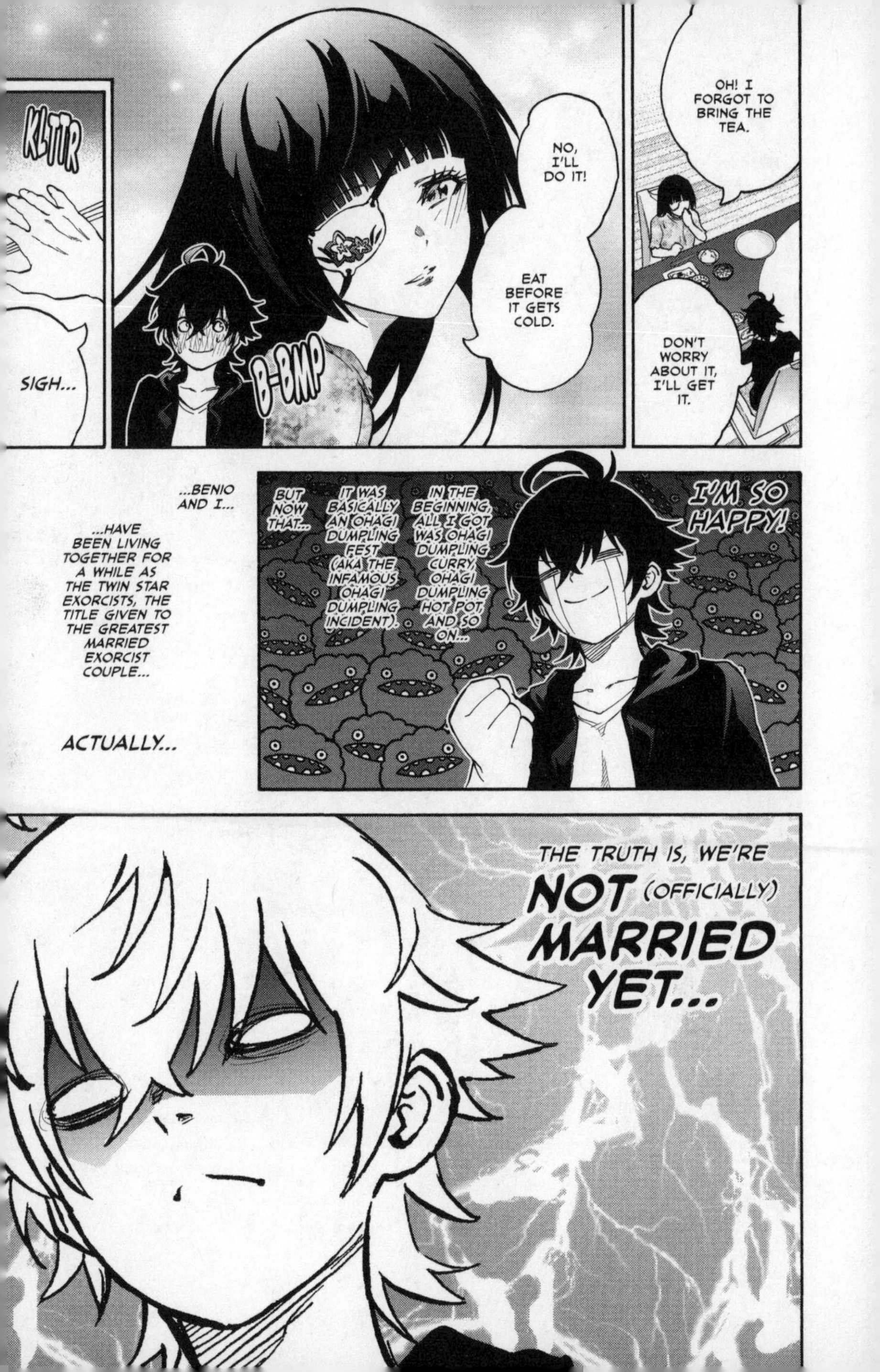
OH! I FORGOT TO BRING THE TEA.
DON'T WORRY ABOUT IT, I'LL GET IT.
NO, I'LL DO IT!
EAT BEFORE IT GETS COLD.
B-BMP
KLTTR
SIGH...
I'M SO HAPPY!
IN THE BEGINNING, ALL I GOT WAS OHAGI DUMPLING CURRY, OHAGI DUMPLING HOT POT, AND SO ON...
IT WAS BASICALLY AN OHAGI DUMPLING FEST (AKA THE INFAMOUS OHAGI DUMPLING INCIDENT).
BUT NOW THAT...
...BENIO AND I...
...HAVE BEEN LIVING TOGETHER FOR A WHILE AS THE TWIN STAR EXORCISTS, THE TITLE GIVEN TO THE GREATEST MARRIED EXORCIST COUPLE...
ACTUALLY...
THE TRUTH IS, WE'RE NOT (OFFICIALLY) MARRIED YET...

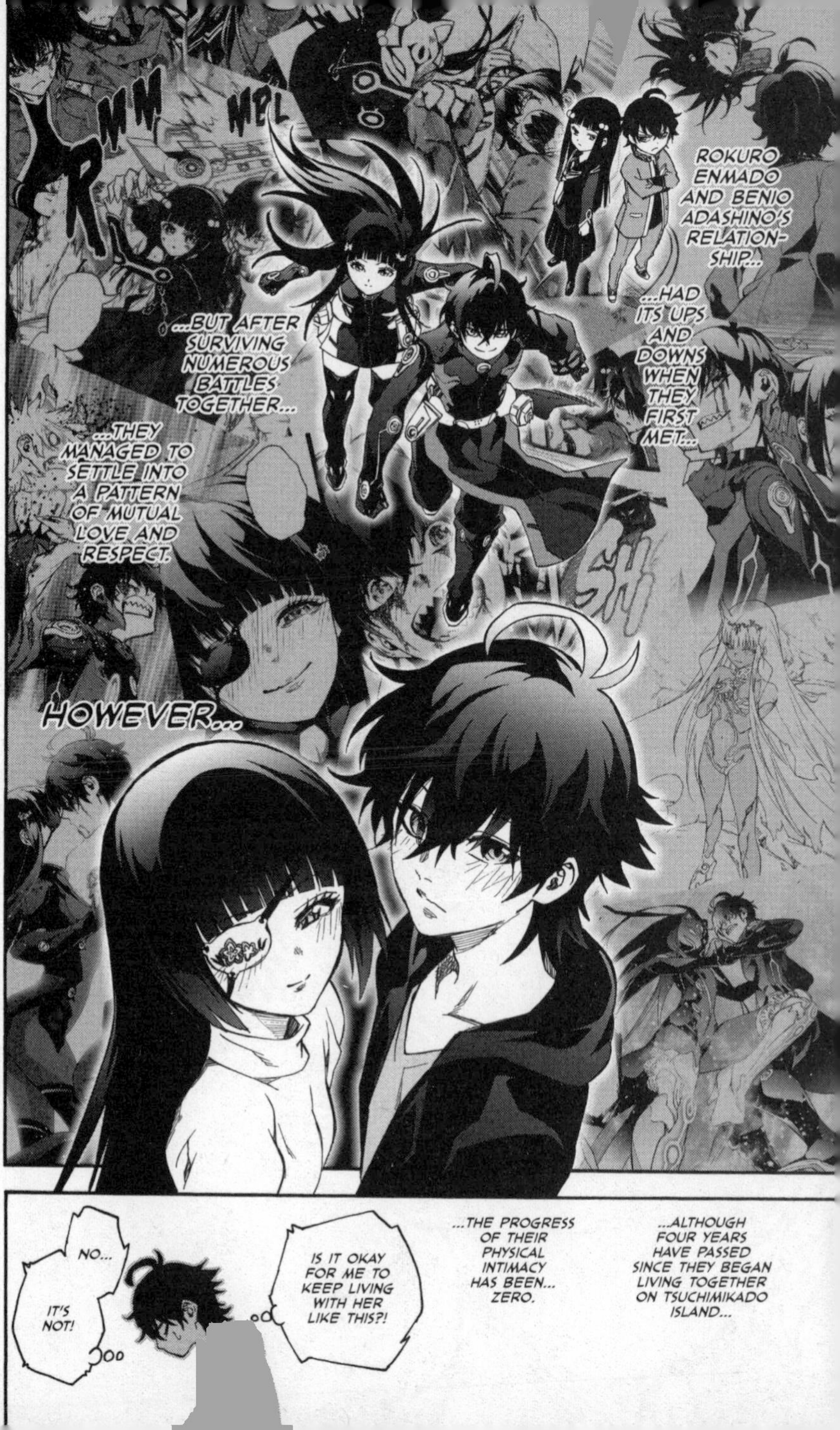
ROKURO ENMADO AND BENIO ADASHINO'S RELATIONSHIP...
...HAD ITS UPS AND DOWNS WHEN THEY FIRST MET...
...BUT AFTER SURVIVING NUMEROUS BATTLES TOGETHER...
...THEY MANAGED TO SETTLE INTO A PATTERN OF MUTUAL LOVE AND RESPECT.
HOWEVER...
...ALTHOUGH FOUR YEARS HAVE PASSED SINCE THEY BEGAN LIVING TOGETHER ON TSUCHIMIKADO ISLAND...
...THE PROGRESS OF THEIR PHYSICAL INTIMACY HAS BEEN... ZERO.
IS IT OKAY FOR ME TO KEEP LIVING WITH HER LIKE THIS?!
NO...
IT'S NOT!

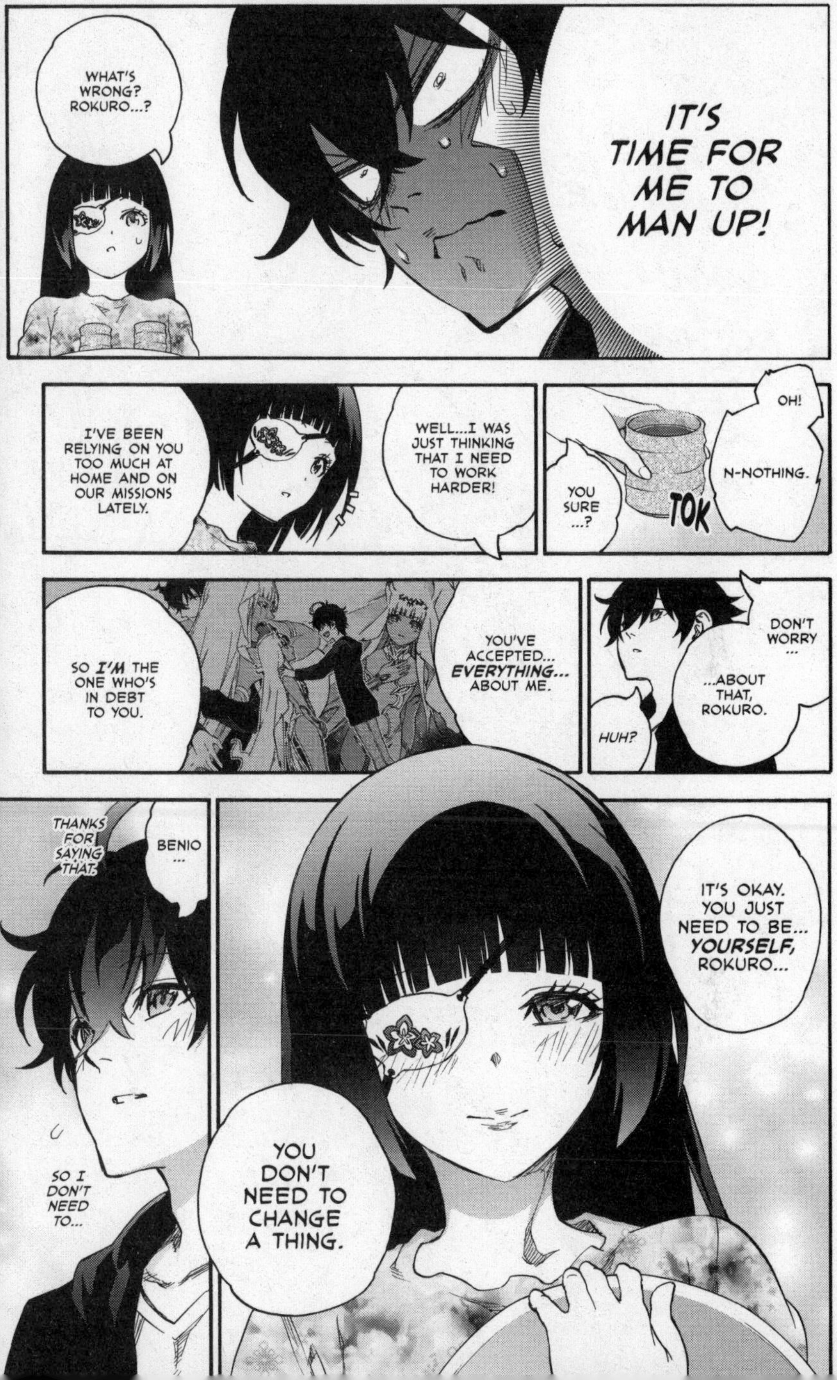
IT'S TIME FOR ME TO MAN UP!
WHAT'S WRONG? ROKURO...?
OH!
N-NOTHING.
TOK
YOU SURE ...?
WELL...I WAS JUST THINKING THAT I NEED TO WORK HARDER!
I'VE BEEN RELYING ON YOU TOO MUCH AT HOME AND ON OUR MISSIONS LATELY.
DON'T WORRY ...
...ABOUT THAT, ROKURO.
HUH?
YOU'VE ACCEPTED... EVERYTHING... ABOUT ME.
SO I'M THE ONE WHO'S IN DEBT TO YOU.
IT'S OKAY. YOU JUST NEED TO BE... YOURSELF, ROKURO...
YOU DON'T NEED TO CHANGE A THING.
BENIO ...
THANKS FOR SAYING THAT.
SO I DON'T NEED TO...

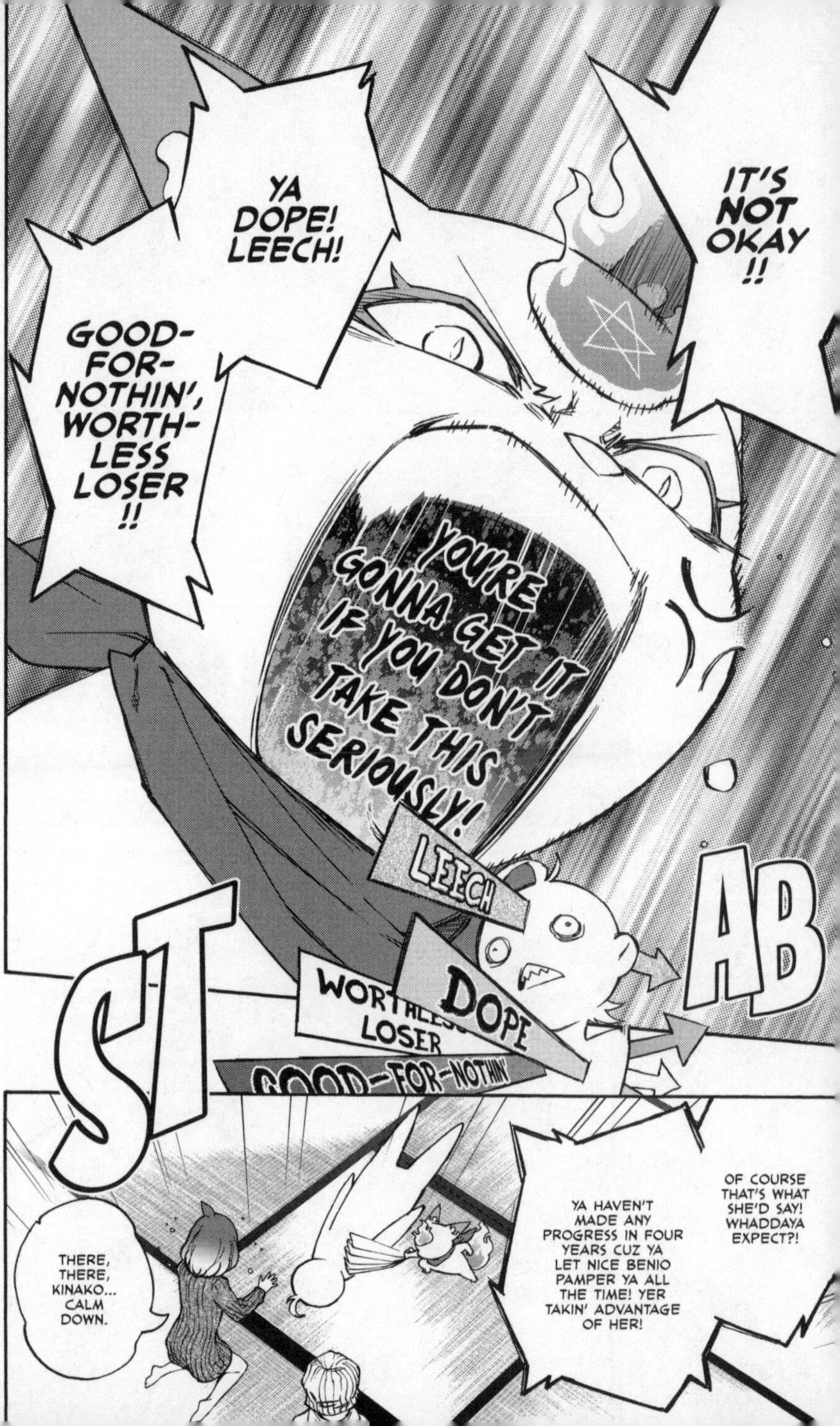
IT'S NOT OKAY!!
YA DOPE! LEECH!
GOOD-FOR-NOTHIN', WORTHLESS LOSER!!
YOU'RE GONNA GET IT IF YOU DON'T TAKE THIS SERIOUSLY!
LEECH
DOPE
WORTHLESS LOSER
GOOD-FOR-NOTHIN'
ST
AB
OF COURSE THAT'S WHAT SHE'D SAY! WHADDAYA EXPECT?!
YA HAVEN'T MADE ANY PROGRESS IN FOUR YEARS CUZ YA LET NICE BENIO PAMPER YA ALL THE TIME! YER TAKIN' ADVANTAGE OF HER!
THERE, THERE, KINAKO... CALM DOWN.

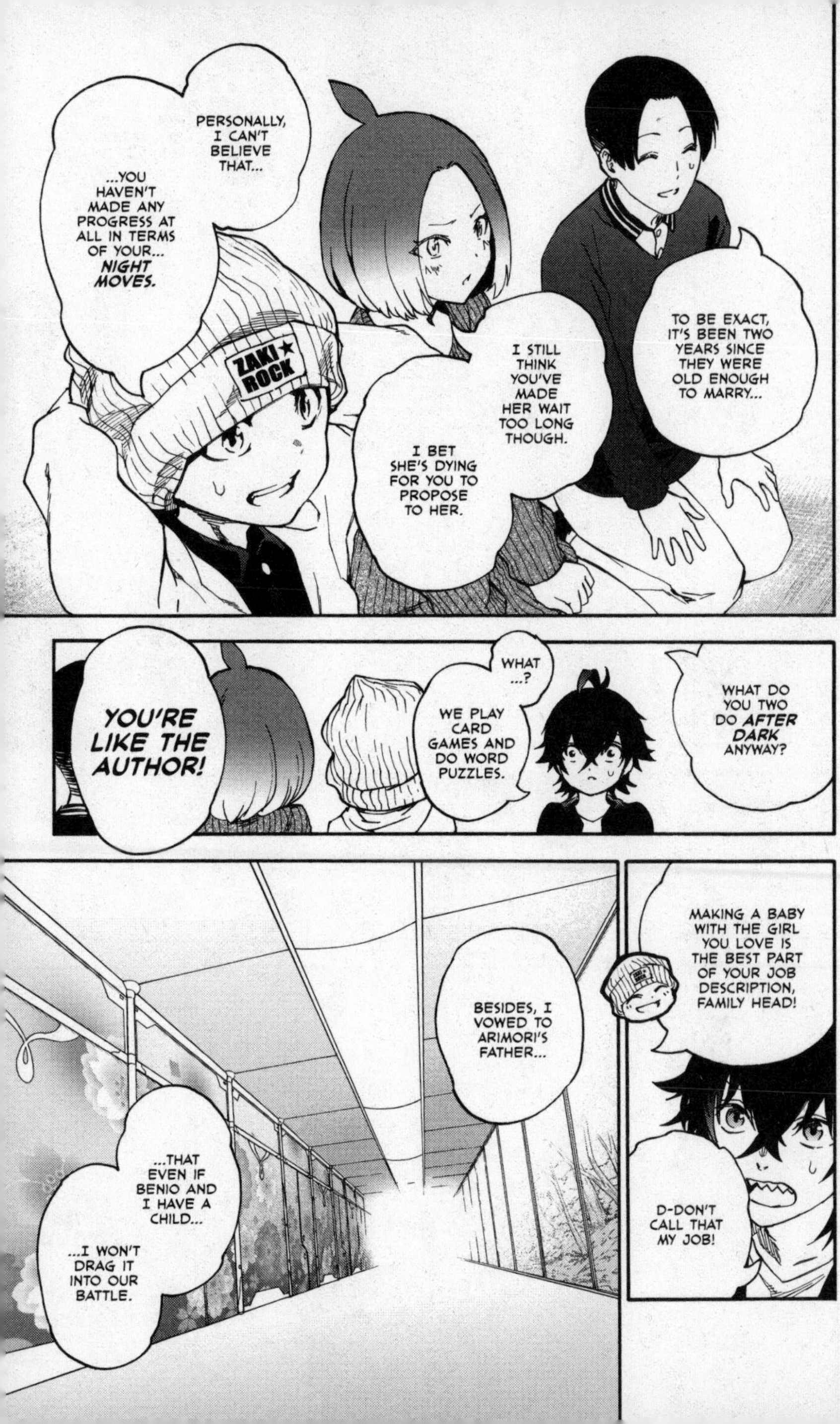
PERSONALLY, I CAN'T BELIEVE THAT...
...YOU HAVEN'T MADE ANY PROGRESS AT ALL IN TERMS OF YOUR... NIGHT MOVES.
ZAKI★ROCK
I STILL THINK YOU'VE MADE HER WAIT TOO LONG THOUGH.
I BET SHE'S DYING FOR YOU TO PROPOSE TO HER.
TO BE EXACT, IT'S BEEN TWO YEARS SINCE THEY WERE OLD ENOUGH TO MARRY...
WHAT DO YOU TWO DO AFTER DARK ANYWAY?
WHAT ...?
WE PLAY CARD GAMES AND DO WORD PUZZLES.
YOU'RE LIKE THE AUTHOR!
MAKING A BABY WITH THE GIRL YOU LOVE IS THE BEST PART OF YOUR JOB DESCRIPTION, FAMILY HEAD!
D-DON'T CALL THAT MY JOB!
BESIDES, I VOWED TO ARIMORI'S FATHER...
...THAT EVEN IF BENIO AND I HAVE A CHILD...
...I WON'T DRAG IT INTO OUR BATTLE.

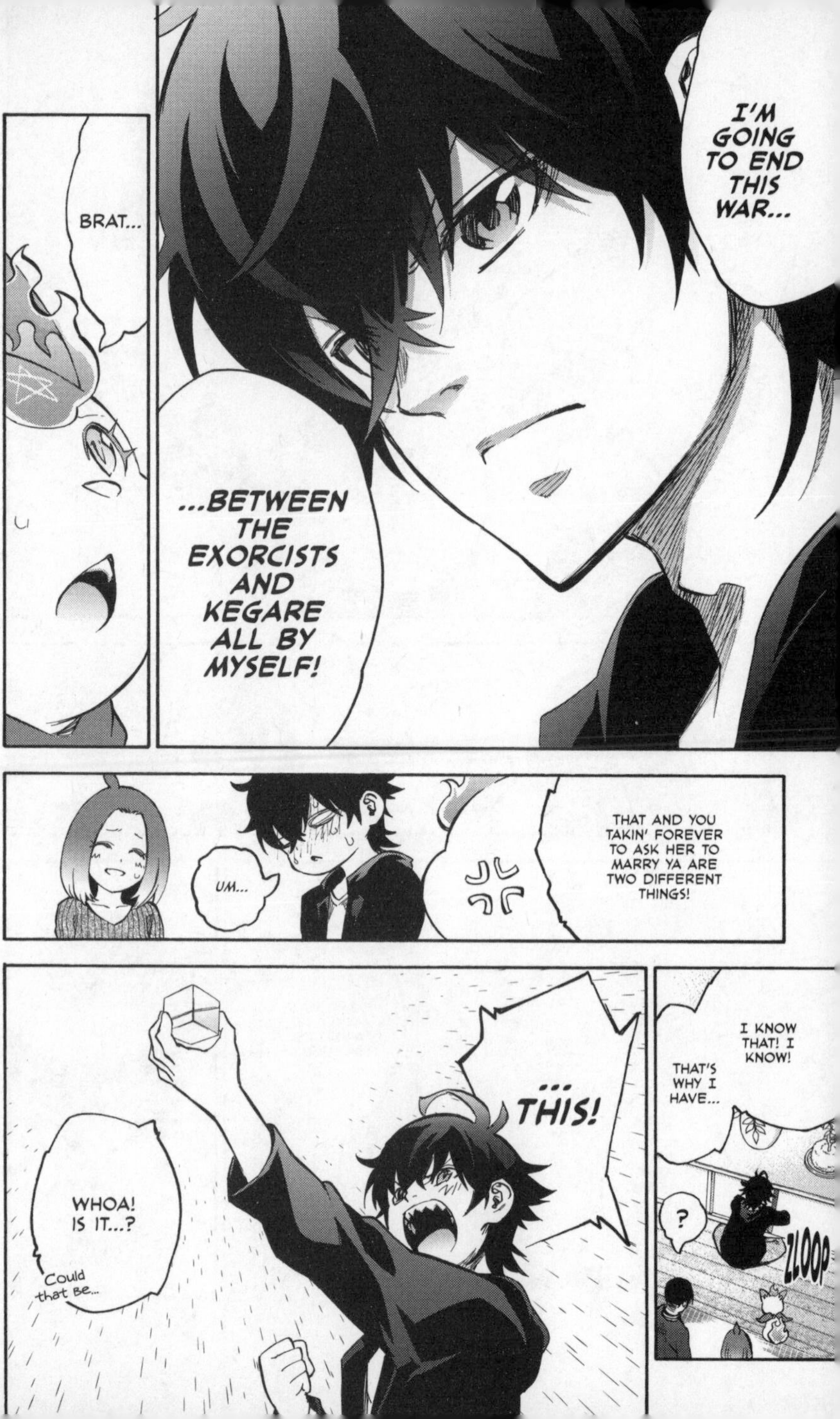
I'M GOING TO END THIS WAR...
...BETWEEN THE EXORCISTS AND KEGARE ALL BY MYSELF!
BRAT...
THAT AND YOU TAKIN' FOREVER TO ASK HER TO MARRY YA ARE TWO DIFFERENT THINGS!
UM...
I KNOW THAT! I KNOW!
THAT'S WHY I HAVE...
?
ZLOOP
...THIS!
WHOA! IS IT...?
Could that be...

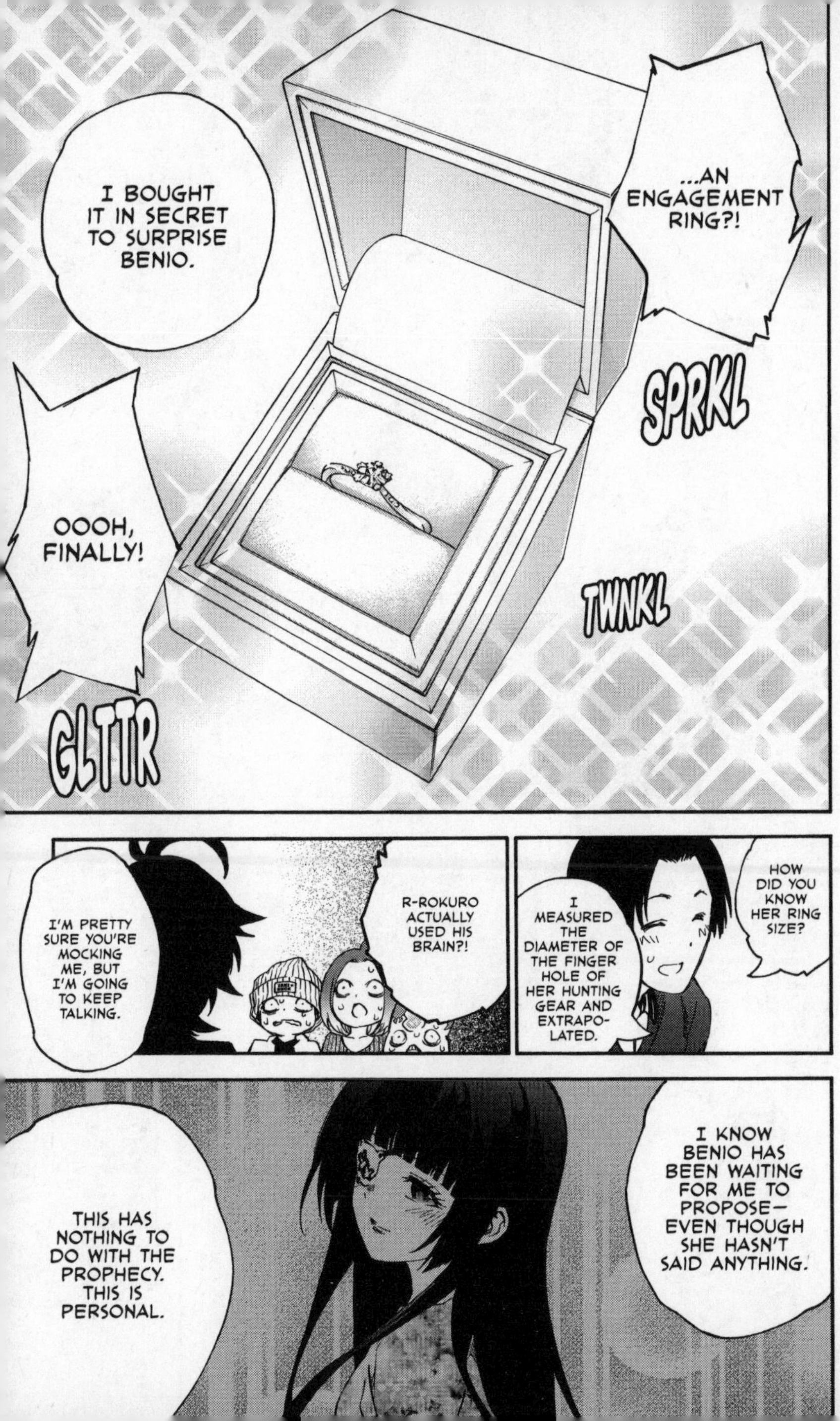
...AN ENGAGEMENT RING?!
I BOUGHT IT IN SECRET TO SURPRISE BENIO.
SPRKL
OOOH, FINALLY!
TWNKL
GLTTR
HOW DID YOU KNOW HER RING SIZE?
I MEASURED THE DIAMETER OF THE FINGER HOLE OF HER HUNTING GEAR AND EXTRAPO-LATED.
R-ROKURO ACTUALLY USED HIS BRAIN?!
I'M PRETTY SURE YOU'RE MOCKING ME, BUT I'M GOING TO KEEP TALKING.
I KNOW BENIO HAS BEEN WAITING FOR ME TO PROPOSE— EVEN THOUGH SHE HASN'T SAID ANYTHING.
THIS HAS NOTHING TO DO WITH THE PROPHECY. THIS IS PERSONAL.

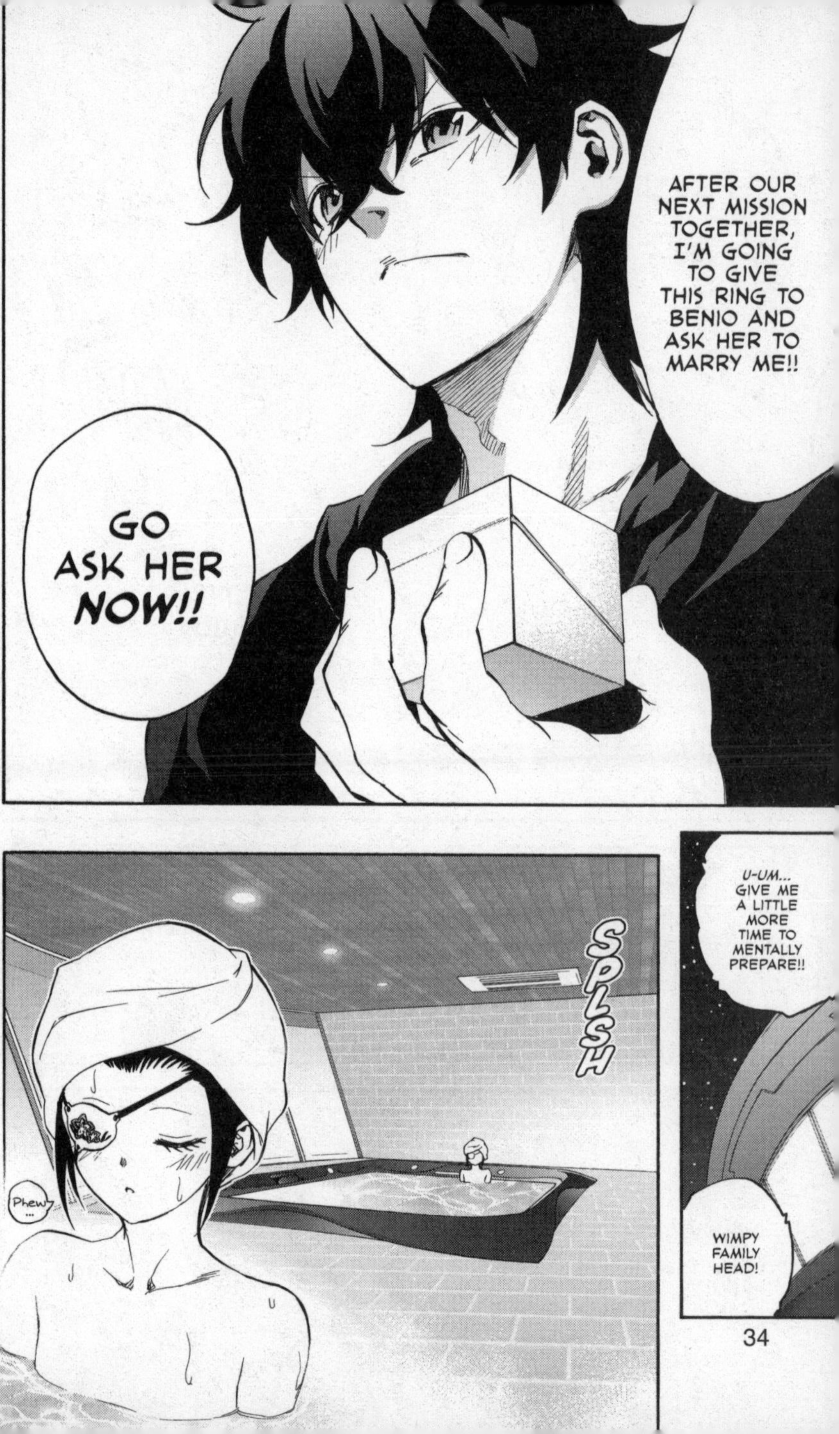
AFTER OUR NEXT MISSION TOGETHER, I'M GOING TO GIVE THIS RING TO BENIO AND ASK HER TO MARRY ME!!
GO ASK HER NOW!!
U-UM... GIVE ME A LITTLE MORE TIME TO MENTALLY PREPARE!!
WIMPY FAMILY HEAD!
SPLSH
Phew...

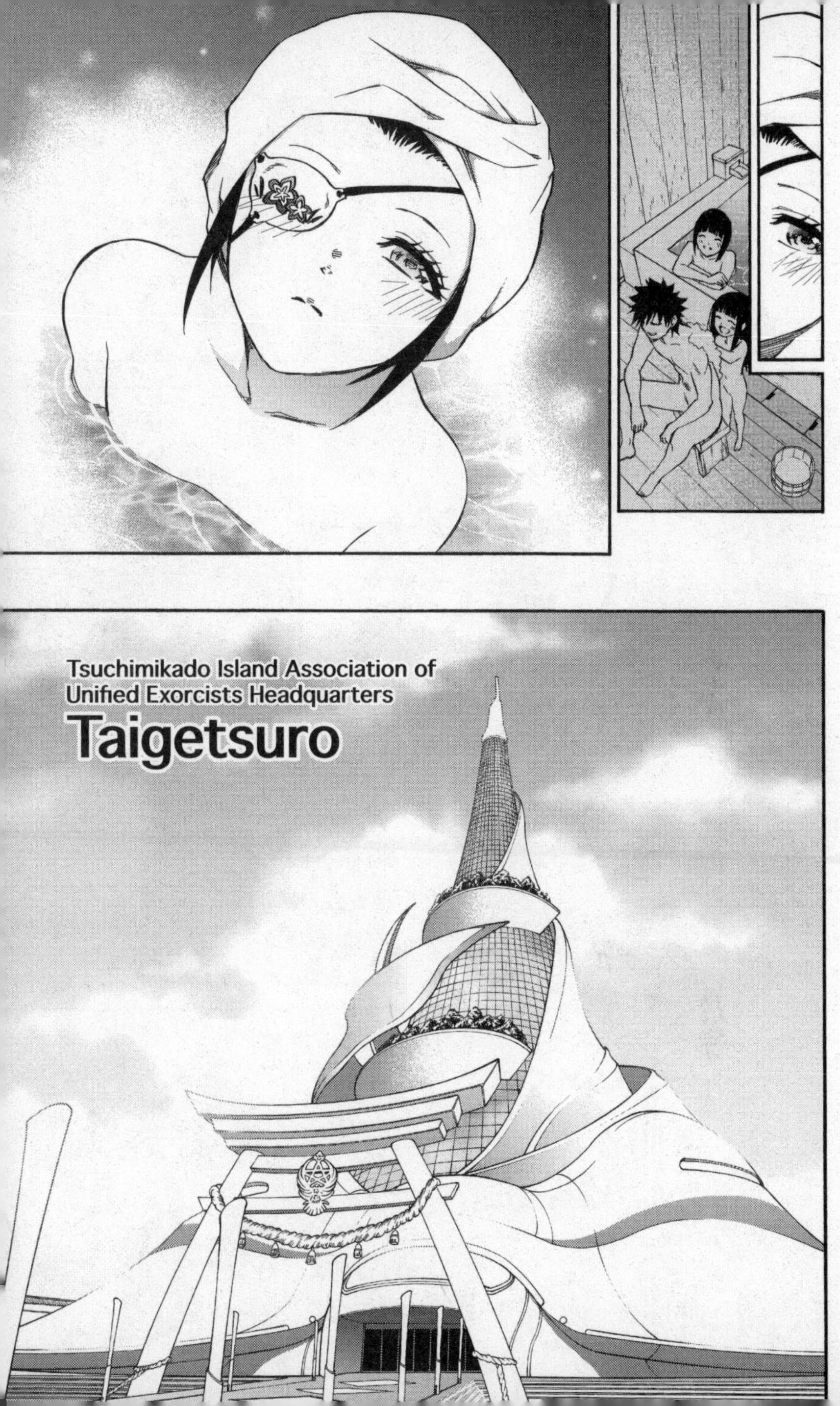
Tsuchimikado Island Association of
Unified Exorcists Headquarters
Taigetsuro

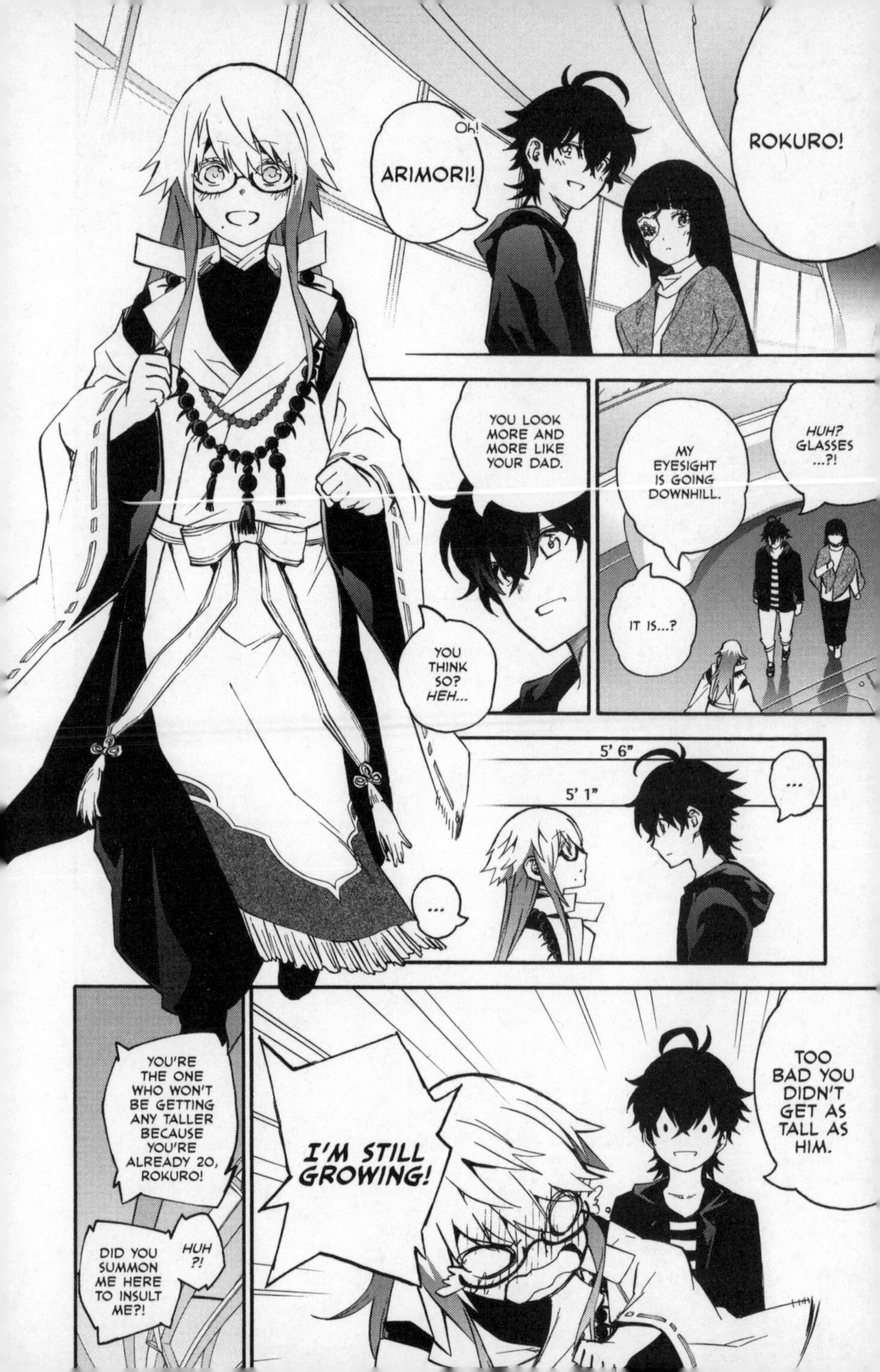
ROKURO!
Oh!
ARIMORI!
HUH? GLASSES ...?!
MY EYESIGHT IS GOING DOWNHILL.
IT IS...?
YOU LOOK MORE AND MORE LIKE YOUR DAD.
YOU THINK SO? HEH...
5' 6"
...
5' 1"
...
TOO BAD YOU DIDN'T GET AS TALL AS HIM.
I'M STILL GROWING!
YOU'RE THE ONE WHO WON'T BE GETTING ANY TALLER BECAUSE YOU'RE ALREADY 20, ROKURO!
HUH ?!
DID YOU SUMMON ME HERE TO INSULT ME?!

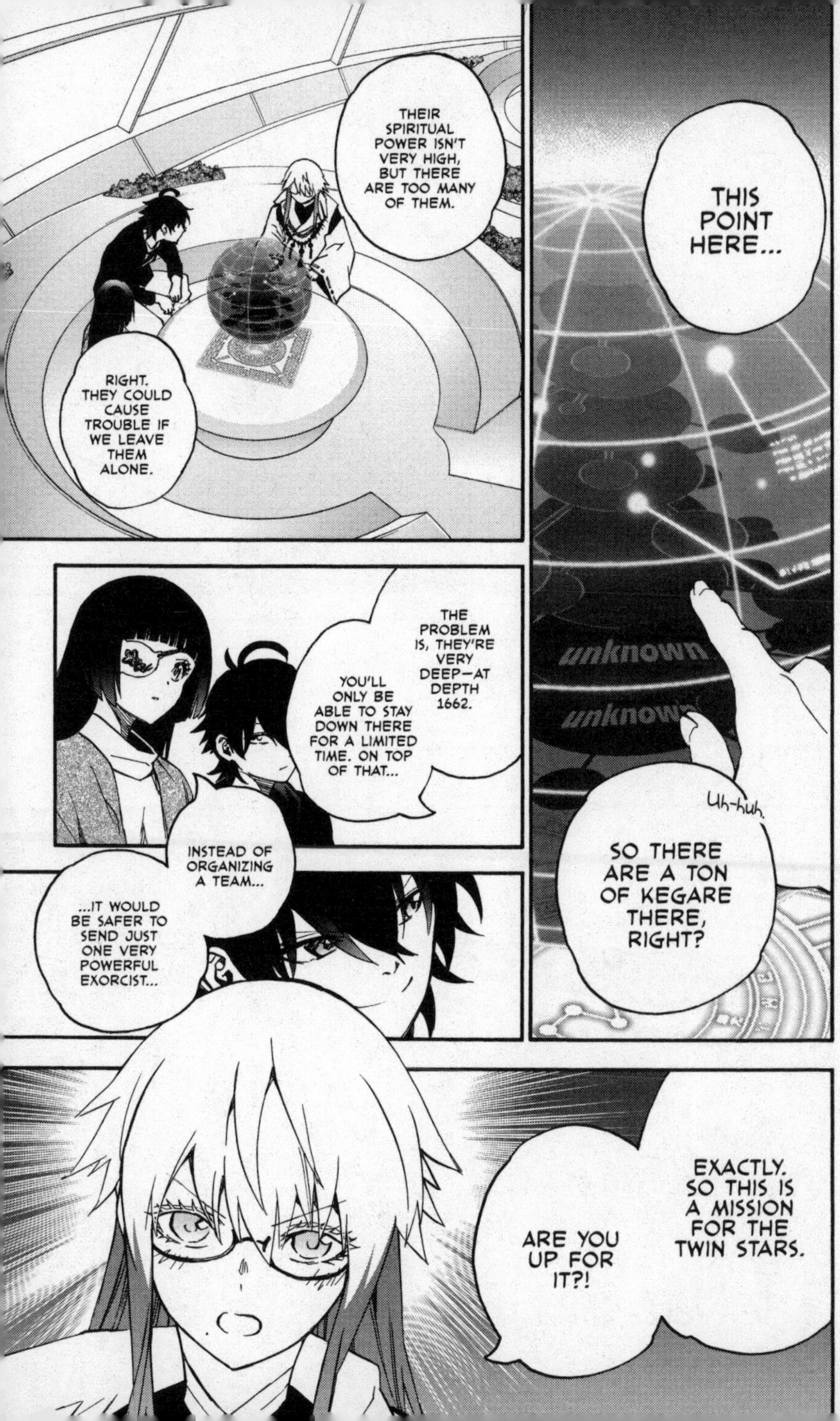
THIS POINT HERE...
Uh-huh.
SO THERE ARE A TON OF KEGARE THERE, RIGHT?
THEIR SPIRITUAL POWER ISN'T VERY HIGH, BUT THERE ARE TOO MANY OF THEM.
RIGHT. THEY COULD CAUSE TROUBLE IF WE LEAVE THEM ALONE.
THE PROBLEM IS, THEY'RE VERY DEEP—AT DEPTH 1662.
YOU'LL ONLY BE ABLE TO STAY DOWN THERE FOR A LIMITED TIME. ON TOP OF THAT...
unknown
unknown
INSTEAD OF ORGANIZING A TEAM...
...IT WOULD BE SAFER TO SEND JUST ONE VERY POWERFUL EXORCIST...
EXACTLY. SO THIS IS A MISSION FOR THE TWIN STARS.
ARE YOU UP FOR IT?!

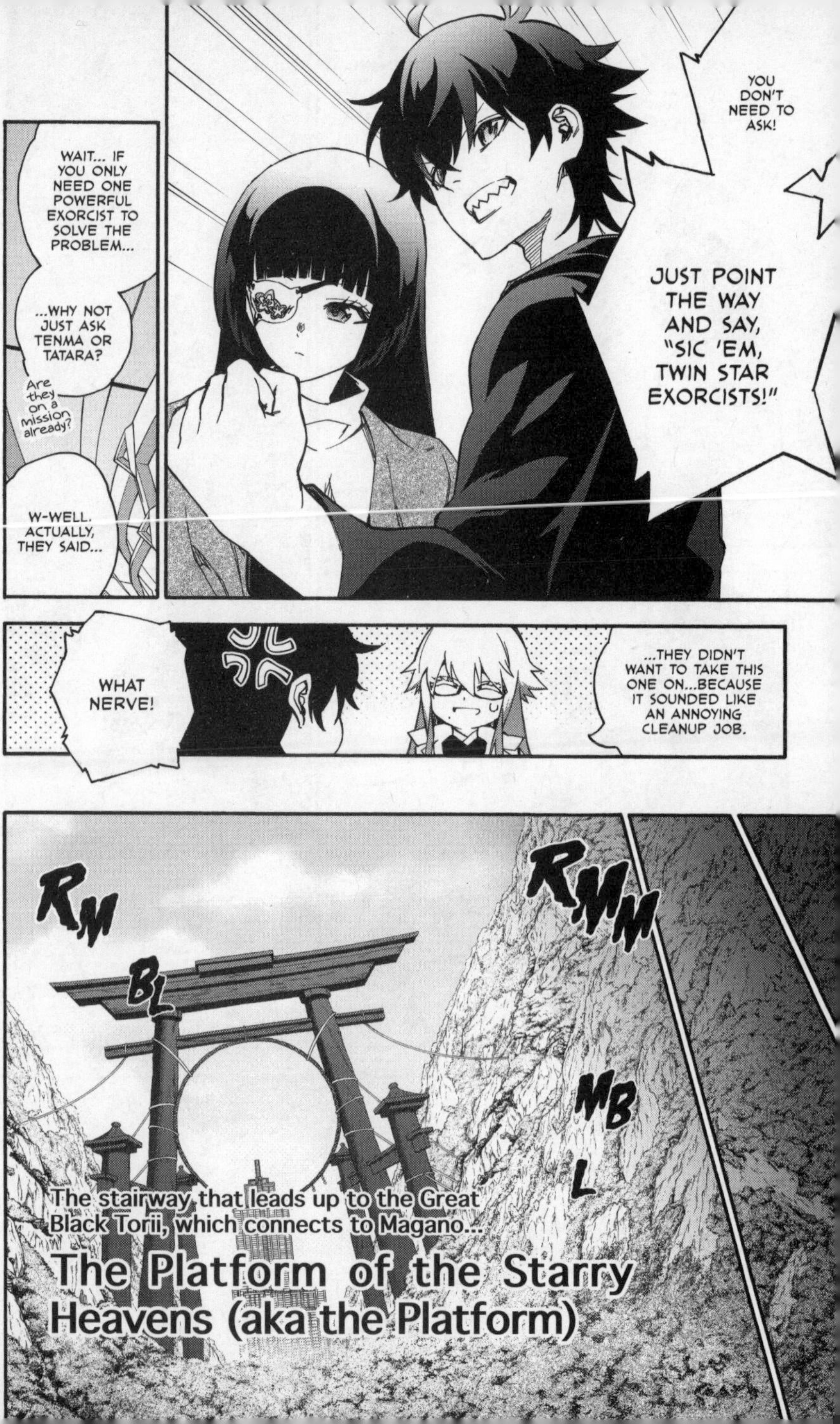
YOU DON'T NEED TO ASK!
JUST POINT THE WAY AND SAY, "SIC 'EM, TWIN STAR EXORCISTS!"
WAIT... IF YOU ONLY NEED ONE POWERFUL EXORCIST TO SOLVE THE PROBLEM...
...WHY NOT JUST ASK TENMA OR TATARA?
Are they on a mission already?
W-WELL. ACTUALLY, THEY SAID...
...THEY DIDN'T WANT TO TAKE THIS ONE ON...BECAUSE IT SOUNDED LIKE AN ANNOYING CLEANUP JOB.
WHAT NERVE!
RMMMBL
RMBL
The stairway that leads up to the Great Black Torii, which connects to Magano...
The Platform of the Starry Heavens (aka the Platform)

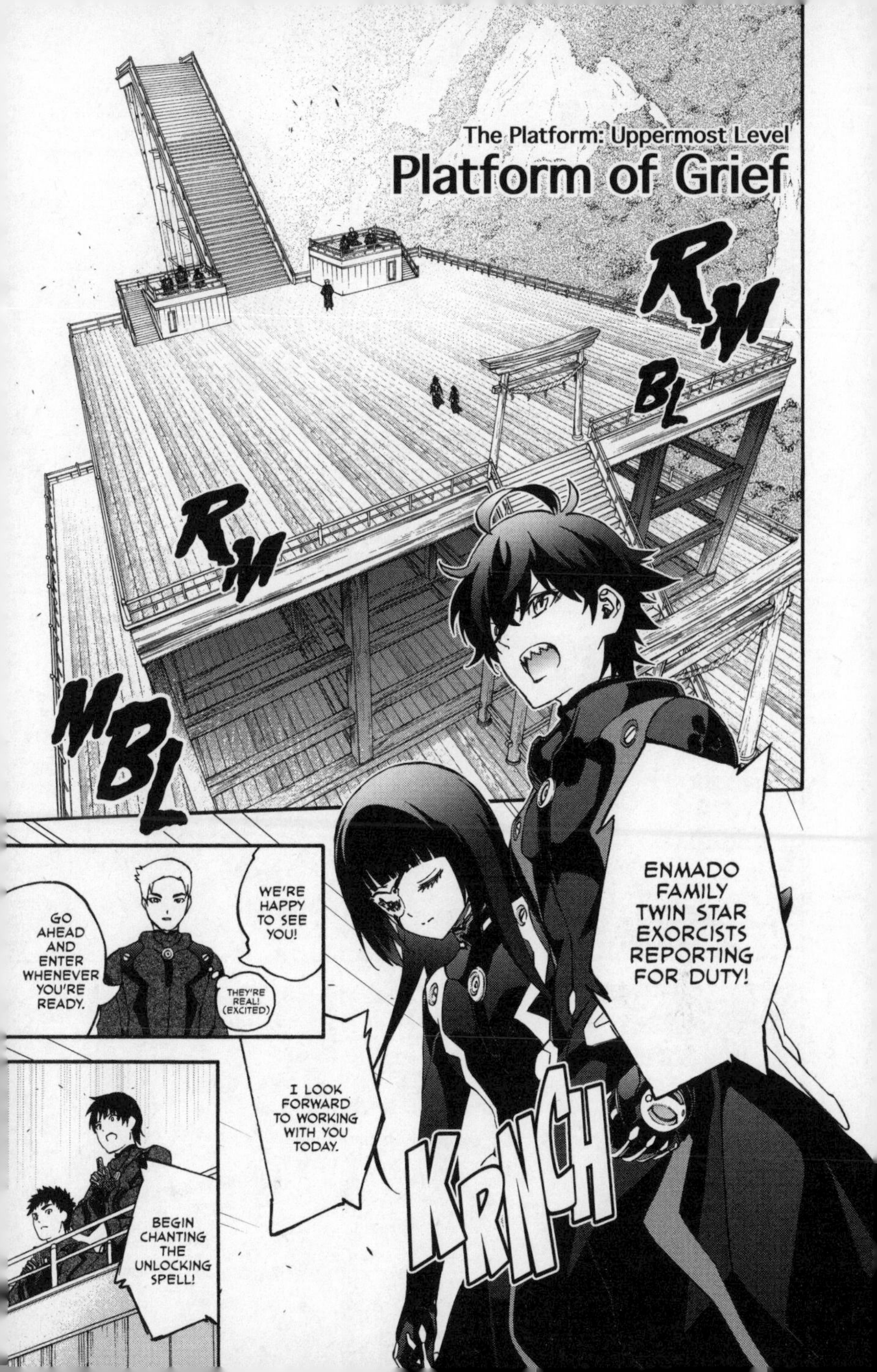
The Platform: Uppermost Level
Platform of Grief
RMBL
RMBL
ENMADO FAMILY TWIN STAR EXORCISTS REPORTING FOR DUTY!
WE'RE HAPPY TO SEE YOU!
GO AHEAD AND ENTER WHENEVER YOU'RE READY.
THEY'RE REAL! (EXCITED)
I LOOK FORWARD TO WORKING WITH YOU TODAY.
KRNCH
BEGIN CHANTING THE UNLOCKING SPELL!

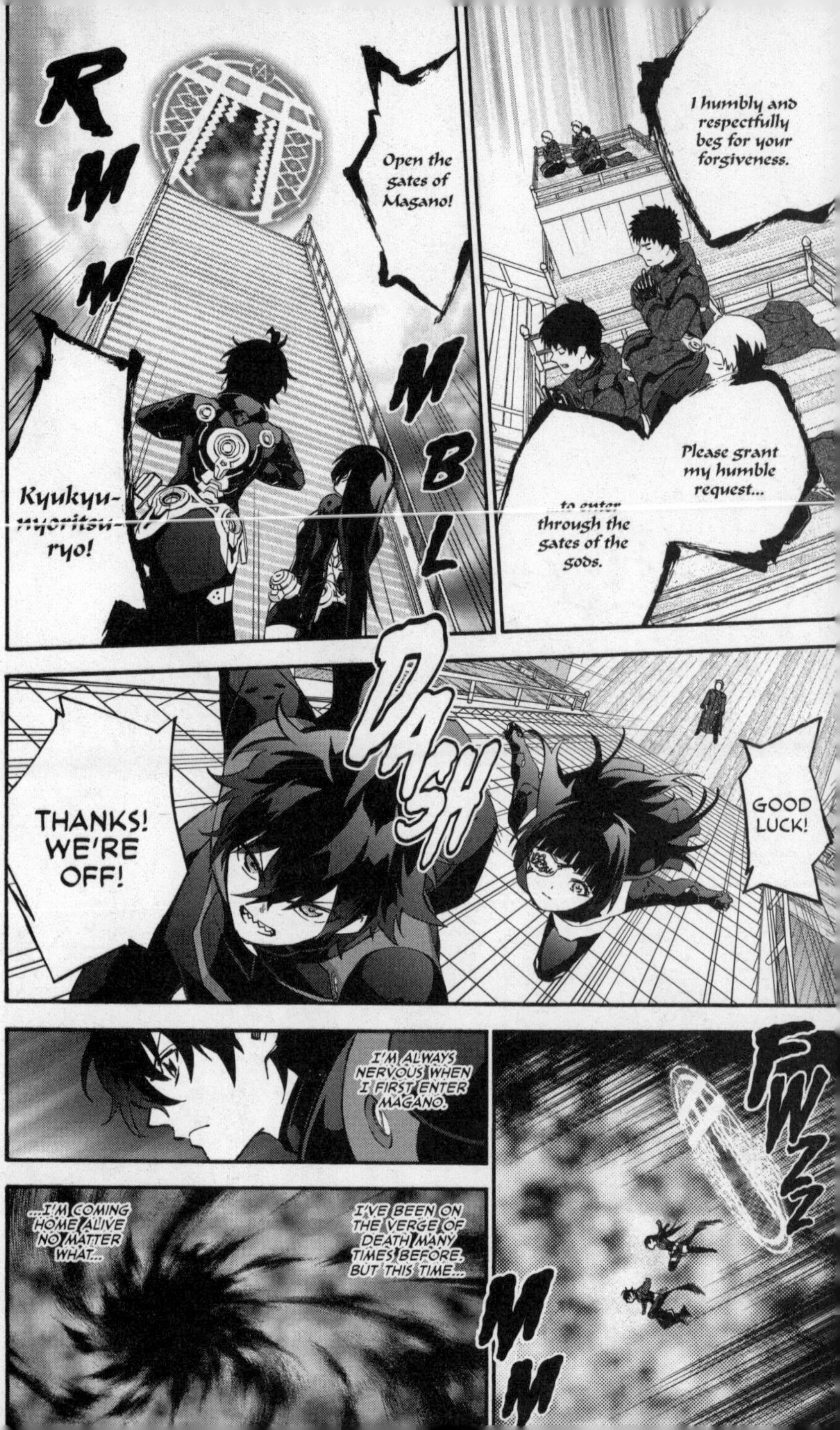
I humbly and respectfully beg for your forgiveness.
Please grant my humble request...
...to enter through the gates of the gods.
Open the gates of Magano!
RMMMBL
Kyukyu-nyoritsu-ryo!
GOOD LUCK!
DASH
THANKS! WE'RE OFF!
I'M ALWAYS NERVOUS WHEN I FIRST ENTER MAGANO.
I'VE BEEN ON THE VERGE OF DEATH MANY TIMES BEFORE, BUT THIS TIME...
...I'M COMING HOME ALIVE NO MATTER WHAT...
FWZZ
MMM

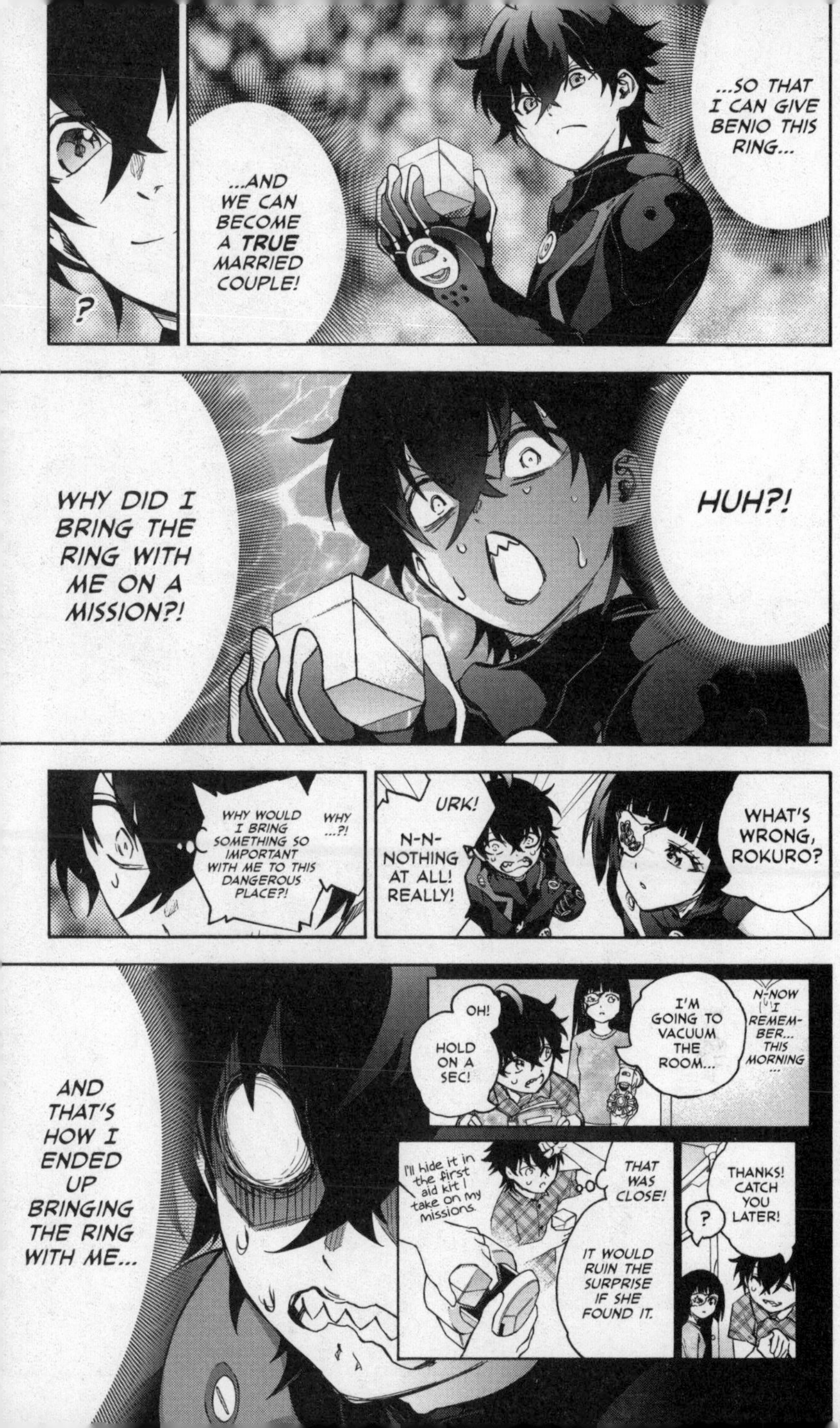
...SO THAT I CAN GIVE BENIO THIS RING...
...AND WE CAN BECOME A **TRUE** MARRIED COUPLE!
?
HUH?!
WHY DID I BRING THE RING WITH ME ON A MISSION?!
WHAT'S WRONG, ROKURO?
URK!
N-N-NOTHING AT ALL! REALLY!
WHY ...?!
WHY WOULD I BRING SOMETHING SO IMPORTANT WITH ME TO THIS DANGEROUS PLACE?!
N-NOW I REMEMBER... THIS MORNING...
I'M GOING TO VACUUM THE ROOM...
OH!
HOLD ON A SEC!
THANKS! CATCH YOU LATER!
?
THAT WAS CLOSE!
IT WOULD RUIN THE SURPRISE IF SHE FOUND IT.
I'll hide it in the first aid kit I take on my missions.
AND THAT'S HOW I ENDED UP BRINGING THE RING WITH ME...

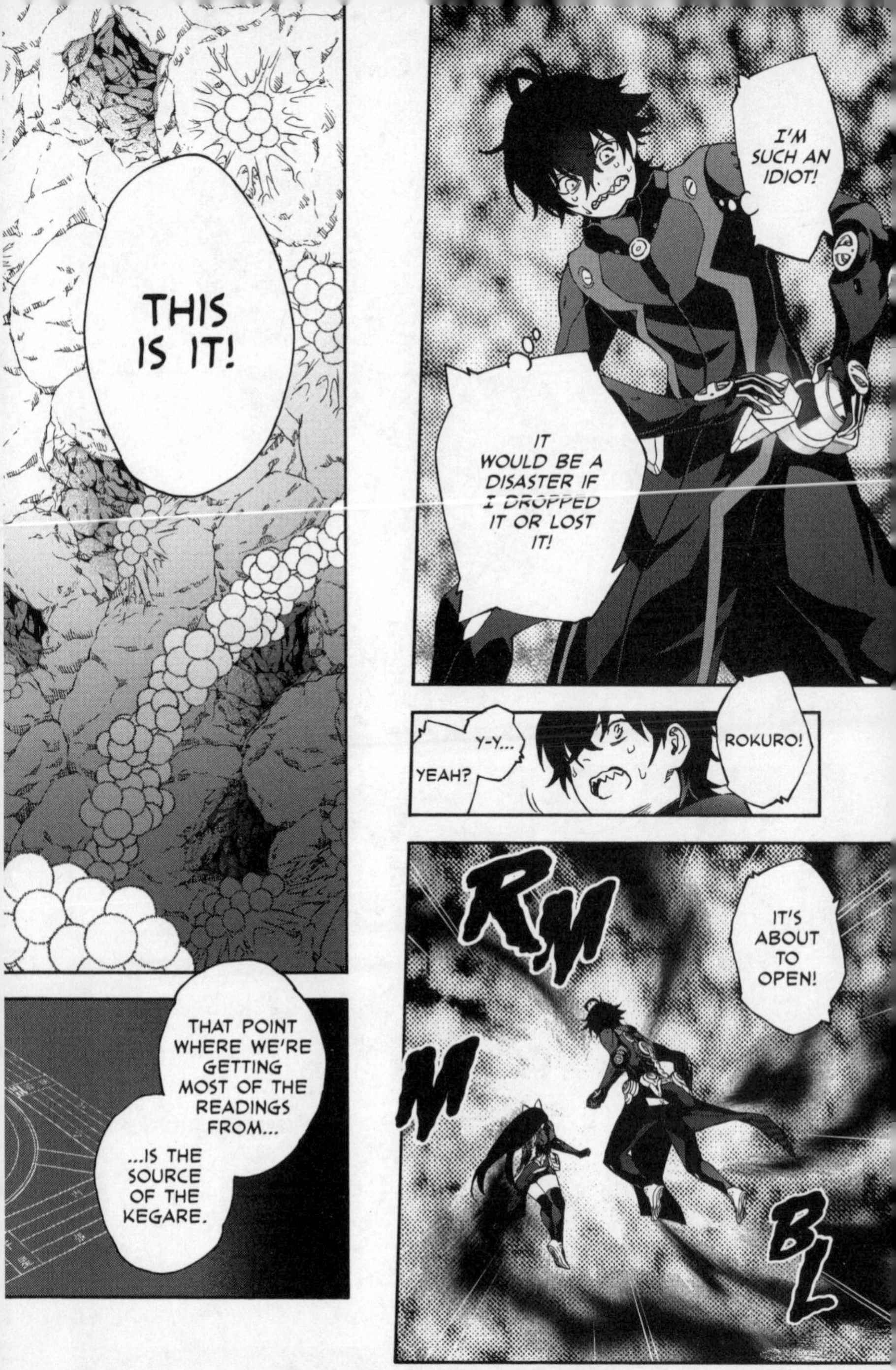
I'M SUCH AN IDIOT!
IT WOULD BE A DISASTER IF I DROPPED IT OR LOST IT!
ROKURO!
Y-Y... YEAH?
IT'S ABOUT TO OPEN!
RMM
BL
THIS IS IT!
THAT POINT WHERE WE'RE GETTING MOST OF THE READINGS FROM...
...IS THE SOURCE OF THE KEGARE.

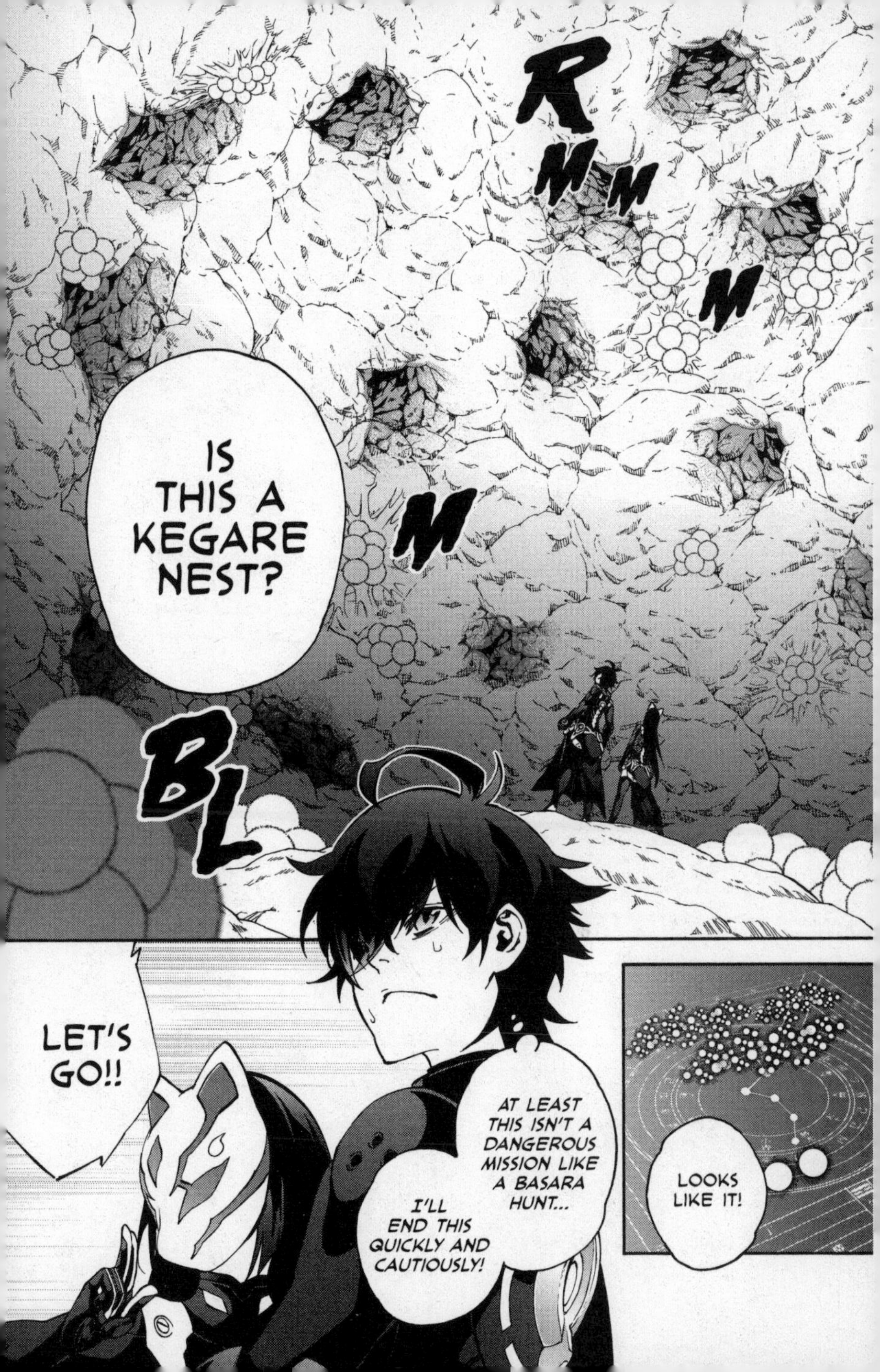
RMMMMM
IS THIS A KEGARE NEST?
BL
LOOKS LIKE IT!
AT LEAST THIS ISN'T A DANGEROUS MISSION LIKE A BASARA HUNT...
I'LL END THIS QUICKLY AND CAUTIOUSLY!
LET'S GO!!

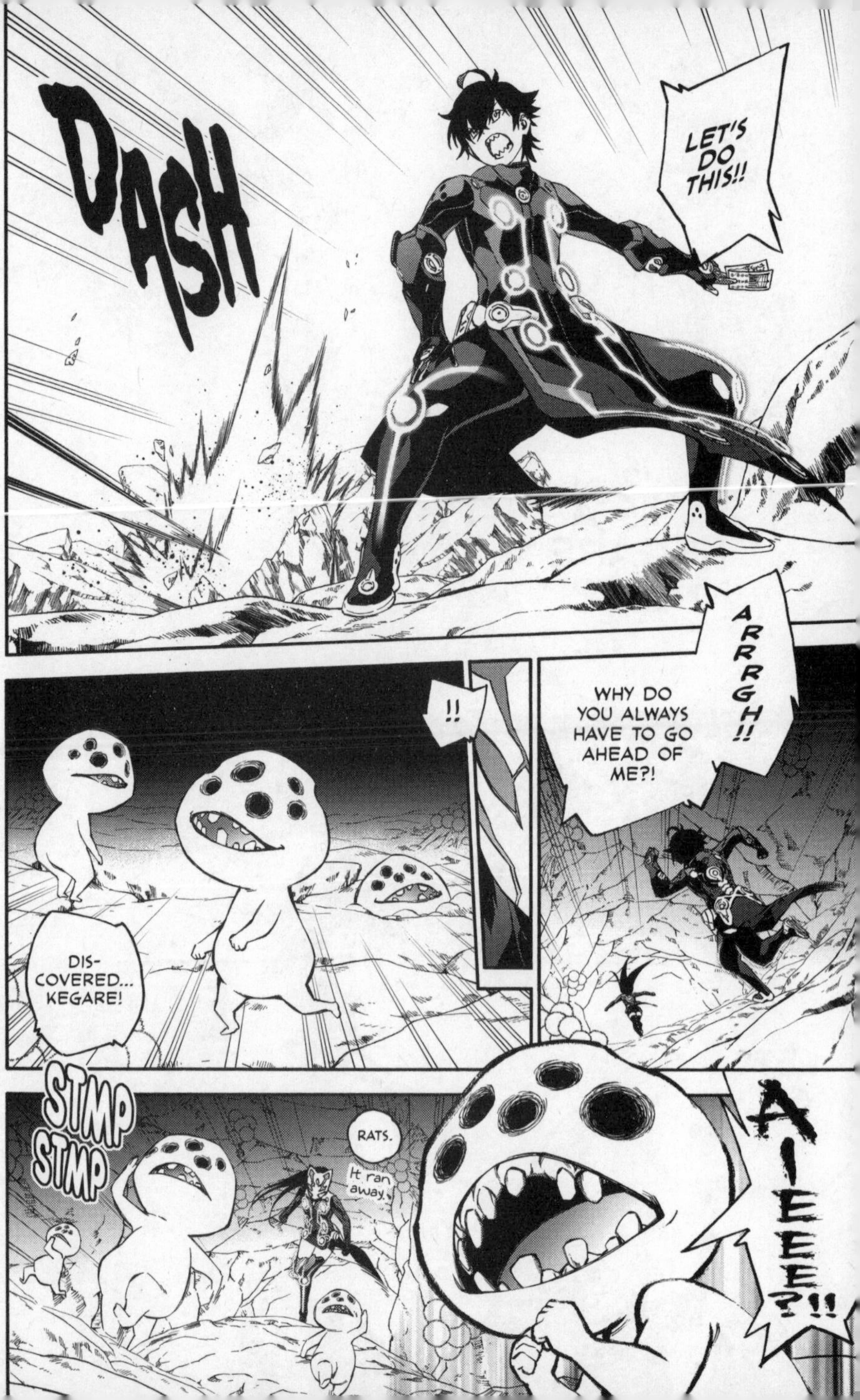
LET'S DO THIS!!
DASH
ARRRGH!!
WHY DO YOU ALWAYS HAVE TO GO AHEAD OF ME?!
!!
DIS-COVERED... KEGARE!
AIEEE?!!
RATS.
It ran away.
STMP STMP

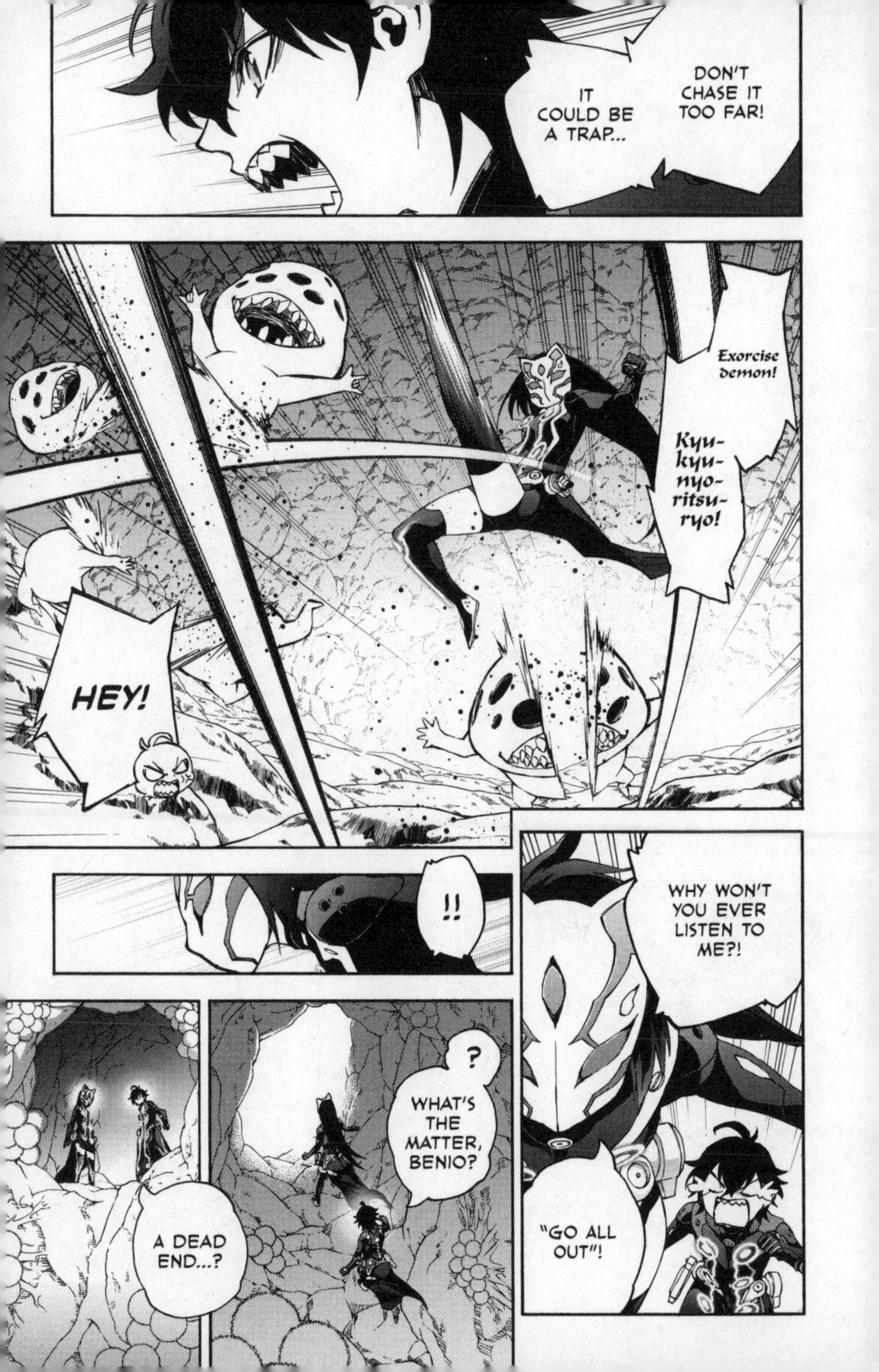
DON'T CHASE IT TOO FAR!
IT COULD BE A TRAP...
Exorcise demon!
Kyu-kyu-nyo-ritsu-ryo!
HEY!
WHY WON'T YOU EVER LISTEN TO ME?!
"GO ALL OUT"!
!!
?
WHAT'S THE MATTER, BENIO?
A DEAD END...?

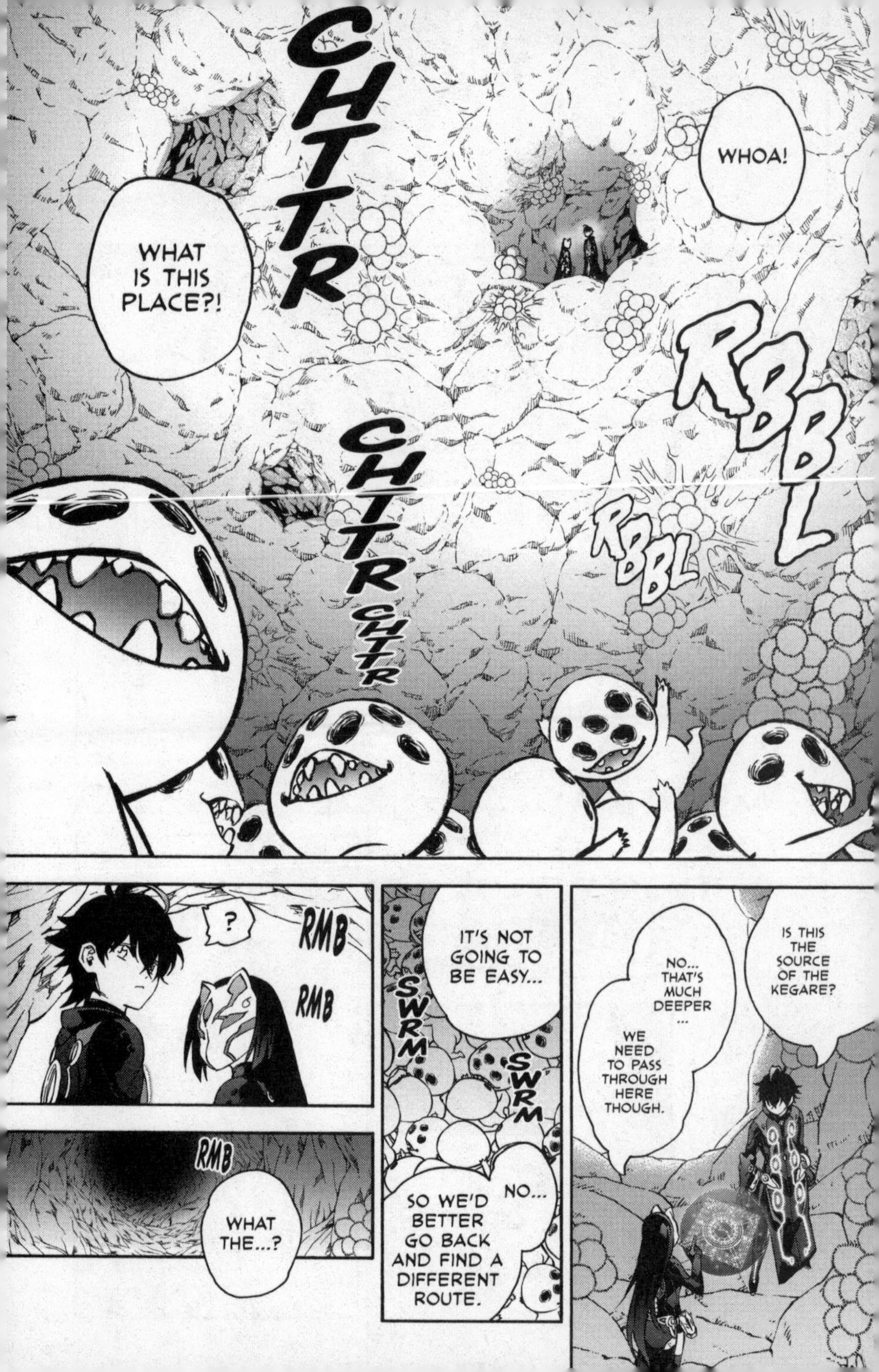
WHOA!
WHAT IS THIS PLACE?!
CHTTR
RBBL
RBBL
CHTTR
CHTTR
IS THIS THE SOURCE OF THE KEGARE?
NO... THAT'S MUCH DEEPER ...
WE NEED TO PASS THROUGH HERE THOUGH.
IT'S NOT GOING TO BE EASY...
SWRM
SWRM
NO...
SO WE'D BETTER GO BACK AND FIND A DIFFERENT ROUTE.
?
RMB
RMB
RMB
WHAT THE...?

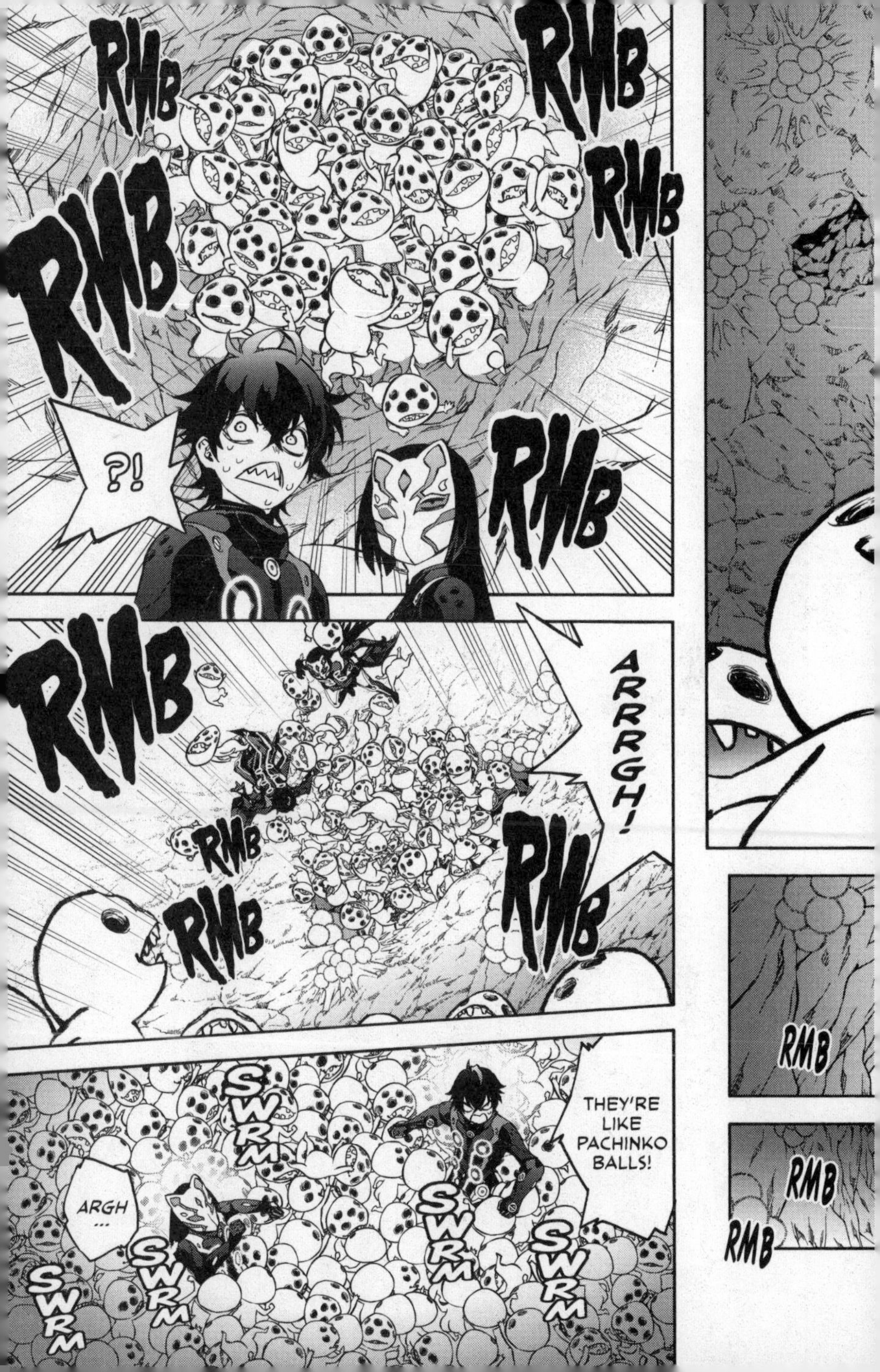
RMB
RMB
RMB
RMB
RMB
RMB
RMB
?!
RMB
ARRRGH!
RMB
RMB
RMB
RMB
THEY'RE LIKE PACHINKO BALLS!
SWRM
SWRM
SWRM
ARGH ...
SWRM
SWRM

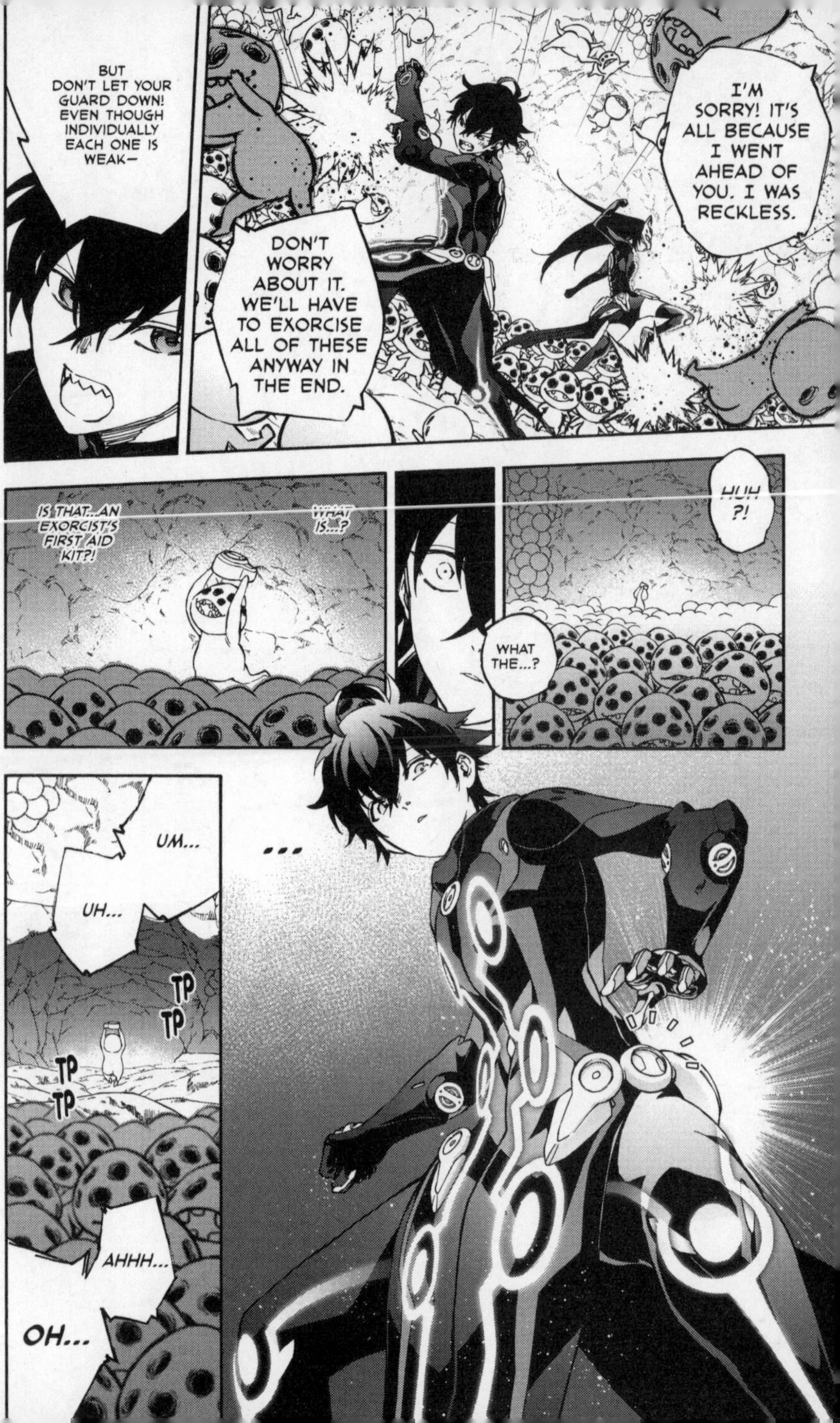
I'M SORRY! IT'S ALL BECAUSE I WENT AHEAD OF YOU. I WAS RECKLESS.
DON'T WORRY ABOUT IT. WE'LL HAVE TO EXORCISE ALL OF THESE ANYWAY IN THE END.
BUT DON'T LET YOUR GUARD DOWN! EVEN THOUGH INDIVIDUALLY EACH ONE IS WEAK—
HUH?!
WHAT THE...?
WHAT IS...?
IS THAT...AN EXORCIST'S FIRST AID KIT?!
...
UM...
UH...
TP TP
TP TP
AHHH...
OH...

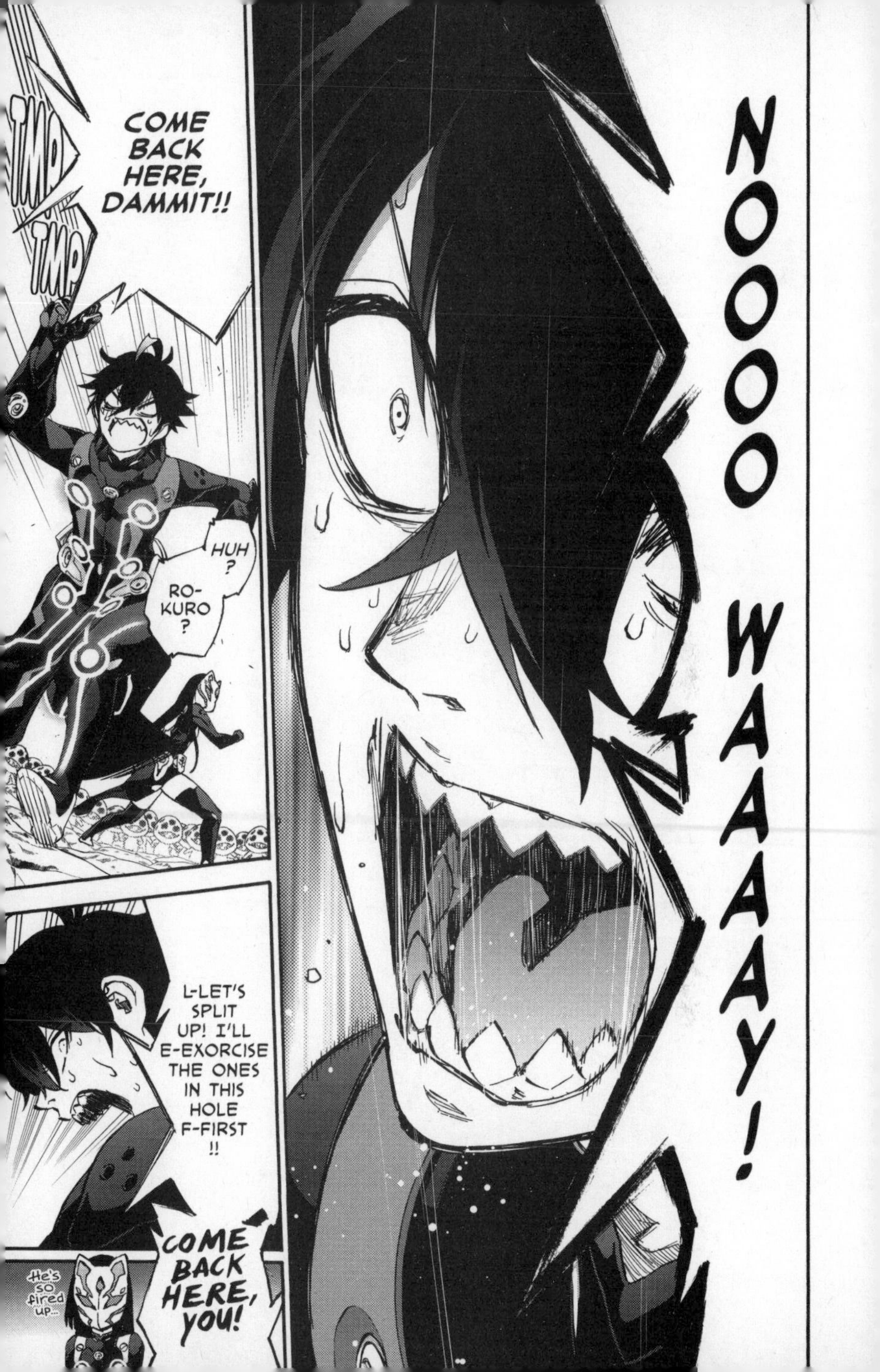
NOOOO WAAAAAY!
COME BACK HERE, DAMMIT!!
TMP TMP
HUH? RO-KURO?
L-LET'S SPLIT UP! I'LL E-EXORCISE THE ONES IN THIS HOLE F-FIRST!!
COME BACK HERE, YOU!
He's so fired up...

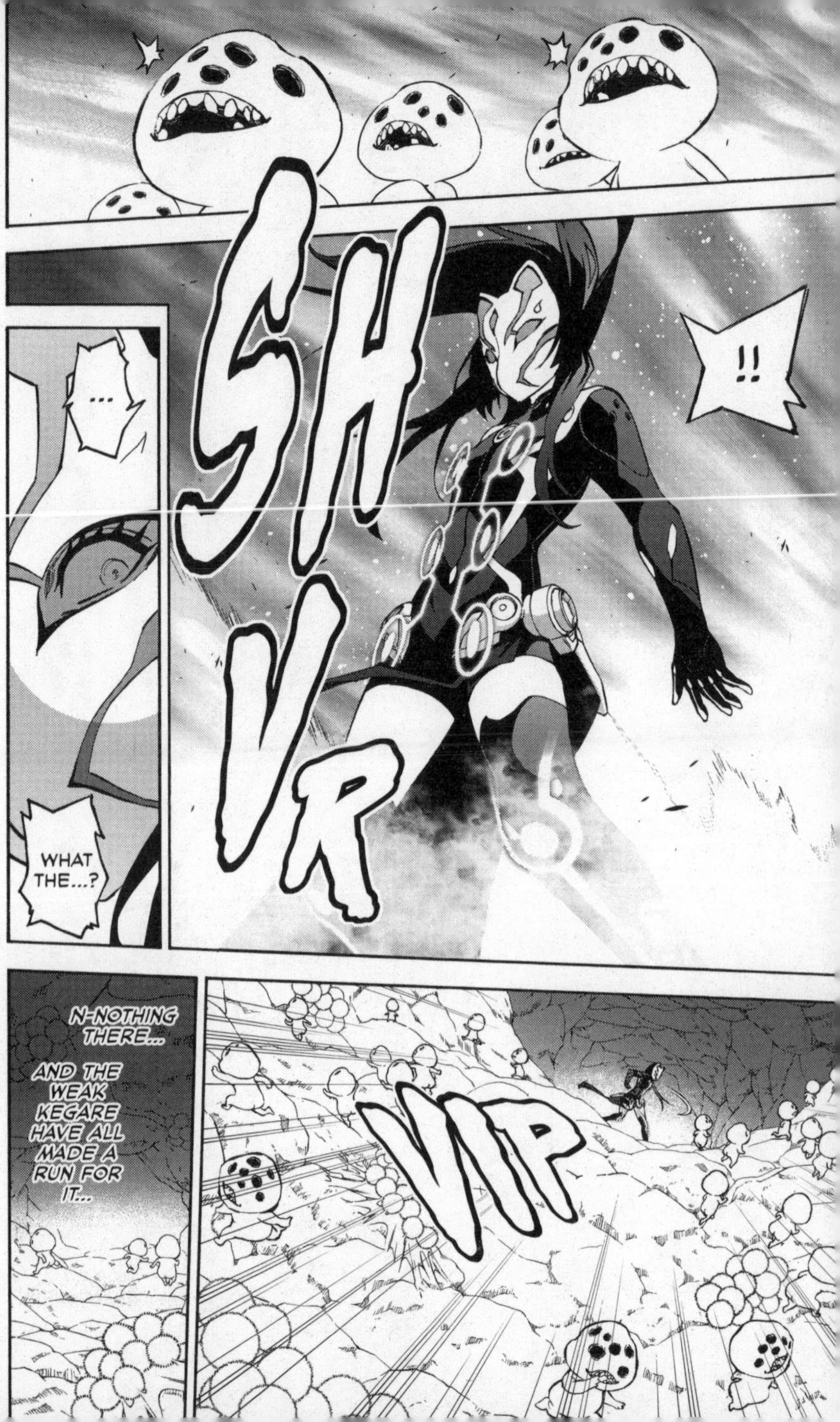
!!
SHVR
...
WHAT THE...?
VIIP
N-NOTHING THERE...
AND THE WEAK KEGARE HAVE ALL MADE A RUN FOR IT...

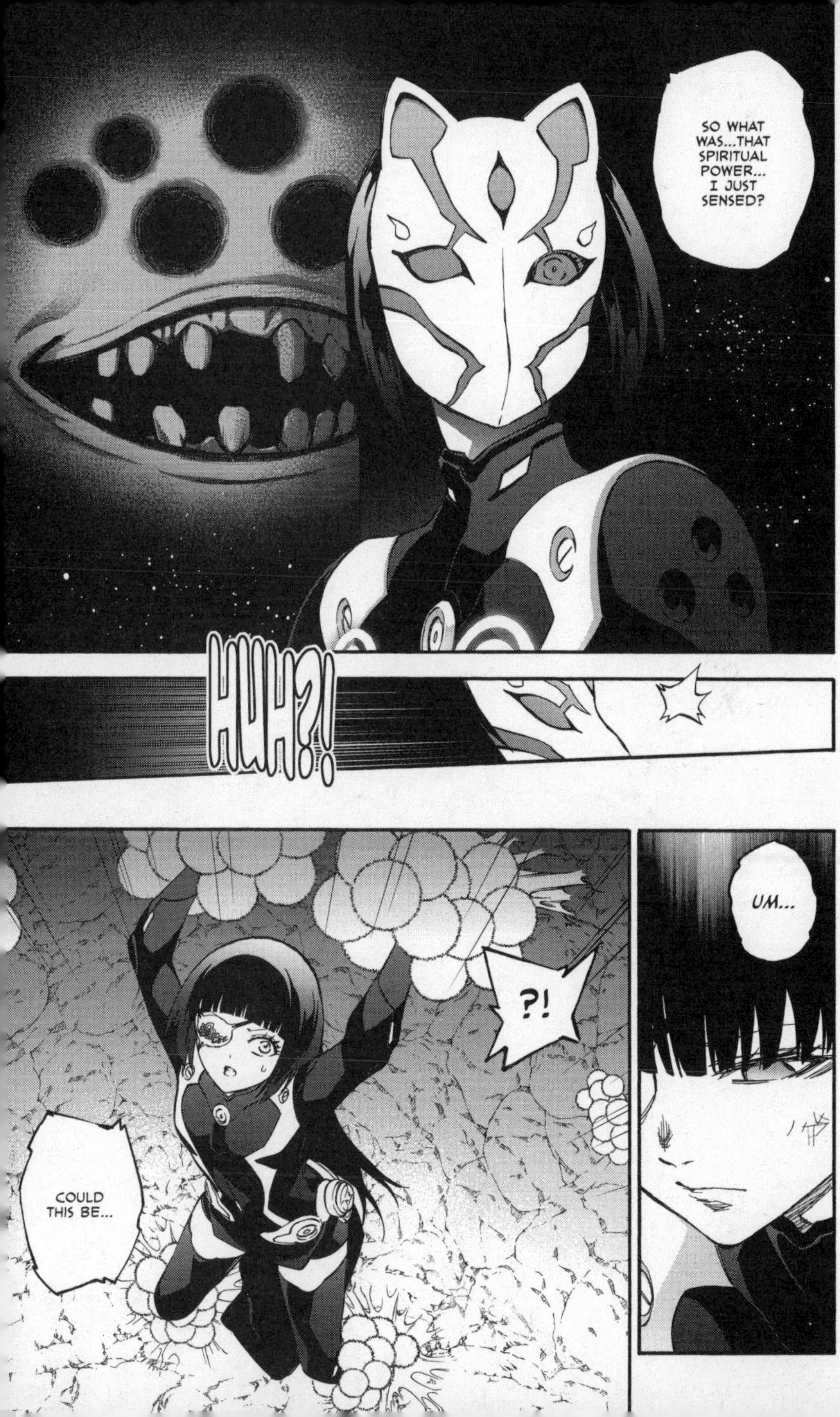
SO WHAT WAS...THAT SPIRITUAL POWER... I JUST SENSED?
HUH?!
UM...
?!
COULD THIS BE...

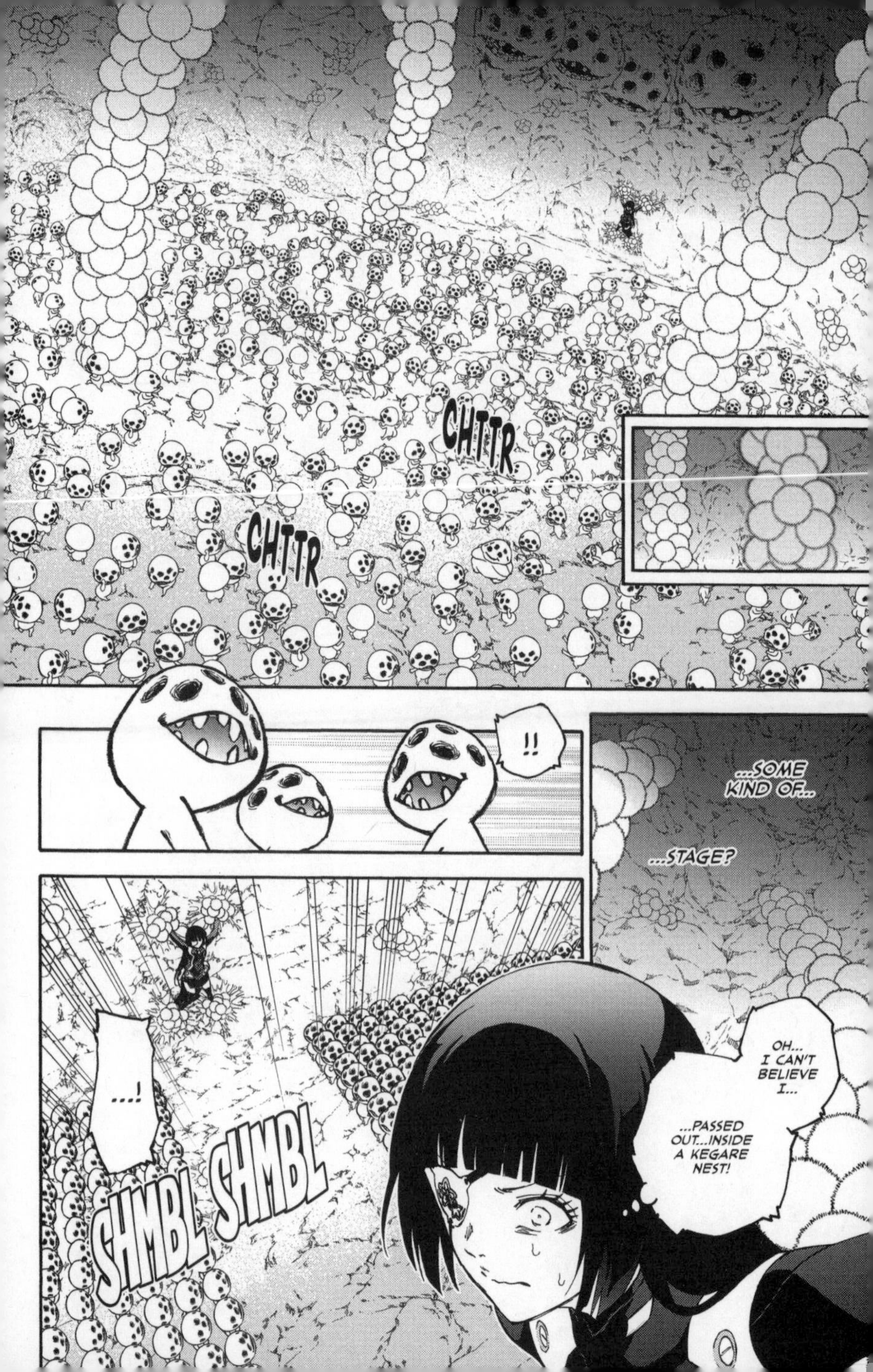
CHTTR
CHTTR
...SOME KIND OF...
...STAGE?
OH... I CAN'T BELIEVE I...
...PASSED OUT...INSIDE A KEGARE NEST!
!!
...!
SHMBL SHMBL

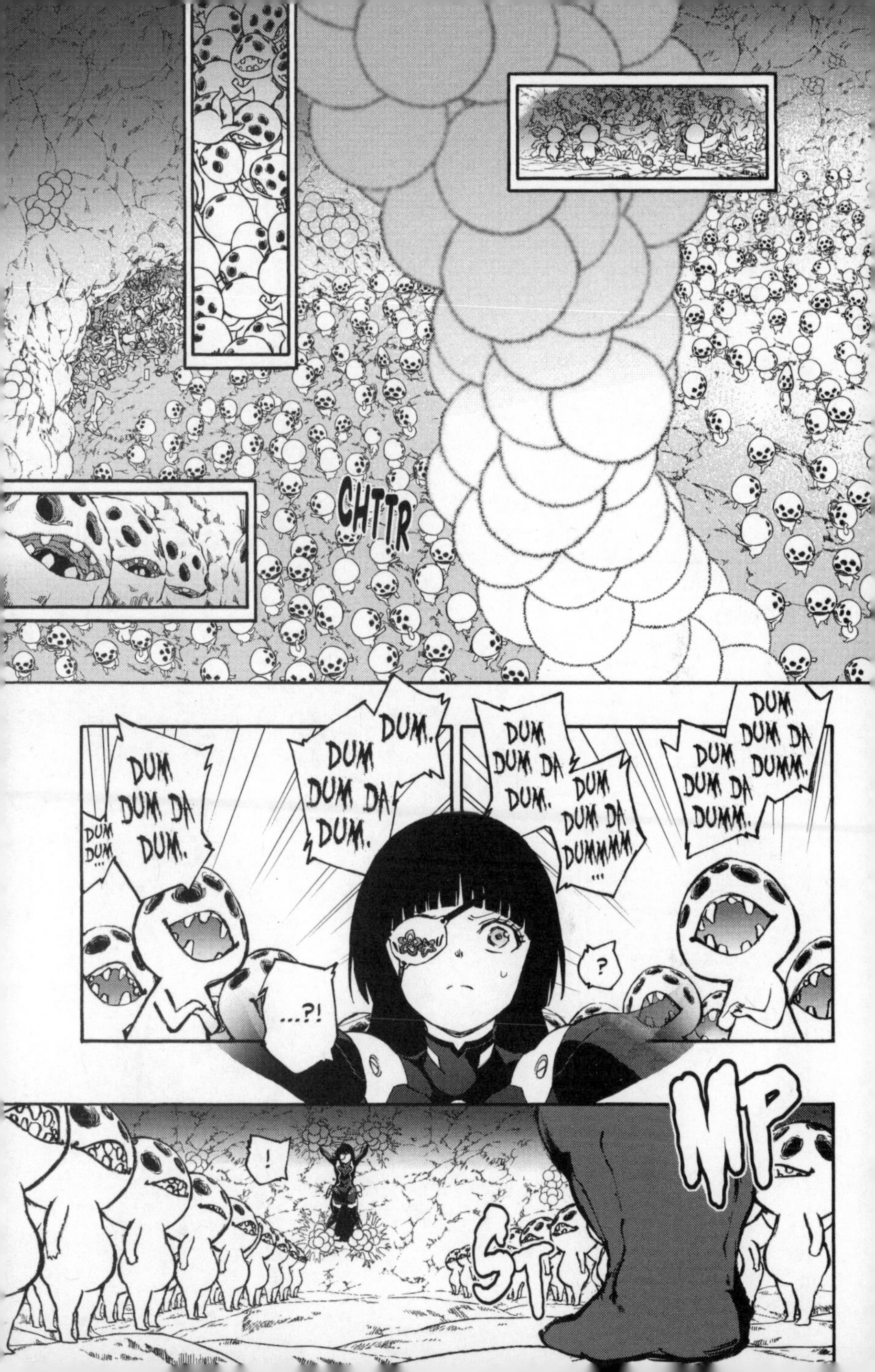
CHTTR
DUM DUM DA DUMM.
DUM DUM DA DUMM.
DUM DUM DA DUM.
DUM DUM DA DUMMMM ...
?
DUM. DUM DUM DA DUM.
DUM DUM DA DUM.
DUM DUM ...
...?!
STMP
!

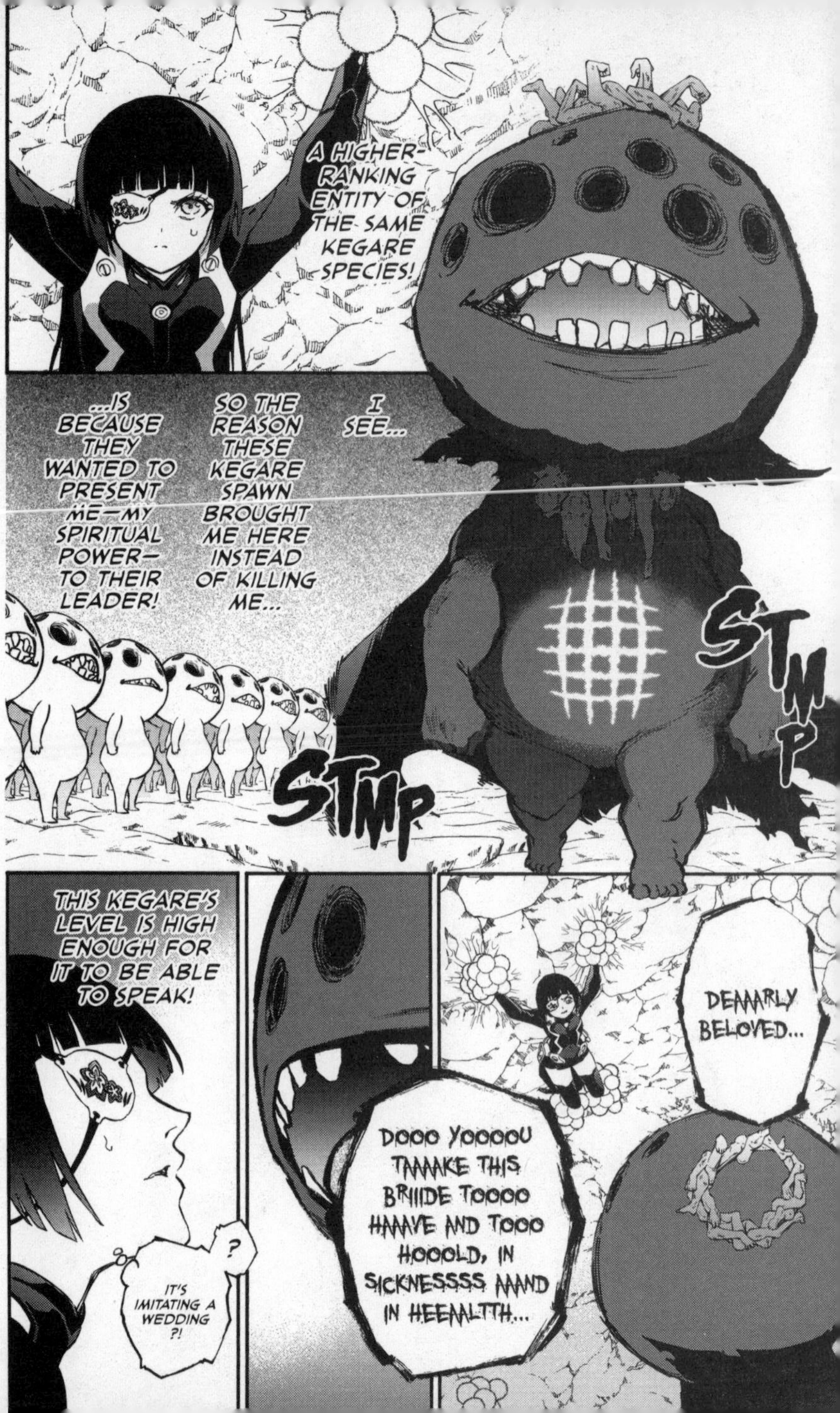
A HIGHER-RANKING ENTITY OF THE SAME KEGARE SPECIES!
I SEE...
SO THE REASON THESE KEGARE SPAWN BROUGHT ME HERE INSTEAD OF KILLING ME...
...IS BECAUSE THEY WANTED TO PRESENT ME—MY SPIRITUAL POWER—TO THEIR LEADER!
STMP
STMP
DEAAARLY BELOVED...
DOOO YOOOOU TAAAAKE THIS BRIIDE TOOOO HAAAVE AND TOOO HOOOLD, IN SICKNESSSS AAAND IN HEEAALTTH...
THIS KEGARE'S LEVEL IS HIGH ENOUGH FOR IT TO BE ABLE TO SPEAK!
?
IT'S IMITATING A WEDDING?!

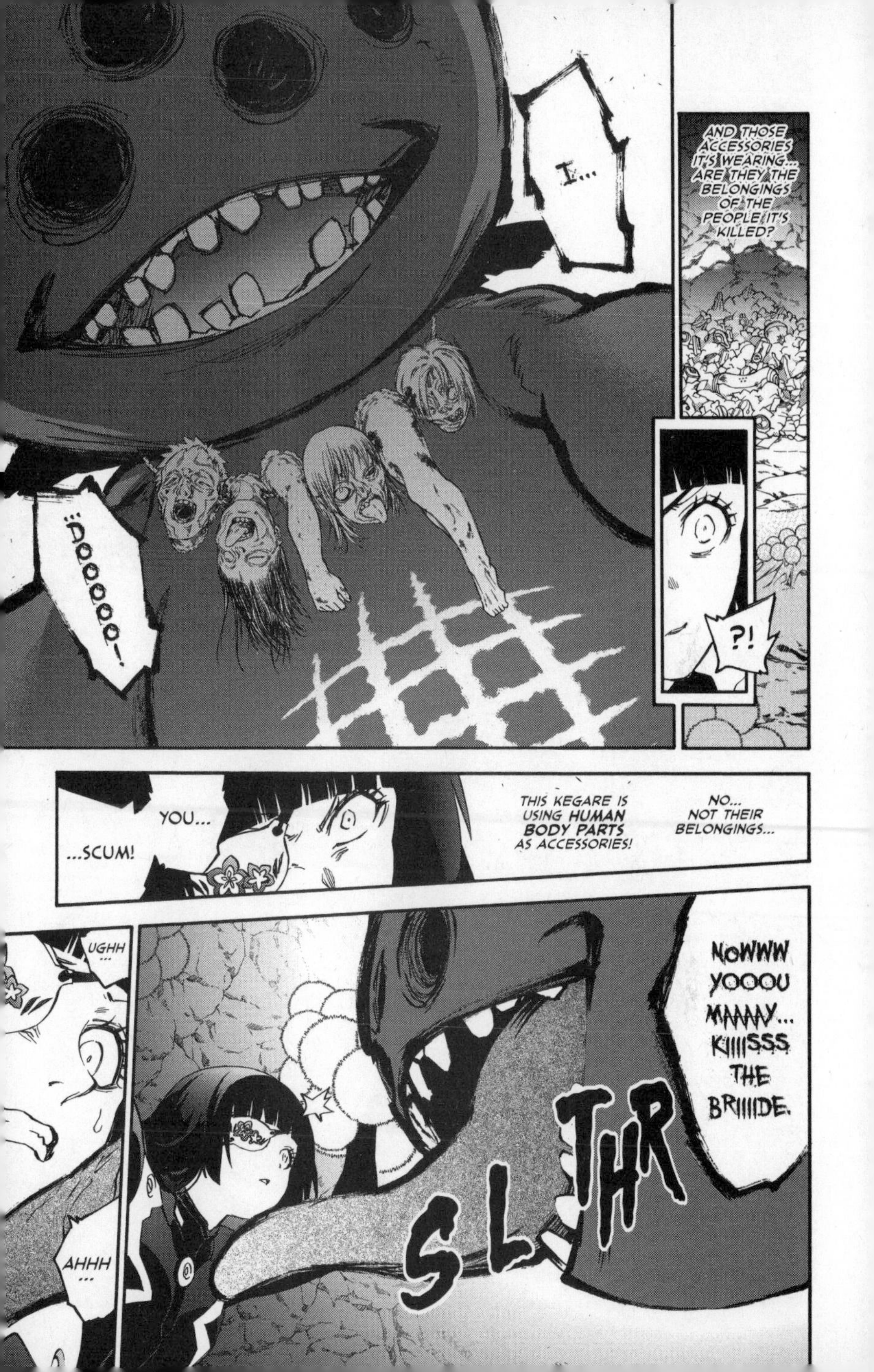
AND THOSE ACCESSORIES IT'S WEARING... ARE THEY THE BELONGINGS OF THE PEOPLE IT'S KILLED?
?!
I...
...DOOOOOO!
NO... NOT THEIR BELONGINGS...
THIS KEGARE IS USING HUMAN BODY PARTS AS ACCESSORIES!
YOU...
...SCUM!
NOWWW YOOOU MAAAAY... KIIIISSS THE BRIIIIDE.
SLTHR
UGHH...
AHHH...

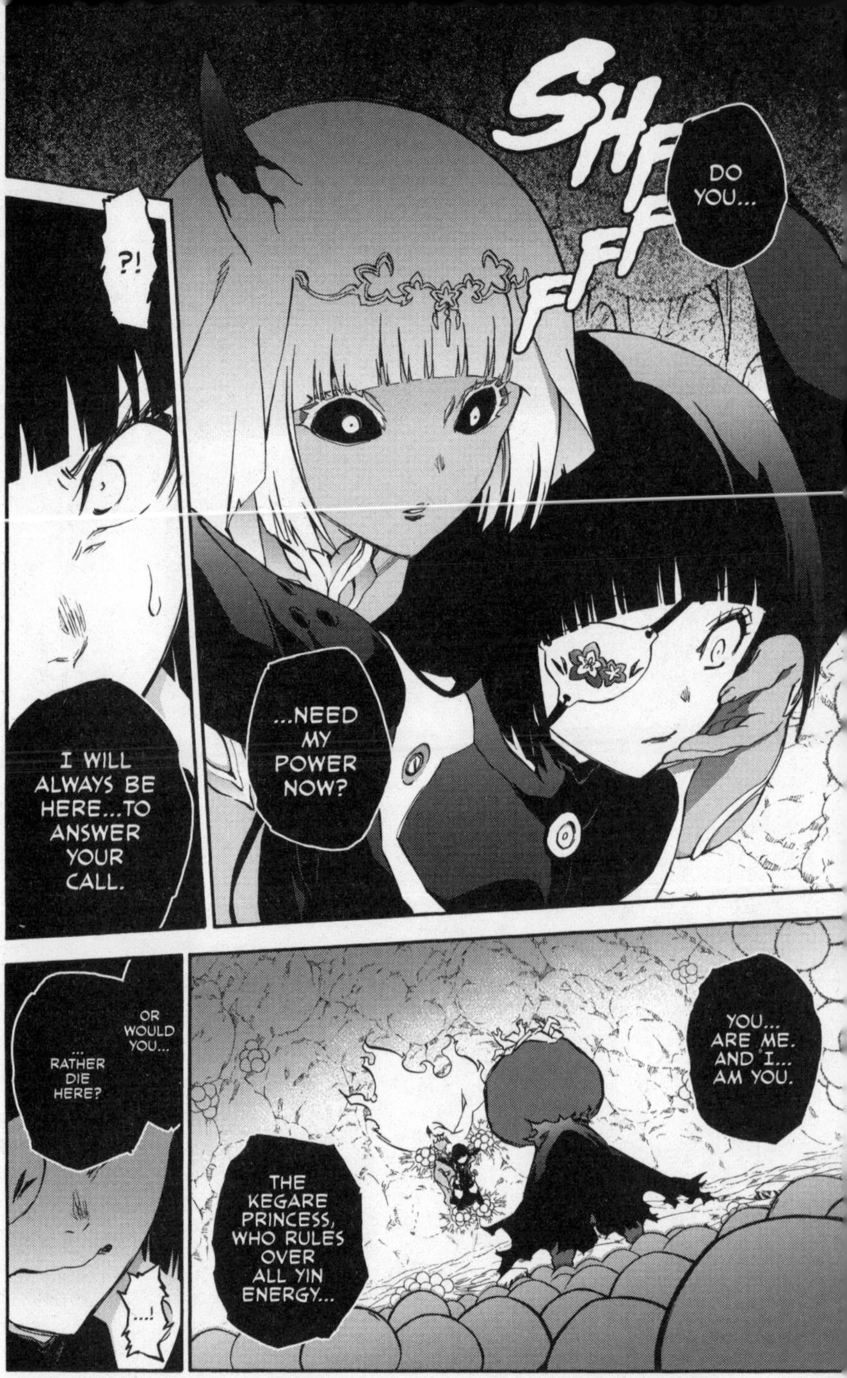
SHFFFF
DO YOU...
...NEED MY POWER NOW?
?!
I WILL ALWAYS BE HERE...TO ANSWER YOUR CALL.
YOU... ARE ME. AND I... AM YOU.
THE KEGARE PRINCESS, WHO RULES OVER ALL YIN ENERGY...
OR WOULD YOU...
...RATHER DIE HERE?
...!

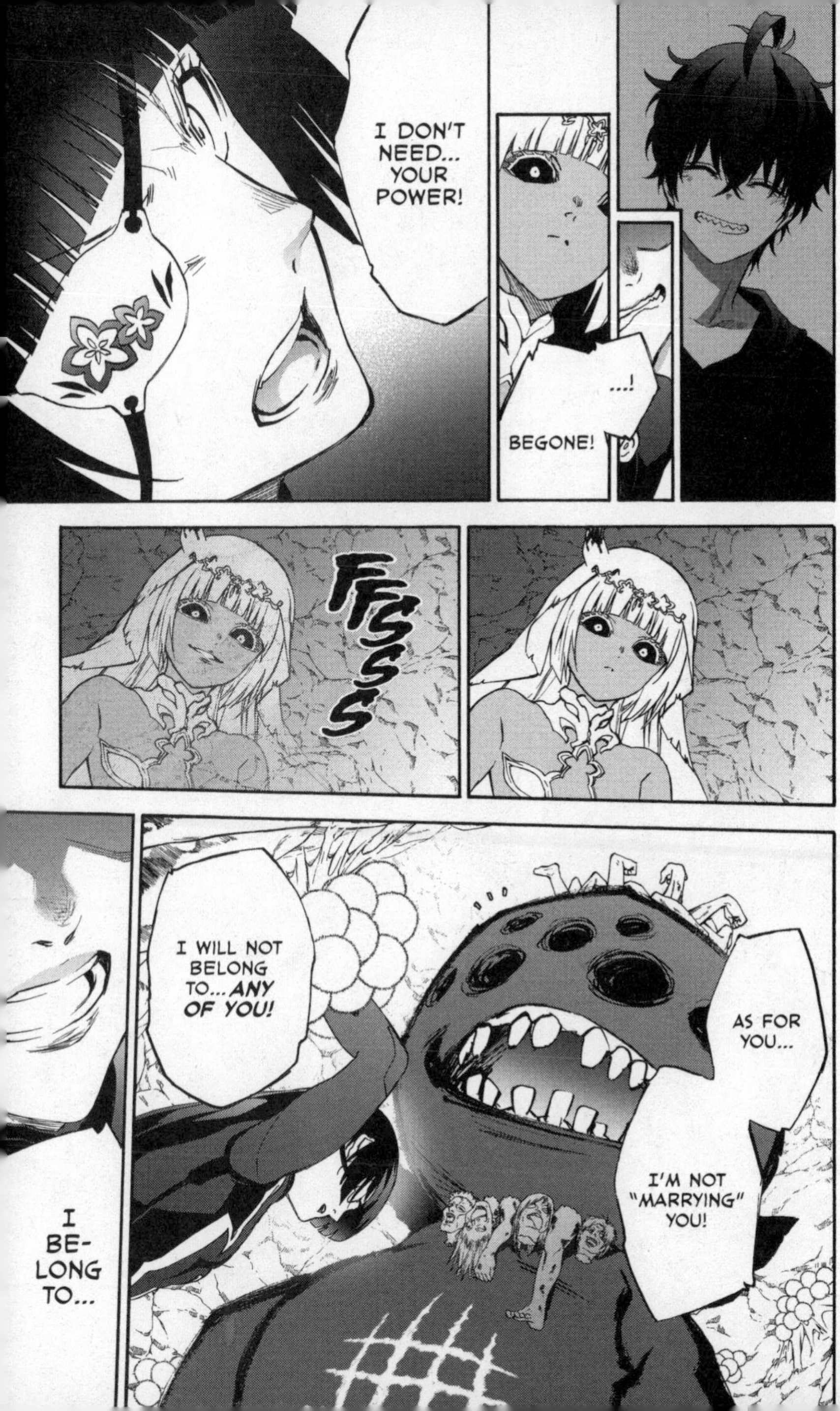
...!
BEGONE!
I DON'T NEED... YOUR POWER!
FFSSS
AS FOR YOU...
I'M NOT "MARRYING" YOU!
I WILL NOT BELONG TO... ANY OF YOU!
I BE-LONG TO...

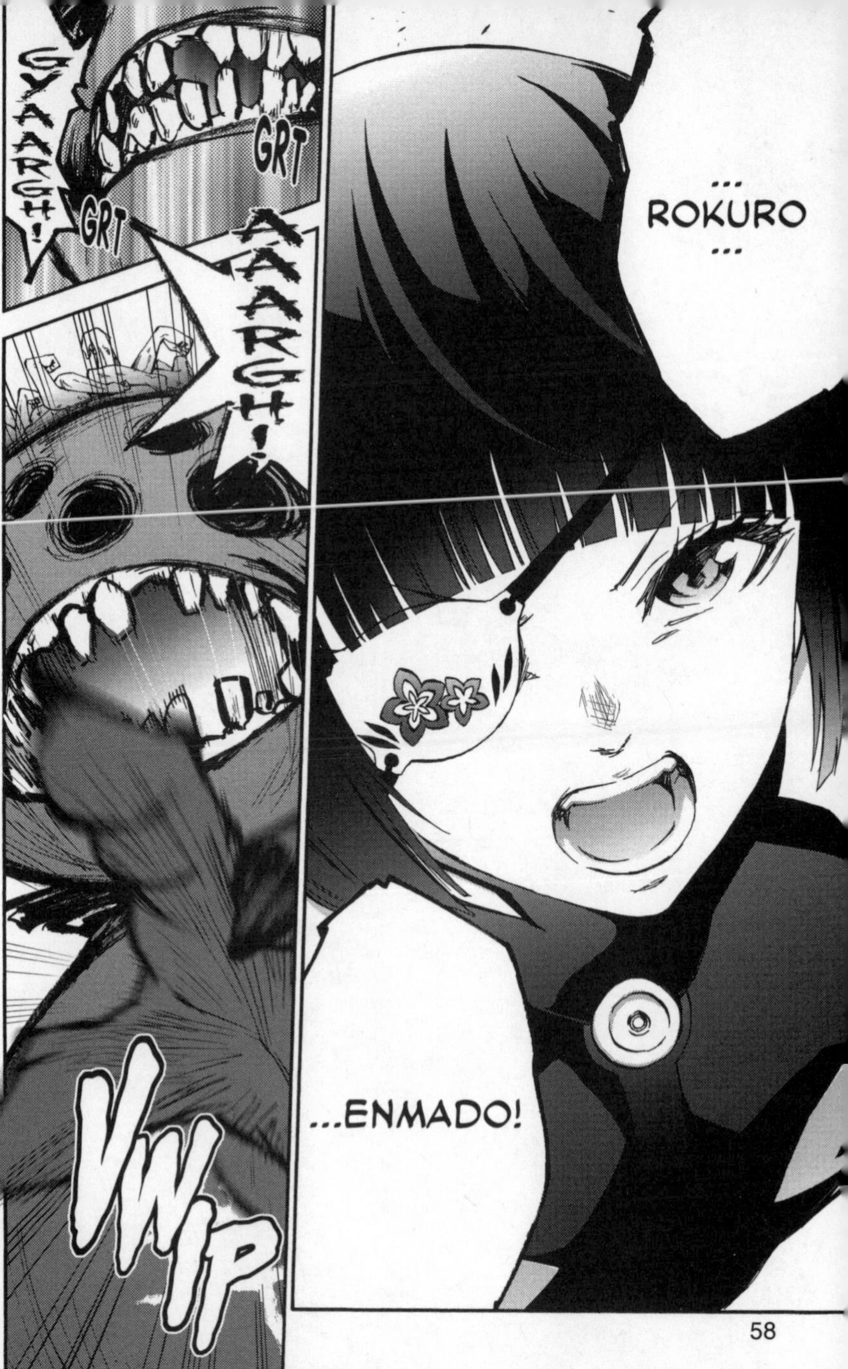
...
ROKURO
...
...ENMADO!
GYAARGH!
GRT
GRT
AAARGH!
VWIP

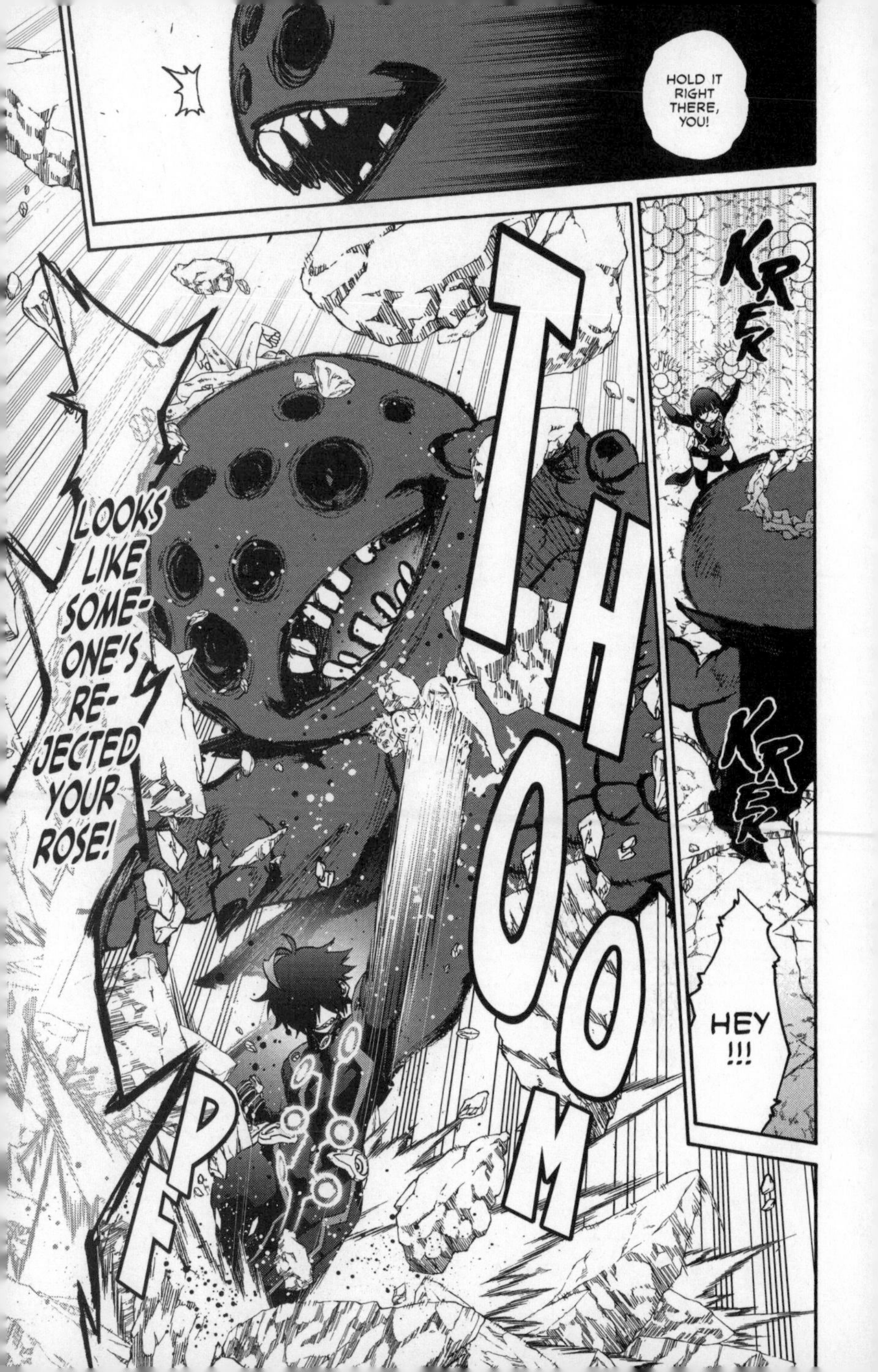
HOLD IT RIGHT THERE, YOU!
KREK
KREK
HEY !!!
THOOM
LOOKS LIKE SOME-ONE'S RE-JECTED YOUR ROSE!
PF

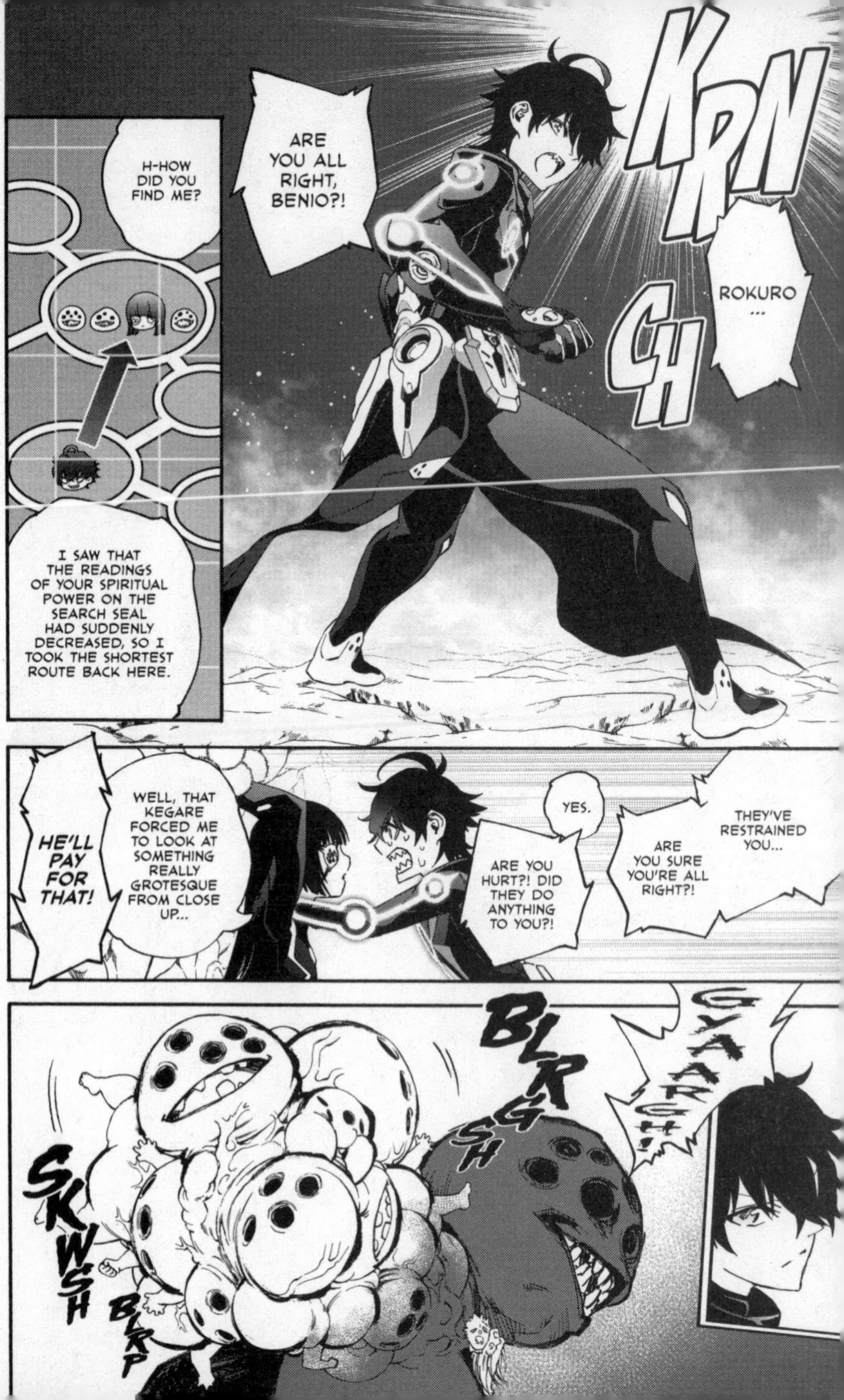
KRN
CH
ROKURO...
ARE YOU ALL RIGHT, BENIO?!
H-HOW DID YOU FIND ME?
I SAW THAT THE READINGS OF YOUR SPIRITUAL POWER ON THE SEARCH SEAL HAD SUDDENLY DECREASED, SO I TOOK THE SHORTEST ROUTE BACK HERE.
THEY'VE RESTRAINED YOU...
ARE YOU SURE YOU'RE ALL RIGHT?!
ARE YOU HURT?! DID THEY DO ANYTHING TO YOU?!
YES.
WELL, THAT KEGARE FORCED ME TO LOOK AT SOMETHING REALLY GROTESQUE FROM CLOSE UP...
HE'LL PAY FOR THAT!
GYAARGH!!
BLRGSH
SKWSH
BLRP

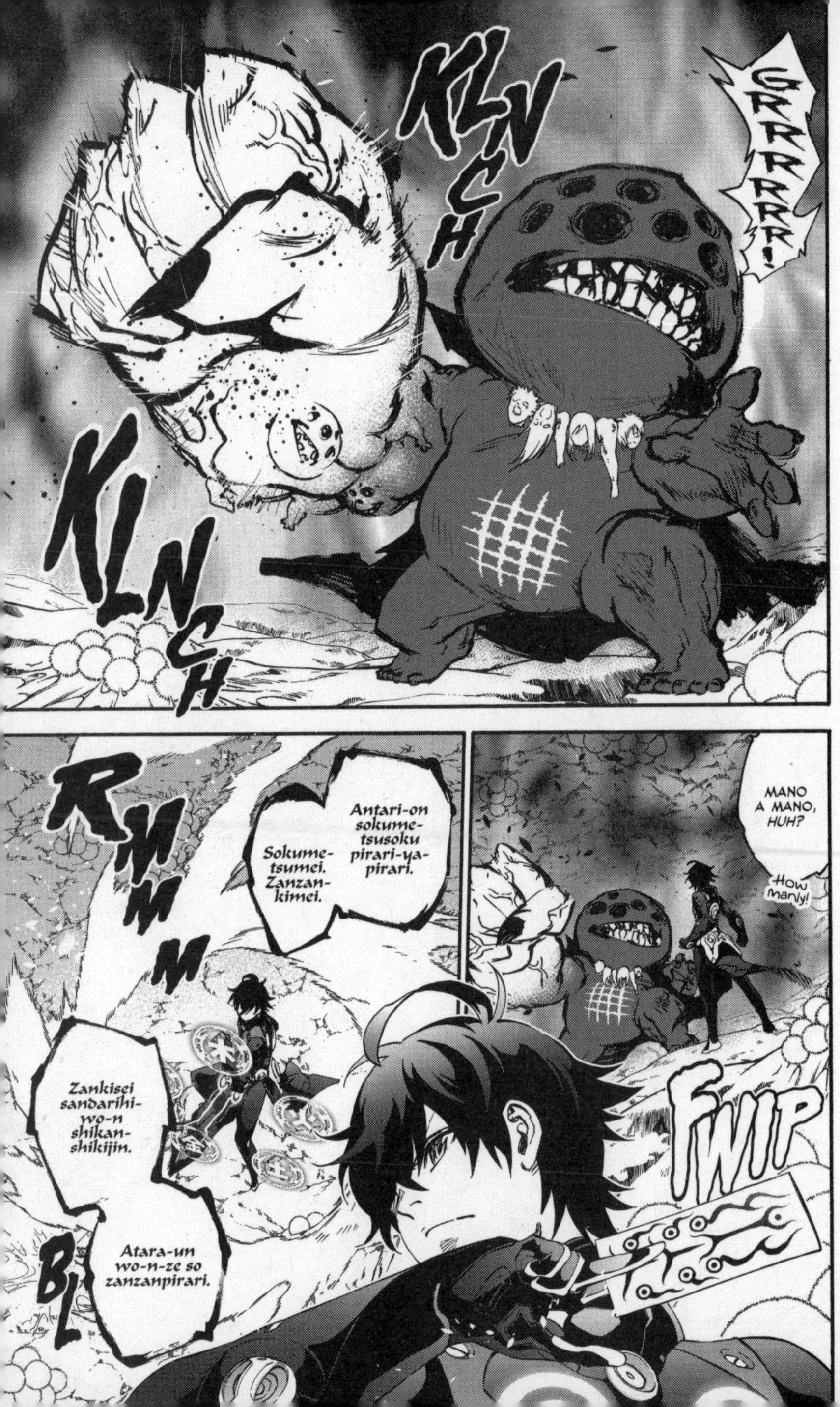
GRRRRRR!
KLNCH
KLNCH
MANO A MANO, HUH?
How manly!
FWIP
RMMM
Antari-on sokume-tsusoku pirari-ya-pirari.
Sokume-tsumei. Zanzan-kimei.
Zankisei sandarihi-wo-n shikan-shikijin.
Atara-un wo-n-ze so zanzanpirari.
BL

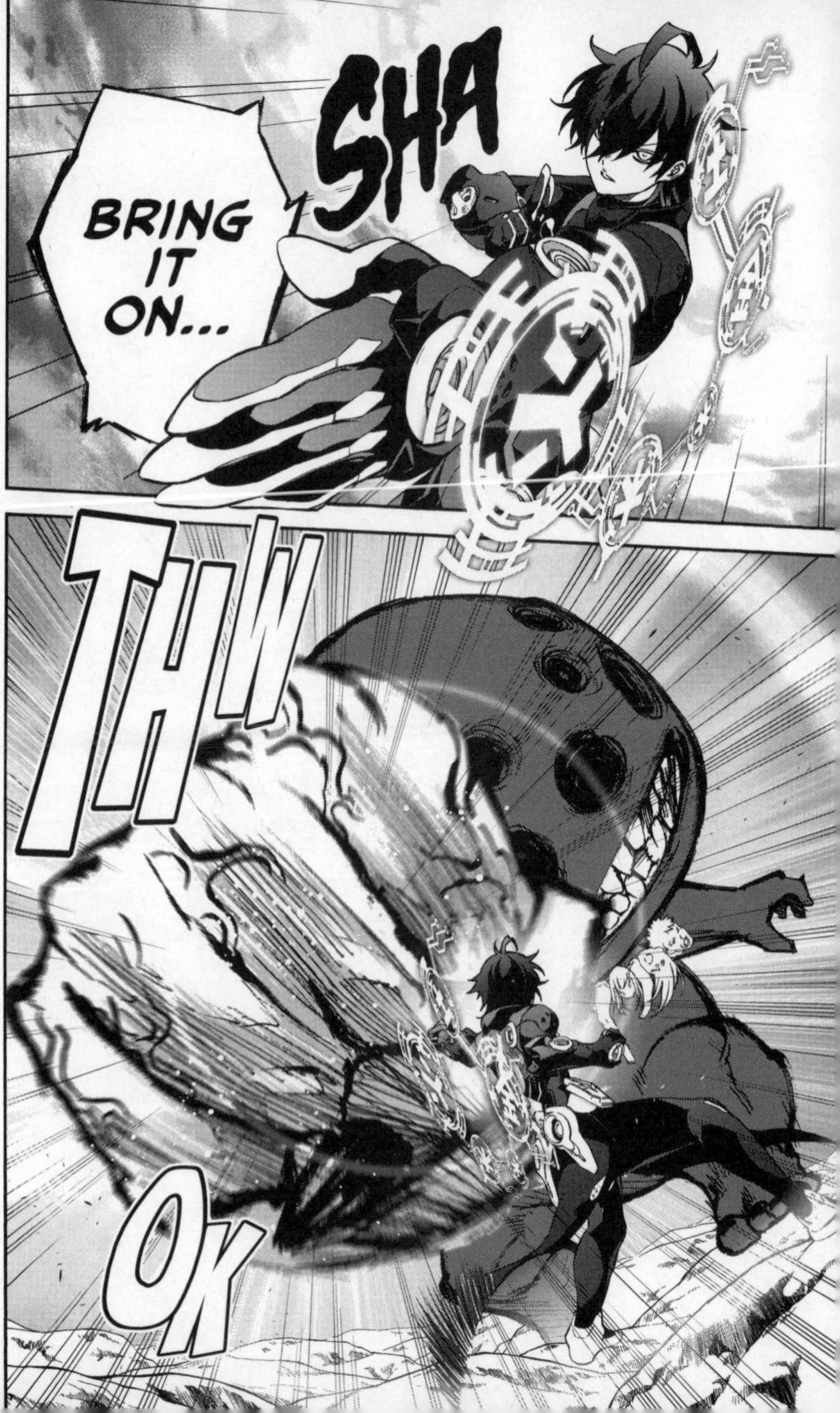
SHA
BRING IT ON...
THWOK

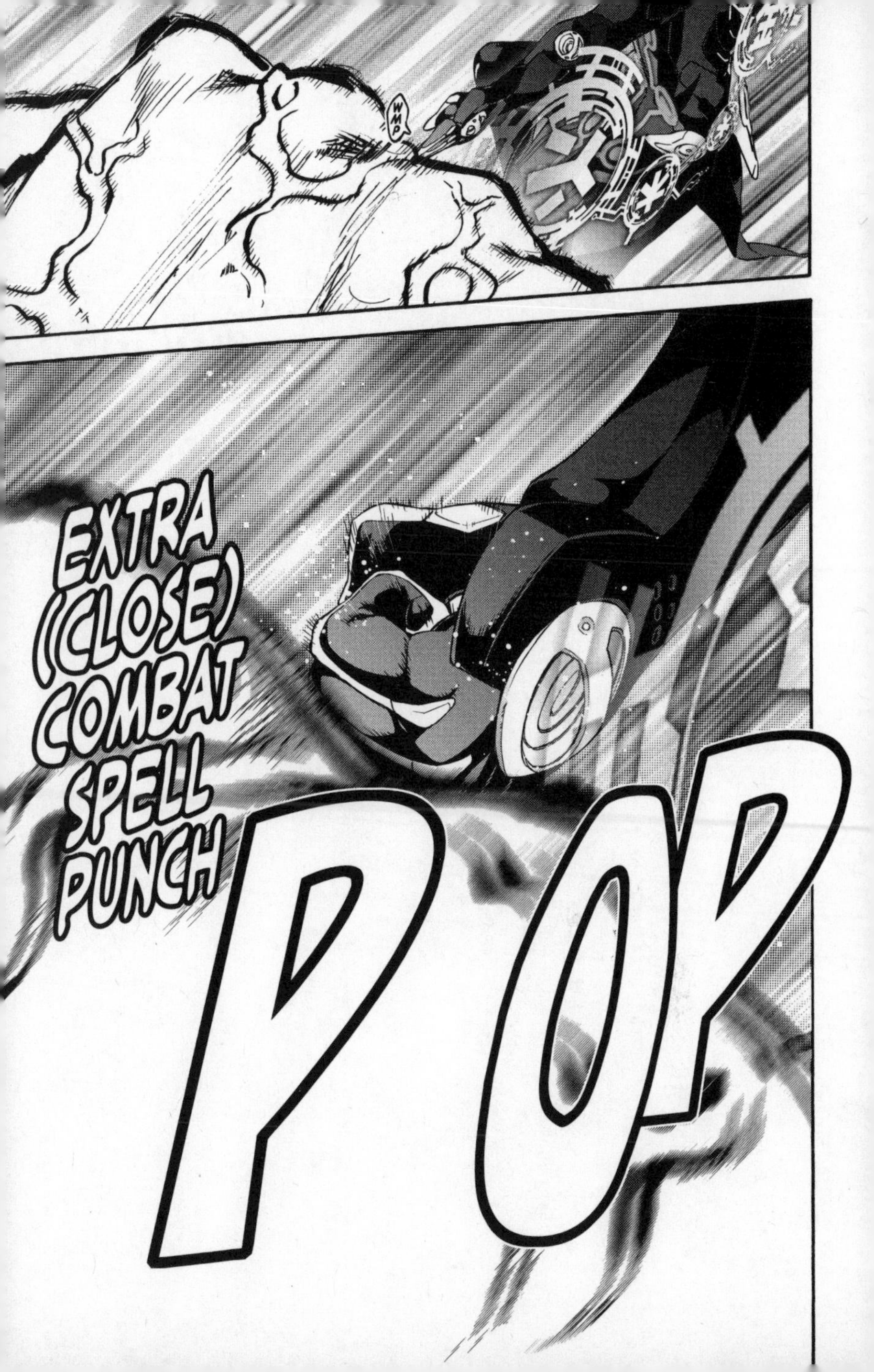
WMP
EXTRA (CLOSE) COMBAT SPELL PUNCH
POP

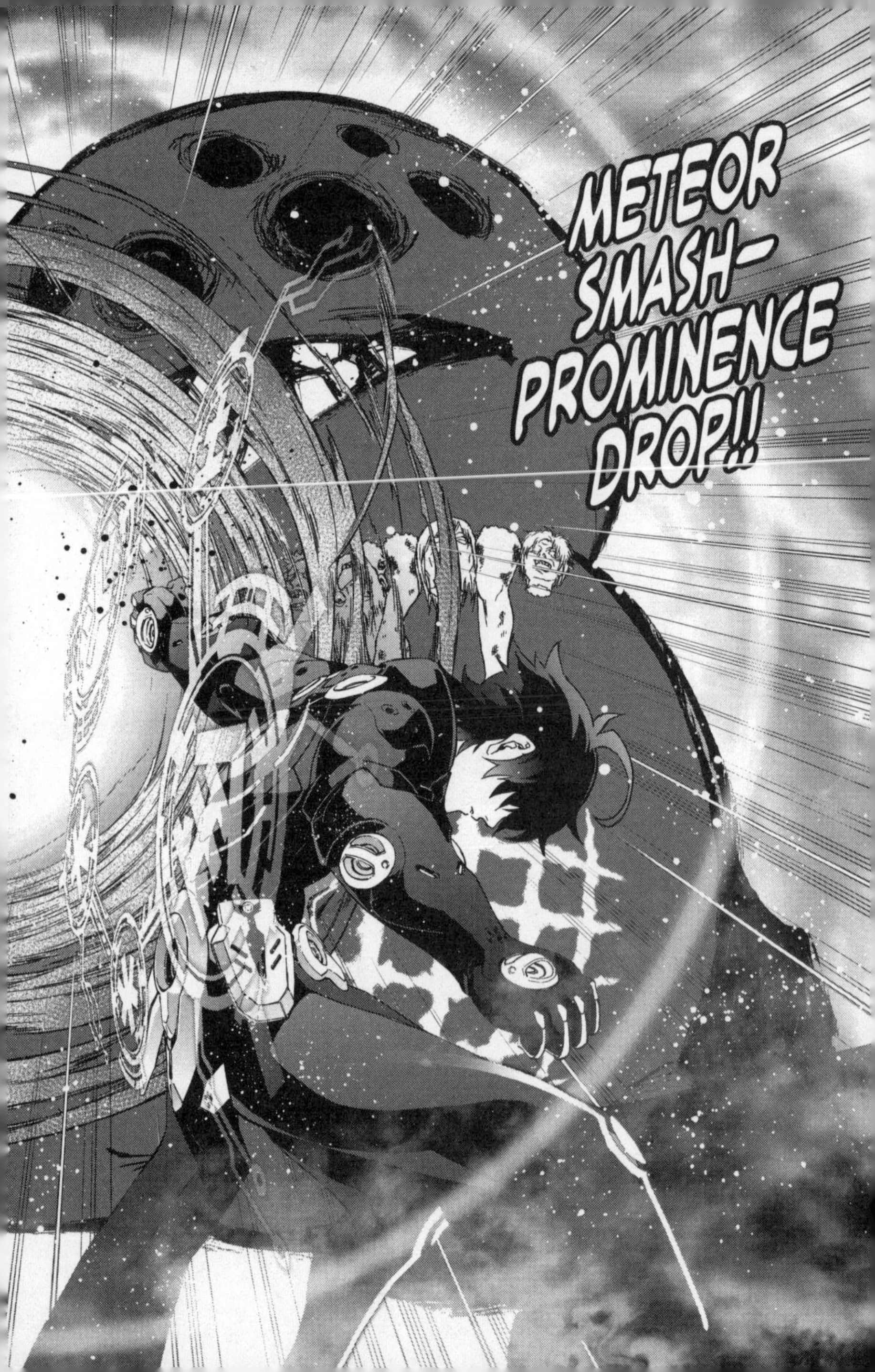
METEOR SMASH-PROMINENCE DROP!!

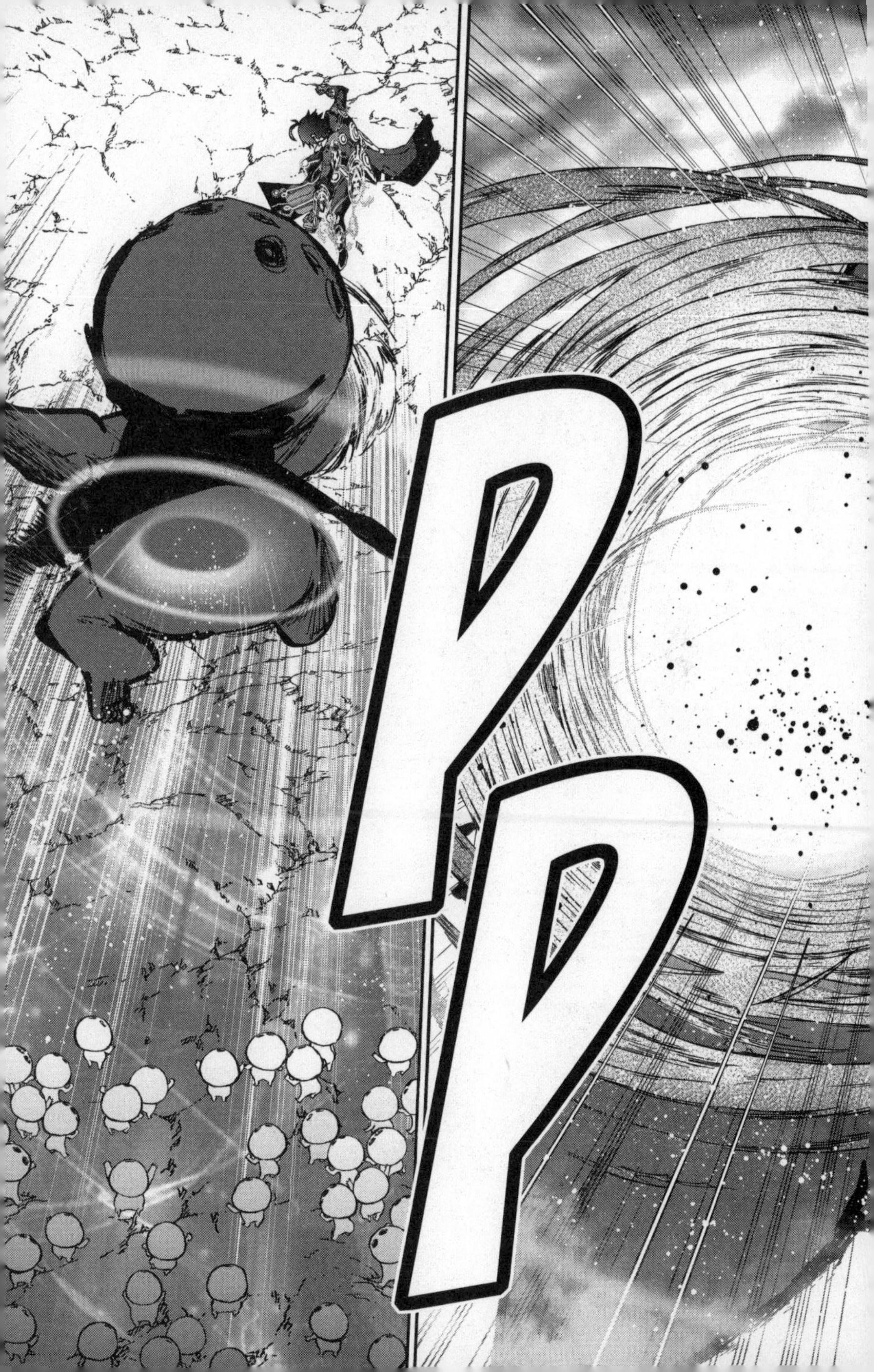

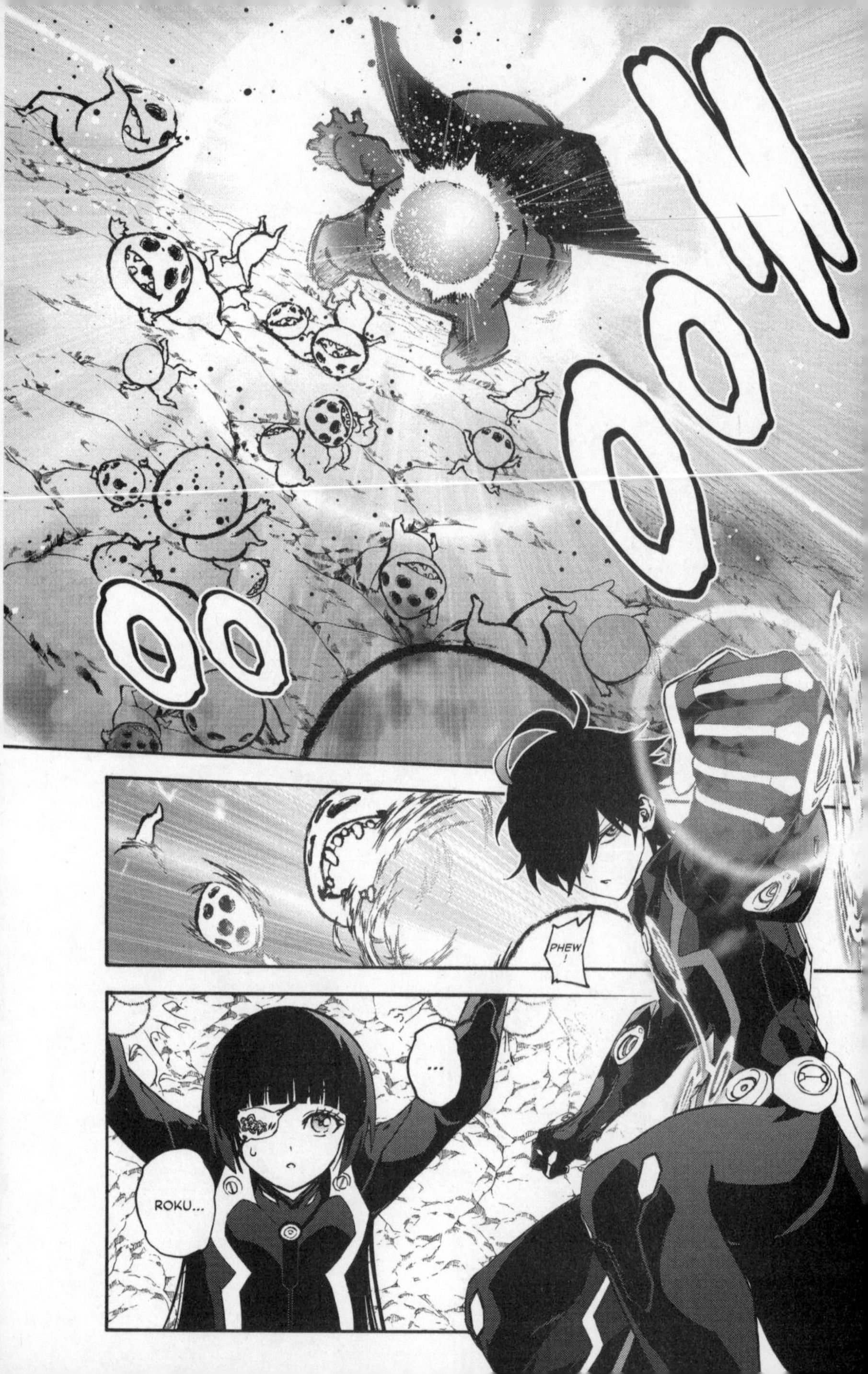
OOOM
OO
PHEW!
...
ROKU...

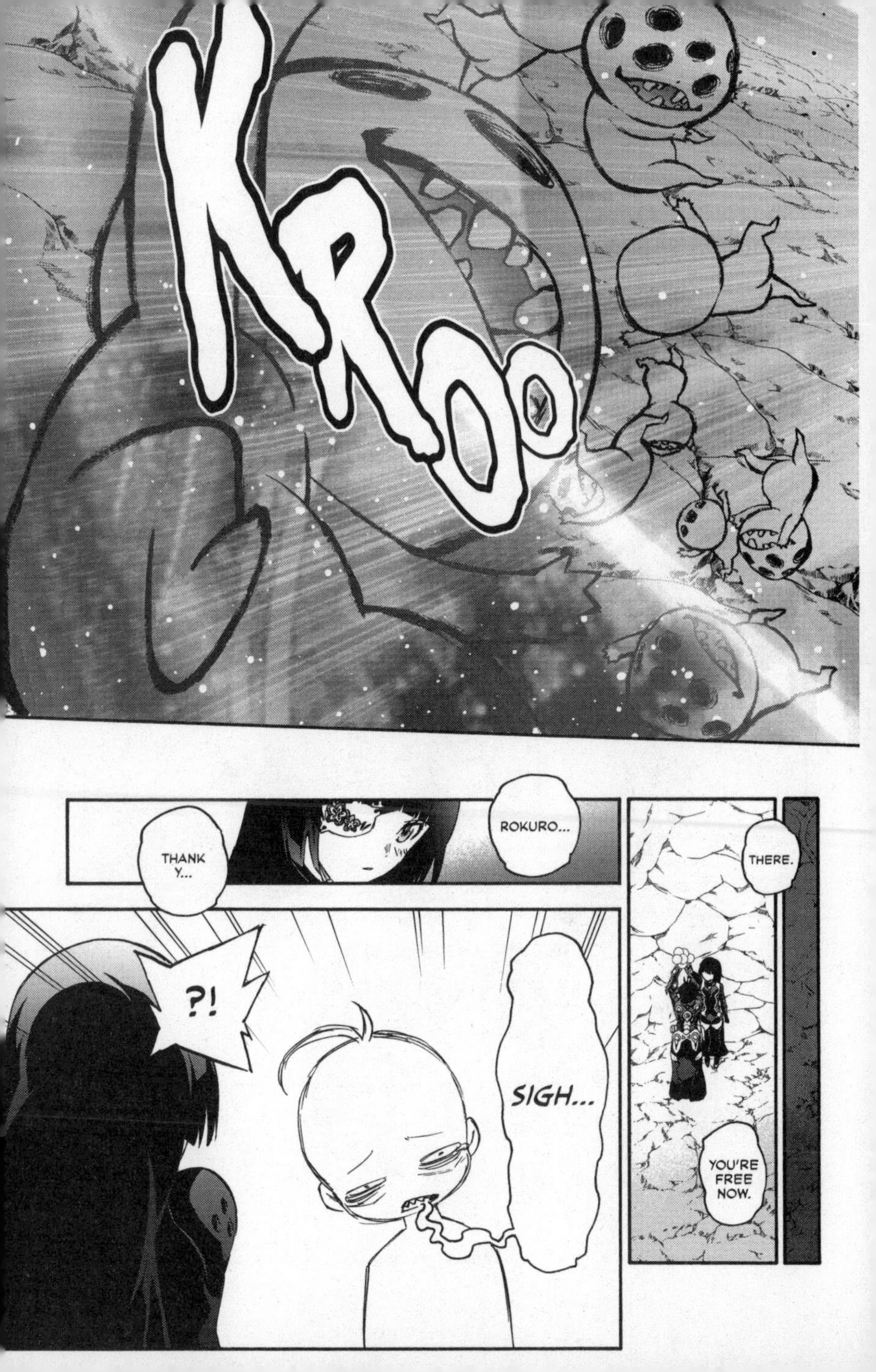
KROOO
THERE.
YOU'RE FREE NOW.
ROKURO...
THANK Y...
SIGH...
?!

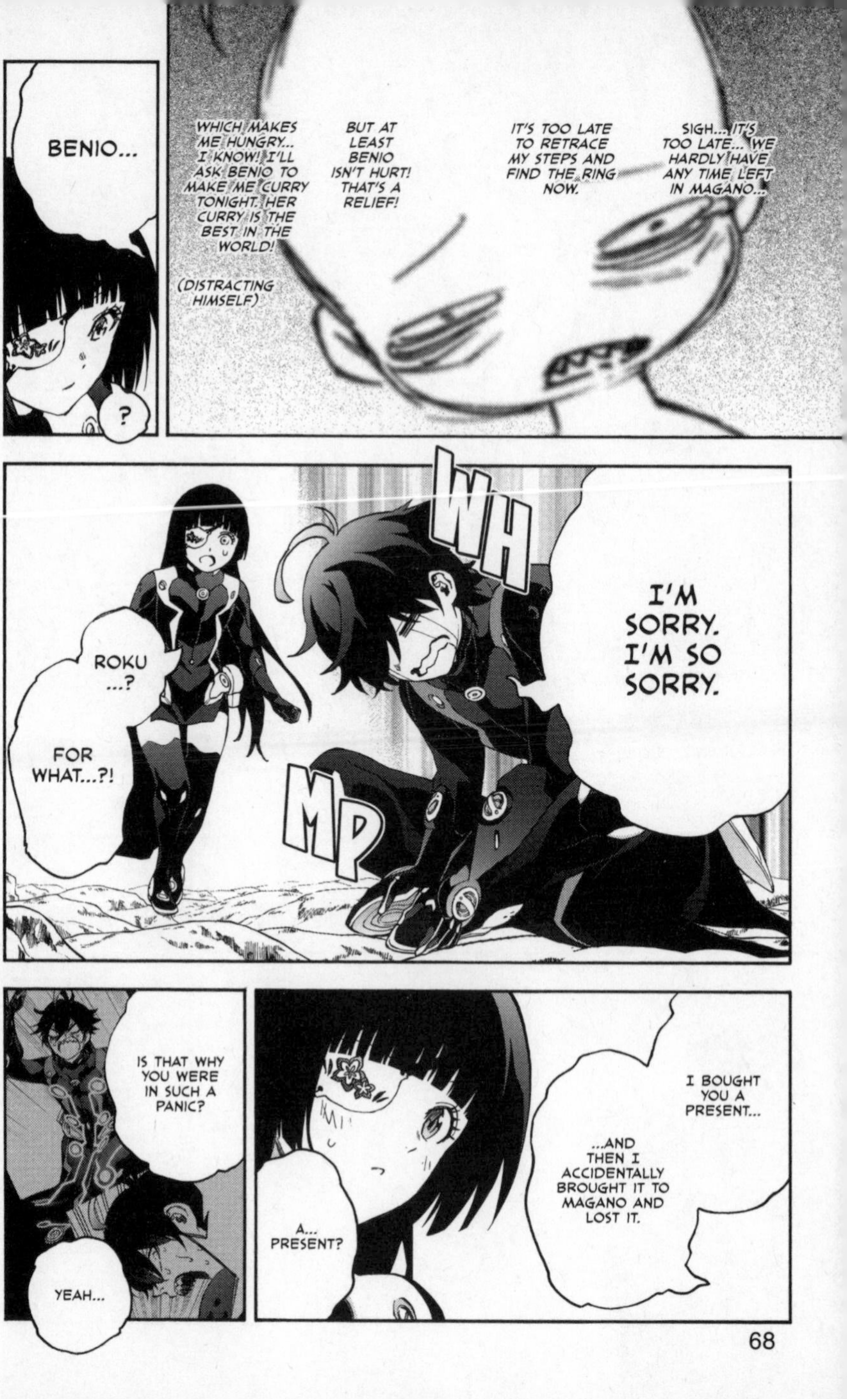
SIGH... IT'S TOO LATE... WE HARDLY HAVE ANY TIME LEFT IN MAGANO...
IT'S TOO LATE TO RETRACE MY STEPS AND FIND THE RING NOW.
BUT AT LEAST BENIO ISN'T HURT! THAT'S A RELIEF!
WHICH MAKES ME HUNGRY... I KNOW! I'LL ASK BENIO TO MAKE ME CURRY TONIGHT. HER CURRY IS THE BEST IN THE WORLD!
(DISTRACTING HIMSELF)
BENIO...
?
I'M SORRY. I'M SO SORRY.
WH
MP
ROKU ...?
FOR WHAT...?!
I BOUGHT YOU A PRESENT...
...AND THEN I ACCIDENTALLY BROUGHT IT TO MAGANO AND LOST IT.
A... PRESENT?
IS THAT WHY YOU WERE IN SUCH A PANIC?
YEAH...

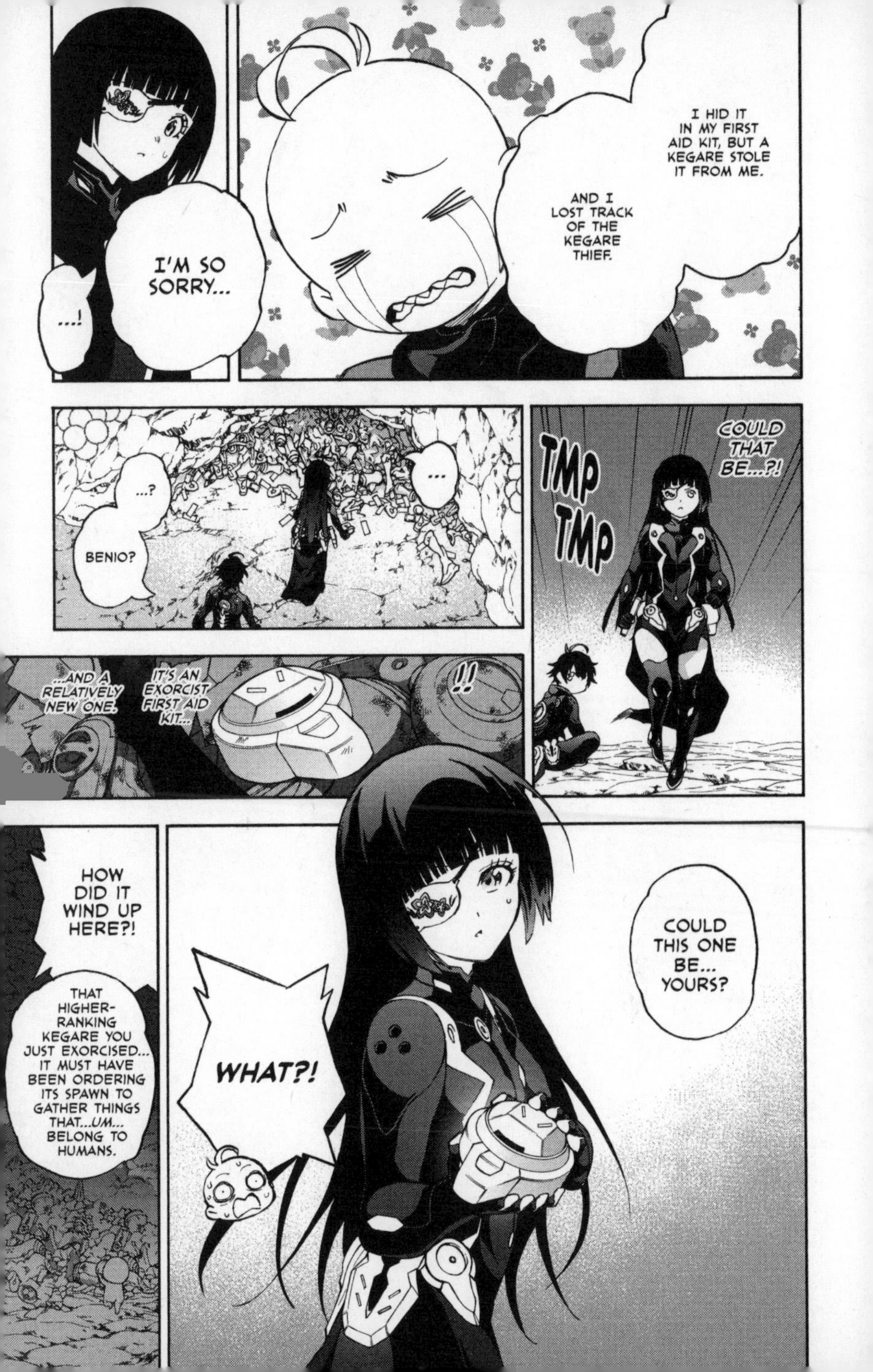

I HID IT IN MY FIRST AID KIT, BUT A KEGARE STOLE IT FROM ME.
AND I LOST TRACK OF THE KEGARE THIEF.
I'M SO SORRY...
...!
COULD THAT BE...?!
TMP TMP
...
...?
BENIO?
!!
IT'S AN EXORCIST FIRST AID KIT...
...AND A RELATIVELY NEW ONE.
COULD THIS ONE BE... YOURS?
WHAT?!
HOW DID IT WIND UP HERE?!
THAT HIGHER-RANKING KEGARE YOU JUST EXORCISED... IT MUST HAVE BEEN ORDERING ITS SPAWN TO GATHER THINGS THAT...UM... BELONG TO HUMANS.

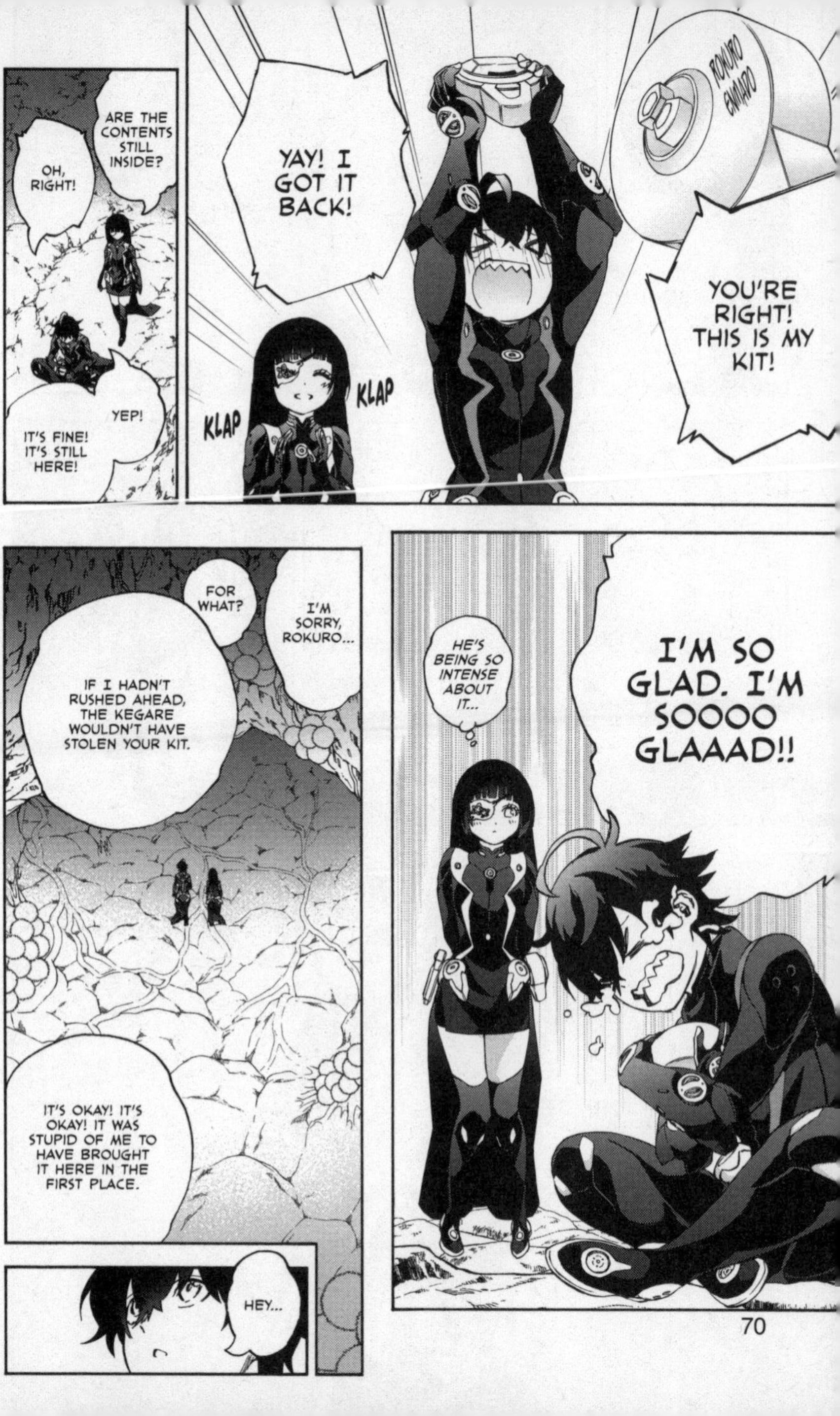
ROKURO ENMADO
YOU'RE RIGHT! THIS IS MY KIT!
YAY! I GOT IT BACK!
KLAP
KLAP
ARE THE CONTENTS STILL INSIDE?
OH, RIGHT!
YEP!
IT'S FINE! IT'S STILL HERE!
I'M SO GLAD. I'M SOOOO GLAAAD!!
HE'S BEING SO INTENSE ABOUT IT...
I'M SORRY, ROKURO...
FOR WHAT?
IF I HADN'T RUSHED AHEAD, THE KEGARE WOULDN'T HAVE STOLEN YOUR KIT.
IT'S OKAY! IT'S OKAY! IT WAS STUPID OF ME TO HAVE BROUGHT IT HERE IN THE FIRST PLACE.
HEY...

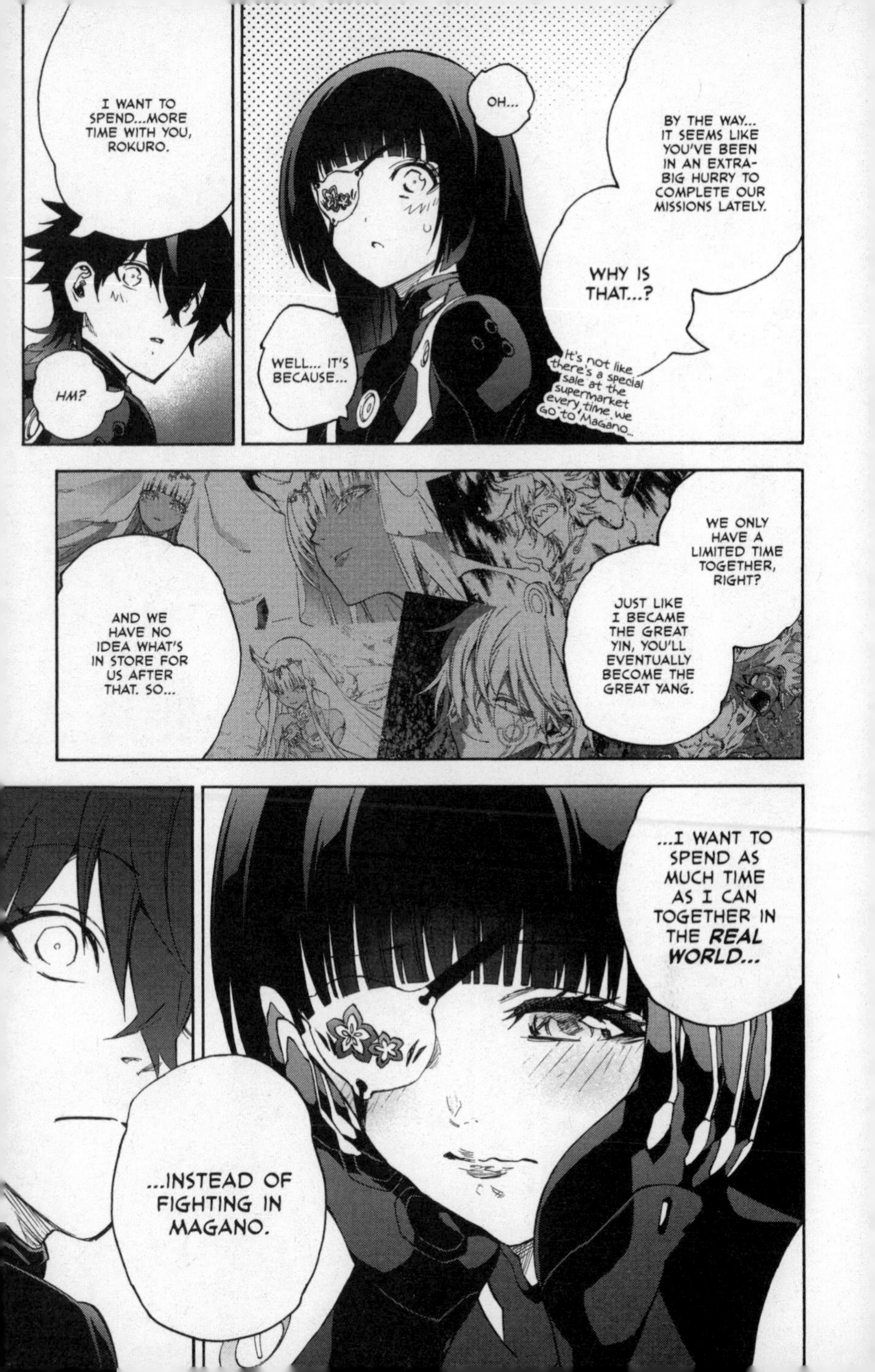
BY THE WAY... IT SEEMS LIKE YOU'VE BEEN IN AN EXTRA-BIG HURRY TO COMPLETE OUR MISSIONS LATELY.
WHY IS THAT...?
It's not like there's a special sale at the supermarket every time we go to Magano...
OH...
WELL... IT'S BECAUSE...
I WANT TO SPEND...MORE TIME WITH YOU, ROKURO.
HM?
WE ONLY HAVE A LIMITED TIME TOGETHER, RIGHT?
JUST LIKE I BECAME THE GREAT YIN, YOU'LL EVENTUALLY BECOME THE GREAT YANG.
AND WE HAVE NO IDEA WHAT'S IN STORE FOR US AFTER THAT. SO...
...I WANT TO SPEND AS MUCH TIME AS I CAN TOGETHER IN THE *REAL WORLD*...
...INSTEAD OF FIGHTING IN MAGANO.

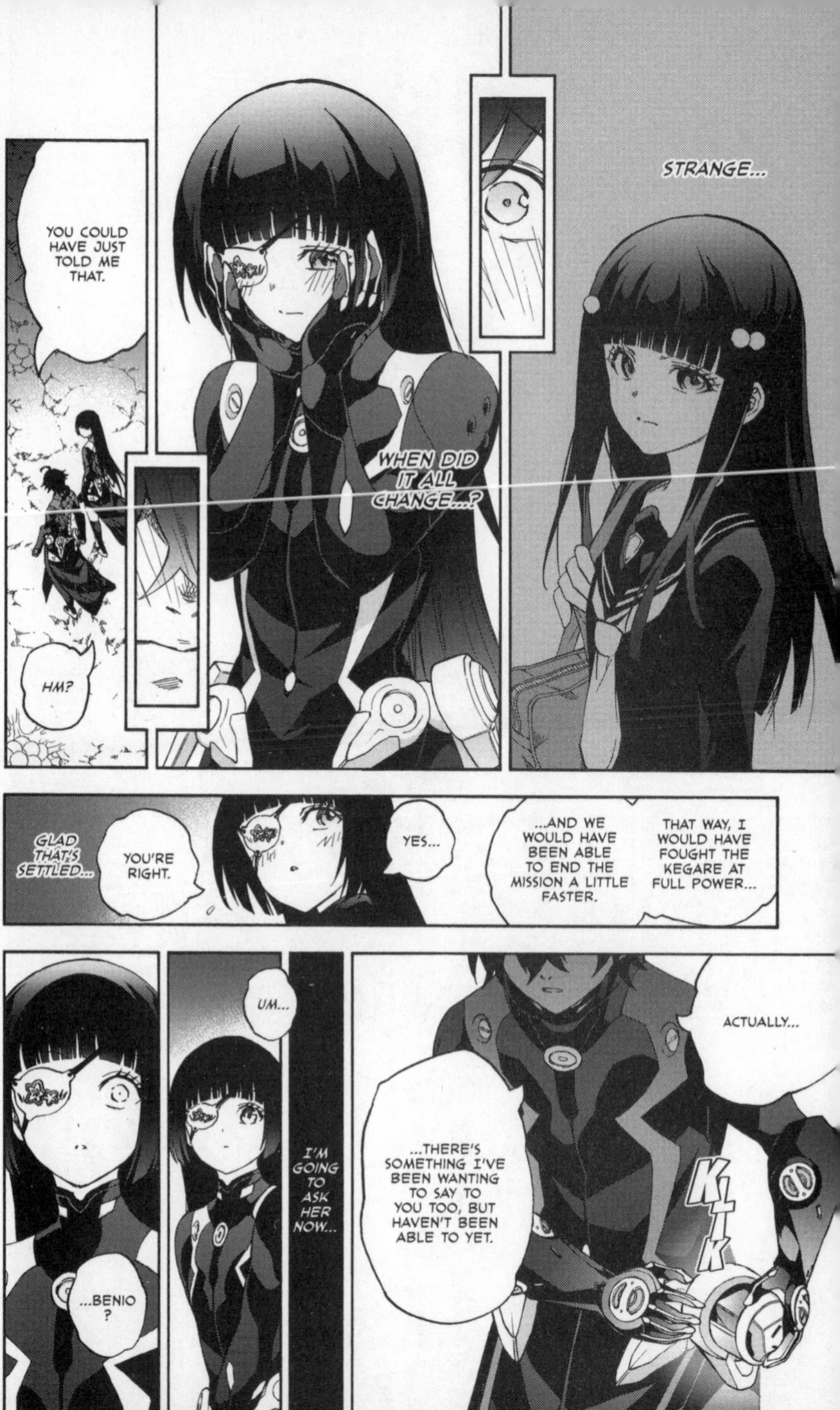
STRANGE...
WHEN DID IT ALL CHANGE...?
YOU COULD HAVE JUST TOLD ME THAT.
HM?
THAT WAY, I WOULD HAVE FOUGHT THE KEGARE AT FULL POWER...
...AND WE WOULD HAVE BEEN ABLE TO END THE MISSION A LITTLE FASTER.
YES...
YOU'RE RIGHT.
GLAD THAT'S SETTLED...
ACTUALLY...
...THERE'S SOMETHING I'VE BEEN WANTING TO SAY TO YOU TOO, BUT HAVEN'T BEEN ABLE TO YET.
KLIK
I'M GOING TO ASK HER NOW...
UM...
...BENIO?

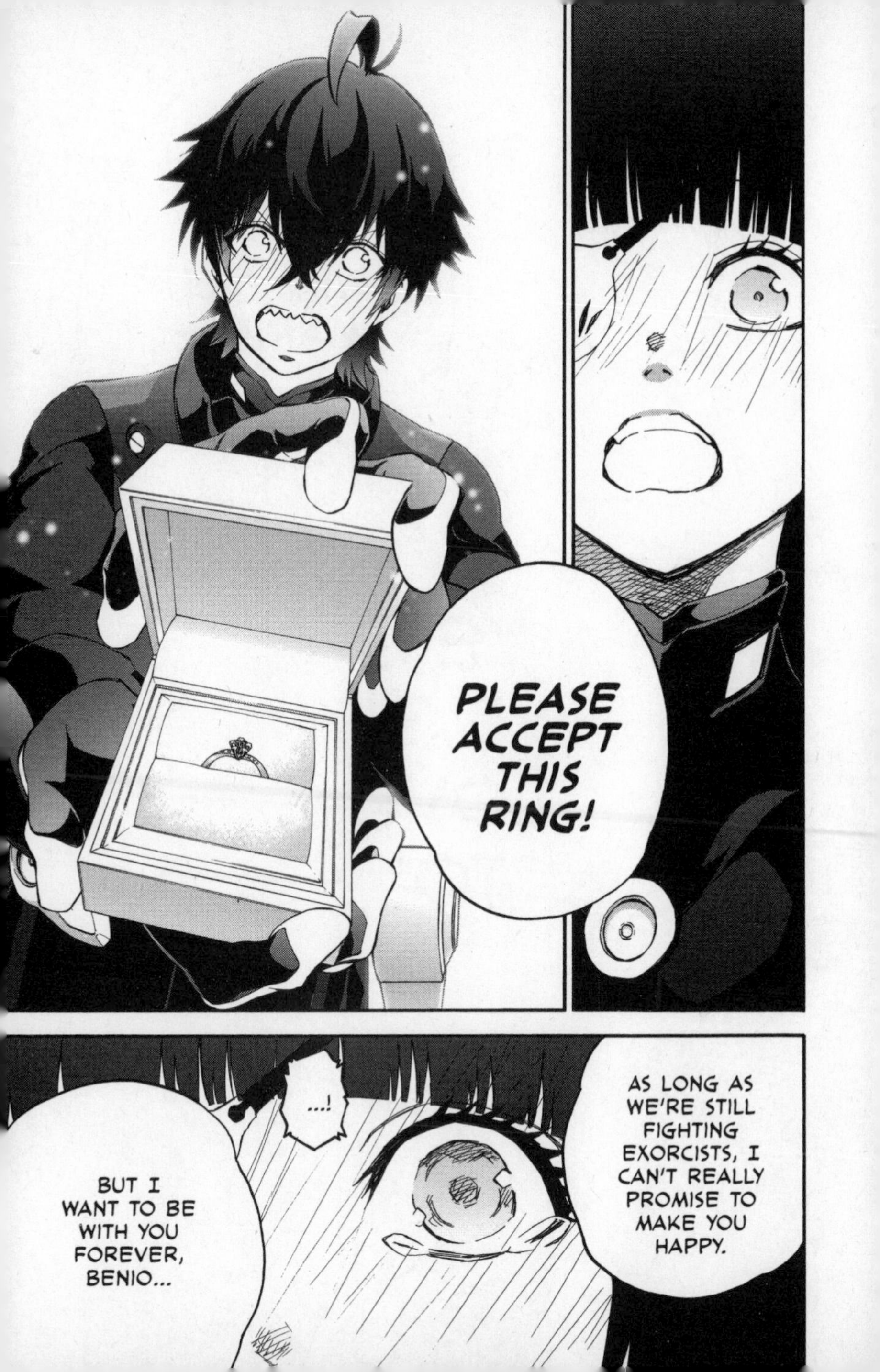
PLEASE ACCEPT THIS RING!
AS LONG AS WE'RE STILL FIGHTING EXORCISTS, I CAN'T REALLY PROMISE TO MAKE YOU HAPPY.
...!
BUT I WANT TO BE WITH YOU FOREVER, BENIO...

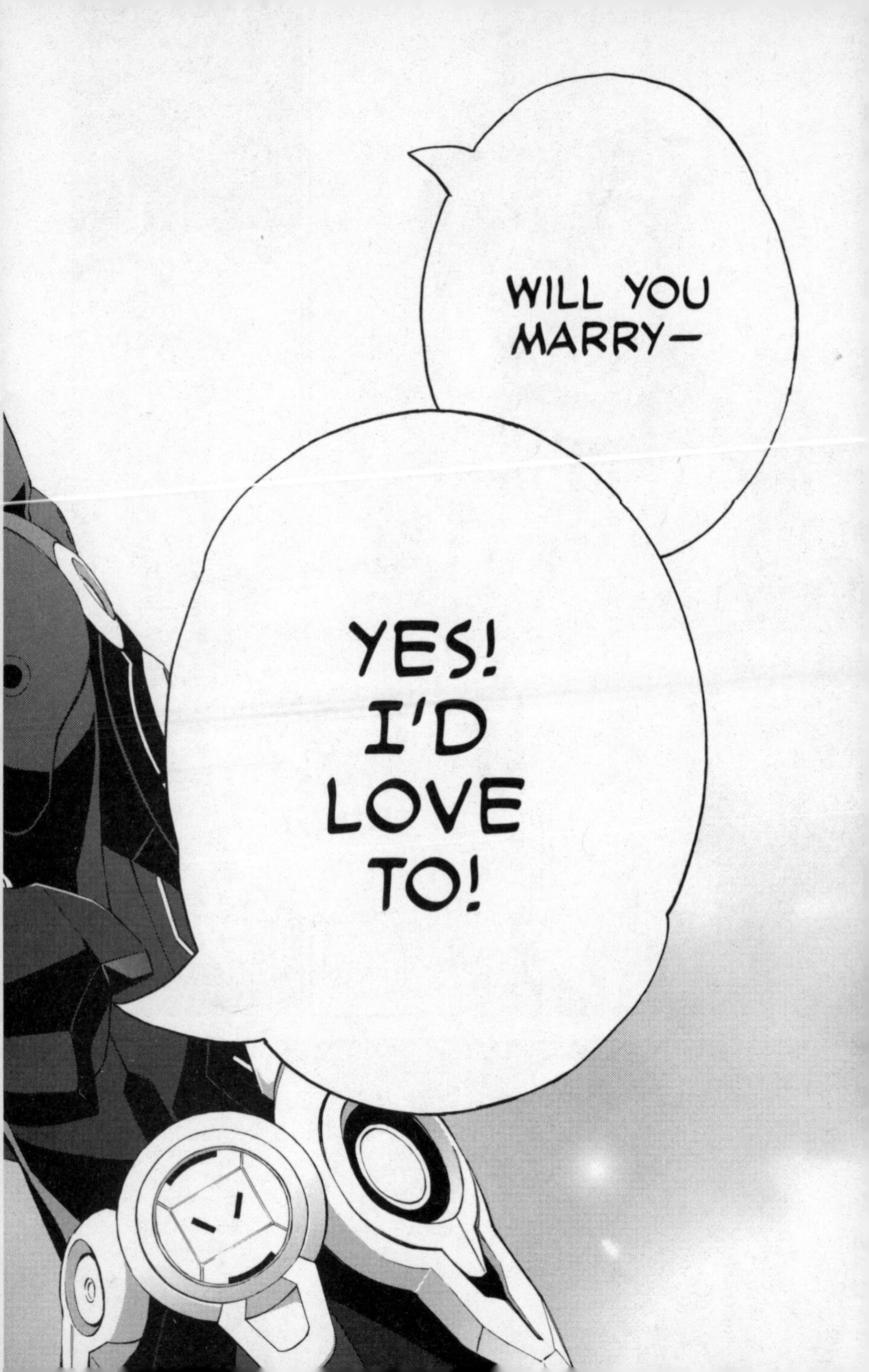
WILL YOU MARRY—
YES! I'D LOVE TO!

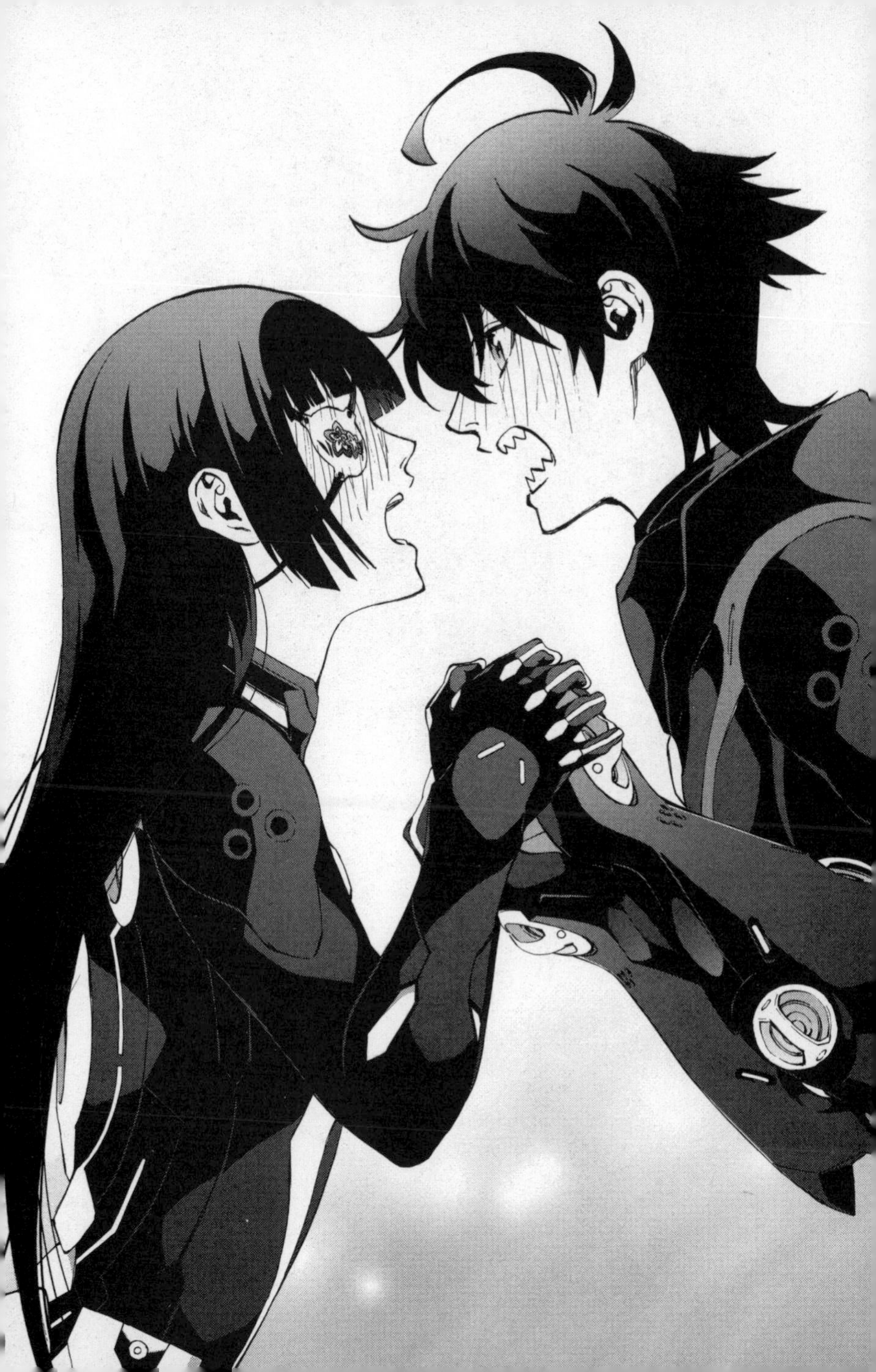

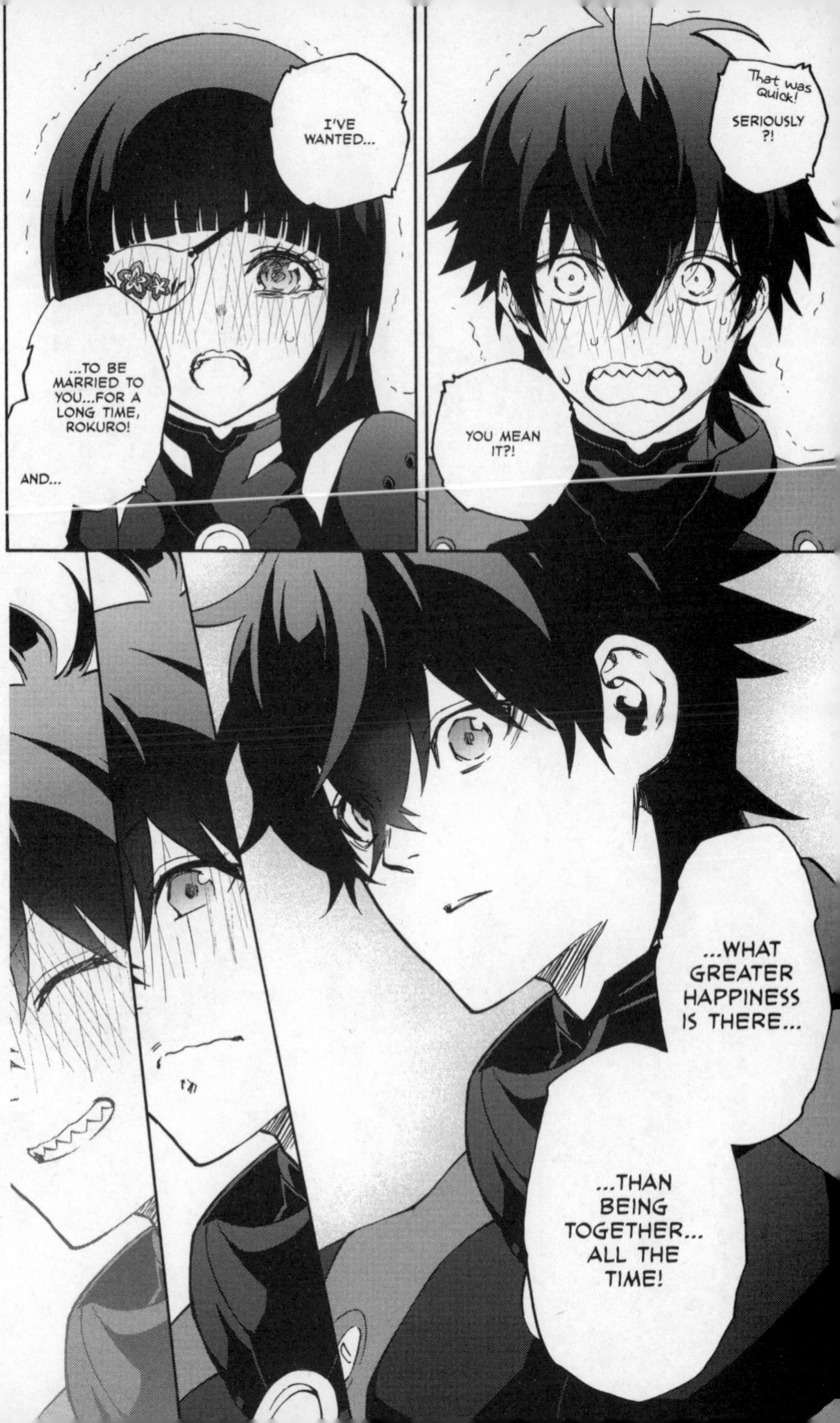
That was Quick!
SERIOUSLY?!
YOU MEAN IT?!
I'VE WANTED...
...TO BE MARRIED TO YOU...FOR A LONG TIME, ROKURO!
AND...
...WHAT GREATER HAPPINESS IS THERE...
...THAN BEING TOGETHER... ALL THE TIME!

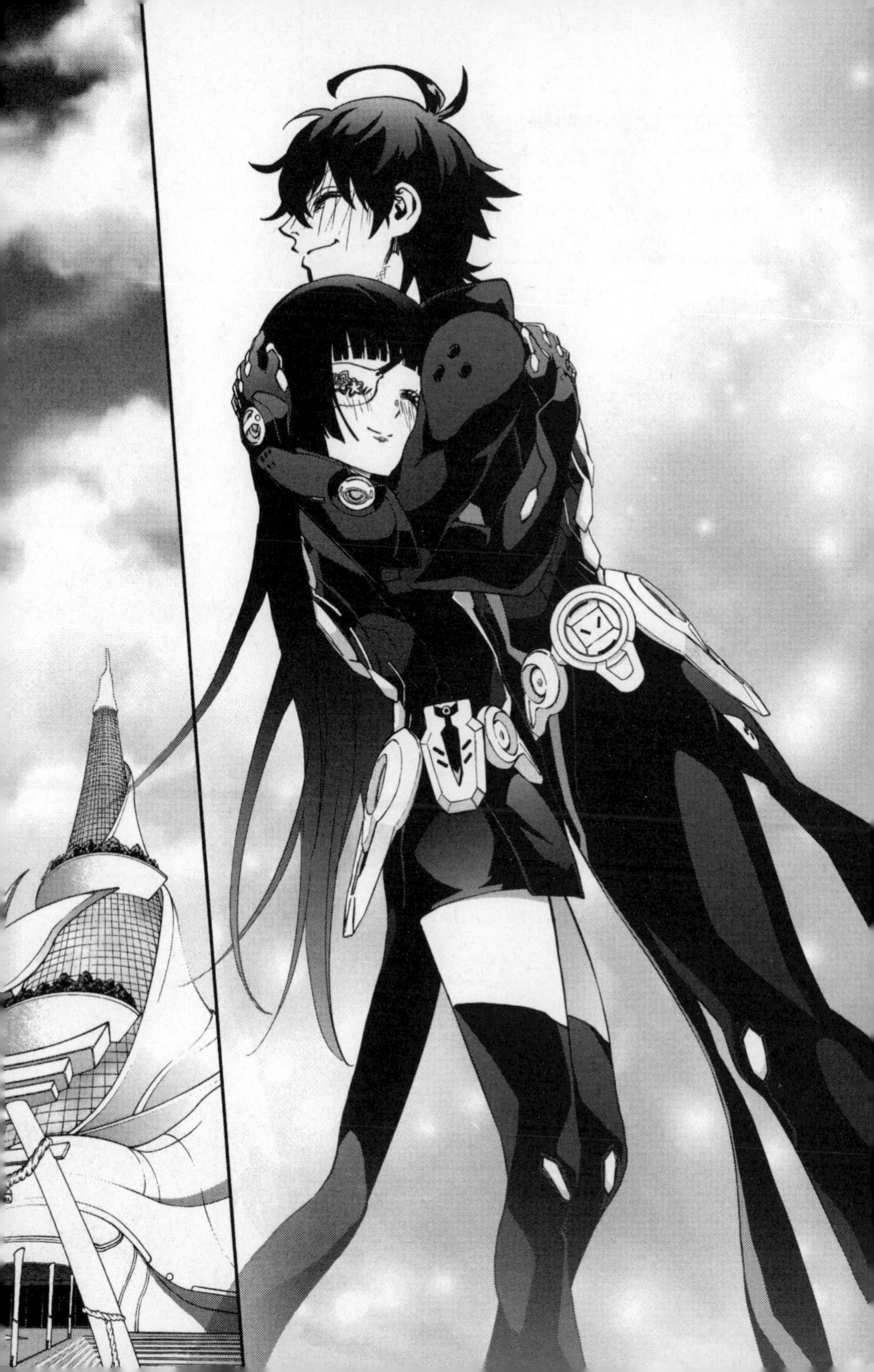

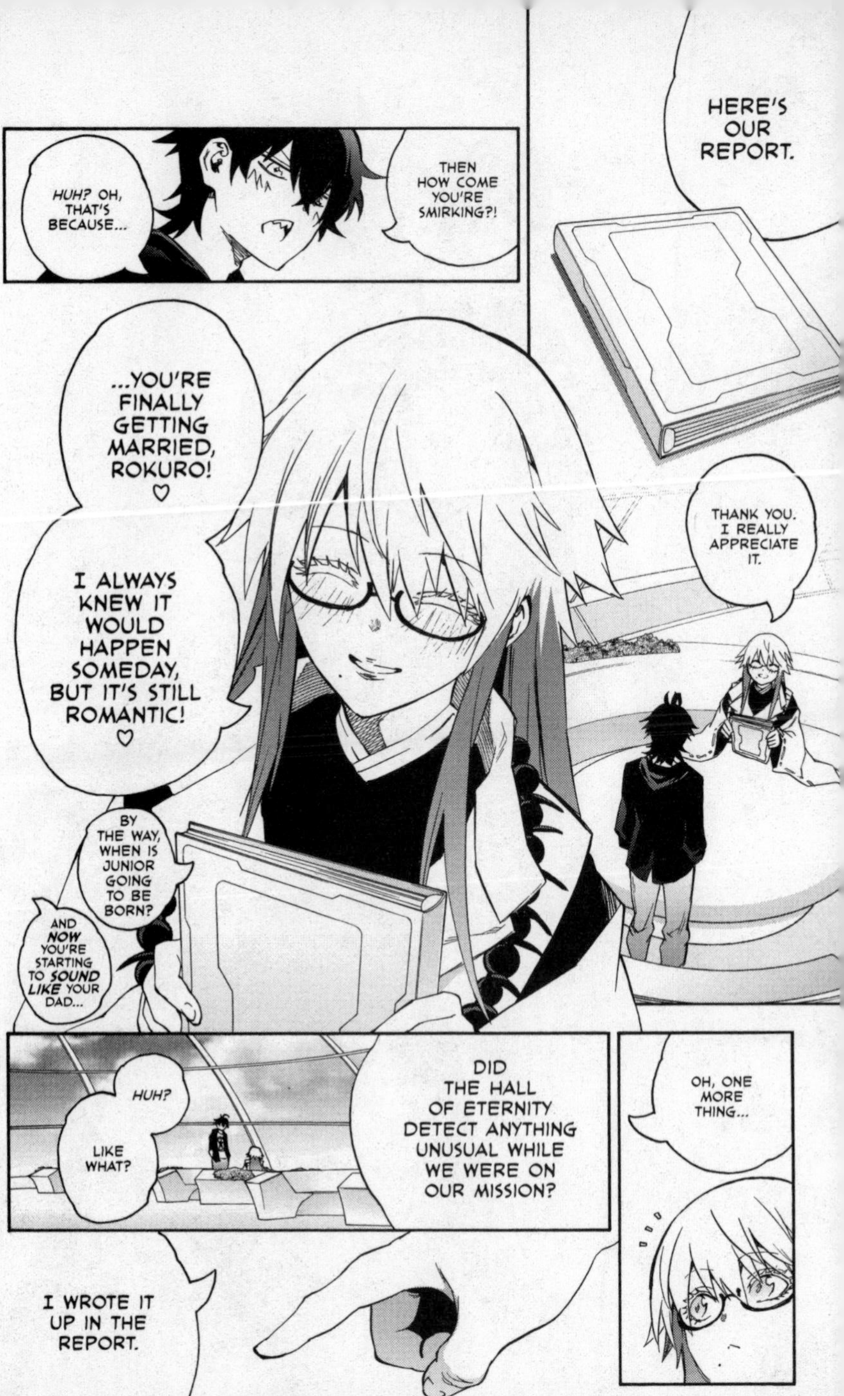
HERE'S OUR REPORT.
THANK YOU. I REALLY APPRECIATE IT.
THEN HOW COME YOU'RE SMIRKING?!
HUH? OH, THAT'S BECAUSE...
...YOU'RE FINALLY GETTING MARRIED, ROKURO! ♡
I ALWAYS KNEW IT WOULD HAPPEN SOMEDAY, BUT IT'S STILL ROMANTIC! ♡
BY THE WAY, WHEN IS JUNIOR GOING TO BE BORN?
AND ***NOW*** YOU'RE STARTING TO ***SOUND LIKE*** YOUR DAD...
OH, ONE MORE THING...
DID THE HALL OF ETERNITY DETECT ANYTHING UNUSUAL WHILE WE WERE ON OUR MISSION?
HUH?
LIKE WHAT?
I WROTE IT UP IN THE REPORT.

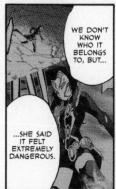

BENIO DETECTED AN UNKNOWN SPIRITUAL ENERGY DURING OUR MISSION.
WHAT?!
WE DON'T KNOW WHO IT BELONGS TO, BUT...
...SHE SAID IT FELT EXTREMELY DANGEROUS.
M-MAYBE IT WAS A BASARA!
BUT IF IT WERE A BASARA, THE OPERATORS WOULD KNOW ABOUT IT, RIGHT?
HAVE YOU RECEIVED ANY OTHER REPORTS ABOUT IT?
NOTHING SO FAR... BUT I'LL LOOK INTO IT.
THANKS.
A SPIRITUAL POWER THAT DOESN'T BELONG TO AN EXORCIST OR A KEGARE...?!

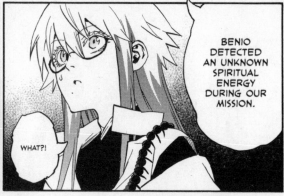

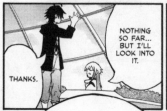

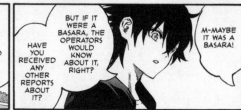

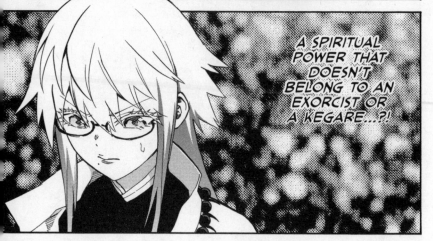

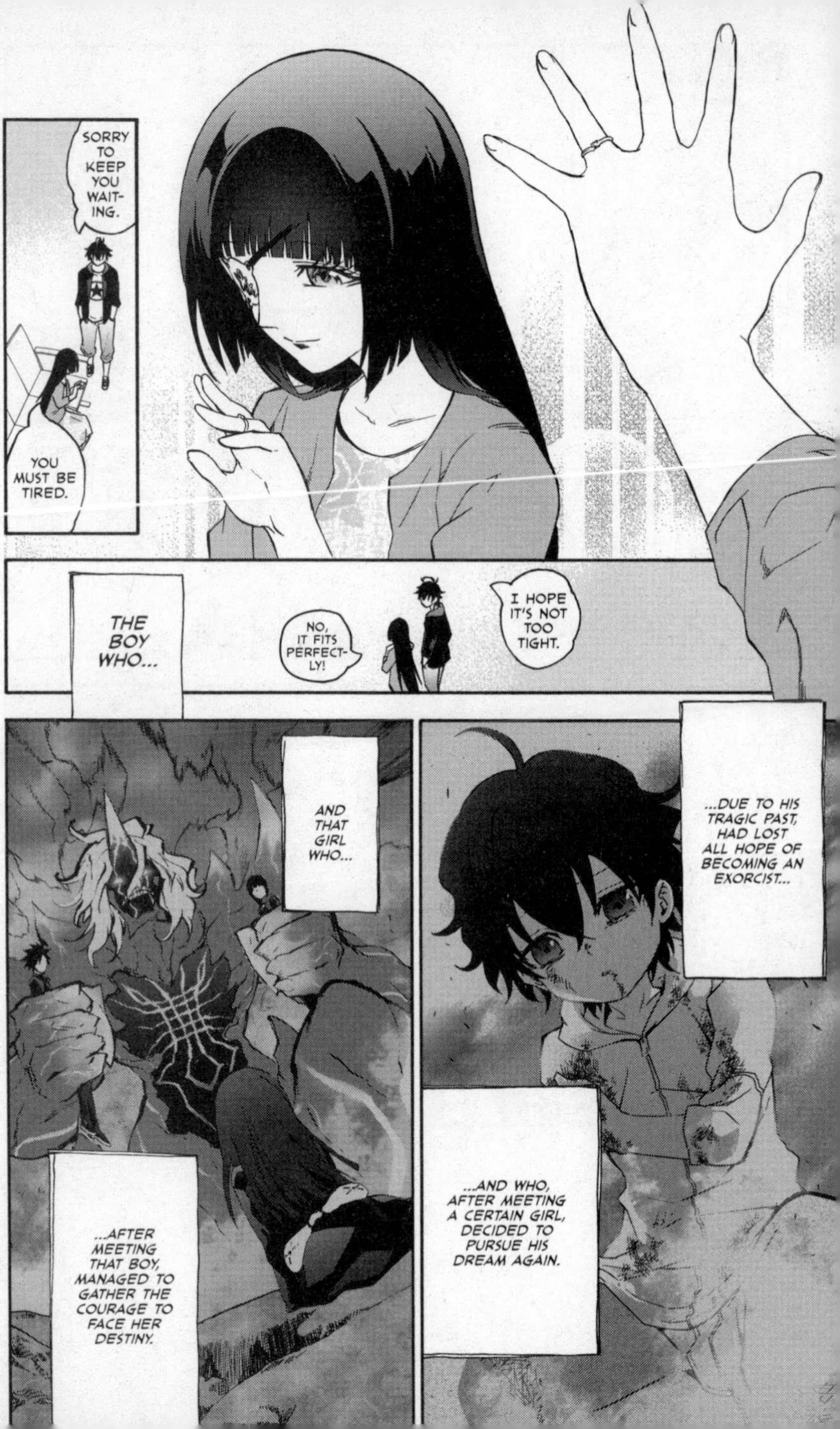
SORRY TO KEEP YOU WAIT-ING.
YOU MUST BE TIRED.
I HOPE IT'S NOT TOO TIGHT.
NO, IT FITS PERFECT-LY!
THE BOY WHO...
...DUE TO HIS TRAGIC PAST, HAD LOST ALL HOPE OF BECOMING AN EXORCIST...
...AND WHO, AFTER MEETING A CERTAIN GIRL, DECIDED TO PURSUE HIS DREAM AGAIN.
AND THAT GIRL WHO...
...AFTER MEETING THAT BOY, MANAGED TO GATHER THE COURAGE TO FACE HER DESTINY.

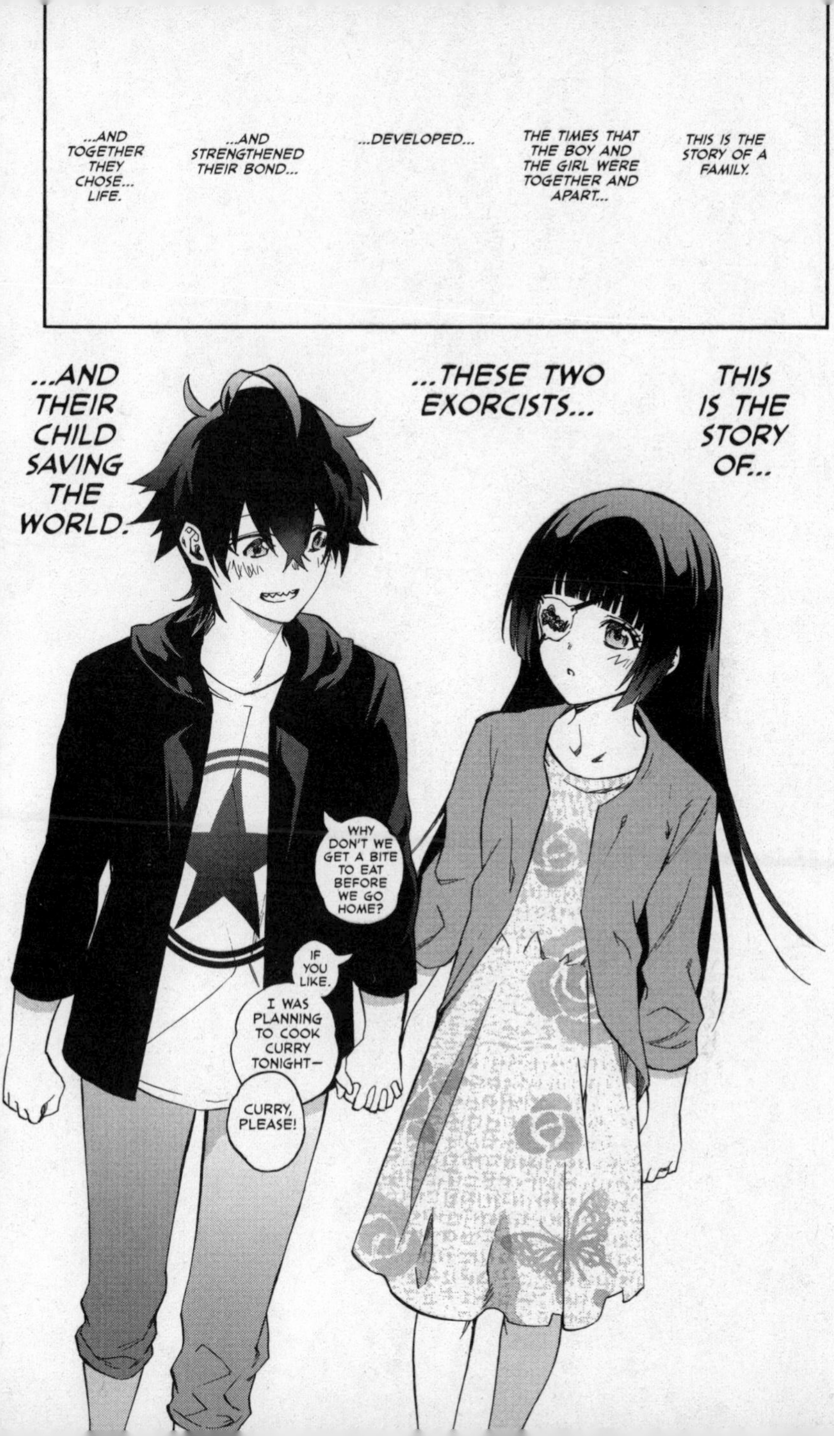
THIS IS THE STORY OF A FAMILY.
THE TIMES THAT THE BOY AND THE GIRL WERE TOGETHER AND APART...
...DEVELOPED...
...AND STRENGTHENED THEIR BOND...
...AND TOGETHER THEY CHOSE... LIFE.
THIS IS THE STORY OF...
...THESE TWO EXORCISTS...
...AND THEIR CHILD SAVING THE WORLD.
WHY DON'T WE GET A BITE TO EAT BEFORE WE GO HOME?
IF YOU LIKE.
I WAS PLANNING TO COOK CURRY TONIGHT—
CURRY, PLEASE!

Twin Star Exorcists

ONMYOJI

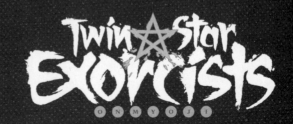

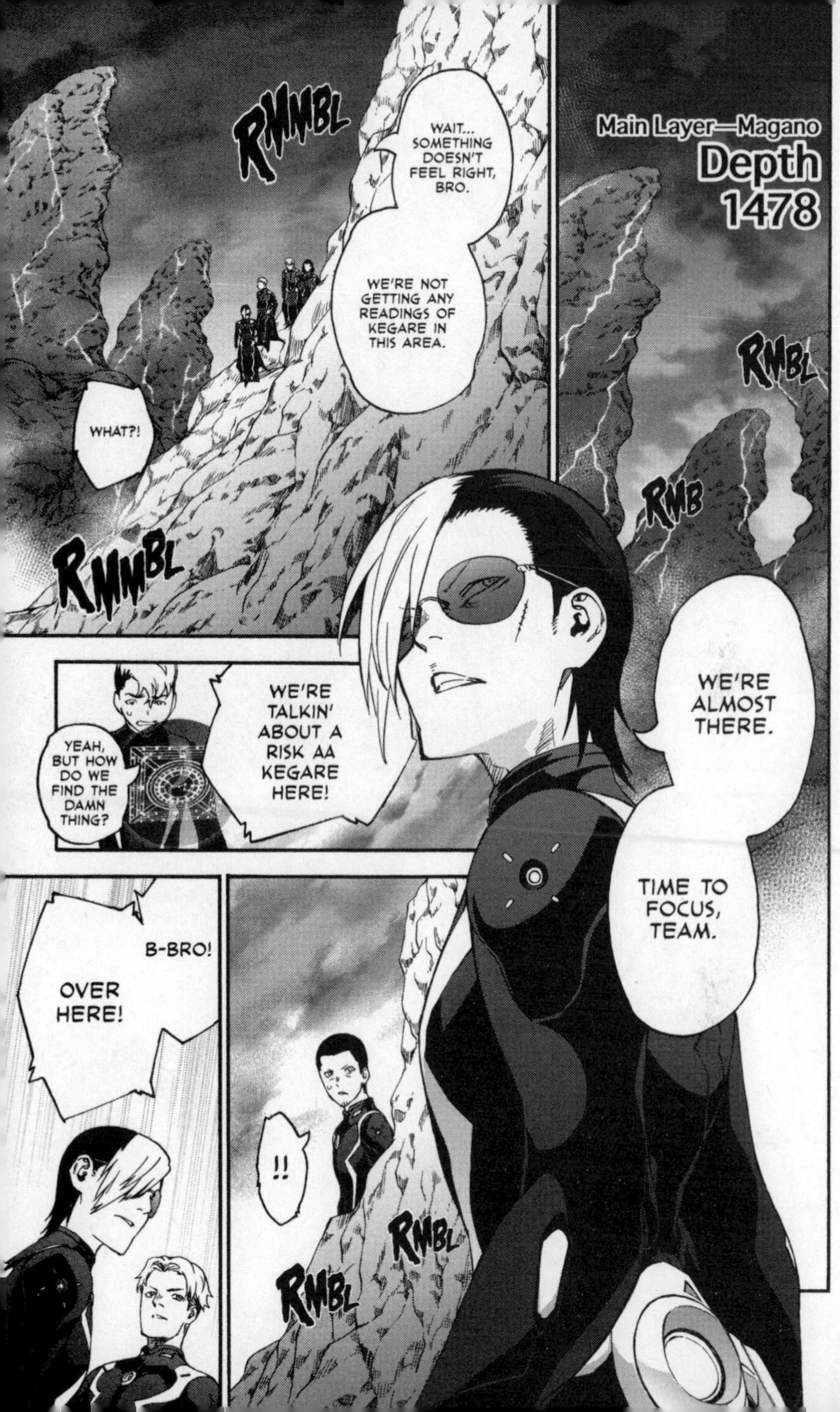
Main Layer—Magano
Depth 1478
RMBL
RMB
WE'RE ALMOST THERE.
TIME TO FOCUS, TEAM.
RMBL
RMBL
RMMBL
WAIT... SOMETHING DOESN'T FEEL RIGHT, BRO.
WE'RE NOT GETTING ANY READINGS OF KEGARE IN THIS AREA.
WHAT?!
RMMBL
WE'RE TALKIN' ABOUT A RISK AA KEGARE HERE!
YEAH, BUT HOW DO WE FIND THE DAMN THING?
!!
B-BRO!
OVER HERE!

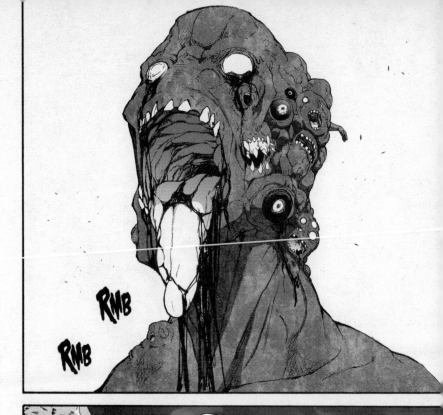

RMB

RMB

A *DEAD* RISK AA KEGARE?!

WHO OR WHAT...

R-MMBL

RMMBL

RMMBL

RMMBL

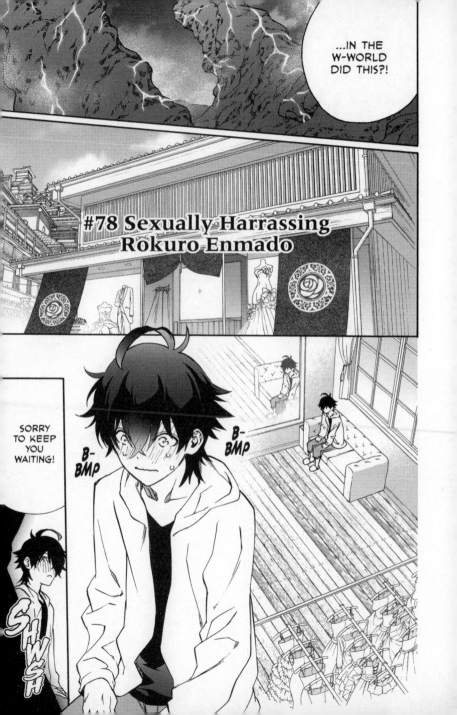

...IN THE W-WORLD DID THIS?!

#78 Sexually Harrassing Rokuro Enmado

SORRY TO KEEP YOU WAITING!

B—BMP

B—BMP

SHWSH

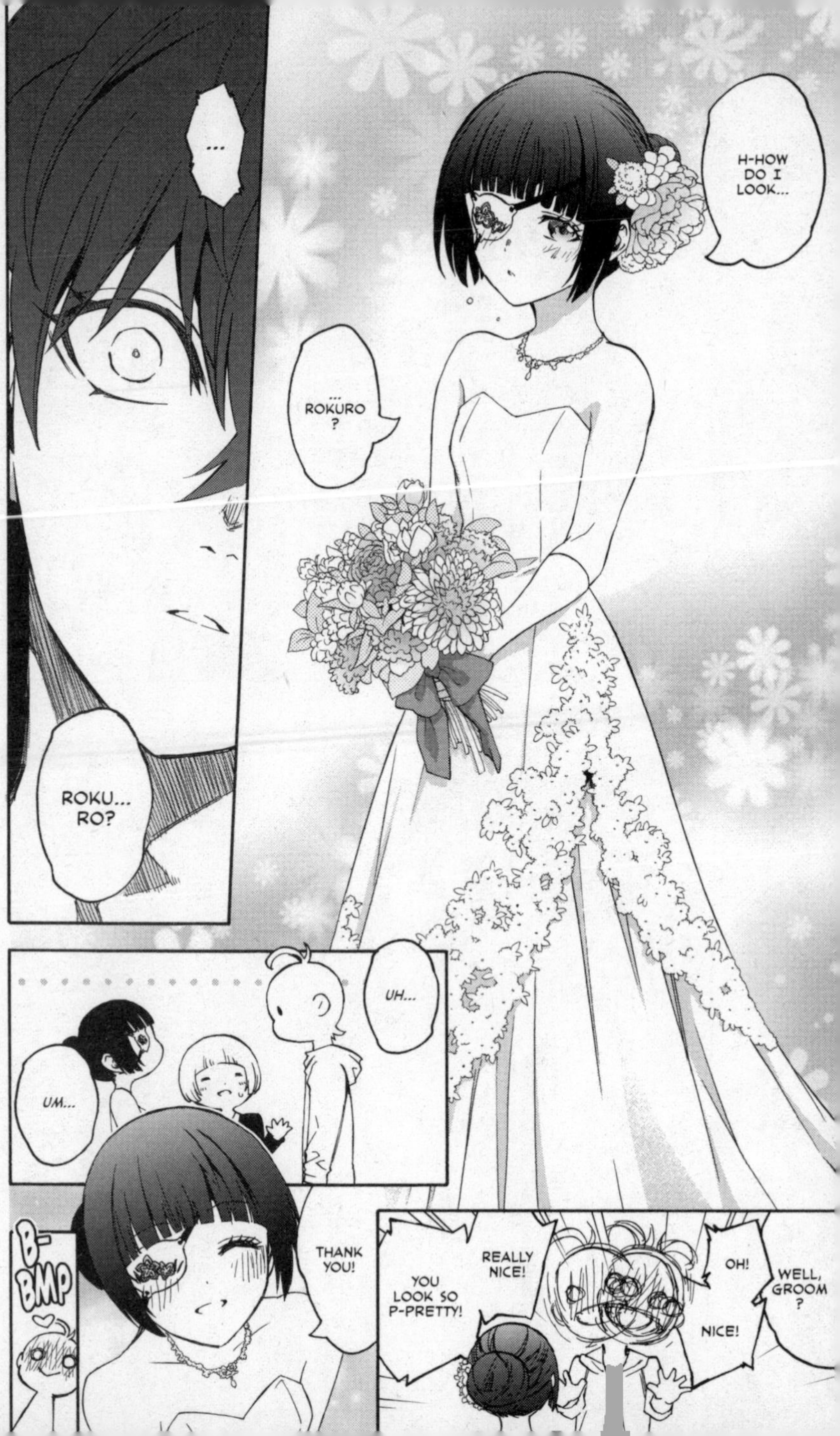
H-HOW DO I LOOK...
... ROKURO ?
...
ROKU... RO?
UH...
UM...
WELL, GROOM ?
OH!
NICE!
REALLY NICE!
YOU LOOK SO P-PRETTY!
THANK YOU!
B-BMP

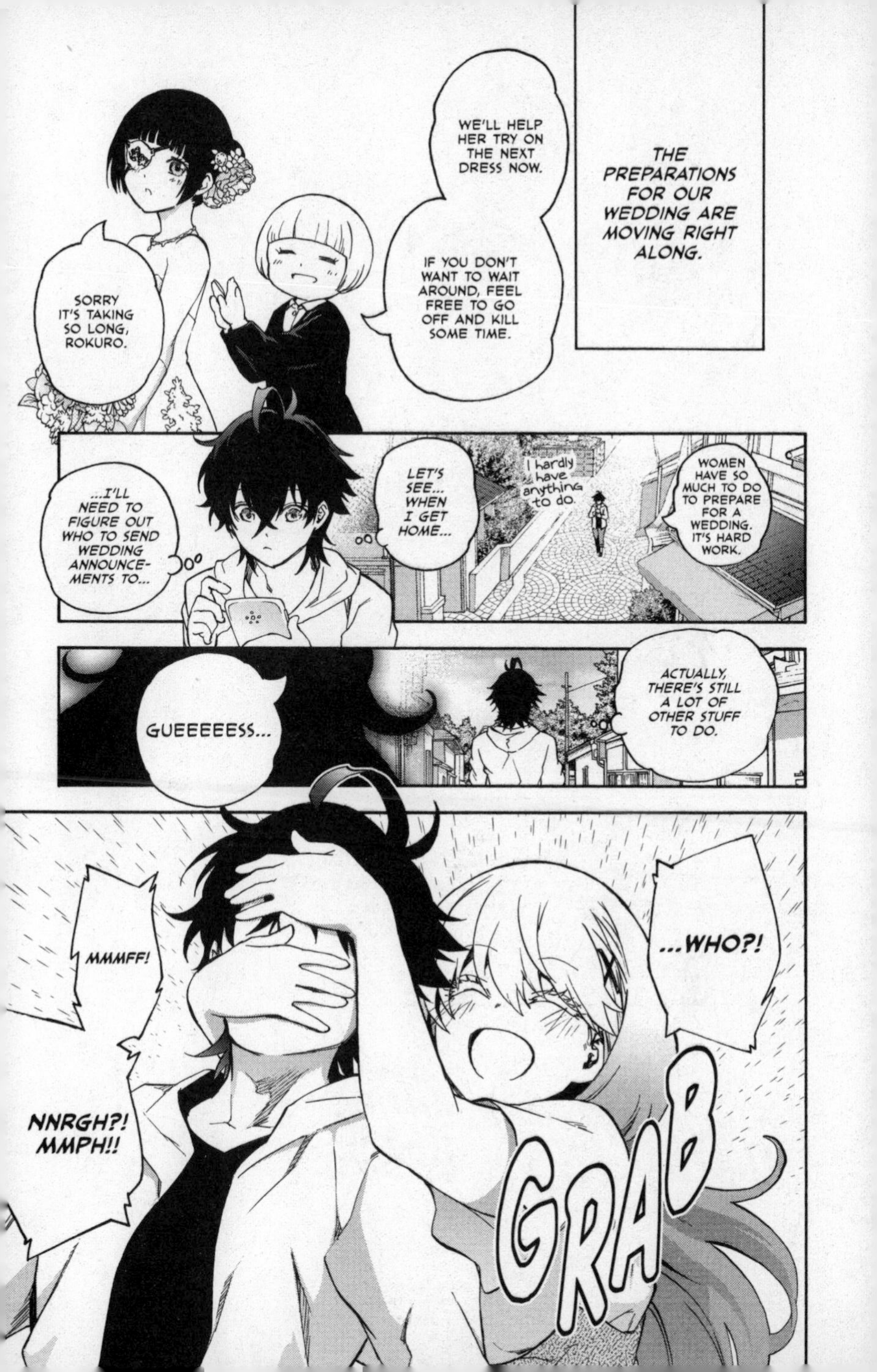
THE PREPARATIONS FOR OUR WEDDING ARE MOVING RIGHT ALONG.
WE'LL HELP HER TRY ON THE NEXT DRESS NOW.
IF YOU DON'T WANT TO WAIT AROUND, FEEL FREE TO GO OFF AND KILL SOME TIME.
SORRY IT'S TAKING SO LONG, ROKURO.
WOMEN HAVE SO MUCH TO DO TO PREPARE FOR A WEDDING. IT'S HARD WORK.
I hardly have anything to do.
LET'S SEE... WHEN I GET HOME...
...I'LL NEED TO FIGURE OUT WHO TO SEND WEDDING ANNOUNCE-MENTS TO...
ACTUALLY, THERE'S STILL A LOT OF OTHER STUFF TO DO.
GUEEEEEESS...
...WHO?!
GRAB
MMMFF!
NNRGH?! MMPH!!

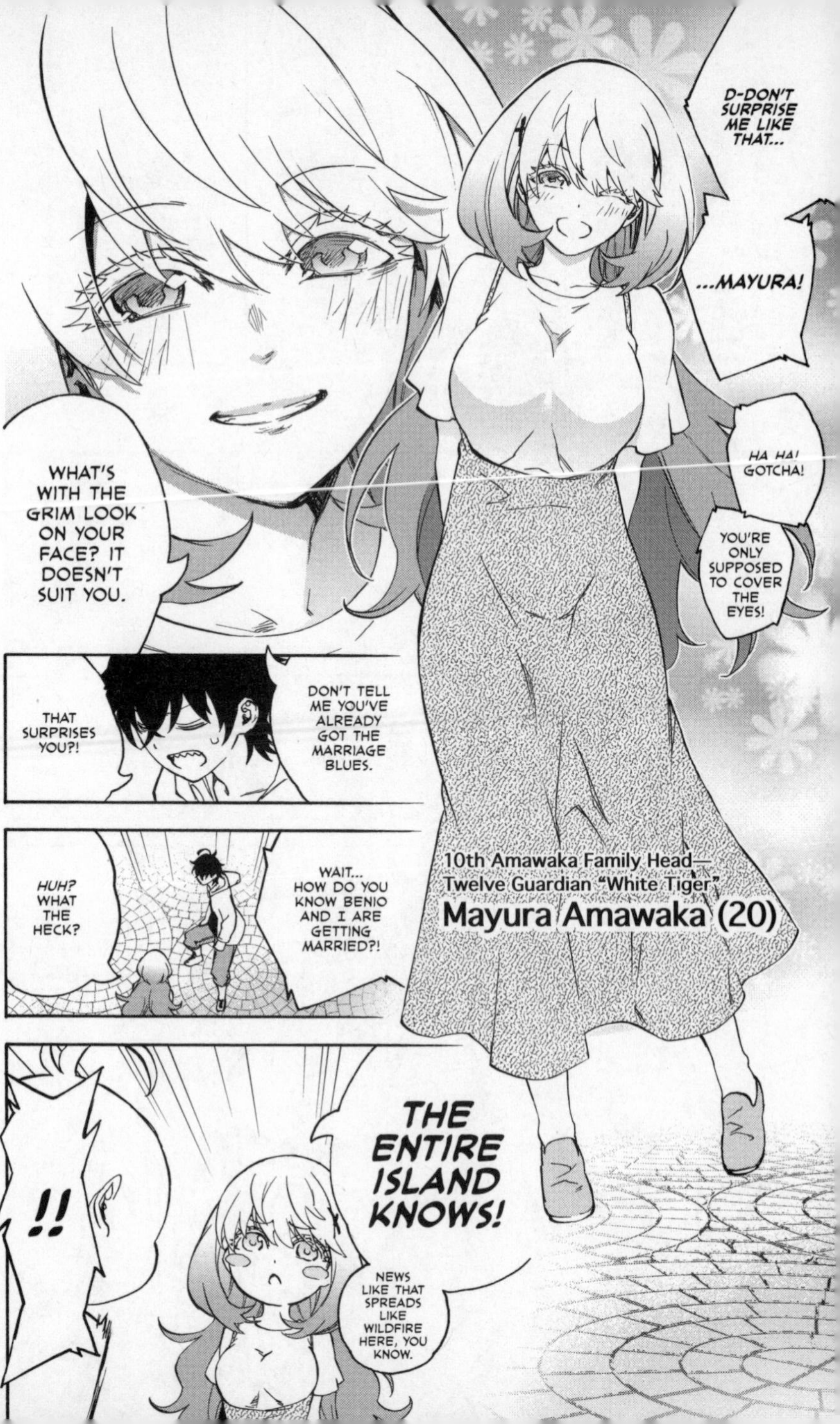
D-DON'T SURPRISE ME LIKE THAT...
...MAYURA!
HA HA! GOTCHA!
YOU'RE ONLY SUPPOSED TO COVER THE EYES!
10th Amawaka Family Head—Twelve Guardian "White Tiger"
Mayura Amawaka (20)
WHAT'S WITH THE GRIM LOOK ON YOUR FACE? IT DOESN'T SUIT YOU.
DON'T TELL ME YOU'VE ALREADY GOT THE MARRIAGE BLUES.
THAT SURPRISES YOU?!
WAIT... HOW DO YOU KNOW BENIO AND I ARE GETTING MARRIED?!
HUH? WHAT THE HECK?
THE ENTIRE ISLAND KNOWS!
!!
NEWS LIKE THAT SPREADS LIKE WILDFIRE HERE, YOU KNOW.

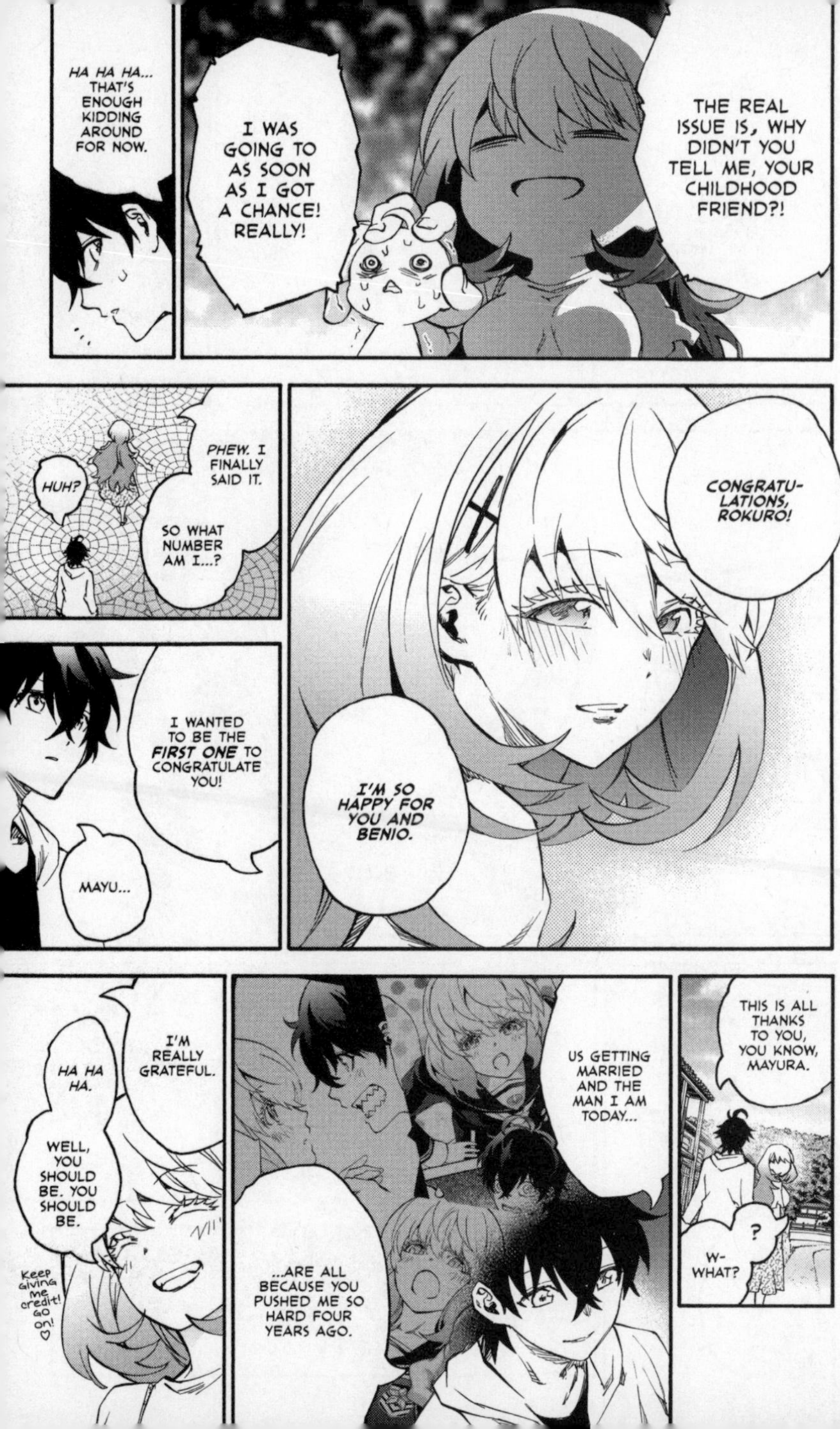
THE REAL ISSUE IS, WHY DIDN'T YOU TELL ME, YOUR CHILDHOOD FRIEND?!
I WAS GOING TO AS SOON AS I GOT A CHANCE! REALLY!
HA HA HA... THAT'S ENOUGH KIDDING AROUND FOR NOW.
CONGRATULATIONS, ROKURO!
I'M SO HAPPY FOR YOU AND BENIO.
PHEW. I FINALLY SAID IT.
SO WHAT NUMBER AM I...?
HUH?
I WANTED TO BE THE FIRST ONE TO CONGRATULATE YOU!
MAYU...
THIS IS ALL THANKS TO YOU, YOU KNOW, MAYURA.
?
W-WHAT?
US GETTING MARRIED AND THE MAN I AM TODAY...
...ARE ALL BECAUSE YOU PUSHED ME SO HARD FOUR YEARS AGO.
I'M REALLY GRATEFUL.
HA HA HA.
WELL, YOU SHOULD BE. YOU SHOULD BE.
Keep giving me credit! Go on! ♡

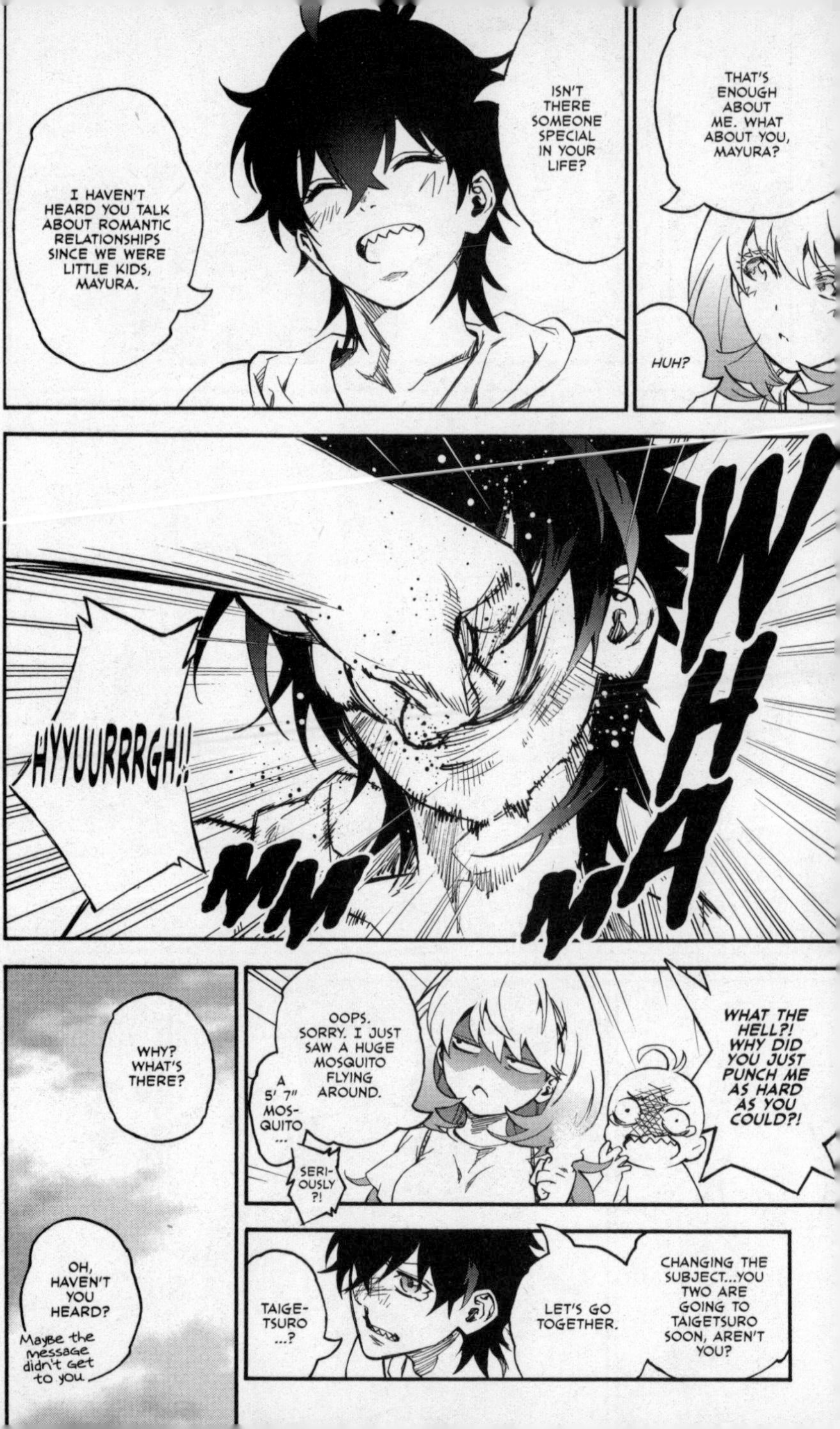
THAT'S ENOUGH ABOUT ME. WHAT ABOUT YOU, MAYURA?
HUH?
ISN'T THERE SOMEONE SPECIAL IN YOUR LIFE?
I HAVEN'T HEARD YOU TALK ABOUT ROMANTIC RELATIONSHIPS SINCE WE WERE LITTLE KIDS, MAYURA.
WHAMMM
HYYUURRRGH!!
WHAT THE HELL?! WHY DID YOU JUST PUNCH ME AS HARD AS YOU COULD?!
OOPS. SORRY. I JUST SAW A HUGE MOSQUITO FLYING AROUND.
A 5' 7" MOSQUITO...
SERIOUSLY?!
CHANGING THE SUBJECT...YOU TWO ARE GOING TO TAIGETSURO SOON, AREN'T YOU?
LET'S GO TOGETHER.
TAIGETSURO...?
WHY? WHAT'S THERE?
OH, HAVEN'T YOU HEARD?
Maybe the message didn't get to you.

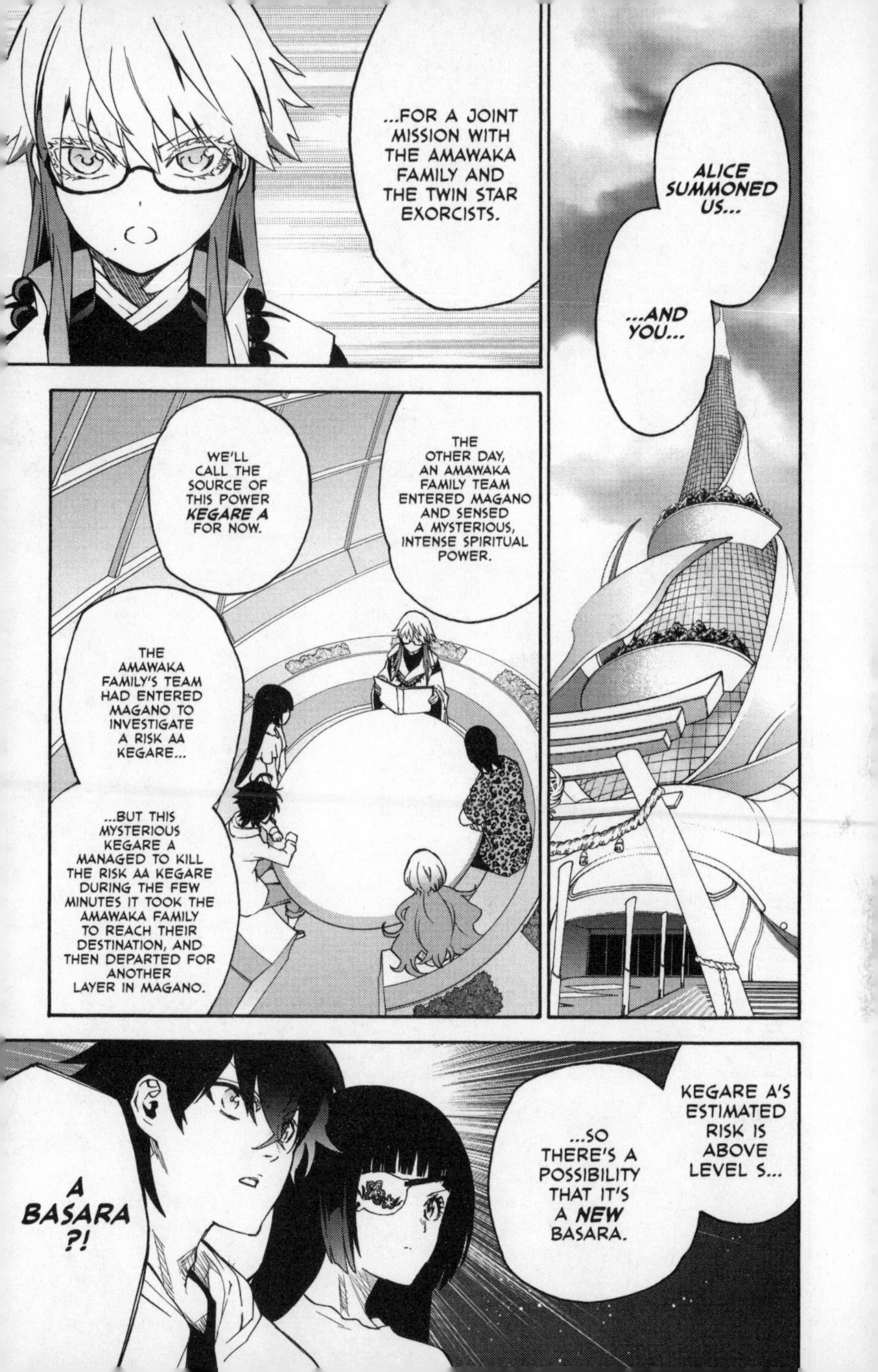
ALICE SUMMONED US...
...AND YOU...
...FOR A JOINT MISSION WITH THE AMAWAKA FAMILY AND THE TWIN STAR EXORCISTS.
THE OTHER DAY, AN AMAWAKA FAMILY TEAM ENTERED MAGANO AND SENSED A MYSTERIOUS, INTENSE SPIRITUAL POWER.
WE'LL CALL THE SOURCE OF THIS POWER *KEGARE A* FOR NOW.
THE AMAWAKA FAMILY'S TEAM HAD ENTERED MAGANO TO INVESTIGATE A RISK AA KEGARE...
...BUT THIS MYSTERIOUS KEGARE A MANAGED TO KILL THE RISK AA KEGARE DURING THE FEW MINUTES IT TOOK THE AMAWAKA FAMILY TO REACH THEIR DESTINATION, AND THEN DEPARTED FOR ANOTHER LAYER IN MAGANO.
KEGARE A'S ESTIMATED RISK IS ABOVE LEVEL S...
...SO THERE'S A POSSIBILITY THAT IT'S A *NEW* BASARA.
A BASARA?!

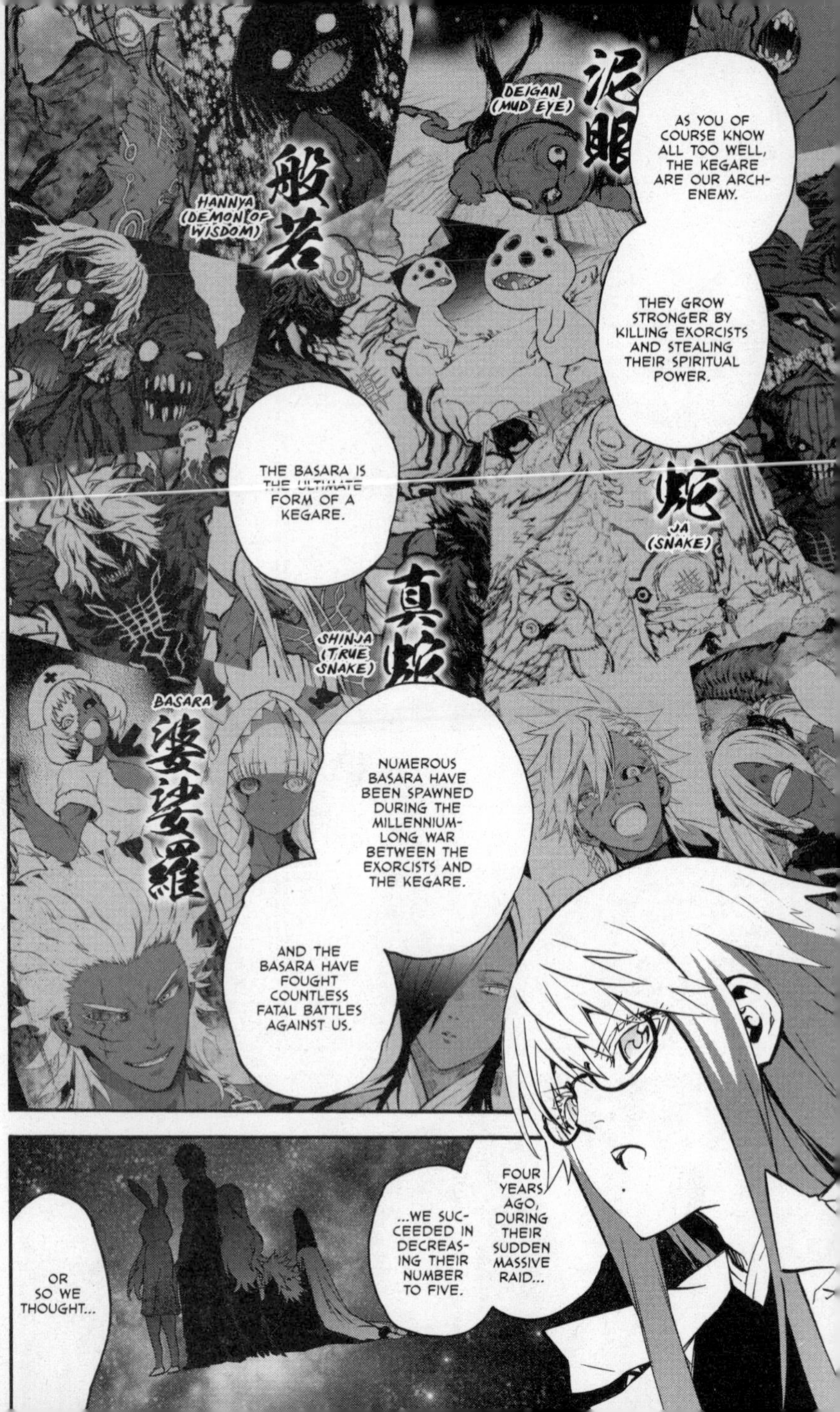
泥眼
DEIGAN (MUD EYE)
AS YOU OF COURSE KNOW ALL TOO WELL, THE KEGARE ARE OUR ARCH-ENEMY.
般若
HANNYA (DEMON OF WISDOM)
THEY GROW STRONGER BY KILLING EXORCISTS AND STEALING THEIR SPIRITUAL POWER.
蛇
JA (SNAKE)
THE BASARA IS THE ULTIMATE FORM OF A KEGARE.
真蛇
SHINJA (TRUE SNAKE)
婆娑羅
BASARA
NUMEROUS BASARA HAVE BEEN SPAWNED DURING THE MILLENNIUM-LONG WAR BETWEEN THE EXORCISTS AND THE KEGARE.
AND THE BASARA HAVE FOUGHT COUNTLESS FATAL BATTLES AGAINST US.
FOUR YEARS AGO, DURING THEIR SUDDEN MASSIVE RAID...
...WE SUCCEEDED IN DECREASING THEIR NUMBER TO FIVE.
OR SO WE THOUGHT...

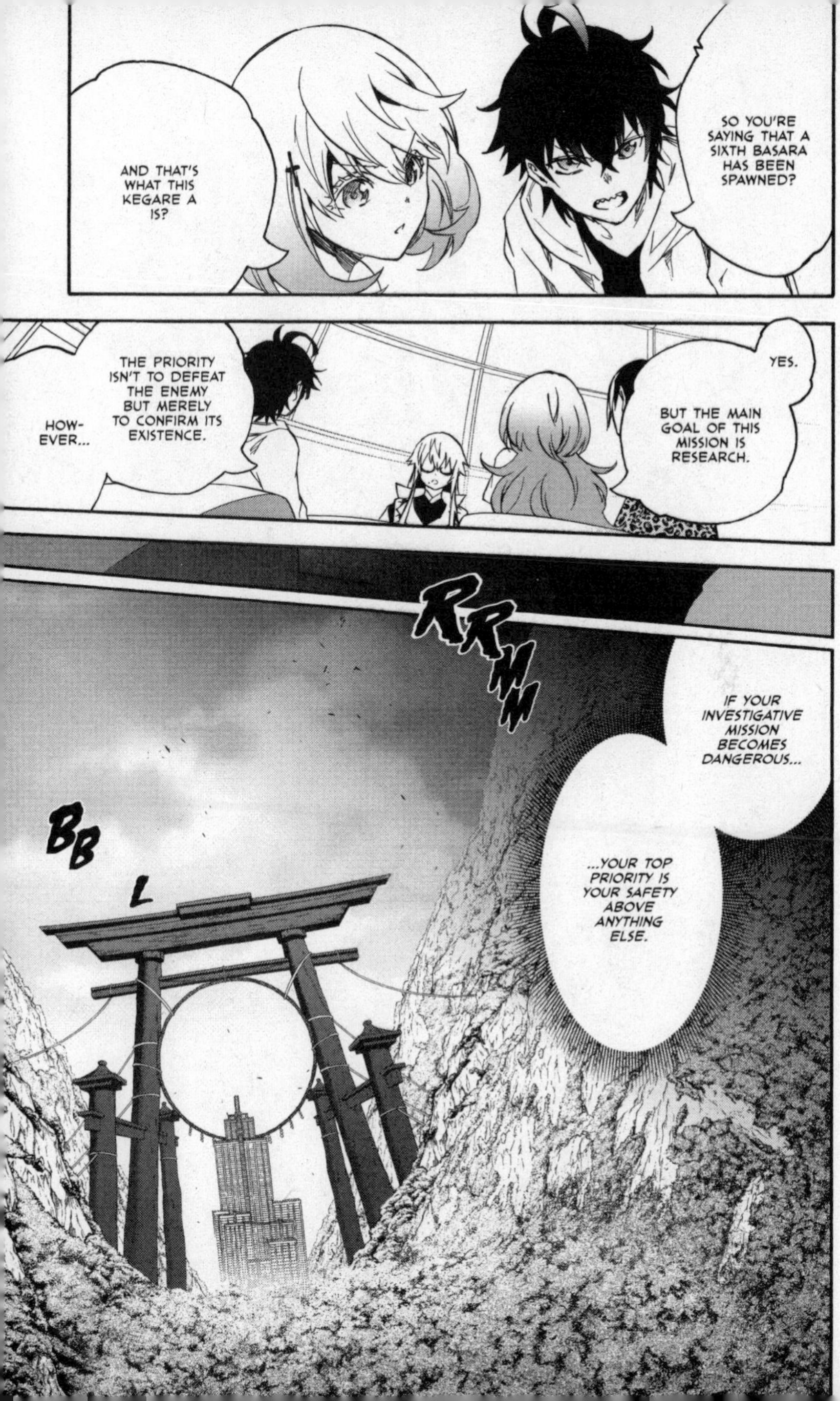
SO YOU'RE SAYING THAT A SIXTH BASARA HAS BEEN SPAWNED?
AND THAT'S WHAT THIS KEGARE A IS?
YES.
BUT THE MAIN GOAL OF THIS MISSION IS RESEARCH.
THE PRIORITY ISN'T TO DEFEAT THE ENEMY BUT MERELY TO CONFIRM ITS EXISTENCE.
HOW-EVER...
RRMM
IF YOUR INVESTIGATIVE MISSION BECOMES DANGEROUS...
...YOUR TOP PRIORITY IS YOUR SAFETY ABOVE ANYTHING ELSE.
BBL

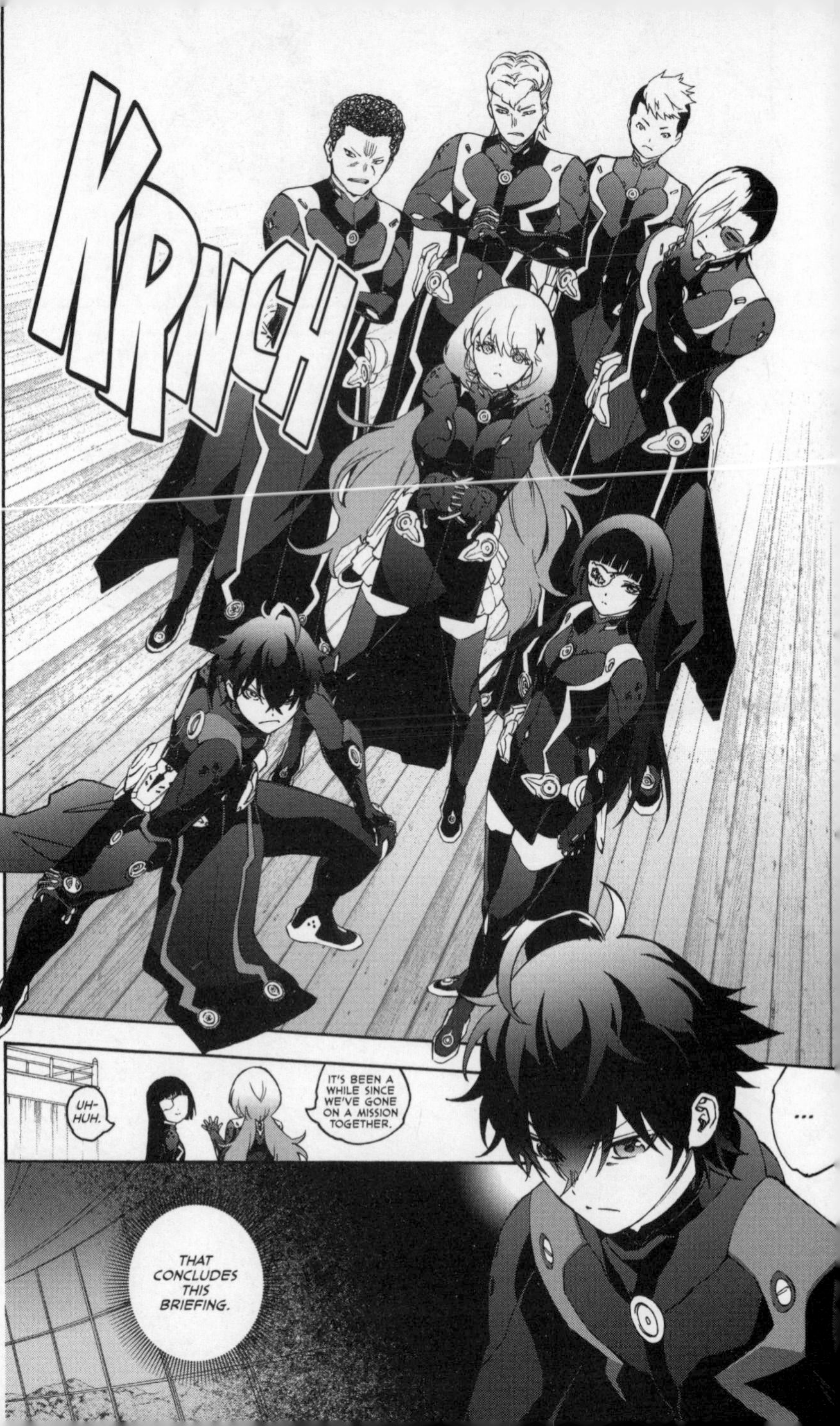
KRNCH
...
IT'S BEEN A WHILE SINCE WE'VE GONE ON A MISSION TOGETHER.
UH-HUH.
THAT CONCLUDES THIS BRIEFING.

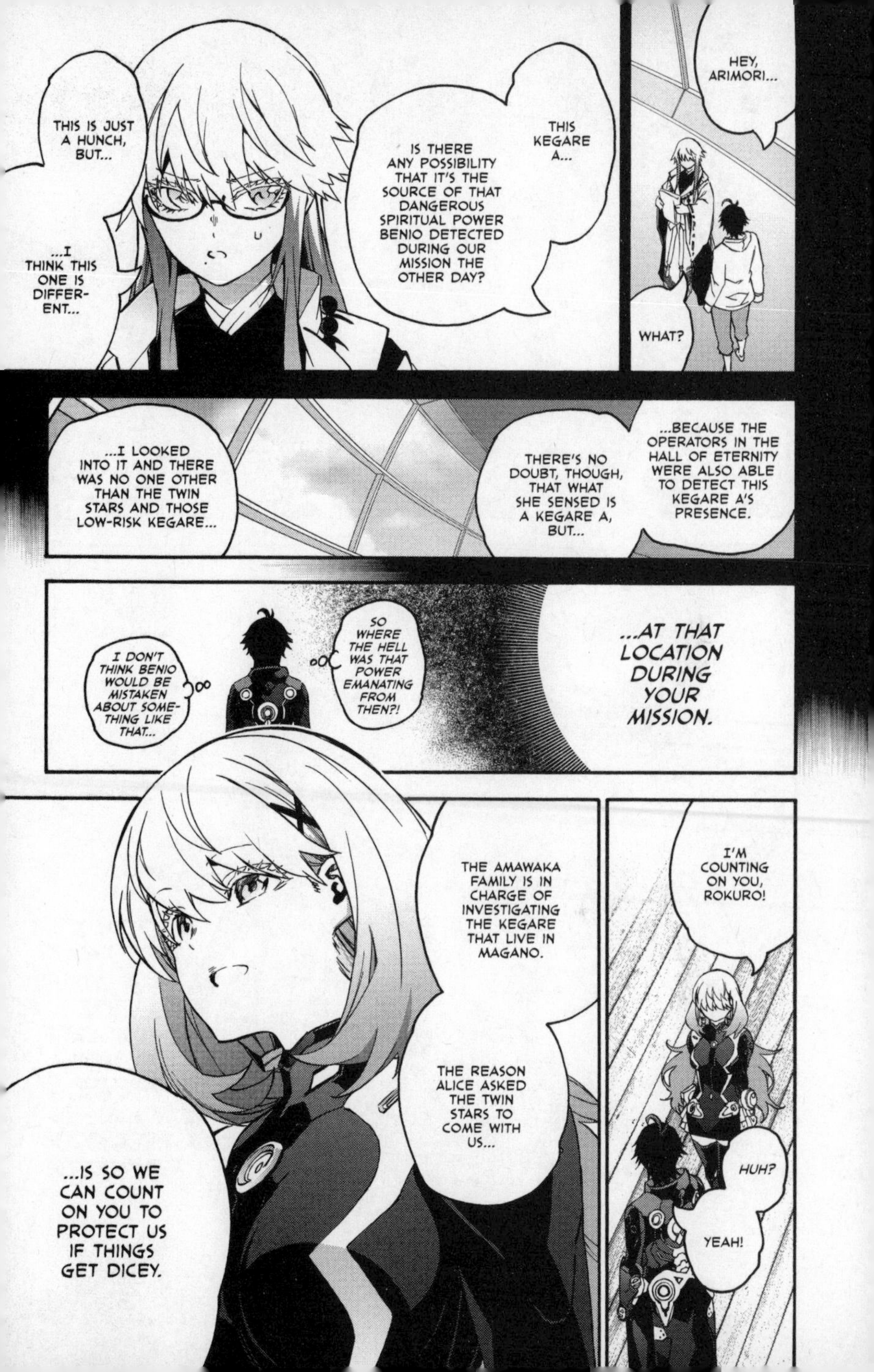
HEY, ARIMORI...
WHAT?
THIS KEGARE A...
IS THERE ANY POSSIBILITY THAT IT'S THE SOURCE OF THAT DANGEROUS SPIRITUAL POWER BENIO DETECTED DURING OUR MISSION THE OTHER DAY?
THIS IS JUST A HUNCH, BUT...
...I THINK THIS ONE IS DIFFERENT...
...BECAUSE THE OPERATORS IN THE HALL OF ETERNITY WERE ALSO ABLE TO DETECT THIS KEGARE A'S PRESENCE.
THERE'S NO DOUBT, THOUGH, THAT WHAT SHE SENSED IS A KEGARE A, BUT...
...I LOOKED INTO IT AND THERE WAS NO ONE OTHER THAN THE TWIN STARS AND THOSE LOW-RISK KEGARE...
...AT THAT LOCATION DURING YOUR MISSION.
SO WHERE THE HELL WAS THAT POWER EMANATING FROM THEN?!
I DON'T THINK BENIO WOULD BE MISTAKEN ABOUT SOMETHING LIKE THAT...
I'M COUNTING ON YOU, ROKURO!
HUH?
YEAH!
THE AMAWAKA FAMILY IS IN CHARGE OF INVESTIGATING THE KEGARE THAT LIVE IN MAGANO.
THE REASON ALICE ASKED THE TWIN STARS TO COME WITH US...
...IS SO WE CAN COUNT ON YOU TO PROTECT US IF THINGS GET DICEY.

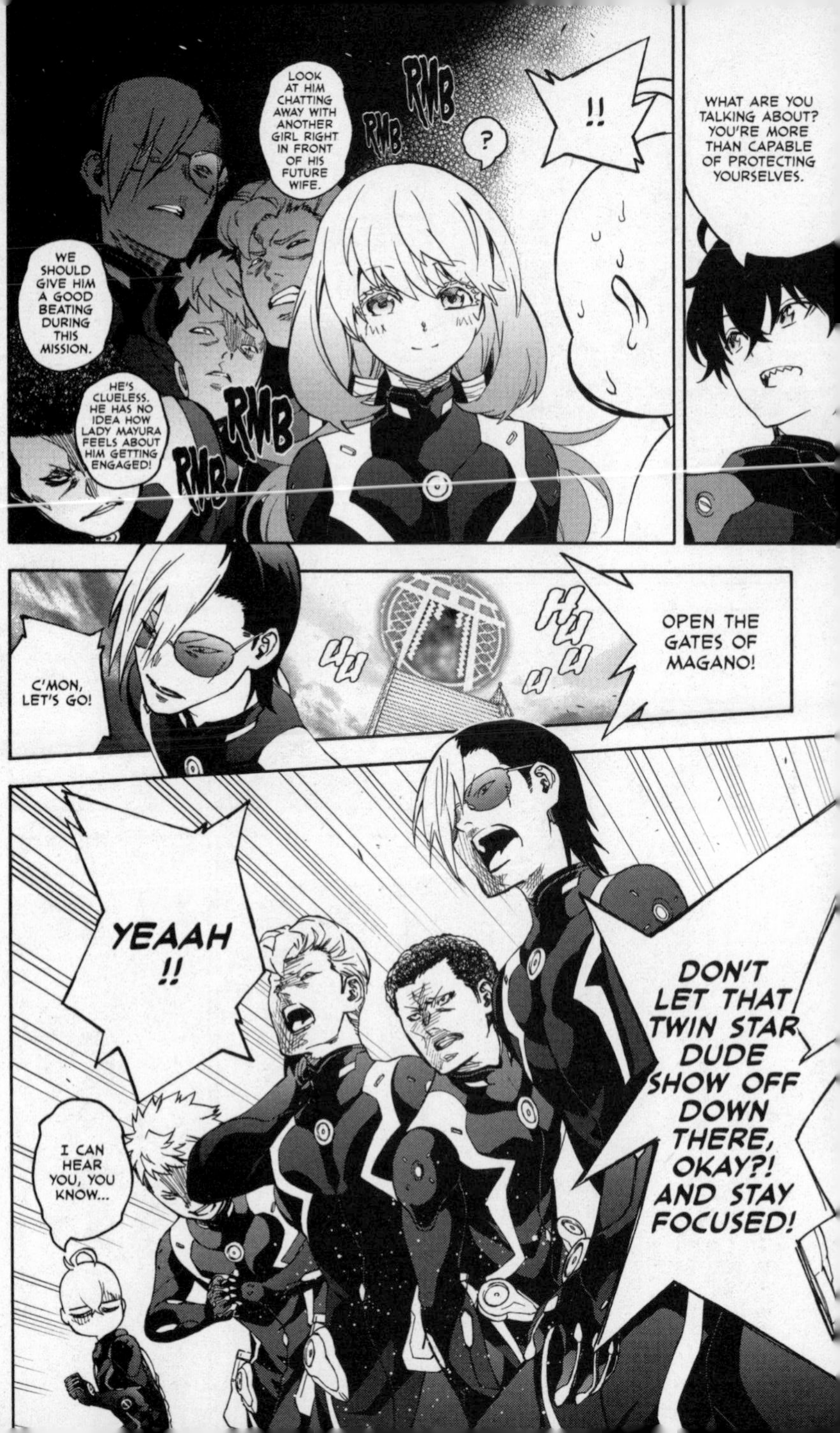
WHAT ARE YOU TALKING ABOUT? YOU'RE MORE THAN CAPABLE OF PROTECTING YOURSELVES.
!!
?
RMB
RMB
LOOK AT HIM CHATTING AWAY WITH ANOTHER GIRL RIGHT IN FRONT OF HIS FUTURE WIFE.
WE SHOULD GIVE HIM A GOOD BEATING DURING THIS MISSION.
RMB
RMB
HE'S CLUELESS. HE HAS NO IDEA HOW LADY MAYURA FEELS ABOUT HIM GETTING ENGAGED!
OPEN THE GATES OF MAGANO!
HUUU
UU
C'MON, LET'S GO!
DON'T LET THAT TWIN STAR DUDE SHOW OFF DOWN THERE, OKAY?! AND STAY FOCUSED!
YEAAH !!
I CAN HEAR YOU, YOU KNOW...

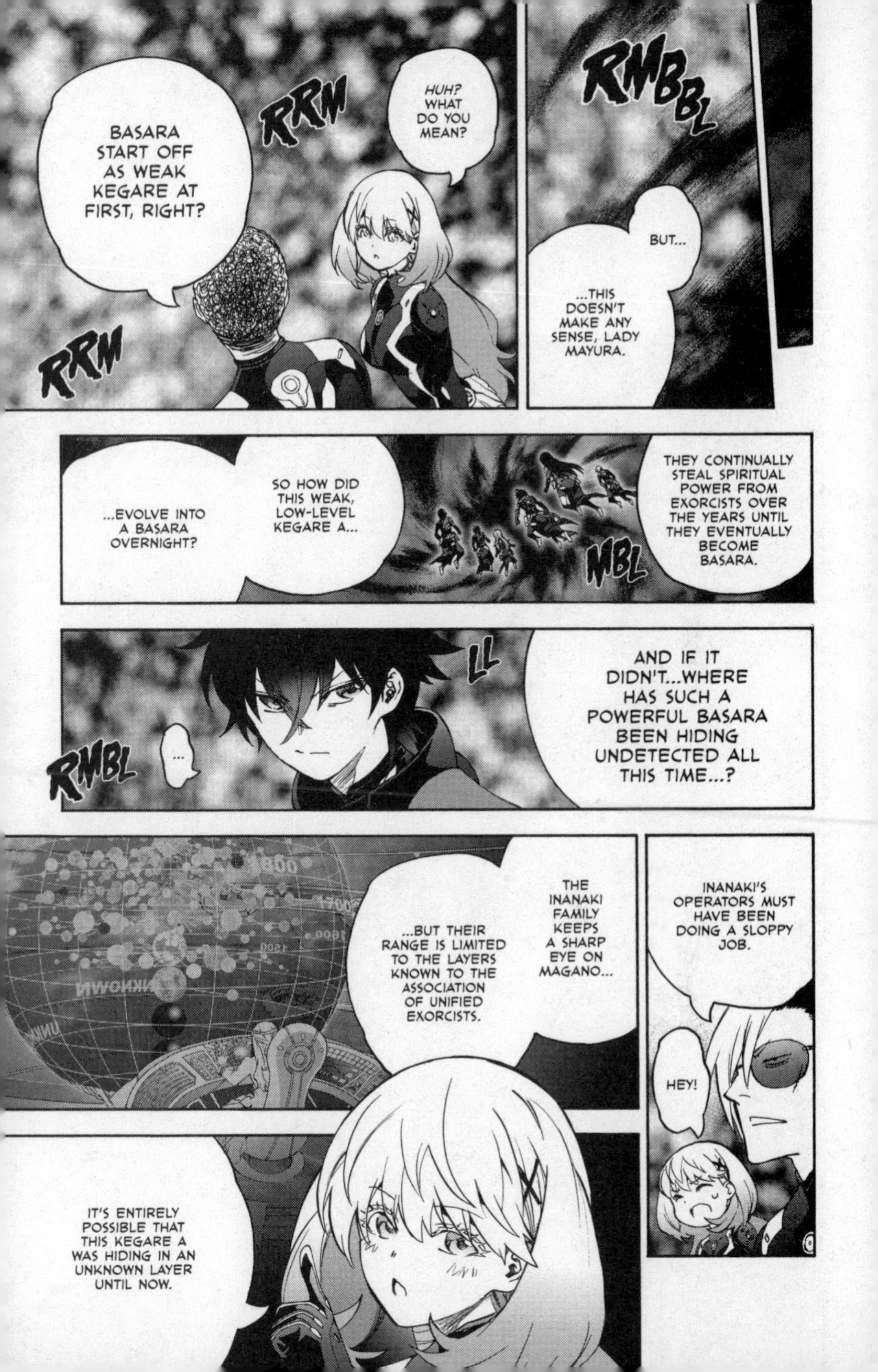
RMBBL
BUT...
...THIS DOESN'T MAKE ANY SENSE, LADY MAYURA.
HUH? WHAT DO YOU MEAN?
RRM
BASARA START OFF AS WEAK KEGARE AT FIRST, RIGHT?
RRM
THEY CONTINUALLY STEAL SPIRITUAL POWER FROM EXORCISTS OVER THE YEARS UNTIL THEY EVENTUALLY BECOME BASARA.
MBL
SO HOW DID THIS WEAK, LOW-LEVEL KEGARE A...
...EVOLVE INTO A BASARA OVERNIGHT?
AND IF IT DIDN'T...WHERE HAS SUCH A POWERFUL BASARA BEEN HIDING UNDETECTED ALL THIS TIME...?
LL
...
RMBL
INANAKI'S OPERATORS MUST HAVE BEEN DOING A SLOPPY JOB.
HEY!
THE INANAKI FAMILY KEEPS A SHARP EYE ON MAGANO...
...BUT THEIR RANGE IS LIMITED TO THE LAYERS KNOWN TO THE ASSOCIATION OF UNIFIED EXORCISTS.
IT'S ENTIRELY POSSIBLE THAT THIS KEGARE A WAS HIDING IN AN UNKNOWN LAYER UNTIL NOW.

IT'S THE JOB OF THE ABOVE-GROUND EXORCISTS TO FIND IT! CONCENTRATE ON YOUR MISSION AND YOUR RESPONSIBILITIES.

SHE'S A REALLY GOOD LEADER.

Y-YES MA'AM.

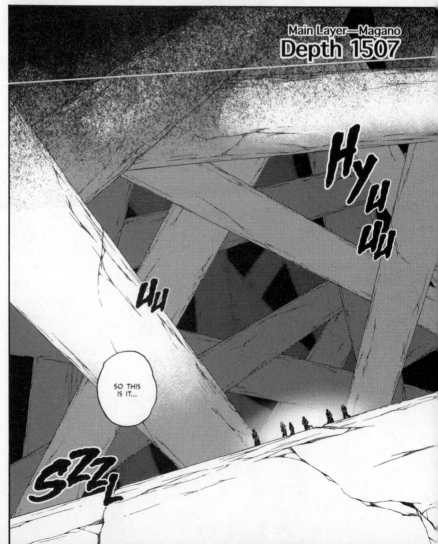

Main Layer—Magano
Depth 1507

HYUUU

UU

SO THIS IS IT...

SZZL

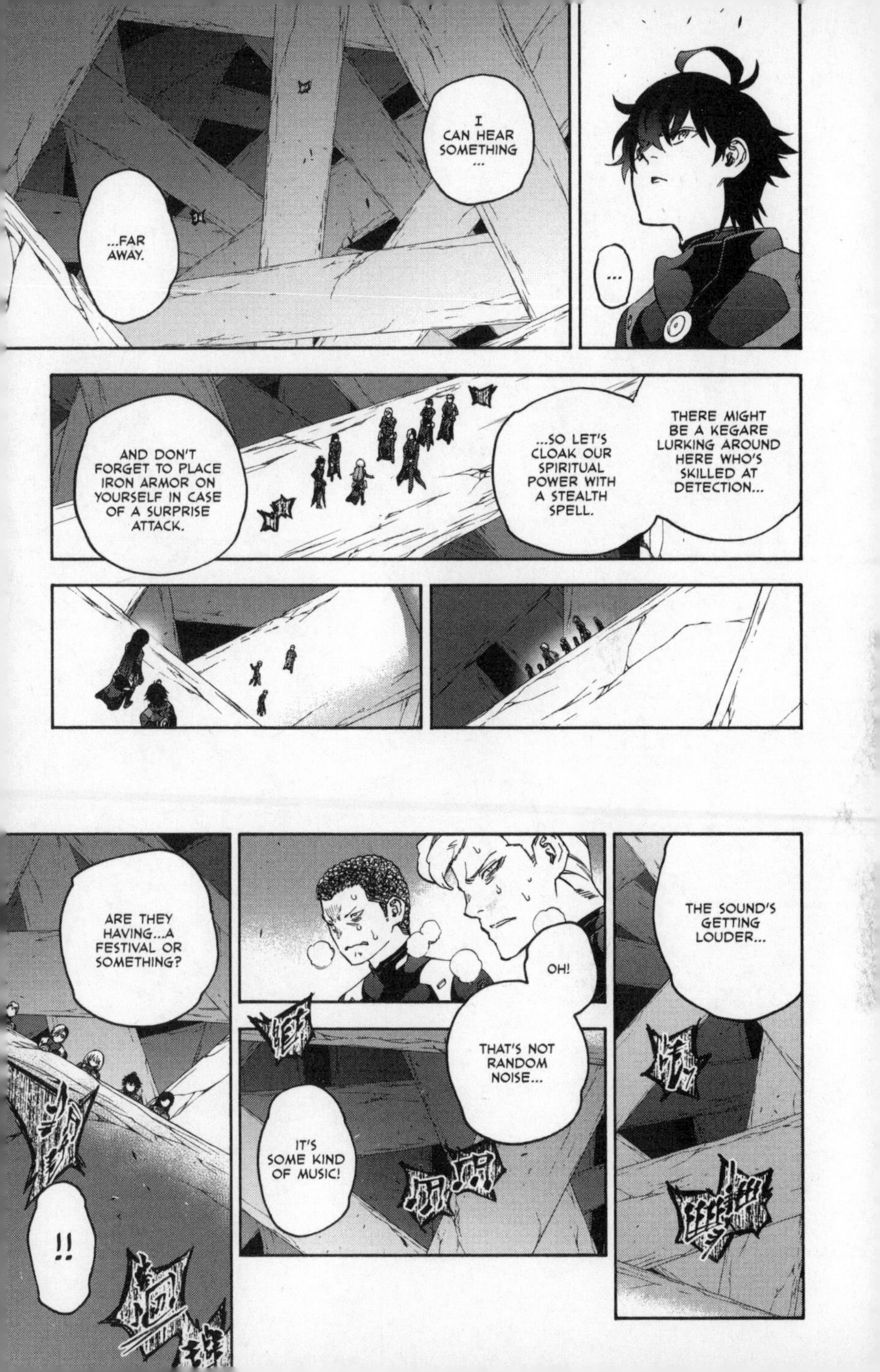
...
I CAN HEAR SOMETHING ...
...FAR AWAY.
THERE MIGHT BE A KEGARE LURKING AROUND HERE WHO'S SKILLED AT DETECTION...
...SO LET'S CLOAK OUR SPIRITUAL POWER WITH A STEALTH SPELL.
AND DON'T FORGET TO PLACE IRON ARMOR ON YOURSELF IN CASE OF A SURPRISE ATTACK.
THE SOUND'S GETTING LOUDER...
OH!
THAT'S NOT RANDOM NOISE...
IT'S SOME KIND OF MUSIC!
ARE THEY HAVING...A FESTIVAL OR SOMETHING?
!!

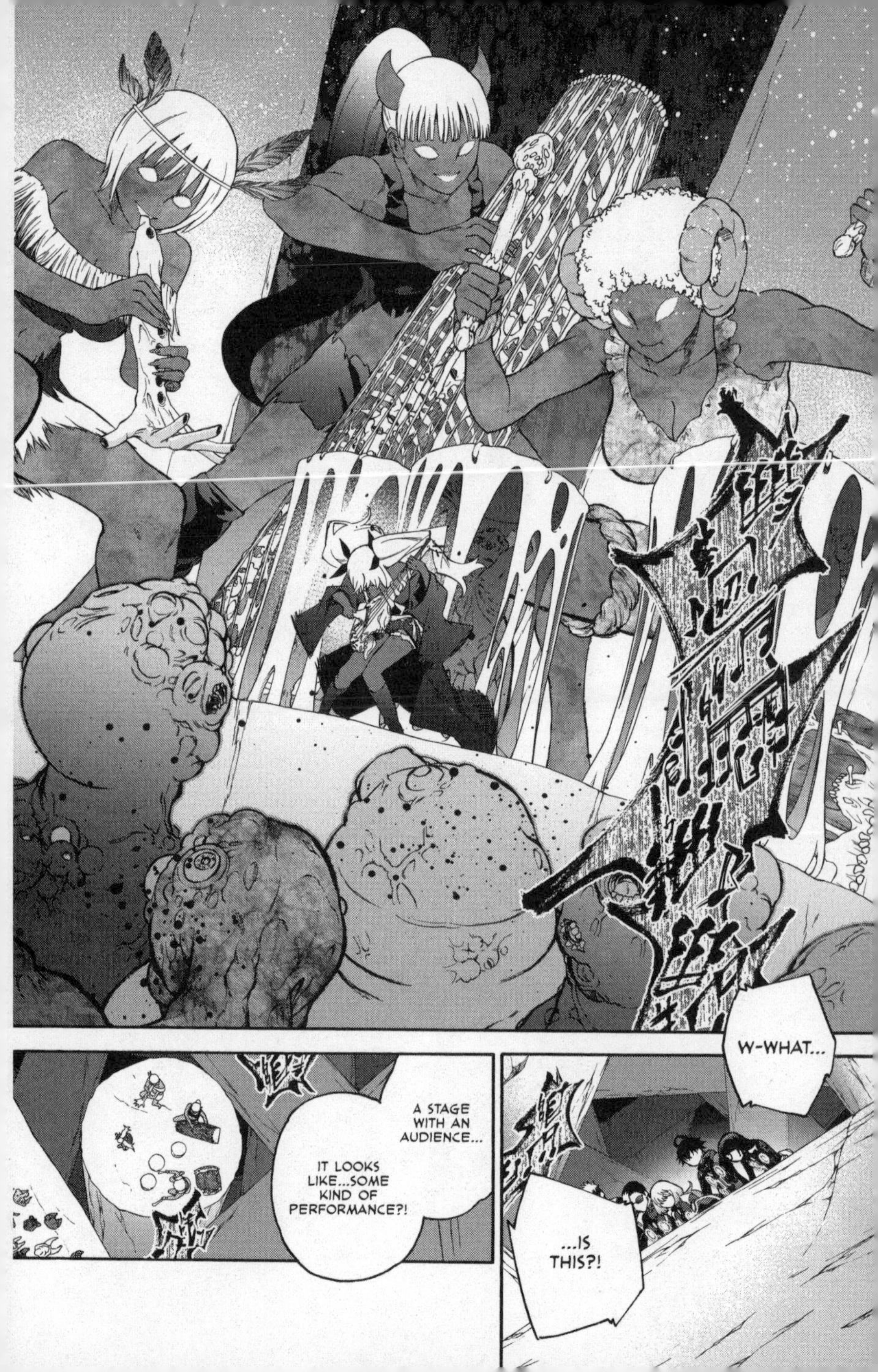
W-WHAT...
...IS THIS?!
A STAGE WITH AN AUDIENCE...
IT LOOKS LIKE...SOME KIND OF PERFORMANCE?!

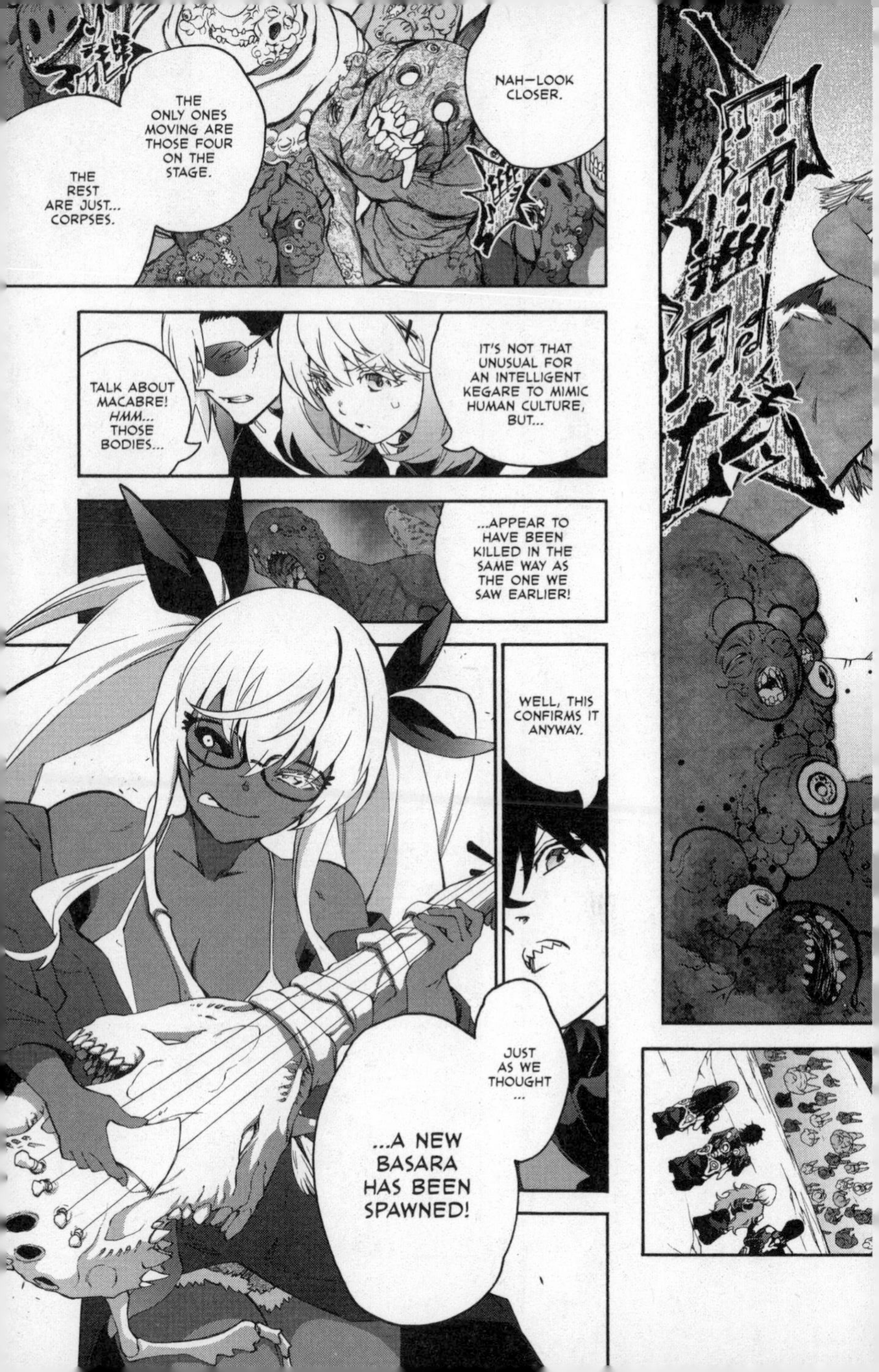
NAH—LOOK CLOSER.
THE ONLY ONES MOVING ARE THOSE FOUR ON THE STAGE.
THE REST ARE JUST... CORPSES.
IT'S NOT THAT UNUSUAL FOR AN INTELLIGENT KEGARE TO MIMIC HUMAN CULTURE, BUT...
TALK ABOUT MACABRE! *HMM...* THOSE BODIES...
...APPEAR TO HAVE BEEN KILLED IN THE SAME WAY AS THE ONE WE SAW EARLIER!
WELL, THIS CONFIRMS IT ANYWAY.
JUST AS WE THOUGHT...
...A NEW BASARA HAS BEEN SPAWNED!

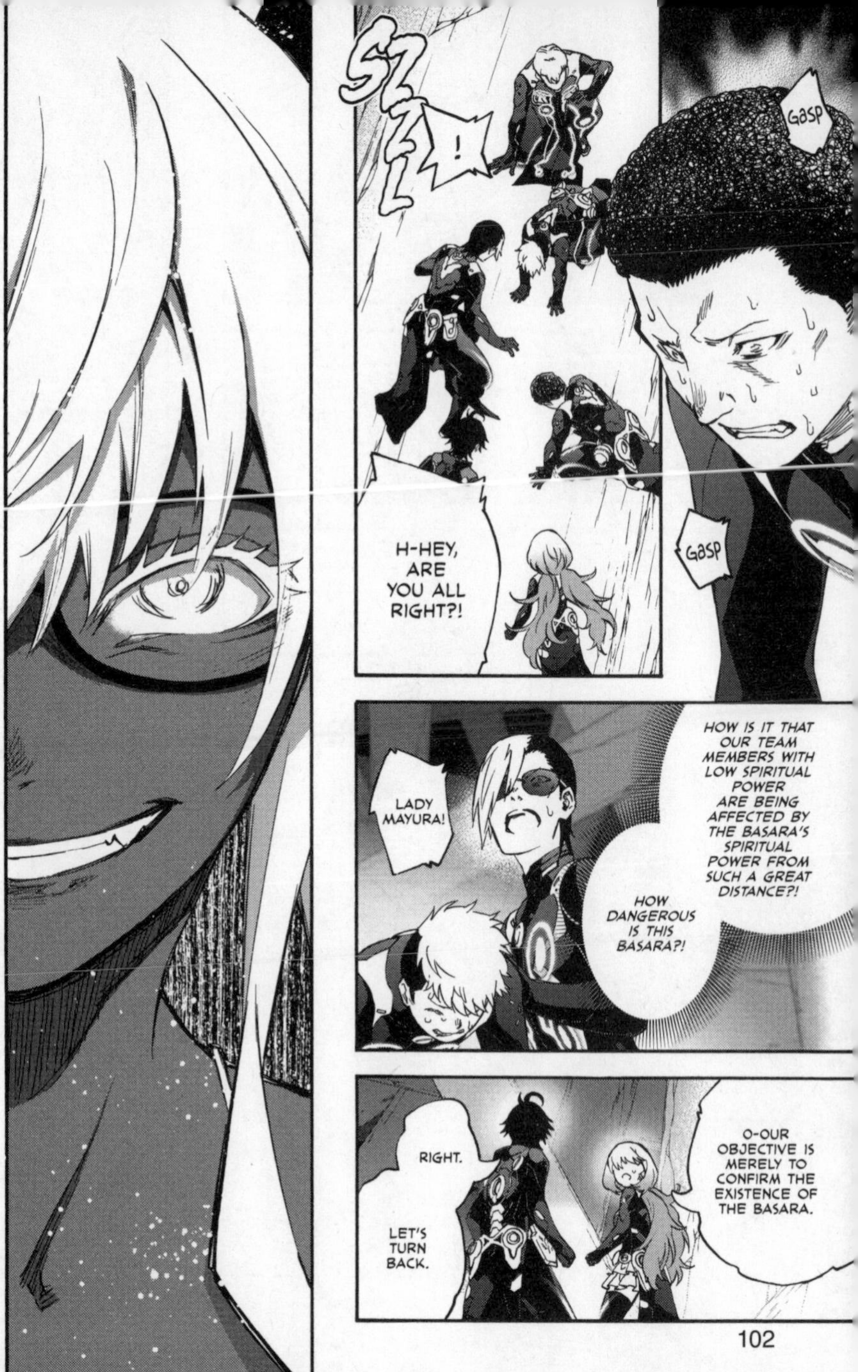
Gasp
Gasp
SZZL
!
H-HEY, ARE YOU ALL RIGHT?!
HOW IS IT THAT OUR TEAM MEMBERS WITH LOW SPIRITUAL POWER ARE BEING AFFECTED BY THE BASARA'S SPIRITUAL POWER FROM SUCH A GREAT DISTANCE?!
HOW DANGEROUS IS THIS BASARA?!
LADY MAYURA!
O-OUR OBJECTIVE IS MERELY TO CONFIRM THE EXISTENCE OF THE BASARA.
RIGHT.
LET'S TURN BACK.

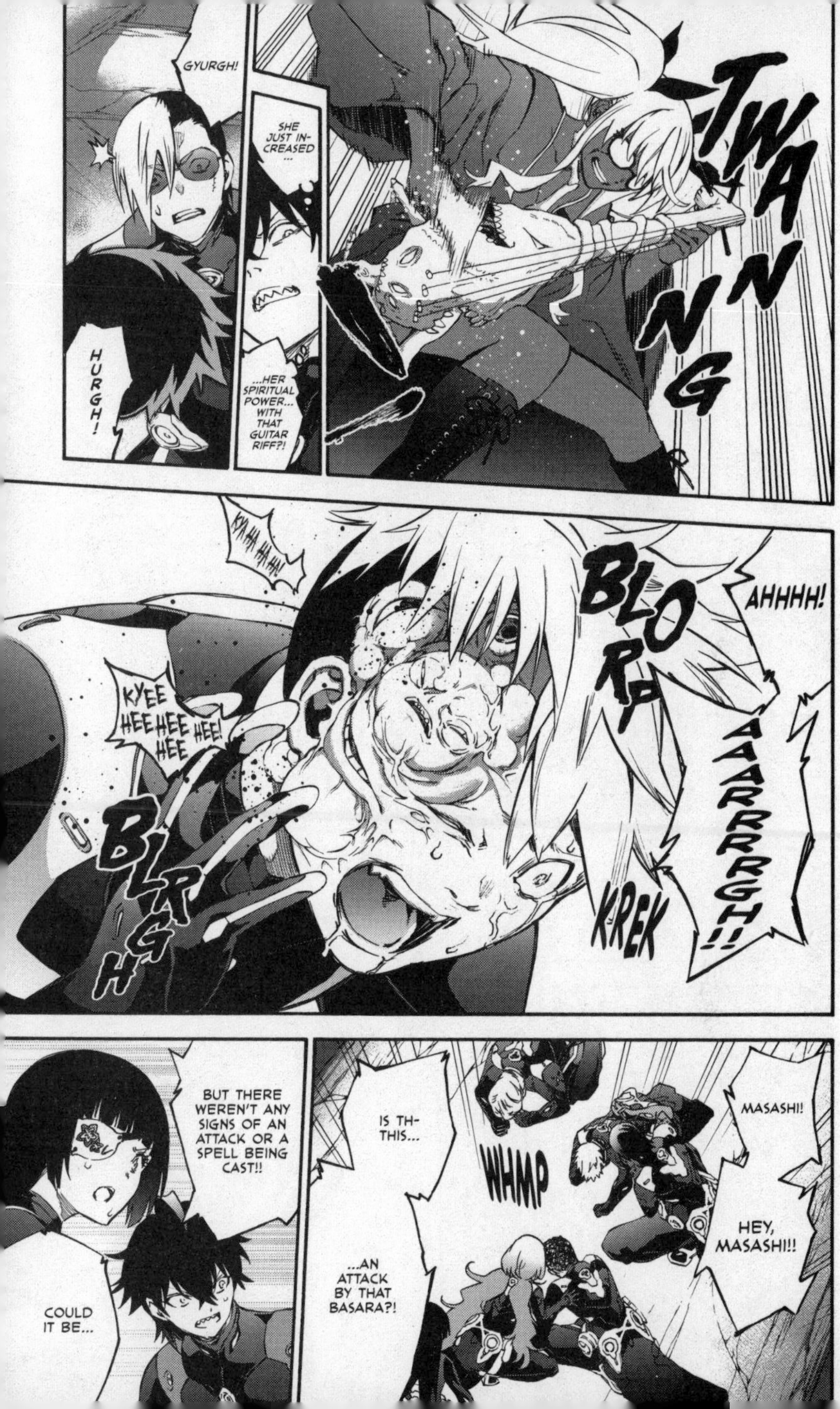
TWANNNG
SHE JUST IN-CREASED...
...HER SPIRITUAL POWER... WITH THAT GUITAR RIFF?!
GYURGH!
HURGH!
AHHHH!
BLORP
AARRRGH!!
KREK
KYA HA HA HA!
KYEE HEE HEE HEE HEE!
BLRGH
MASASHI!
HEY, MASASHI!!
WHMP
IS TH-THIS...
...AN ATTACK BY THAT BASARA?!
BUT THERE WEREN'T ANY SIGNS OF AN ATTACK OR A SPELL BEING CAST!!
COULD IT BE...

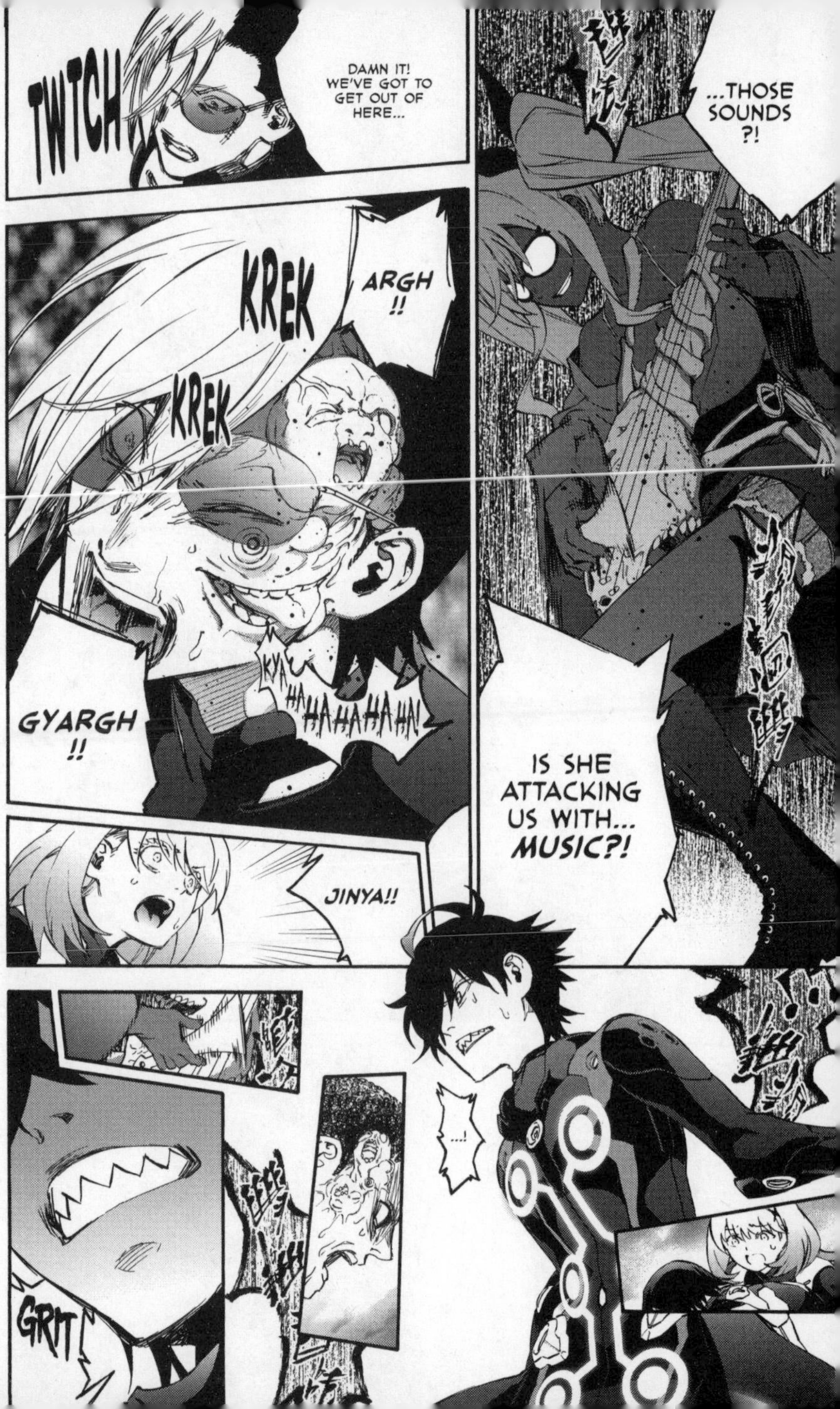
...THOSE SOUNDS ?!
IS SHE ATTACKING US WITH... *MUSIC?!*
TWITCH
DAMN IT! WE'VE GOT TO GET OUT OF HERE...
KREK
ARGH !!
KREK
KYAHAHAHAHAHA!
GYARGH !!
JINYA!!
...!
GRIT

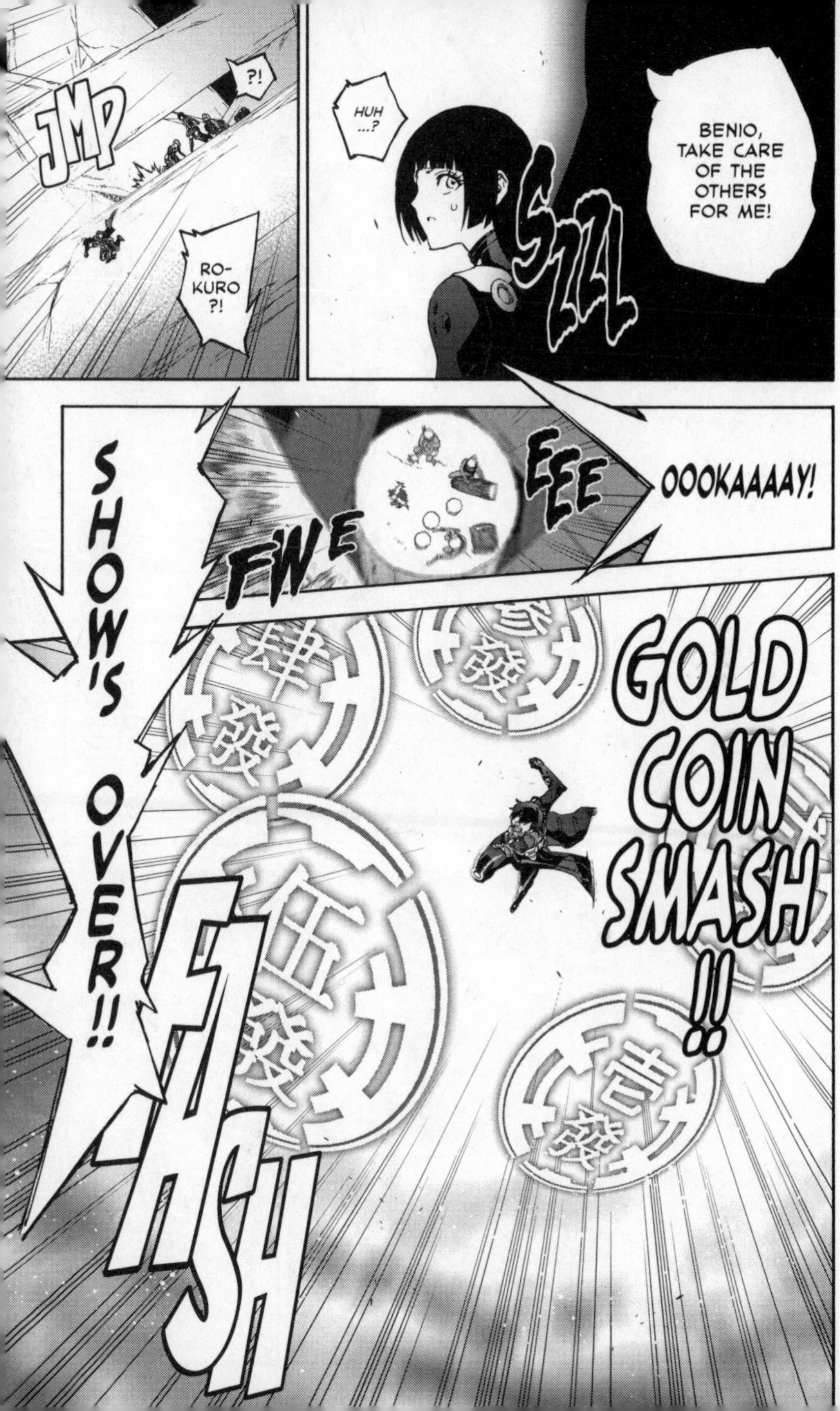
BENIO, TAKE CARE OF THE OTHERS FOR ME!
SZZZ
HUH ...?
?!
JMP
RO-KURO ?!
OOOKAAAAY!
FWEEEE
GOLD COIN SMASH!!
SHOW'S OVER!!

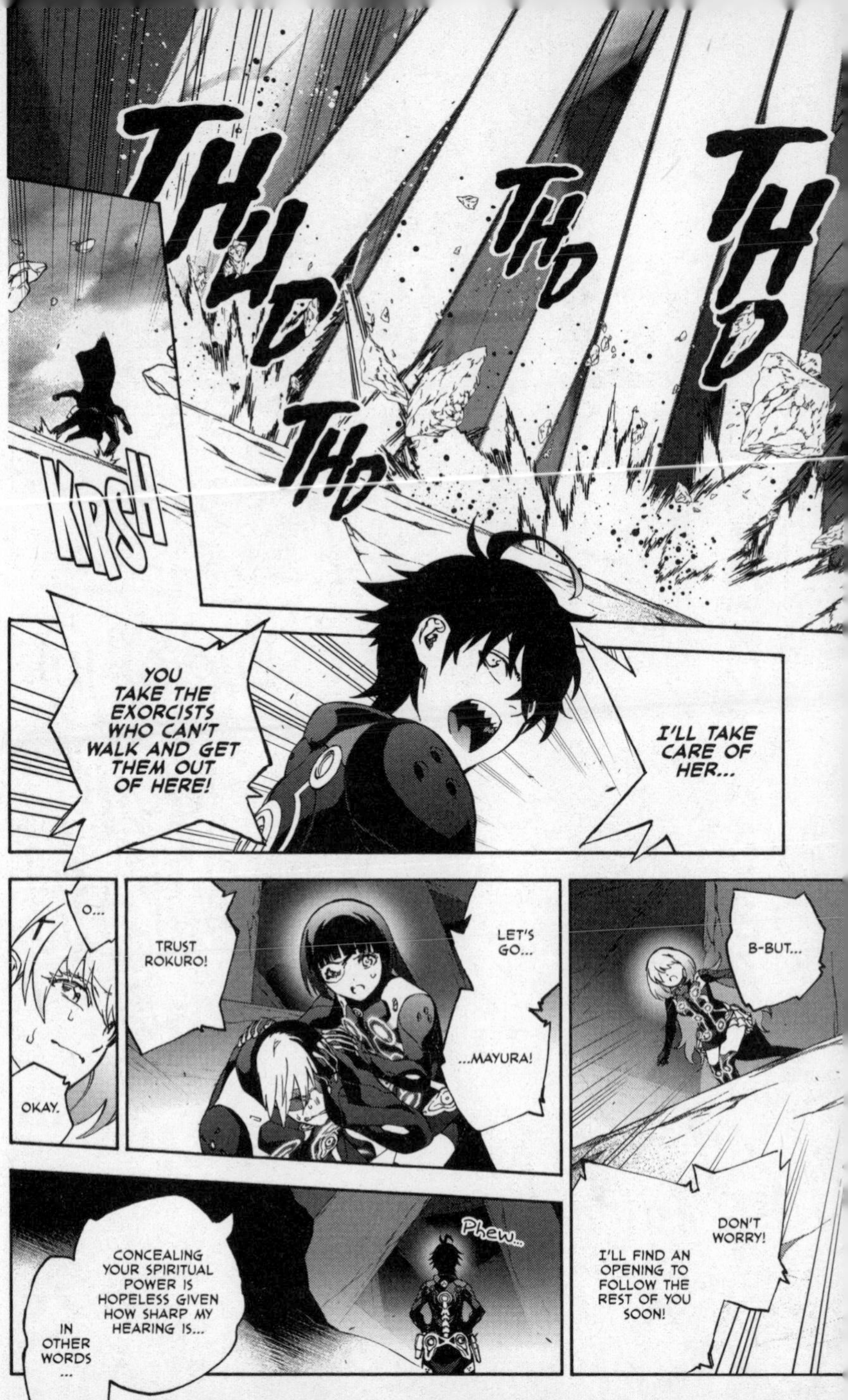
THD
THD
THUD
THD
KRSH
I'LL TAKE CARE OF HER...
YOU TAKE THE EXORCISTS WHO CAN'T WALK AND GET THEM OUT OF HERE!
B-BUT...
LET'S GO...
...MAYURA!
TRUST ROKURO!
O...
OKAY.
DON'T WORRY!
I'LL FIND AN OPENING TO FOLLOW THE REST OF YOU SOON!
Phew...
CONCEALING YOUR SPIRITUAL POWER IS HOPELESS GIVEN HOW SHARP MY HEARING IS...
IN OTHER WORDS ...

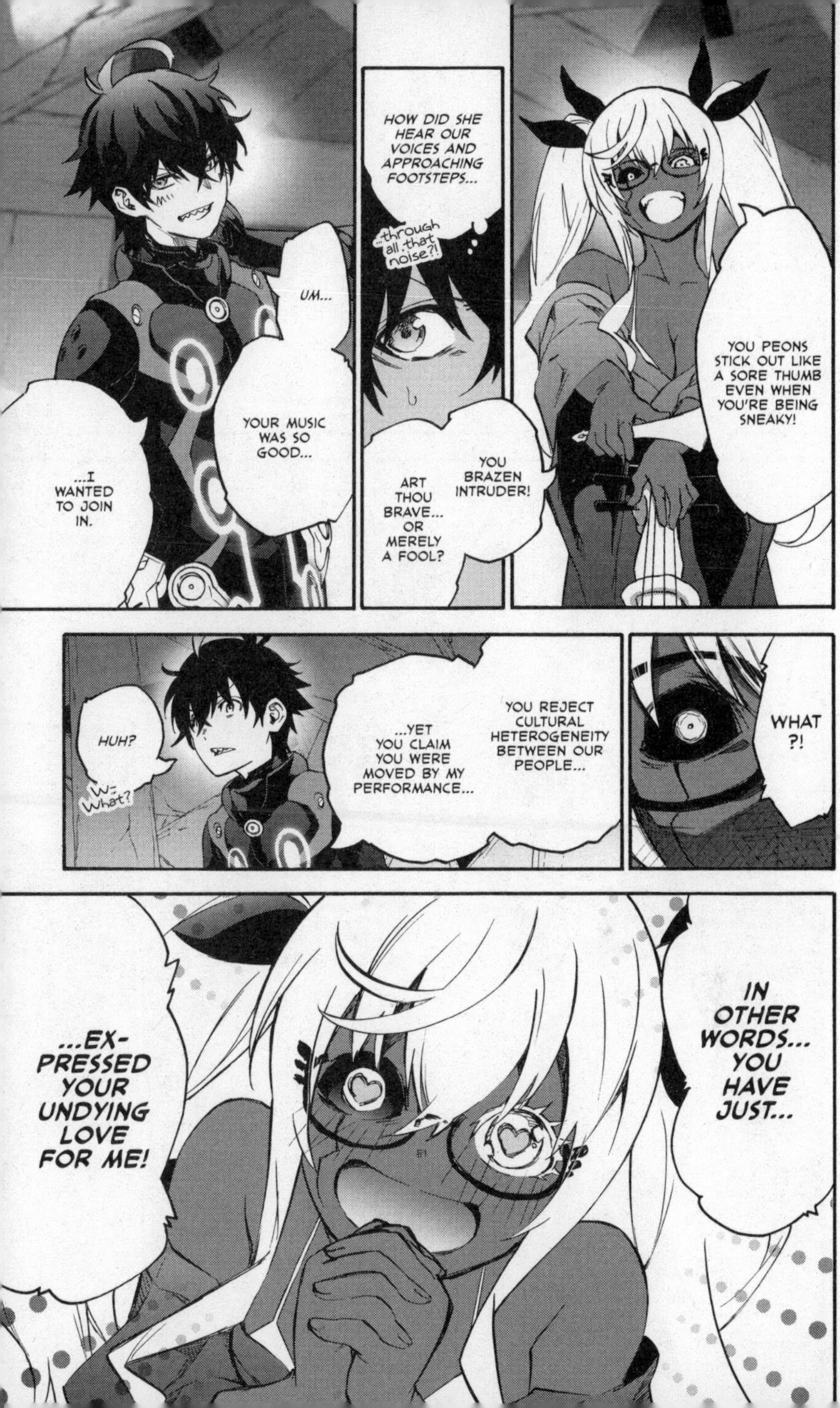

YOU PEONS STICK OUT LIKE A SORE THUMB EVEN WHEN YOU'RE BEING SNEAKY!
HOW DID SHE HEAR OUR VOICES AND APPROACHING FOOTSTEPS...
...through all that noise?!
YOU BRAZEN INTRUDER!
ART THOU BRAVE... OR MERELY A FOOL?
UM...
YOUR MUSIC WAS SO GOOD...
...I WANTED TO JOIN IN.
WHAT?!
YOU REJECT CULTURAL HETEROGENEITY BETWEEN OUR PEOPLE...
...YET YOU CLAIM YOU WERE MOVED BY MY PERFORMANCE...
HUH?
W- What?
IN OTHER WORDS... YOU HAVE JUST...
...EX-PRESSED YOUR UNDYING LOVE FOR ME!

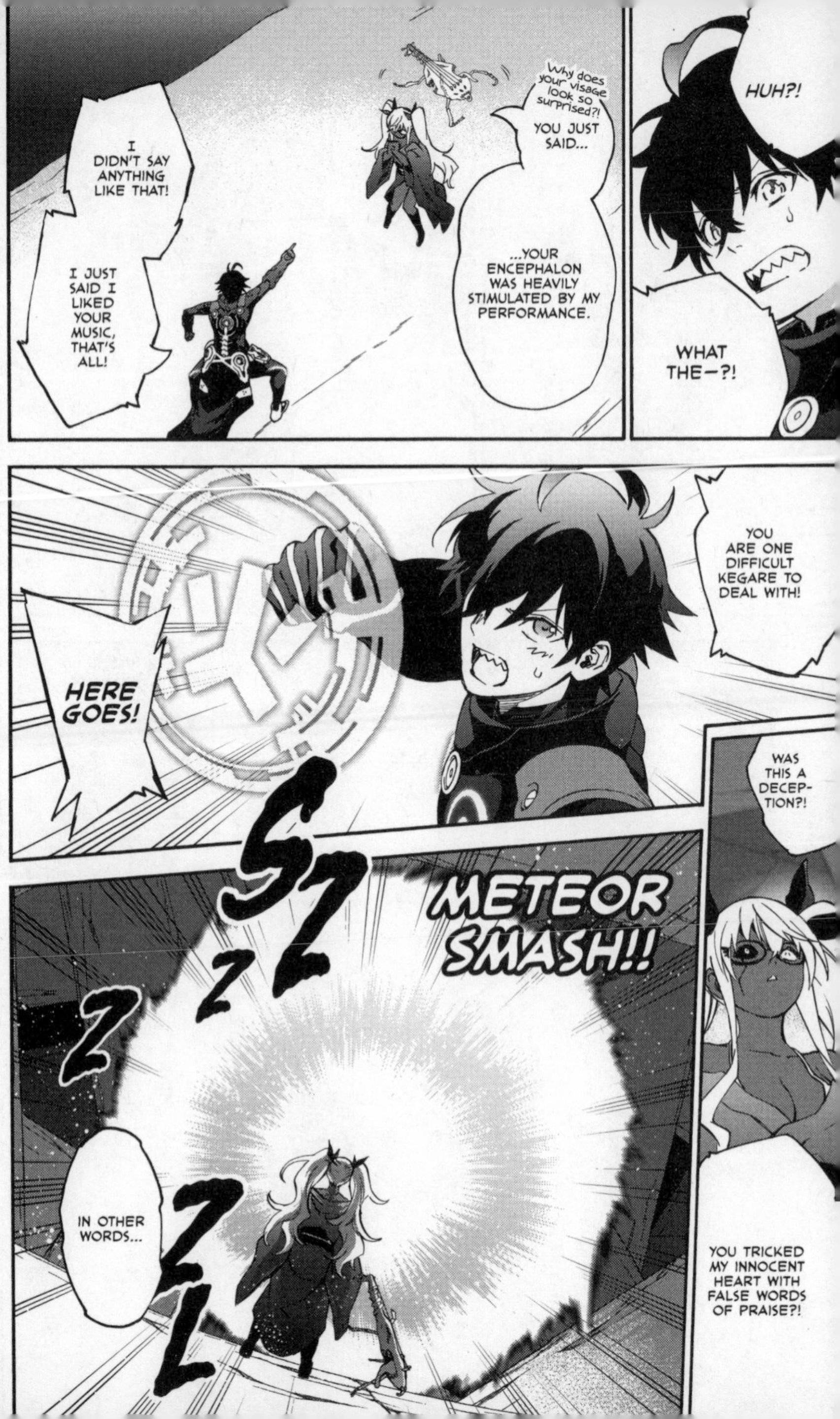
HUH?!
WHAT THE—?!
Why does your visage look so surprised?!
YOU JUST SAID...
...YOUR ENCEPHALON WAS HEAVILY STIMULATED BY MY PERFORMANCE.
I DIDN'T SAY ANYTHING LIKE THAT!
I JUST SAID I LIKED YOUR MUSIC, THAT'S ALL!
YOU ARE ONE DIFFICULT KEGARE TO DEAL WITH!
HERE GOES!
WAS THIS A DECEP-TION?!
YOU TRICKED MY INNOCENT HEART WITH FALSE WORDS OF PRAISE?!
METEOR SMASH!!
SZZZZ
IN OTHER WORDS...

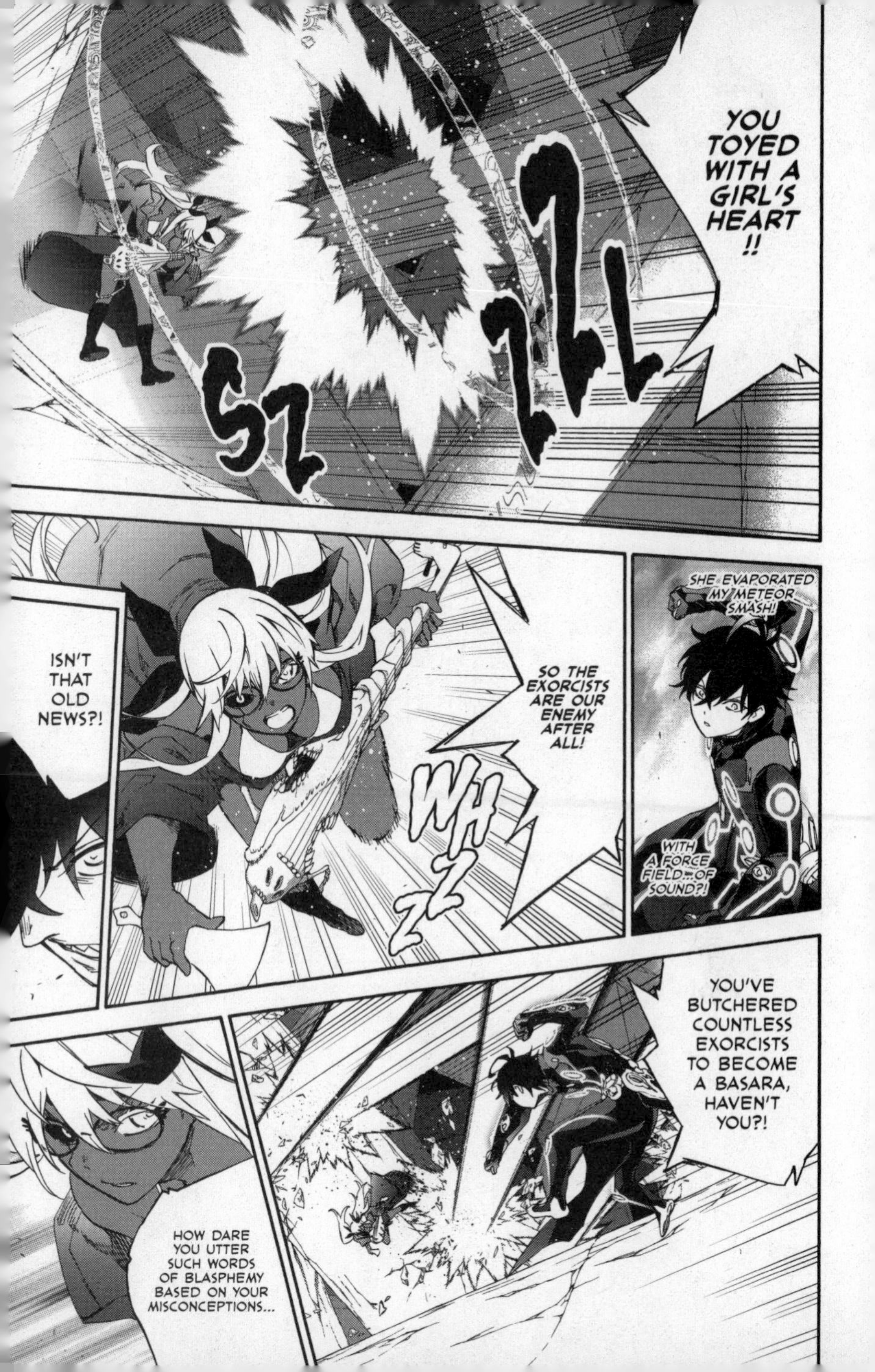
YOU TOYED WITH A GIRL'S HEART !!
SZZZZ
SHE EVAPORATED MY METEOR SMASH!
WITH A FORCE FIELD OF SOUND?!
SO THE EXORCISTS ARE OUR ENEMY AFTER ALL!
WHZZZ
ISN'T THAT OLD NEWS?!
YOU'VE BUTCHERED COUNTLESS EXORCISTS TO BECOME A BASARA, HAVEN'T YOU?!
HOW DARE YOU UTTER SUCH WORDS OF BLASPHEMY BASED ON YOUR MISCONCEPTIONS...

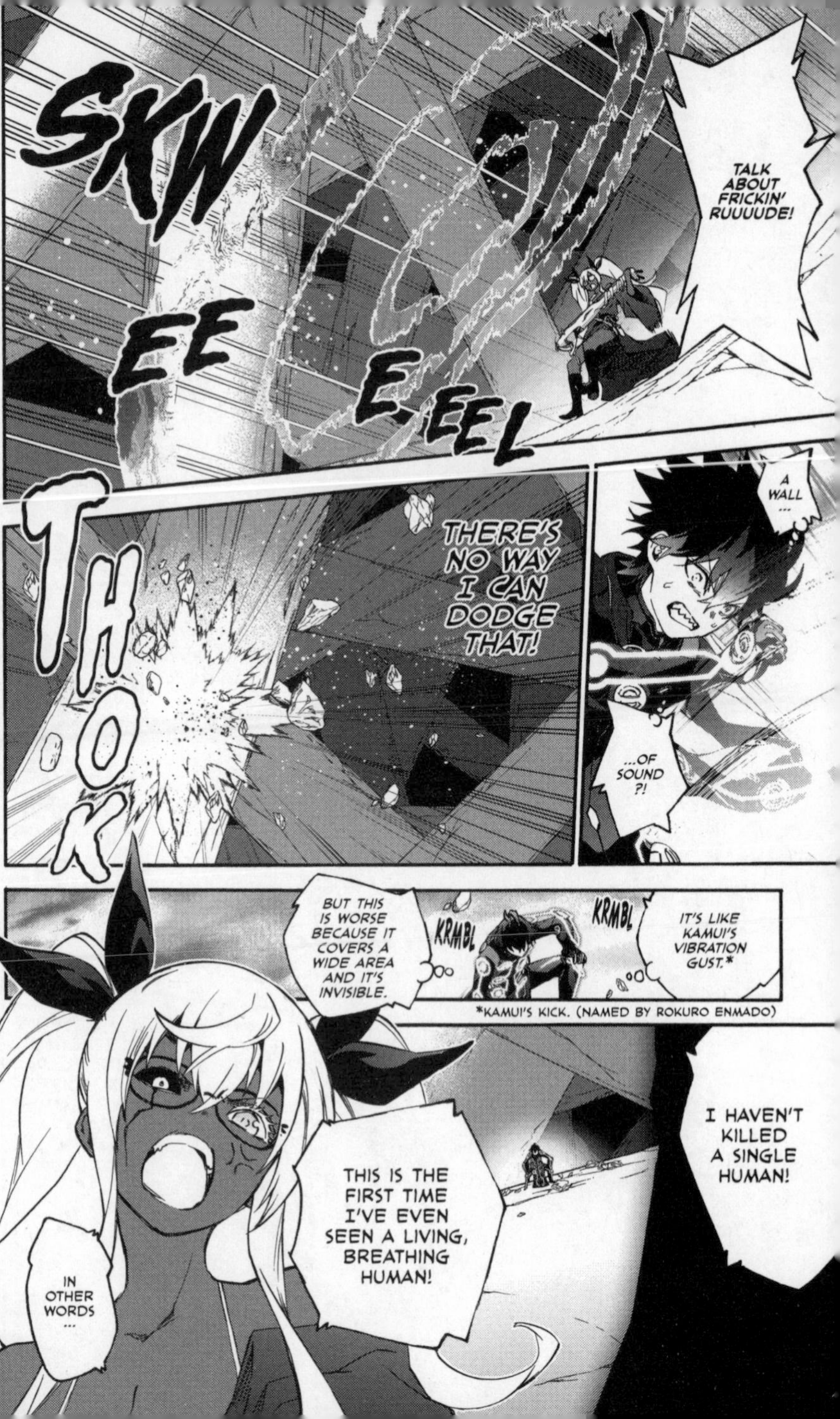
SKWEEEEEL
TALK ABOUT FRICKIN' RUUUUDE!
A WALL ...
...OF SOUND ?!
THERE'S NO WAY I CAN DODGE THAT!
THOK
IT'S LIKE KAMUI'S VIBRATION GUST.*
KRMBL
KRMBL
BUT THIS IS WORSE BECAUSE IT COVERS A WIDE AREA AND IT'S INVISIBLE.
I HAVEN'T KILLED A SINGLE HUMAN!
THIS IS THE FIRST TIME I'VE EVEN SEEN A LIVING, BREATHING HUMAN!
IN OTHER WORDS ...
*KAMUI'S KICK. (NAMED BY ROKURO ENMADO)

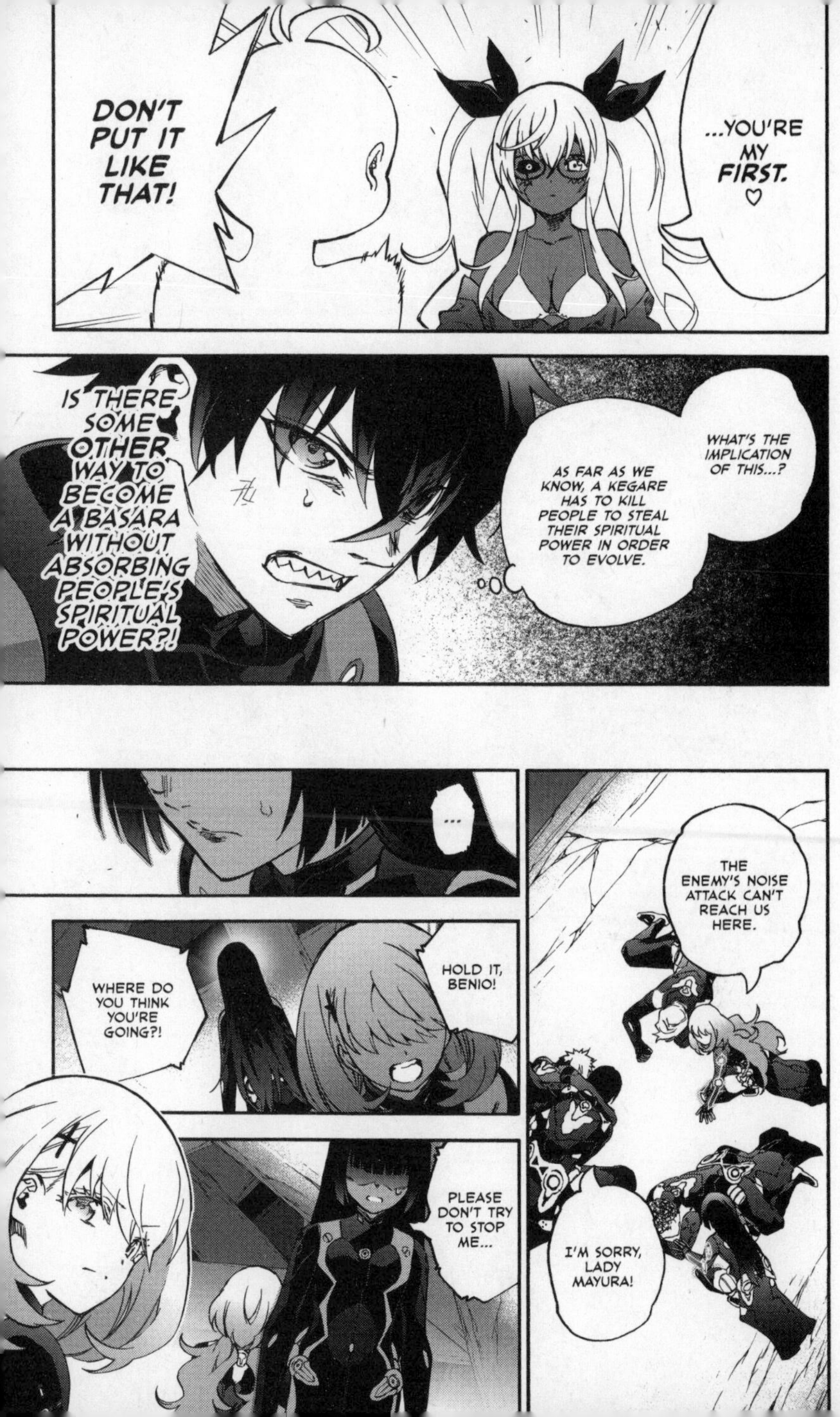
...YOU'RE MY FIRST. ♡
DON'T PUT IT LIKE THAT!
WHAT'S THE IMPLICATION OF THIS...?
AS FAR AS WE KNOW, A KEGARE HAS TO KILL PEOPLE TO STEAL THEIR SPIRITUAL POWER IN ORDER TO EVOLVE.
IS THERE SOME OTHER WAY TO BECOME A BASARA WITHOUT ABSORBING PEOPLE'S SPIRITUAL POWER?!
THE ENEMY'S NOISE ATTACK CAN'T REACH US HERE.
I'M SORRY, LADY MAYURA!
...
HOLD IT, BENIO!
WHERE DO YOU THINK YOU'RE GOING?!
PLEASE DON'T TRY TO STOP ME...

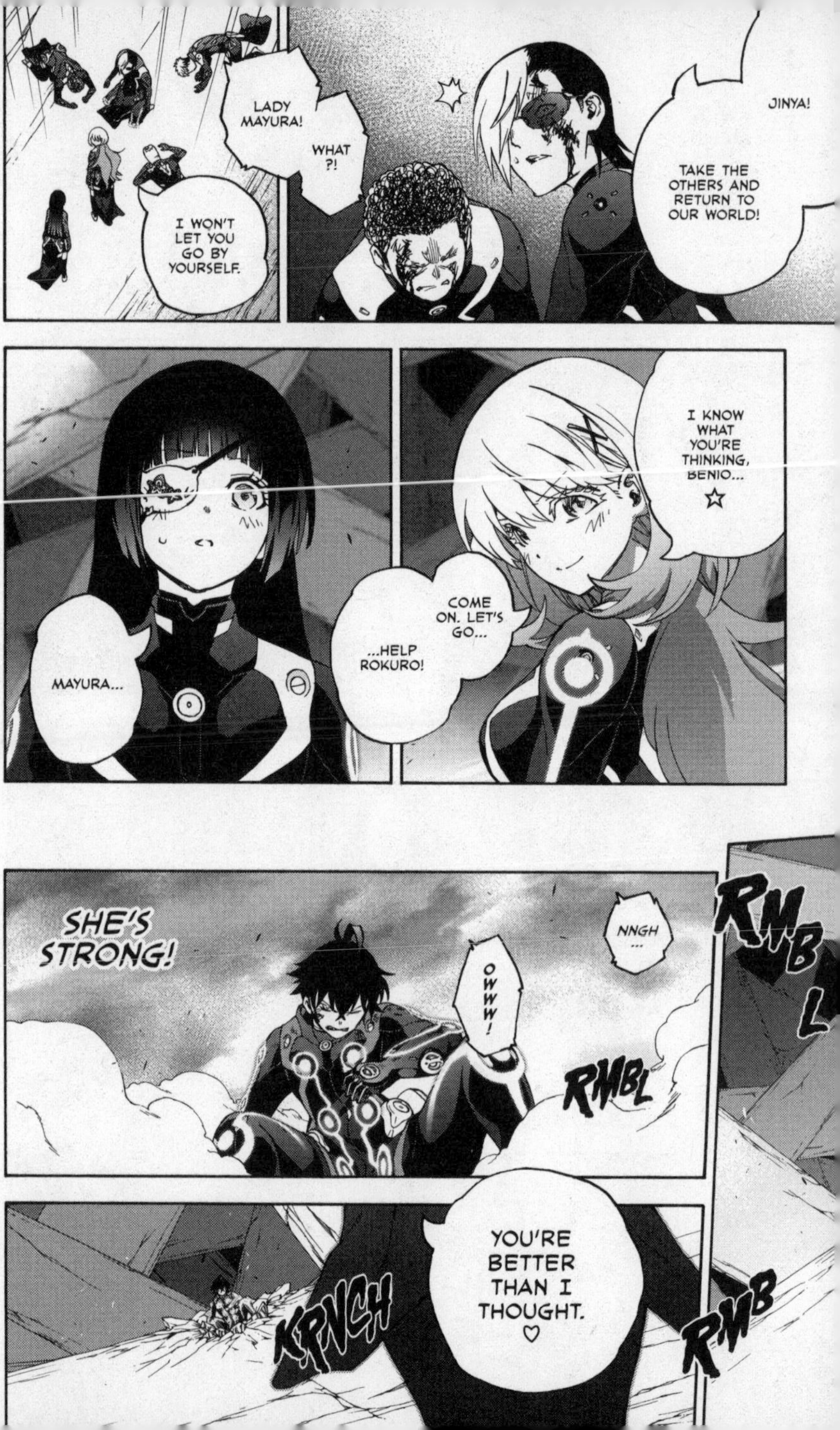
JINYA!
TAKE THE OTHERS AND RETURN TO OUR WORLD!
LADY MAYURA!
WHAT?!
I WON'T LET YOU GO BY YOURSELF.
I KNOW WHAT YOU'RE THINKING, BENIO... ☆
COME ON. LET'S GO...
...HELP ROKURO!
MAYURA...
RMBL
NNGH...
OWWW!
SHE'S STRONG!
RMBL
RMB
YOU'RE BETTER THAN I THOUGHT. ♡
KRNCH

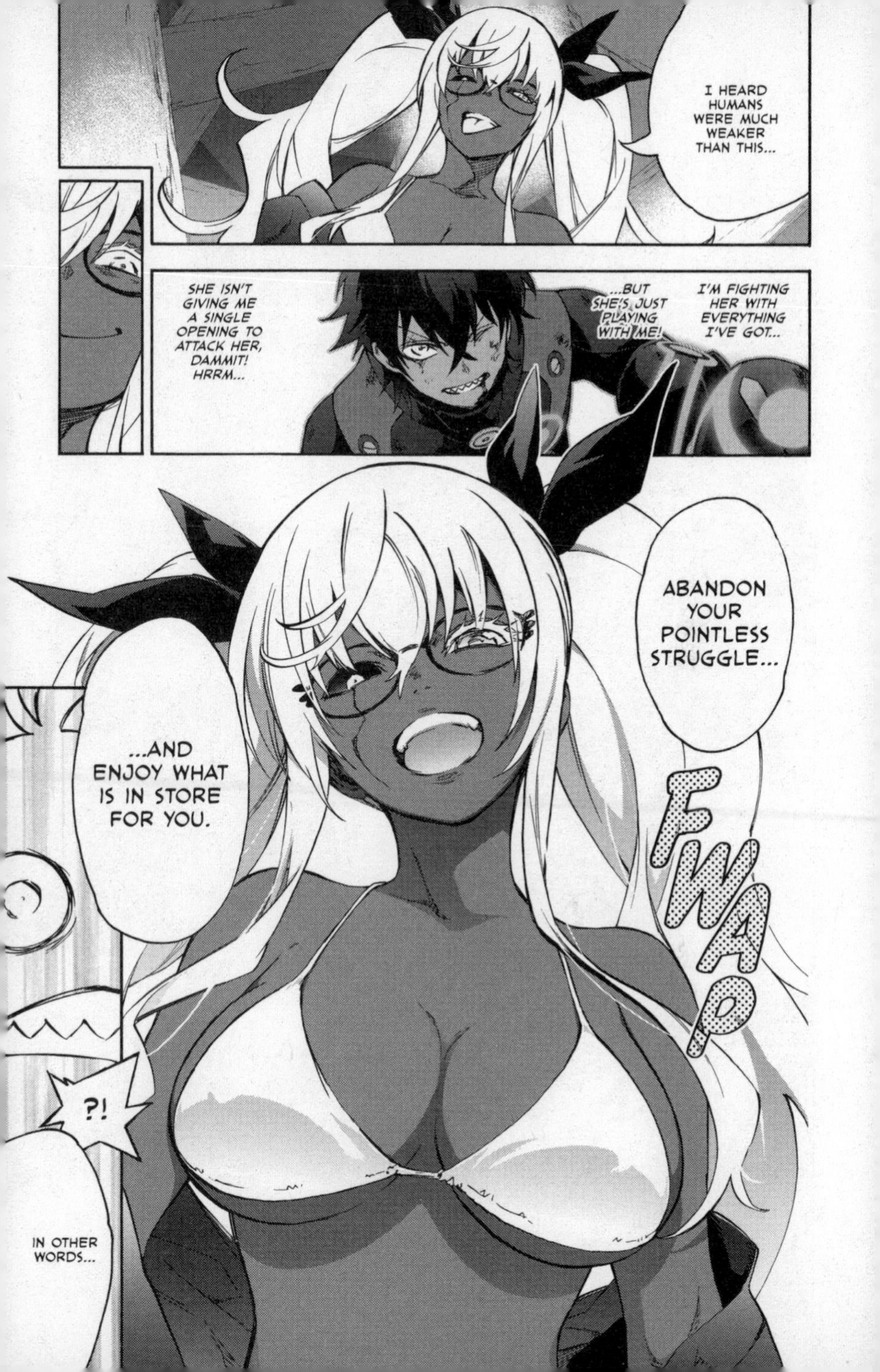
I HEARD HUMANS WERE MUCH WEAKER THAN THIS...
I'M FIGHTING HER WITH EVERYTHING I'VE GOT...
...BUT SHE'S JUST PLAYING WITH ME!
SHE ISN'T GIVING ME A SINGLE OPENING TO ATTACK HER, DAMMIT! HRRM...
ABANDON YOUR POINTLESS STRUGGLE...
FWAP
...AND ENJOY WHAT IS IN STORE FOR YOU.
?!
IN OTHER WORDS...

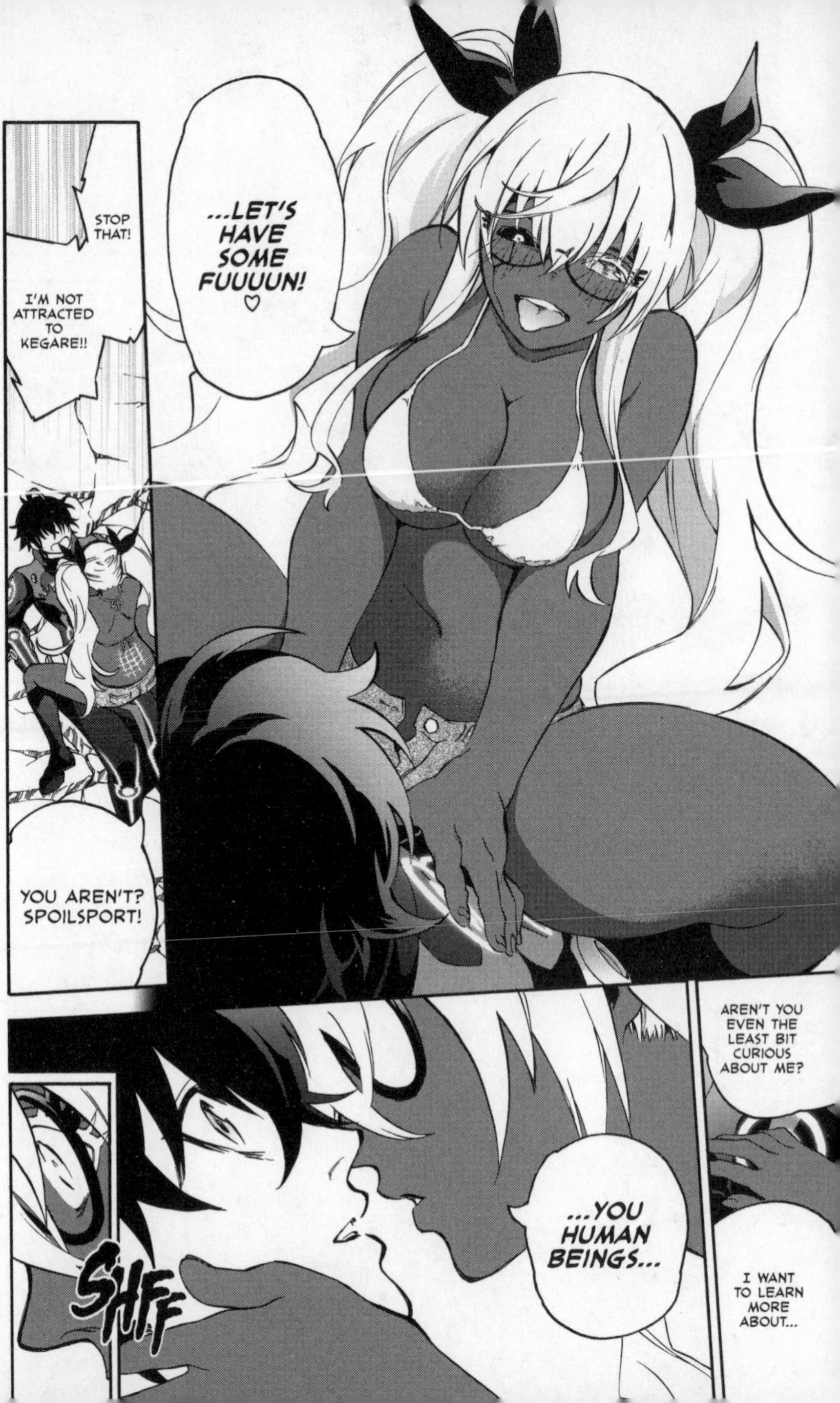
...LET'S HAVE SOME FUUUUN! ♡
STOP THAT!
I'M NOT ATTRACTED TO KEGARE!!
YOU AREN'T? SPOILSPORT!
AREN'T YOU EVEN THE LEAST BIT CURIOUS ABOUT ME?
I WANT TO LEARN MORE ABOUT...
...YOU HUMAN BEINGS...
SHFF

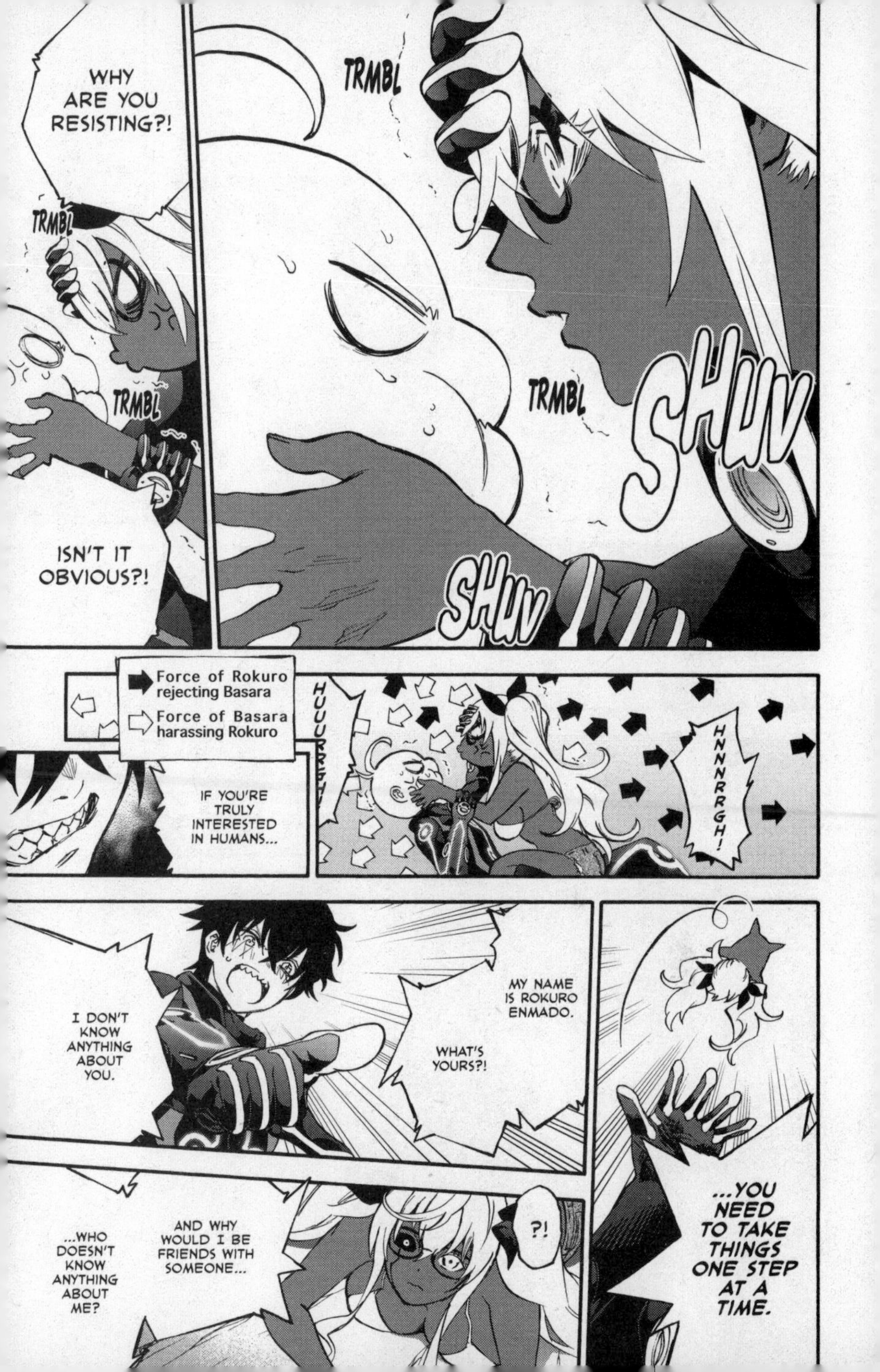
TRMBL
TRMBL
SHUV
SHUV
WHY ARE YOU RESISTING?!
TRMBL
TRMBL
ISN'T IT OBVIOUS?!
HUUURRGH
HNNNRRGH!
Force of Rokuro rejecting Basara
Force of Basara harassing Rokuro
IF YOU'RE TRULY INTERESTED IN HUMANS...
...YOU NEED TO TAKE THINGS ONE STEP AT A TIME.
MY NAME IS ROKURO ENMADO.
WHAT'S YOURS?!
I DON'T KNOW ANYTHING ABOUT YOU.
?!
AND WHY WOULD I BE FRIENDS WITH SOMEONE...
...WHO DOESN'T KNOW ANYTHING ABOUT ME?

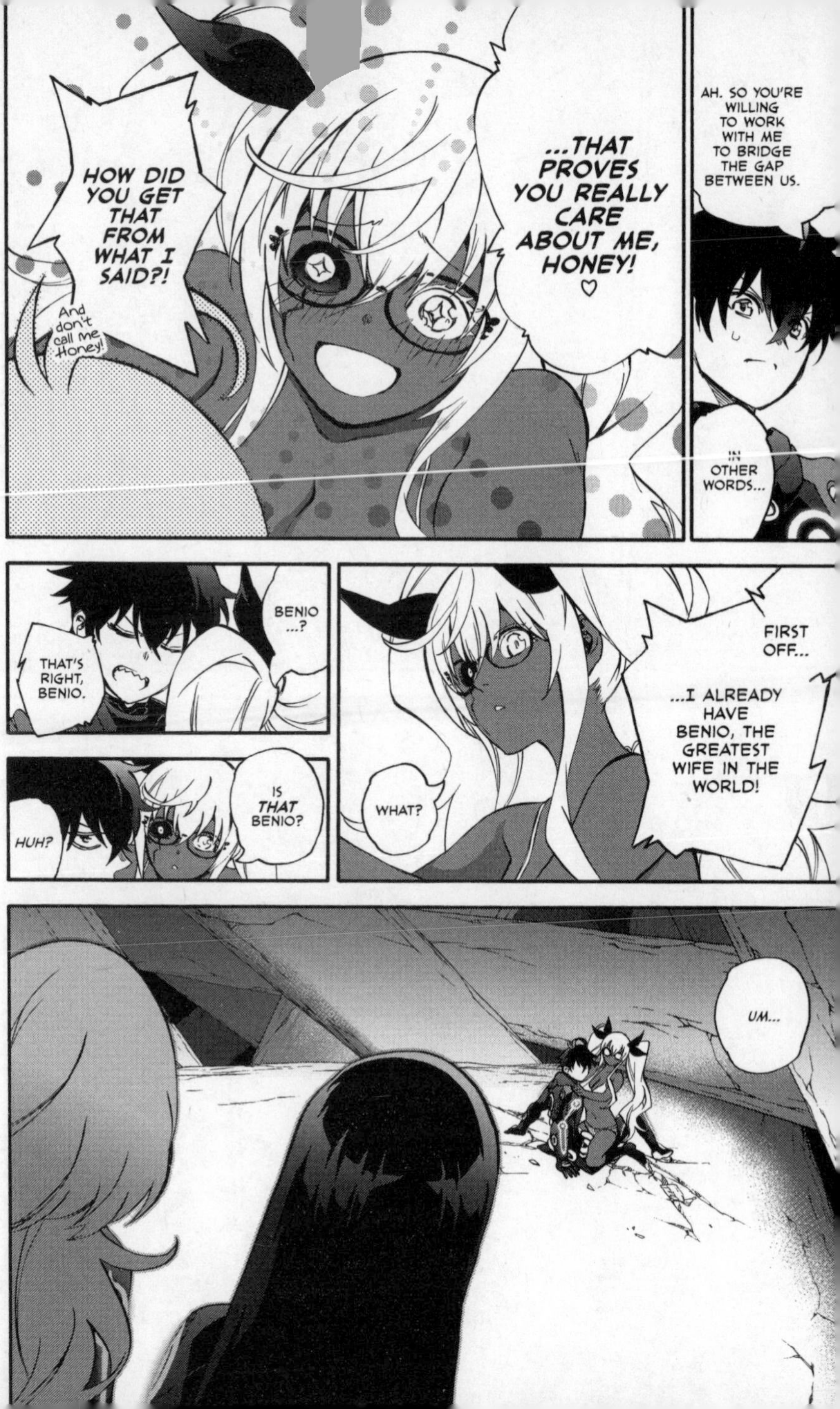
AH. SO YOU'RE WILLING TO WORK WITH ME TO BRIDGE THE GAP BETWEEN US.
IN OTHER WORDS...
...THAT PROVES YOU REALLY CARE ABOUT ME, HONEY! ♡
HOW DID YOU GET THAT FROM WHAT I SAID?!
And don't call me Honey!
FIRST OFF...
...I ALREADY HAVE BENIO, THE GREATEST WIFE IN THE WORLD!
WHAT?
BENIO ...?
THAT'S RIGHT, BENIO.
IS *THAT* BENIO?
HUH?
UM...

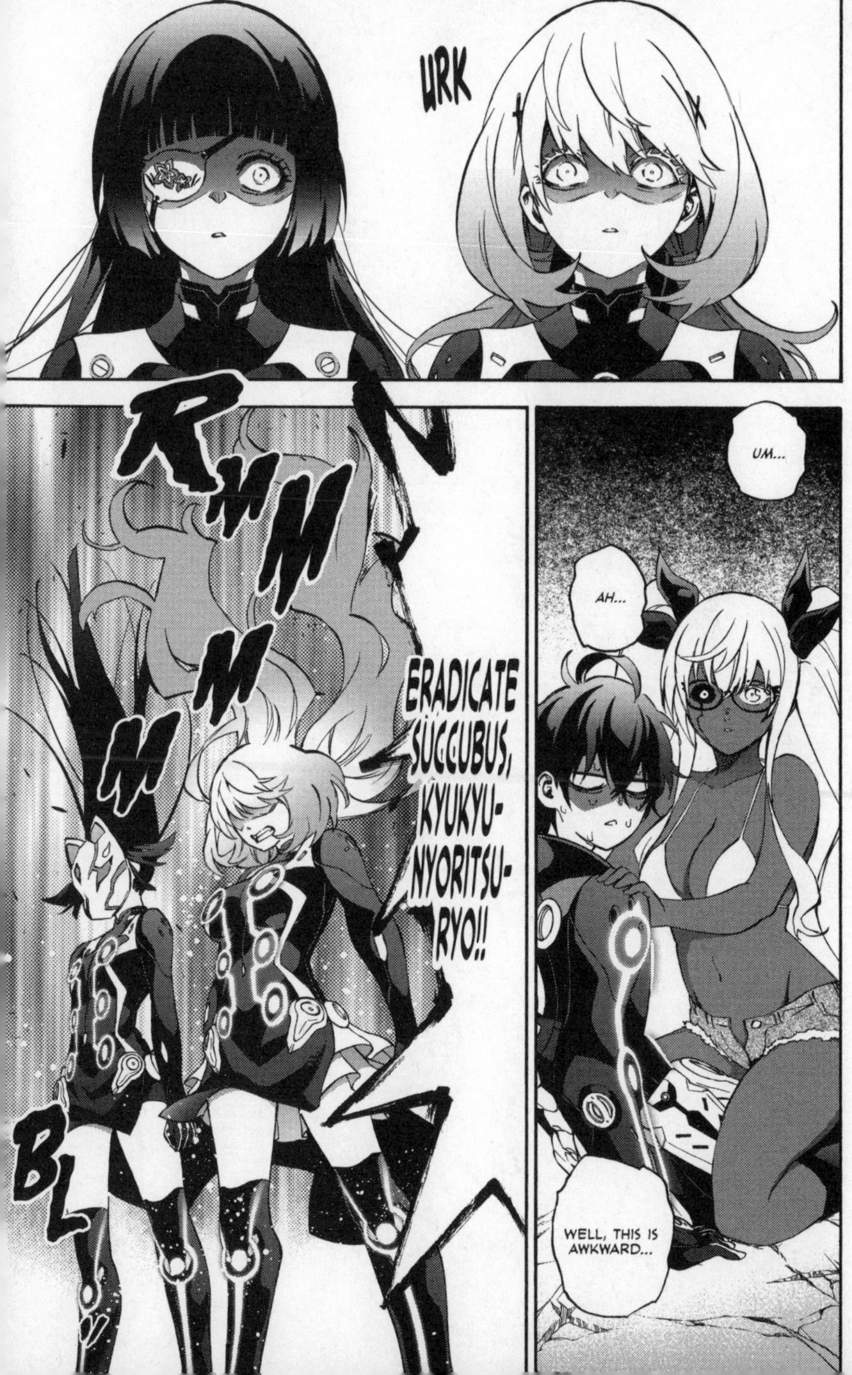
URK
UM...
AH...
WELL, THIS IS AWKWARD...
RMMMMM
ERADICATE SUCCUBUS, KYUKYU-NYORITSU-RYO!!

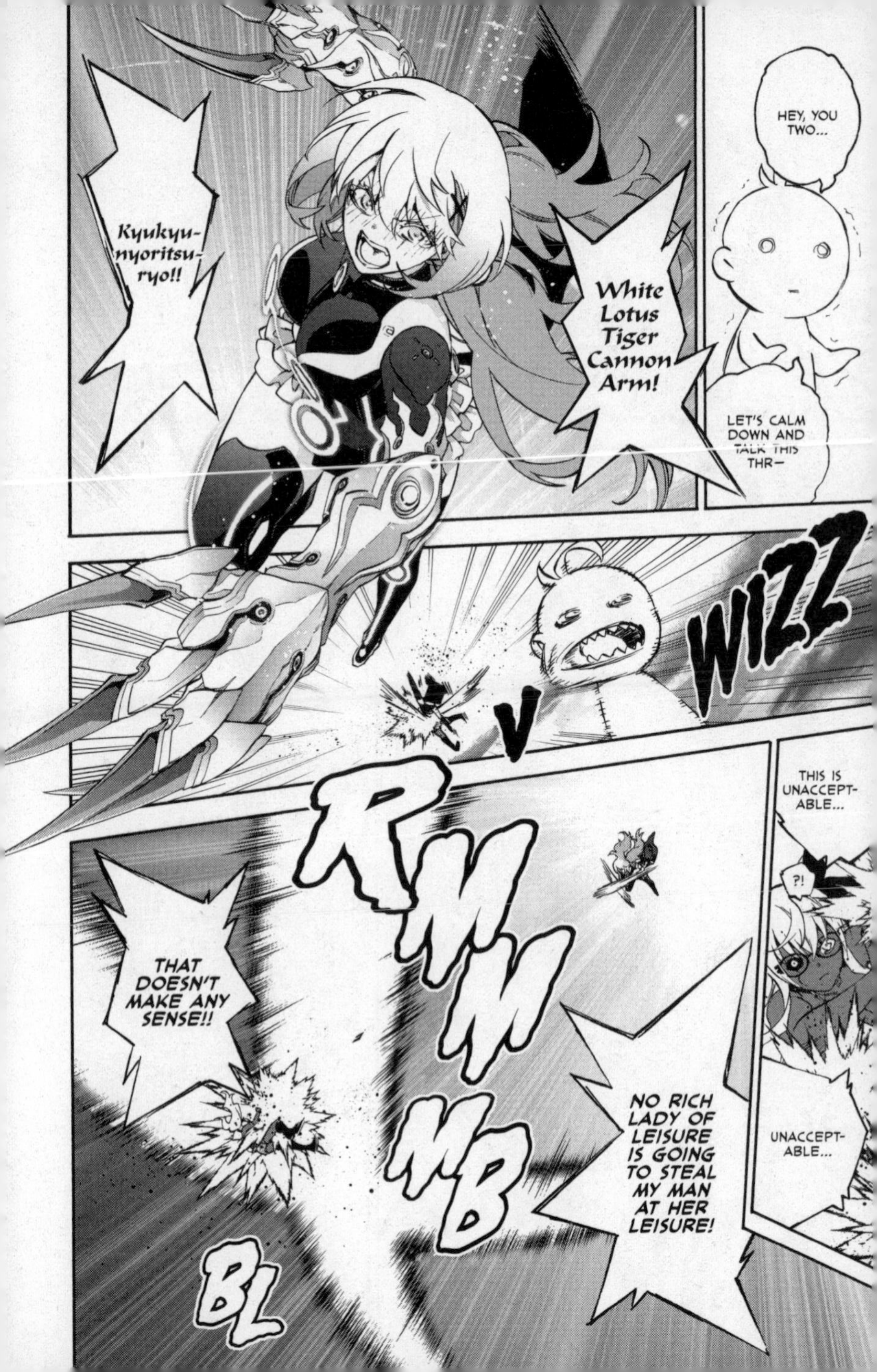
HEY, YOU TWO...
LET'S CALM DOWN AND TALK THIS THR—
White Lotus Tiger Cannon Arm!
Kyukyu-nyoritsu-ryo!!
WIZZ
V
THIS IS UNACCEPTABLE...
?!
UNACCEPTABLE...
NO RICH LADY OF LEISURE IS GOING TO STEAL MY MAN AT HER LEISURE!
RMMMB
THAT DOESN'T MAKE ANY SENSE!!
BL

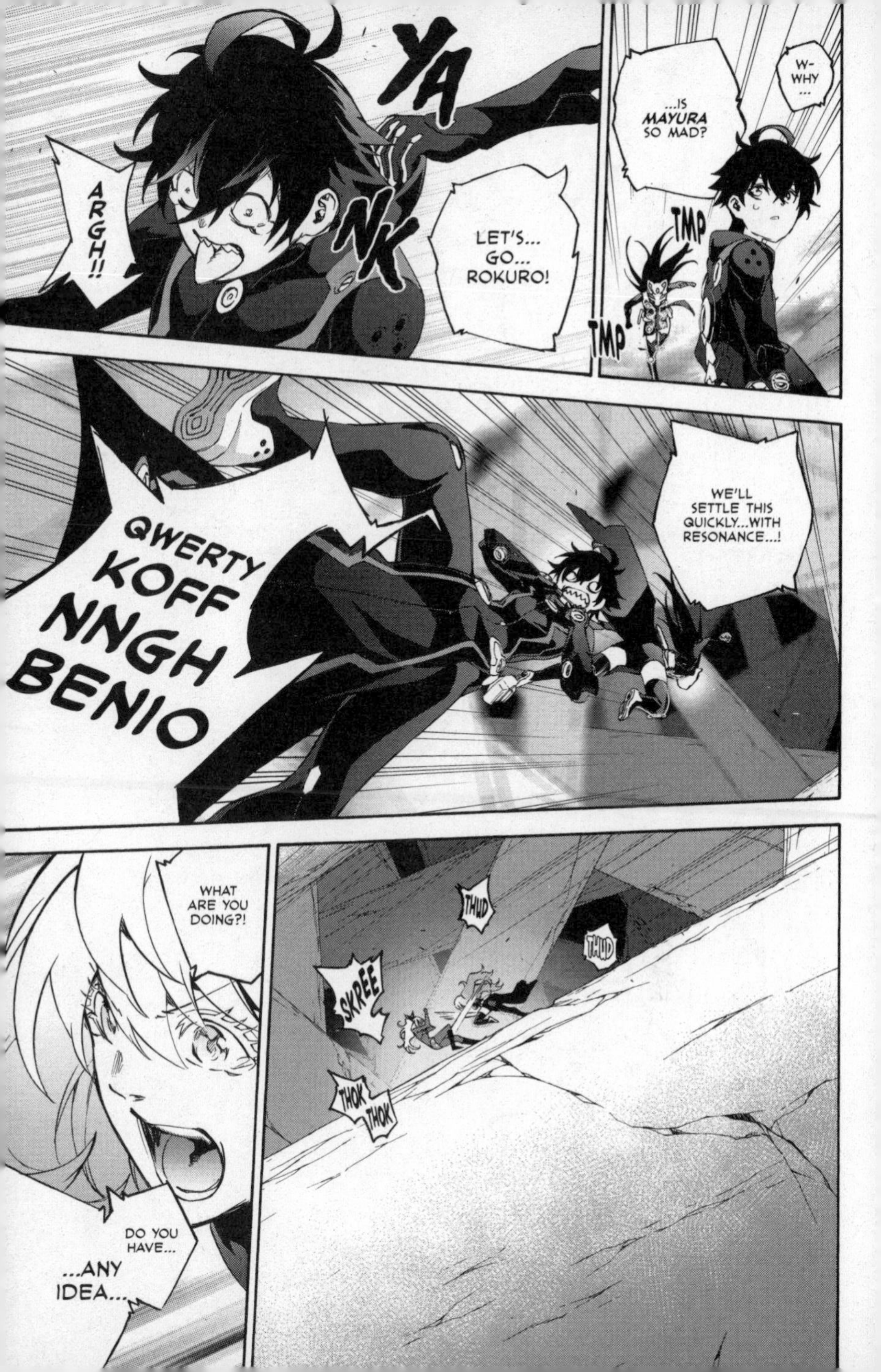
W-WHY...
...IS MAYURA SO MAD?
TMP
TMP
YANK
LET'S... GO... ROKURO!
ARGH!!
WE'LL SETTLE THIS QUICKLY...WITH RESONANCE...!
QWERTY KOFF NNGH BENIO
THUD
THUD
SKREE
THOK THOK
WHAT ARE YOU DOING?!
DO YOU HAVE...
...ANY IDEA...

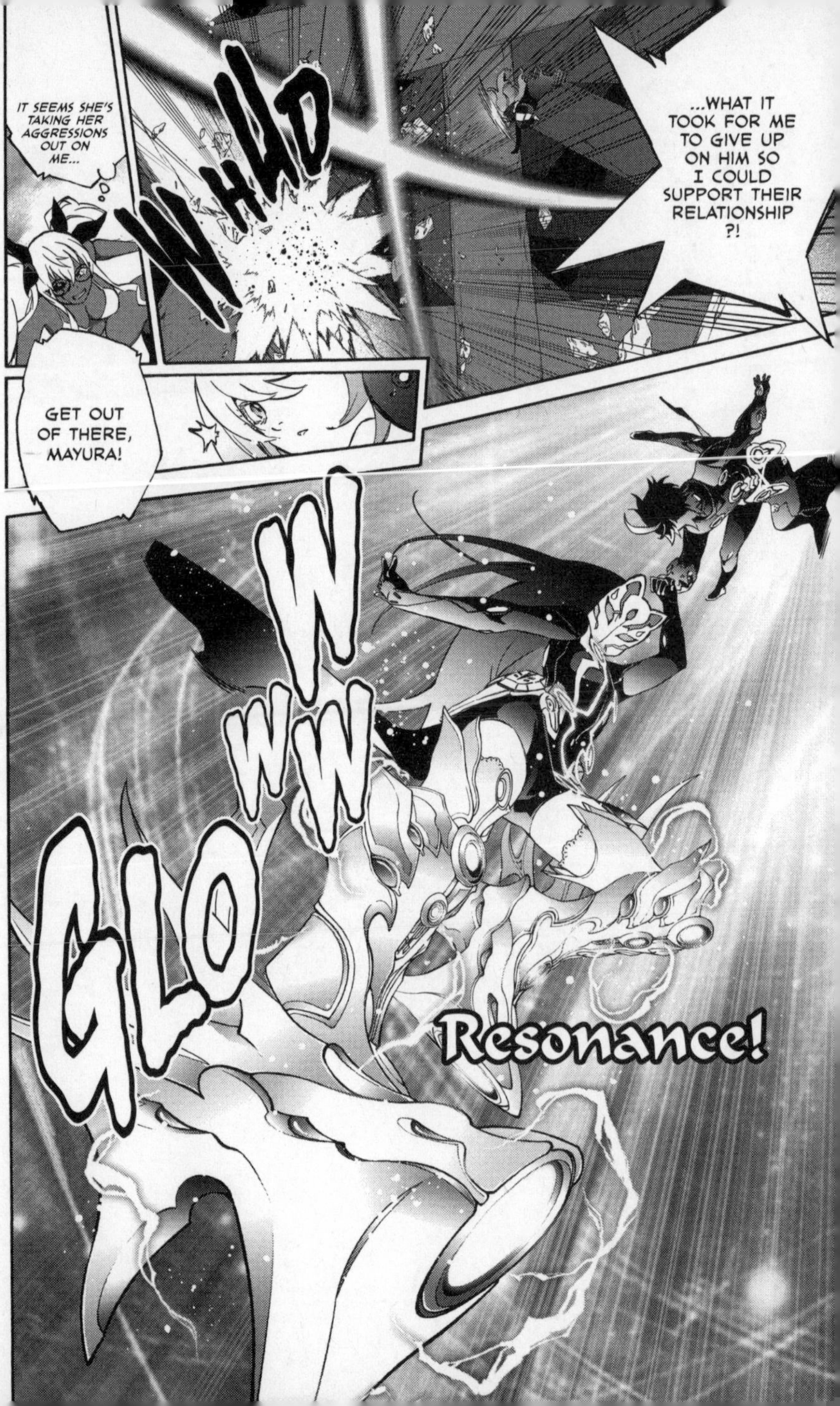
...WHAT IT TOOK FOR ME TO GIVE UP ON HIM SO I COULD SUPPORT THEIR RELATIONSHIP ?!
WHUD
IT SEEMS SHE'S TAKING HER AGGRESSIONS OUT ON ME...
GET OUT OF THERE, MAYURA!
GLOWWWN
Resonance!

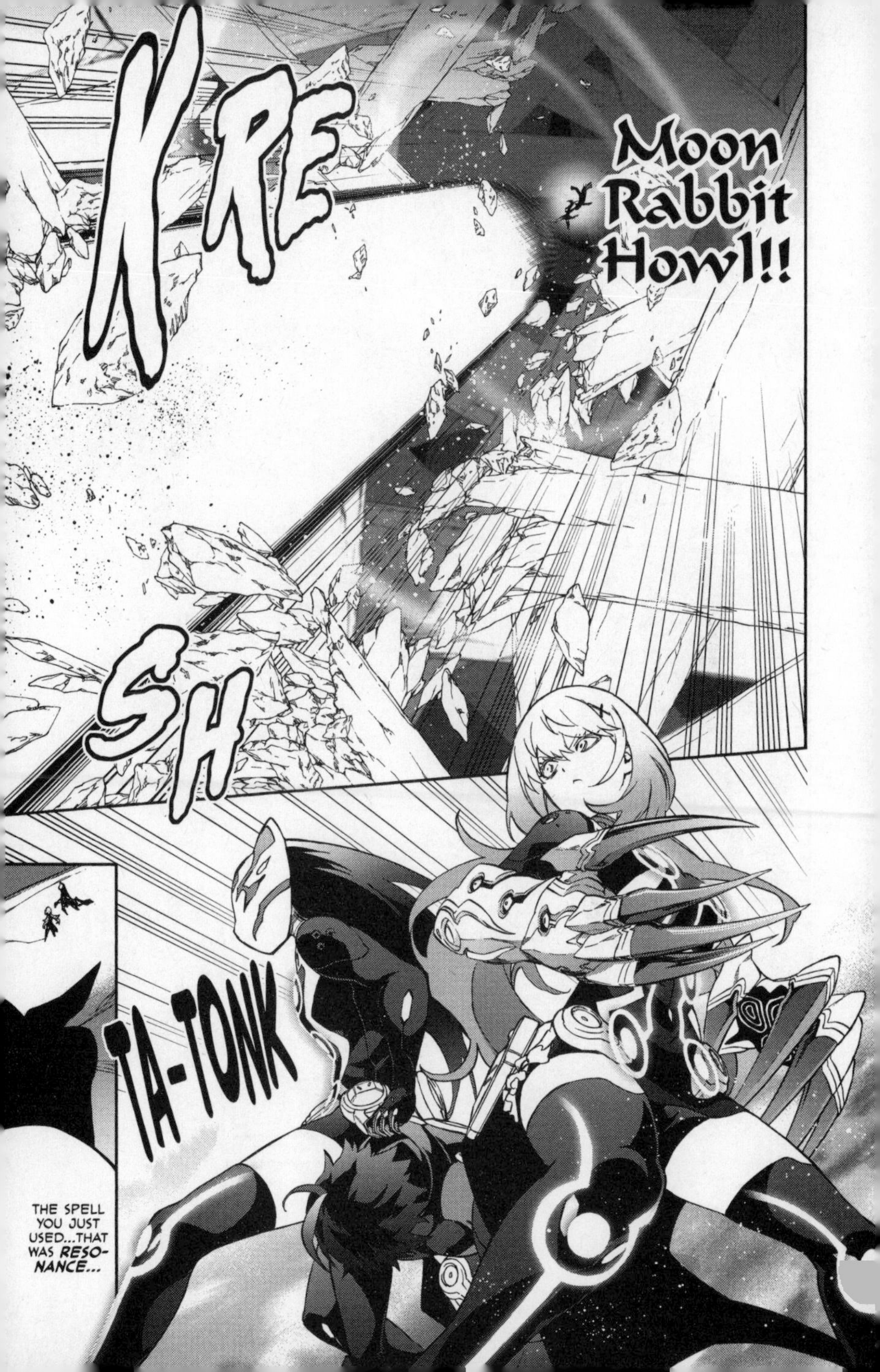
Moon Rabbit Howl!!
KRE
SH
TA-TONK
THE SPELL YOU JUST USED...THAT WAS *RESONANCE...*

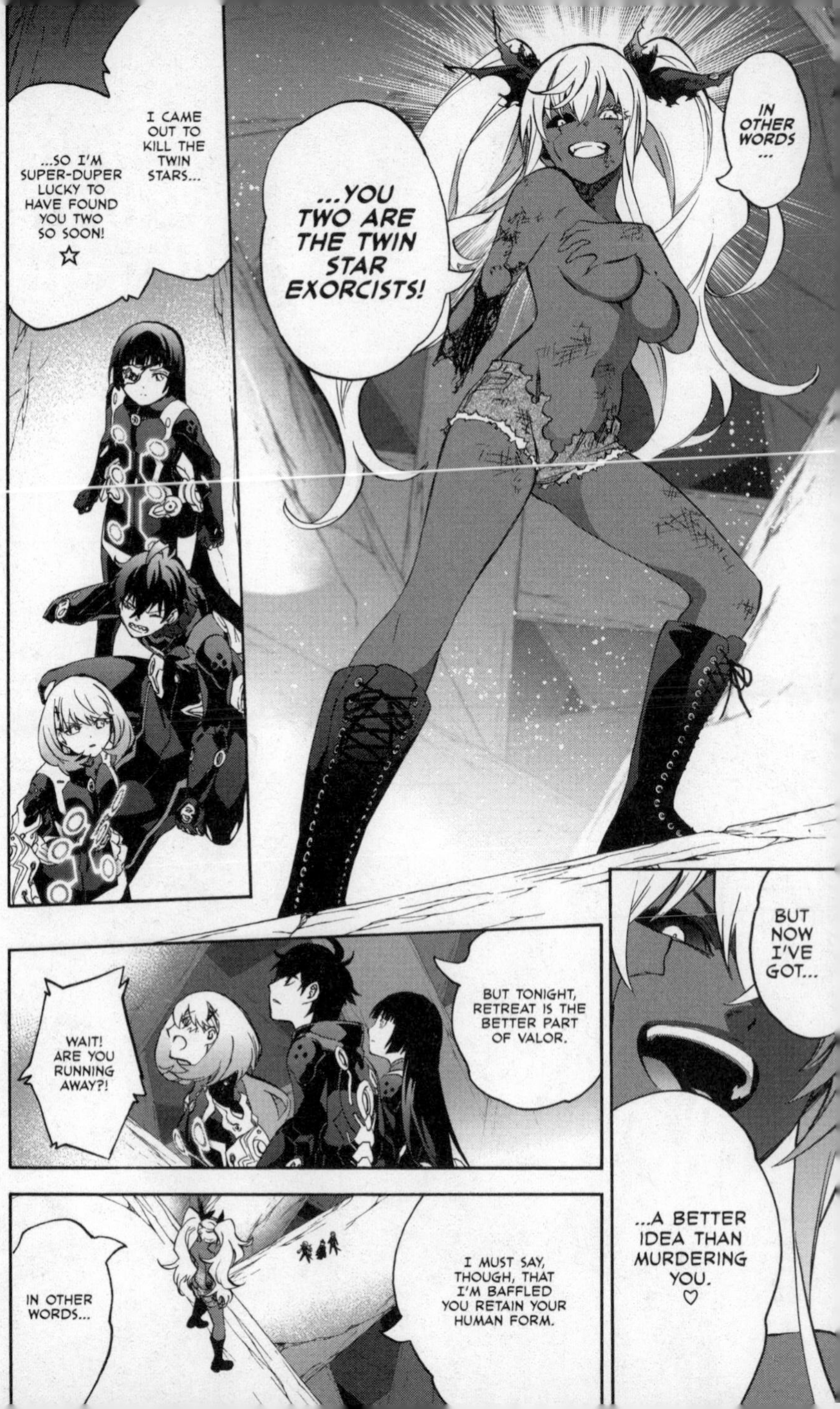
IN OTHER WORDS...
...YOU TWO ARE THE TWIN STAR EXORCISTS!
I CAME OUT TO KILL THE TWIN STARS...
...SO I'M SUPER-DUPER LUCKY TO HAVE FOUND YOU TWO SO SOON! ☆
BUT NOW I'VE GOT...
...A BETTER IDEA THAN MURDERING YOU. ♡
BUT TONIGHT, RETREAT IS THE BETTER PART OF VALOR.
WAIT! ARE YOU RUNNING AWAY?!
I MUST SAY, THOUGH, THAT I'M BAFFLED YOU RETAIN YOUR HUMAN FORM.
IN OTHER WORDS...

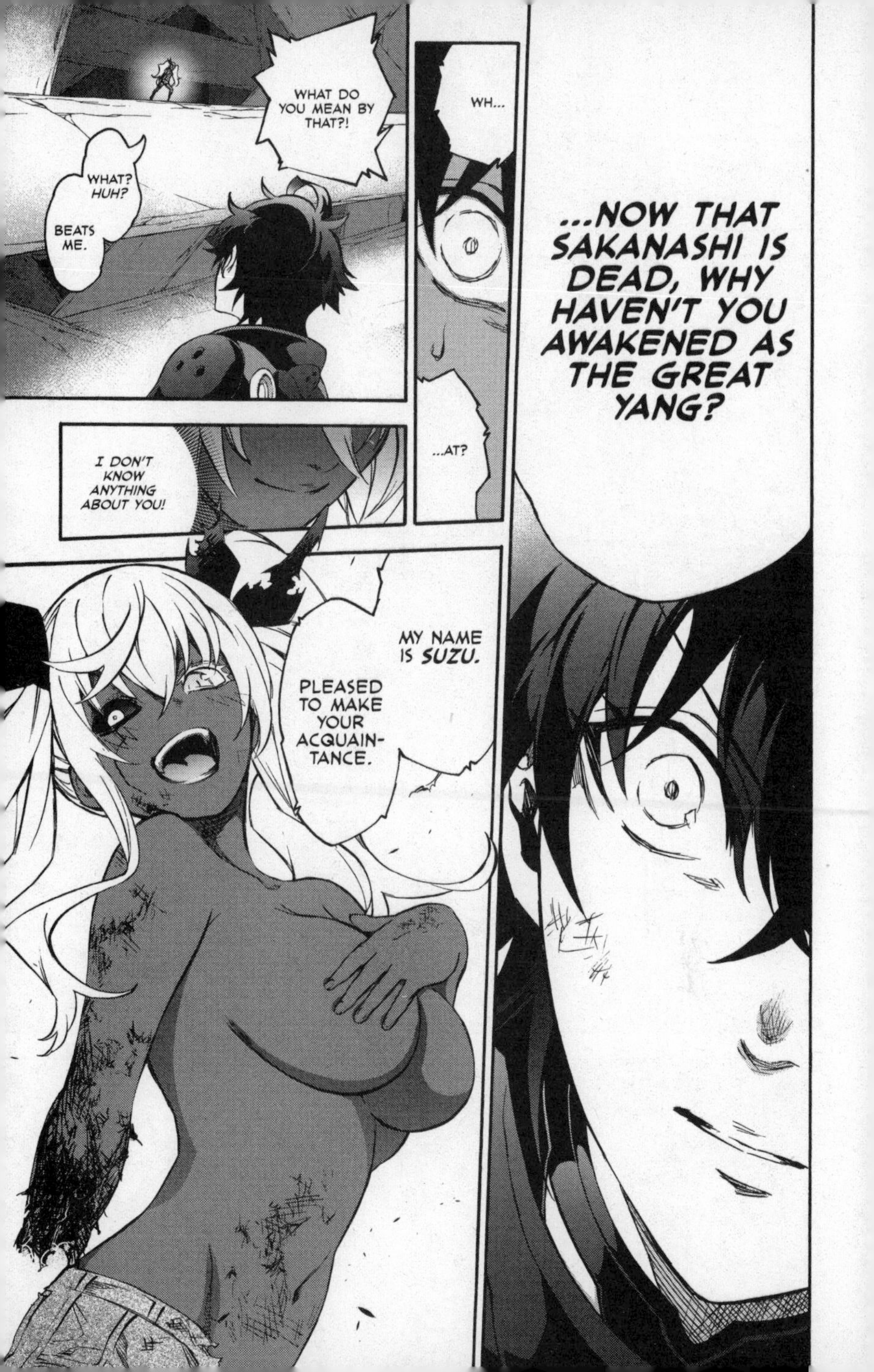
...NOW THAT SAKANASHI IS DEAD, WHY HAVEN'T YOU AWAKENED AS THE GREAT YANG?
WH...
...AT?
WHAT DO YOU MEAN BY THAT?!
WHAT? HUH?
BEATS ME.
I DON'T KNOW ANYTHING ABOUT YOU!
MY NAME IS SUZU.
PLEASED TO MAKE YOUR ACQUAIN-TANCE.

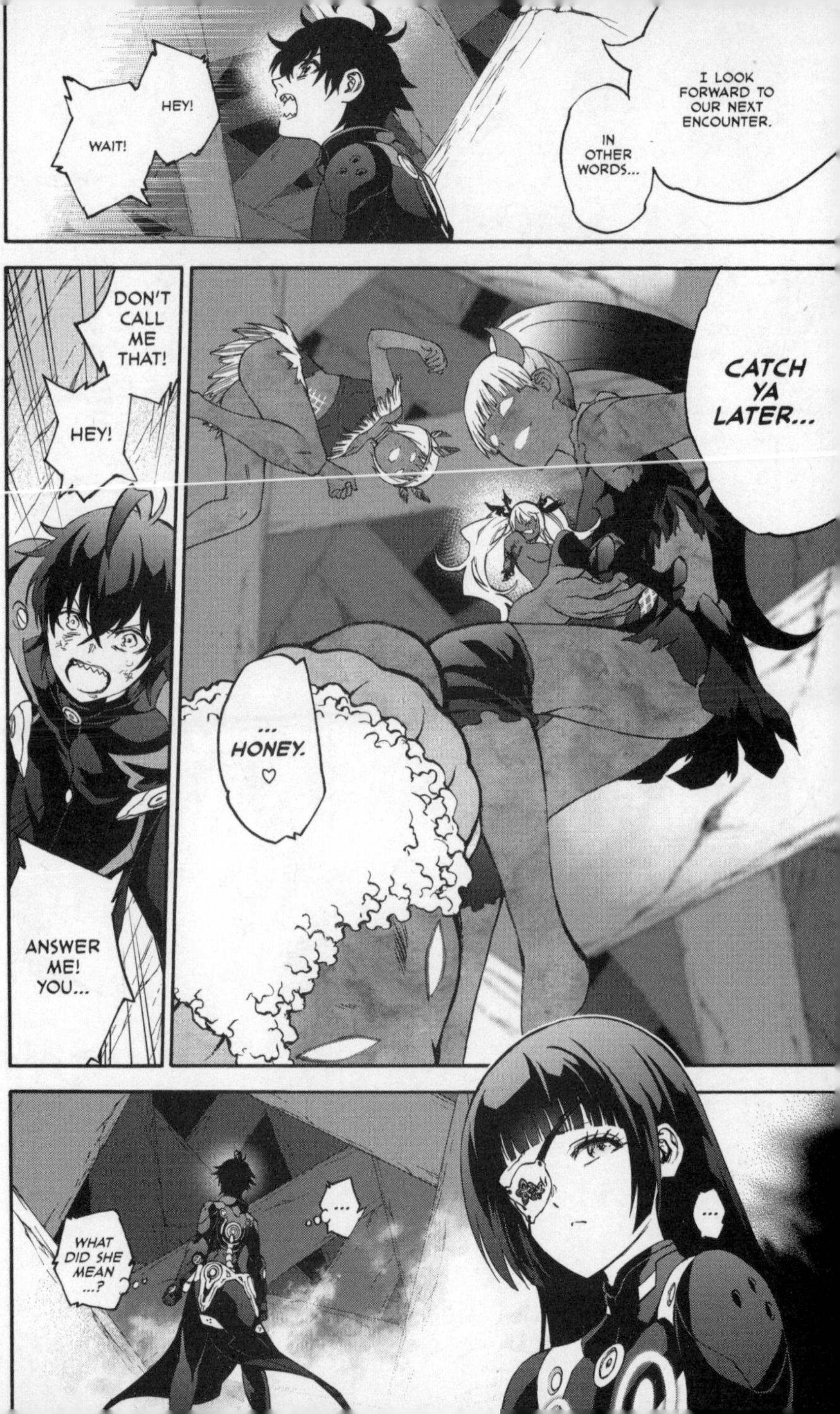
I LOOK FORWARD TO OUR NEXT ENCOUNTER.
IN OTHER WORDS...
HEY!
WAIT!
CATCH YA LATER...
... HONEY. ♡
DON'T CALL ME THAT!
HEY!
ANSWER ME! YOU...
...
...
WHAT DID SHE MEAN ...?

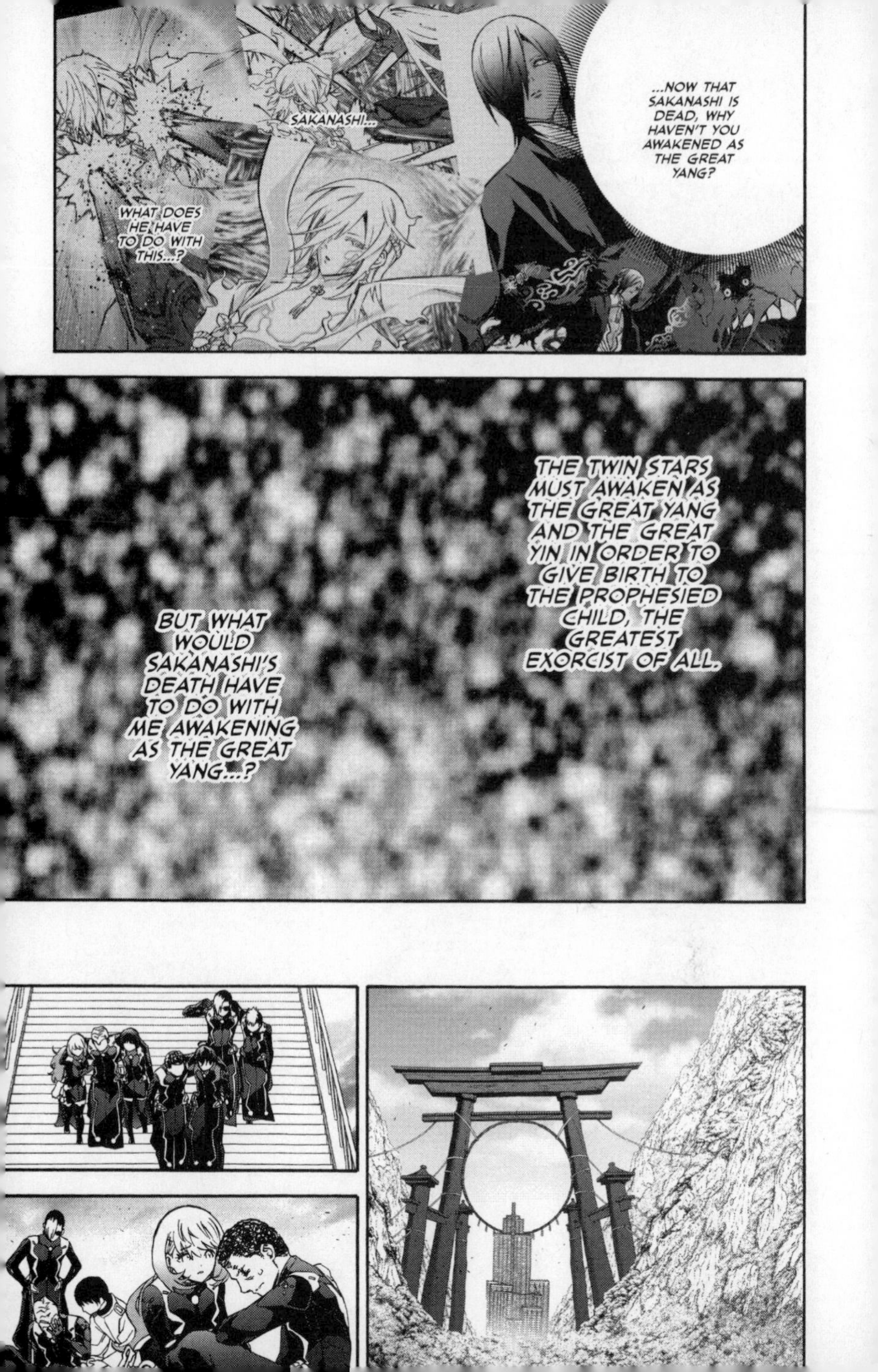
...NOW THAT SAKANASHI IS DEAD, WHY HAVEN'T YOU AWAKENED AS THE GREAT YANG?
SAKANASHI...
WHAT DOES HE HAVE TO DO WITH THIS...?
THE TWIN STARS MUST AWAKEN AS THE GREAT YANG AND THE GREAT YIN IN ORDER TO GIVE BIRTH TO THE PROPHESIED CHILD, THE GREATEST EXORCIST OF ALL.
BUT WHAT WOULD SAKANASHI'S DEATH HAVE TO DO WITH ME AWAKENING AS THE GREAT YANG...?

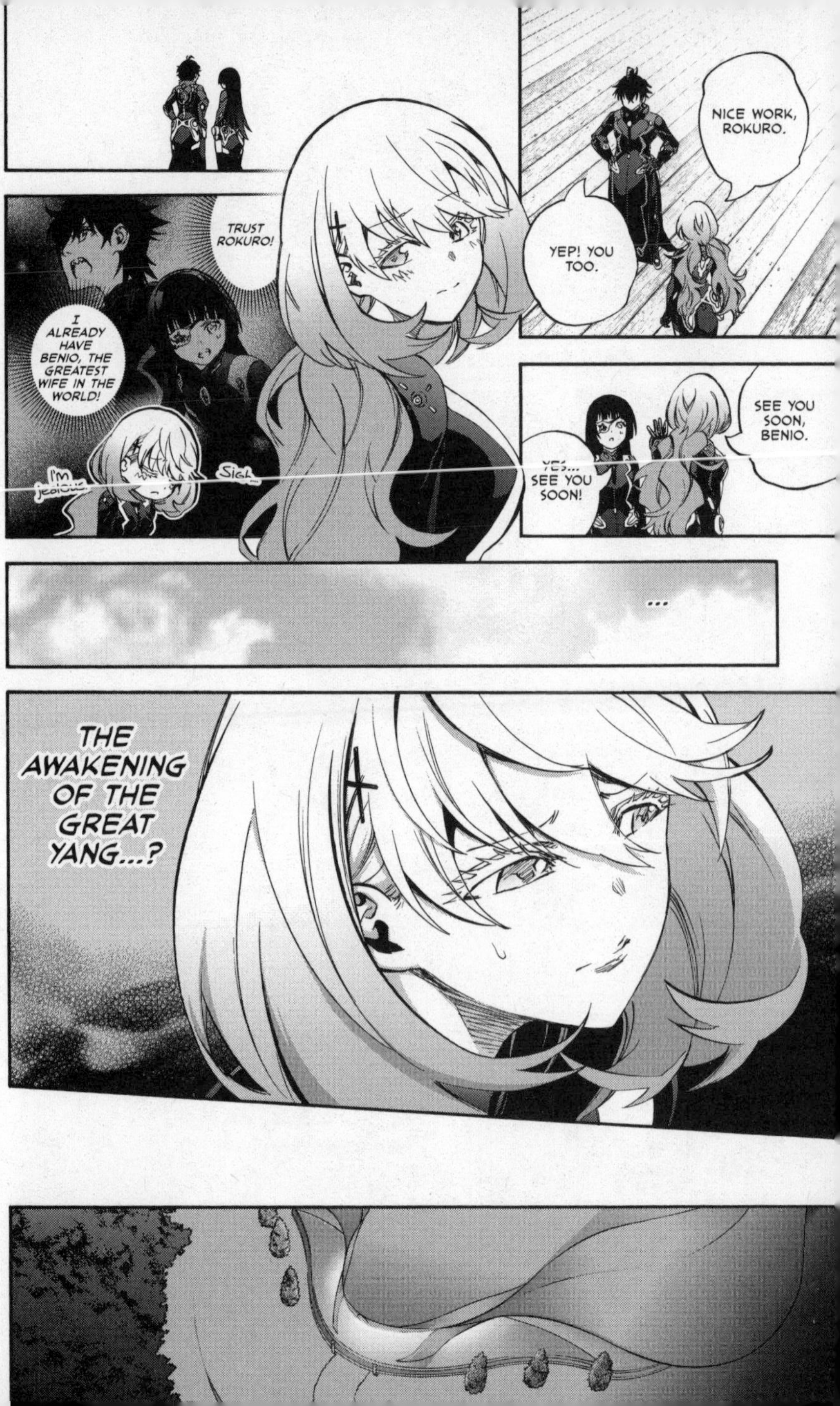
NICE WORK, ROKURO.
YEP! YOU TOO.
SEE YOU SOON, BENIO.
YES... SEE YOU SOON!
TRUST ROKURO!
I ALREADY HAVE BENIO, THE GREATEST WIFE IN THE WORLD!
Sigh...
I'm jealous
...
THE AWAKENING OF THE GREAT YANG...?

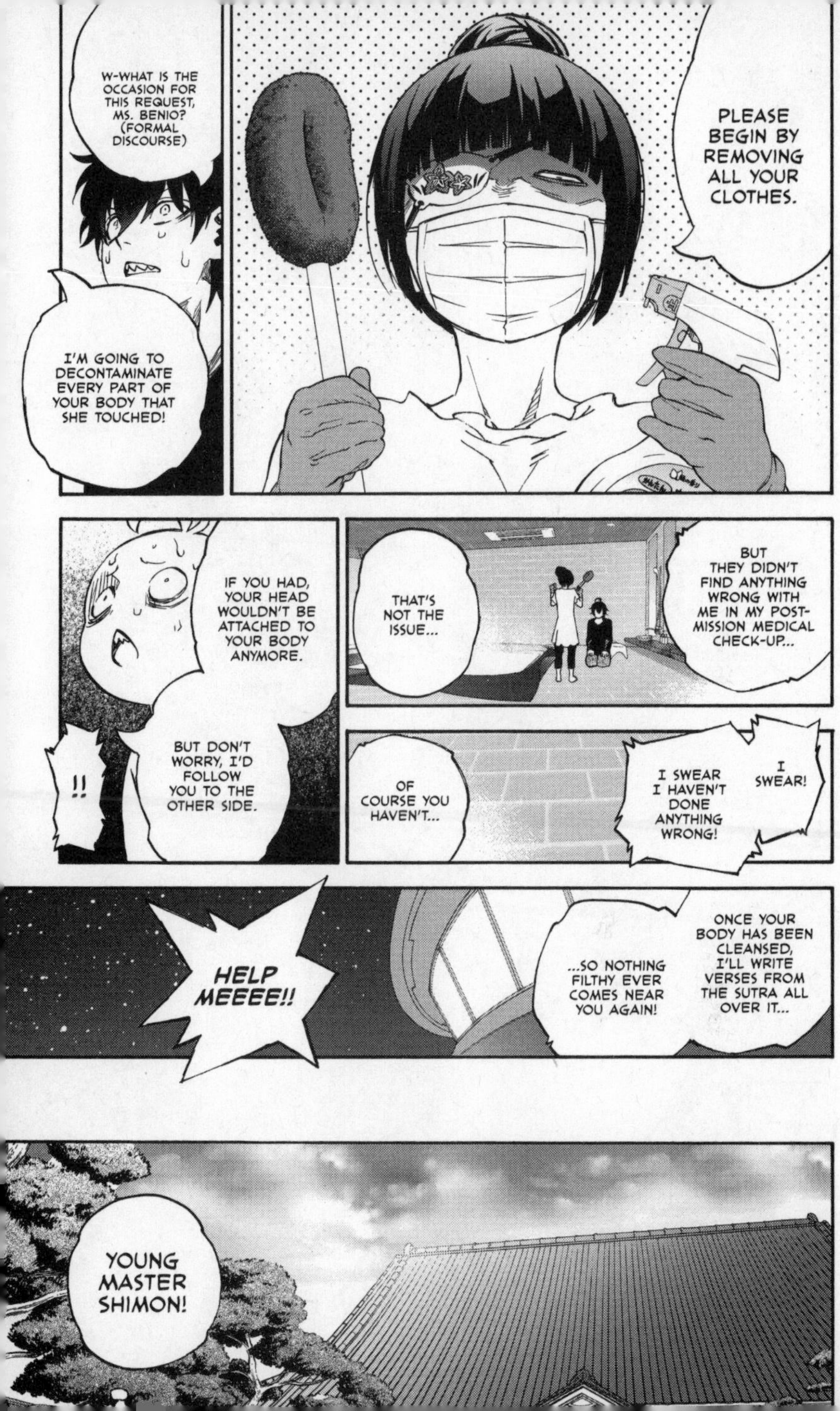
PLEASE BEGIN BY REMOVING ALL YOUR CLOTHES.
W-WHAT IS THE OCCASION FOR THIS REQUEST, MS. BENIO? (FORMAL DISCOURSE)
I'M GOING TO DECONTAMINATE EVERY PART OF YOUR BODY THAT SHE TOUCHED!
BUT THEY DIDN'T FIND ANYTHING WRONG WITH ME IN MY POST-MISSION MEDICAL CHECK-UP...
THAT'S NOT THE ISSUE...
I SWEAR!
I SWEAR I HAVEN'T DONE ANYTHING WRONG!
OF COURSE YOU HAVEN'T...
IF YOU HAD, YOUR HEAD WOULDN'T BE ATTACHED TO YOUR BODY ANYMORE.
BUT DON'T WORRY, I'D FOLLOW YOU TO THE OTHER SIDE.
!!
ONCE YOUR BODY HAS BEEN CLEANSED, I'LL WRITE VERSES FROM THE SUTRA ALL OVER IT...
...SO NOTHING FILTHY EVER COMES NEAR YOU AGAIN!
HELP MEEEE!!
YOUNG MASTER SHIMON!

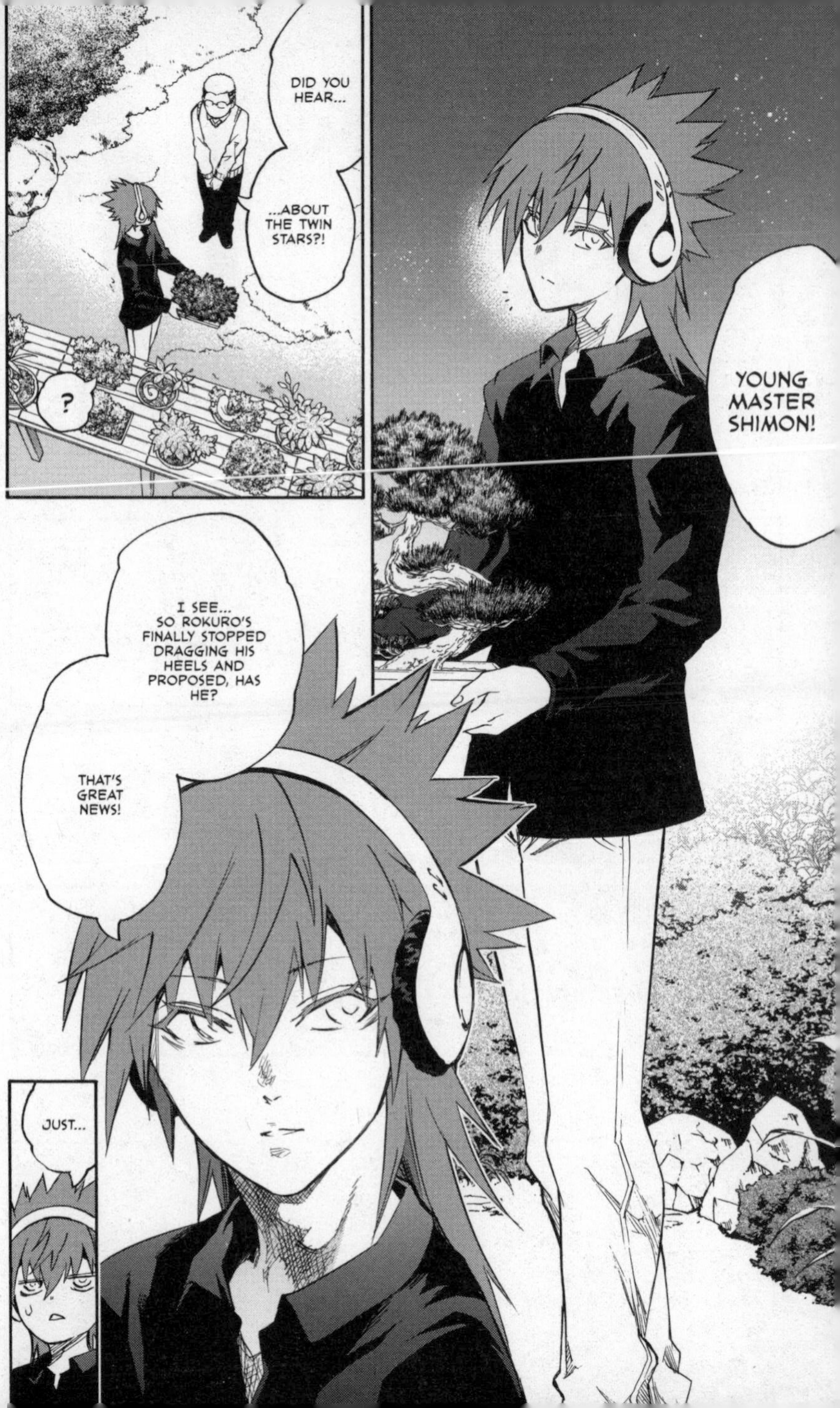
YOUNG MASTER SHIMON!
DID YOU HEAR...
...ABOUT THE TWIN STARS?!
?
I SEE... SO ROKURO'S FINALLY STOPPED DRAGGING HIS HEELS AND PROPOSED, HAS HE?
THAT'S GREAT NEWS!
JUST...

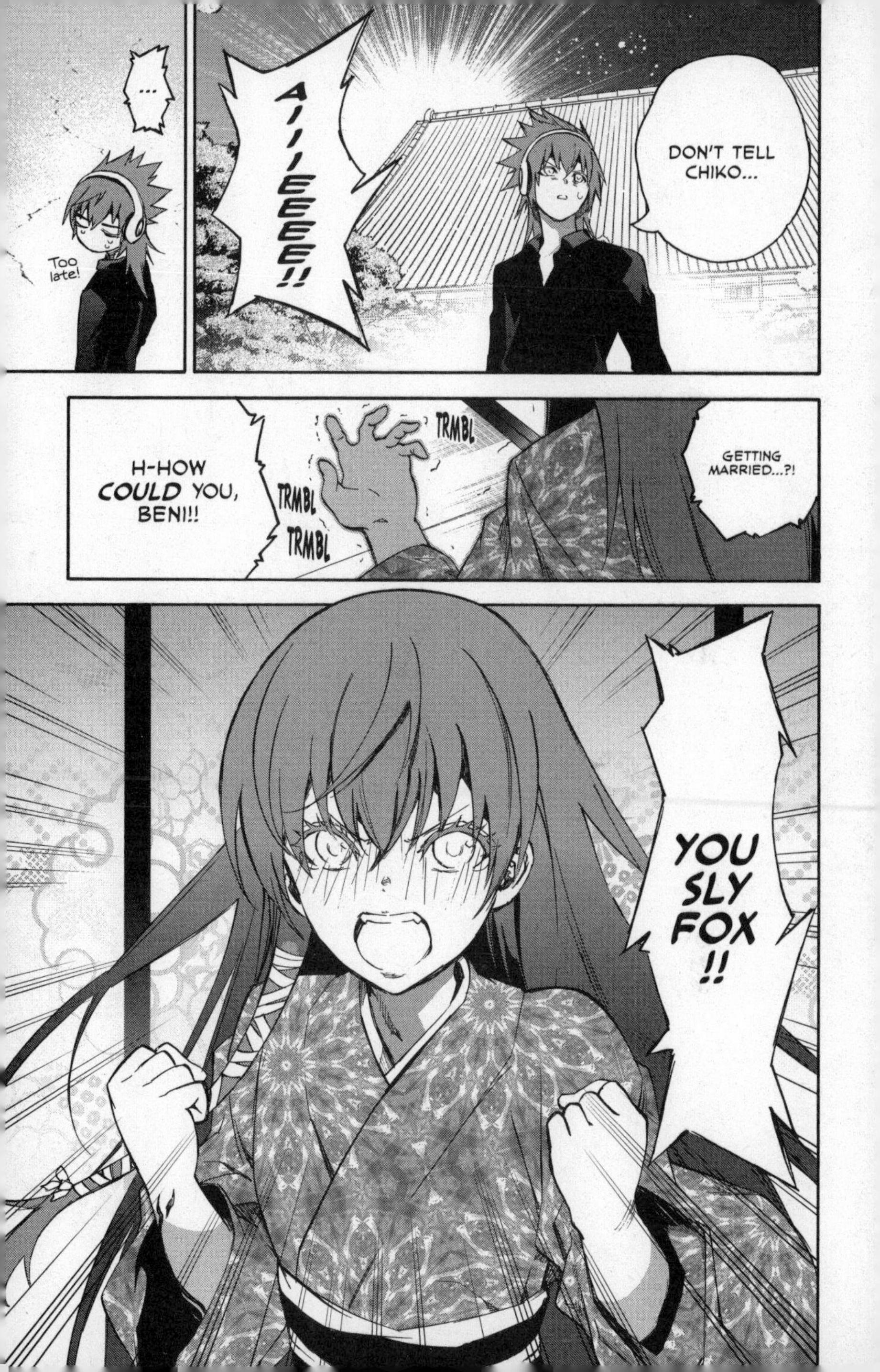

DON'T TELL CHIKO...
AIIIEEEEE!!
...
Too late!
GETTING MARRIED...?!
TRMBL
H-HOW COULD YOU, BENI!!
TRMBL
TRMBL
YOU SLY FOX!!

Suzu's band's musical instruments

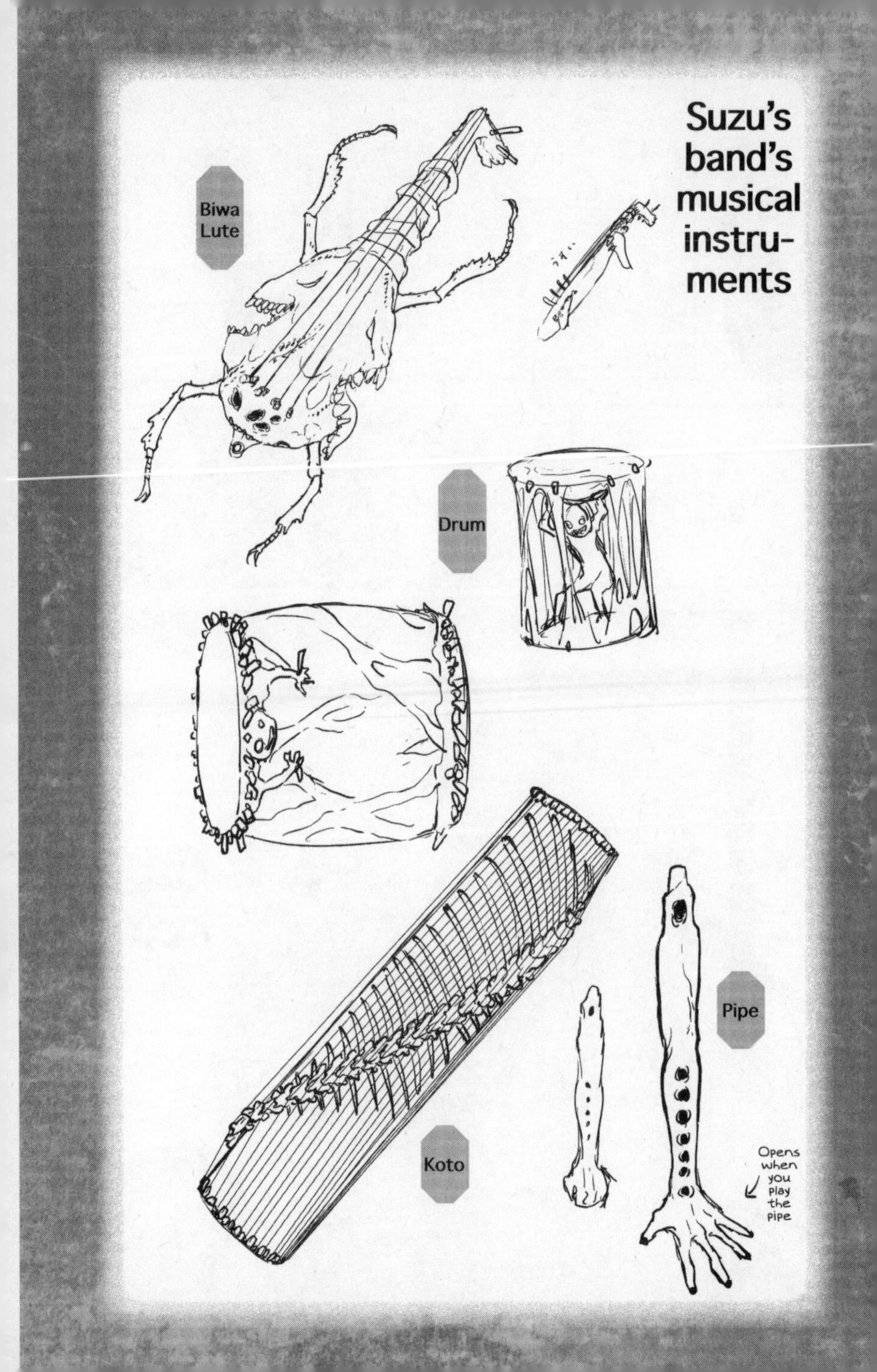
Biwa Lute
Drum
Koto
Pipe
Opens when you play the pipe

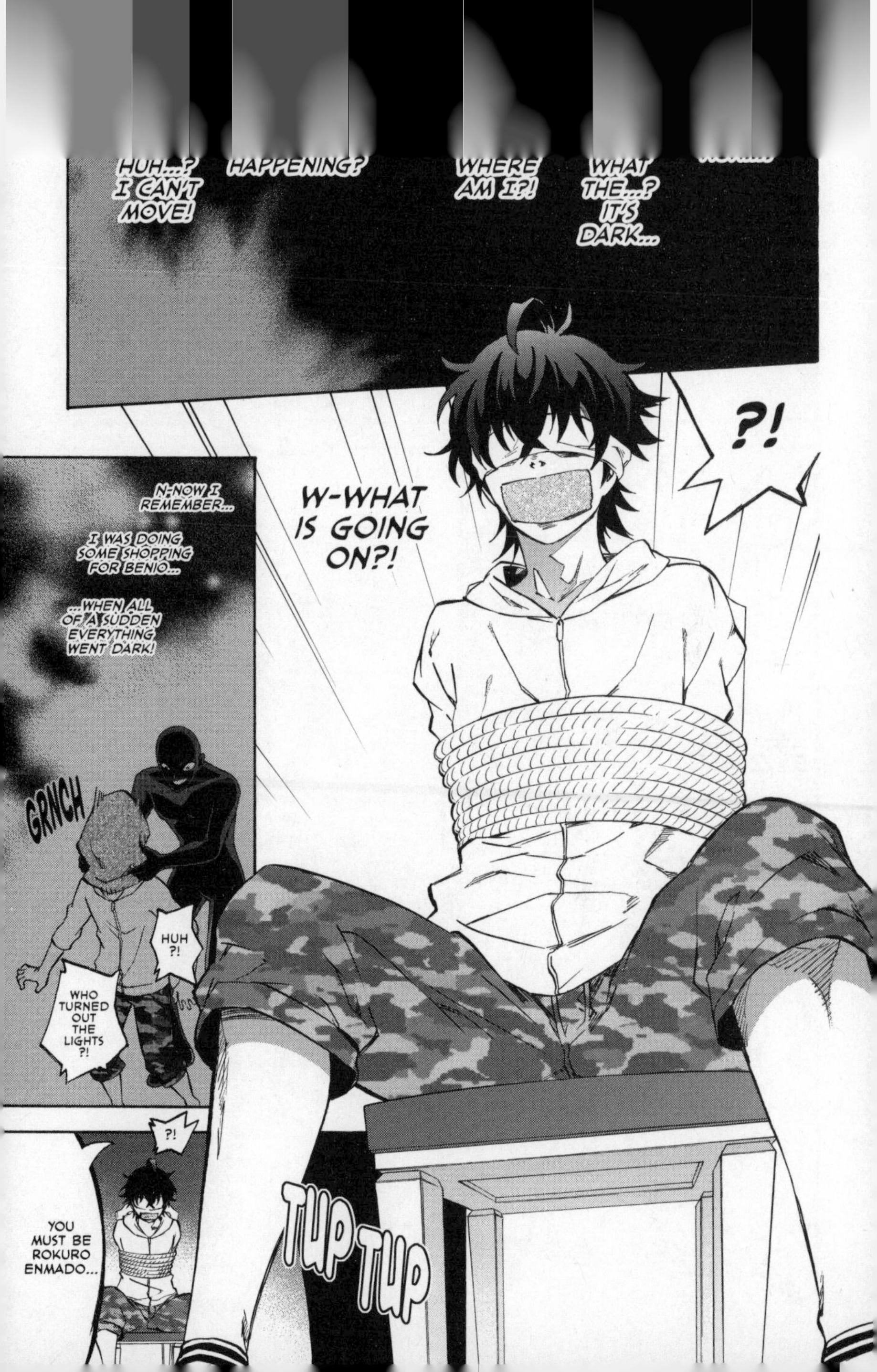
WHAT THE...? IT'S DARK...
WHERE AM I?!
HAPPENING?
HUH...? I CAN'T MOVE!
?!
W-WHAT IS GOING ON?!
TUP TUP
N-NOW I REMEMBER...
I WAS DOING SOME SHOPPING FOR BENIO...
...WHEN ALL OF A SUDDEN EVERYTHING WENT DARK!
GRNCH
HUH ?!
WHO TURNED OUT THE LIGHTS ?!
?!
YOU MUST BE ROKURO ENMADO...

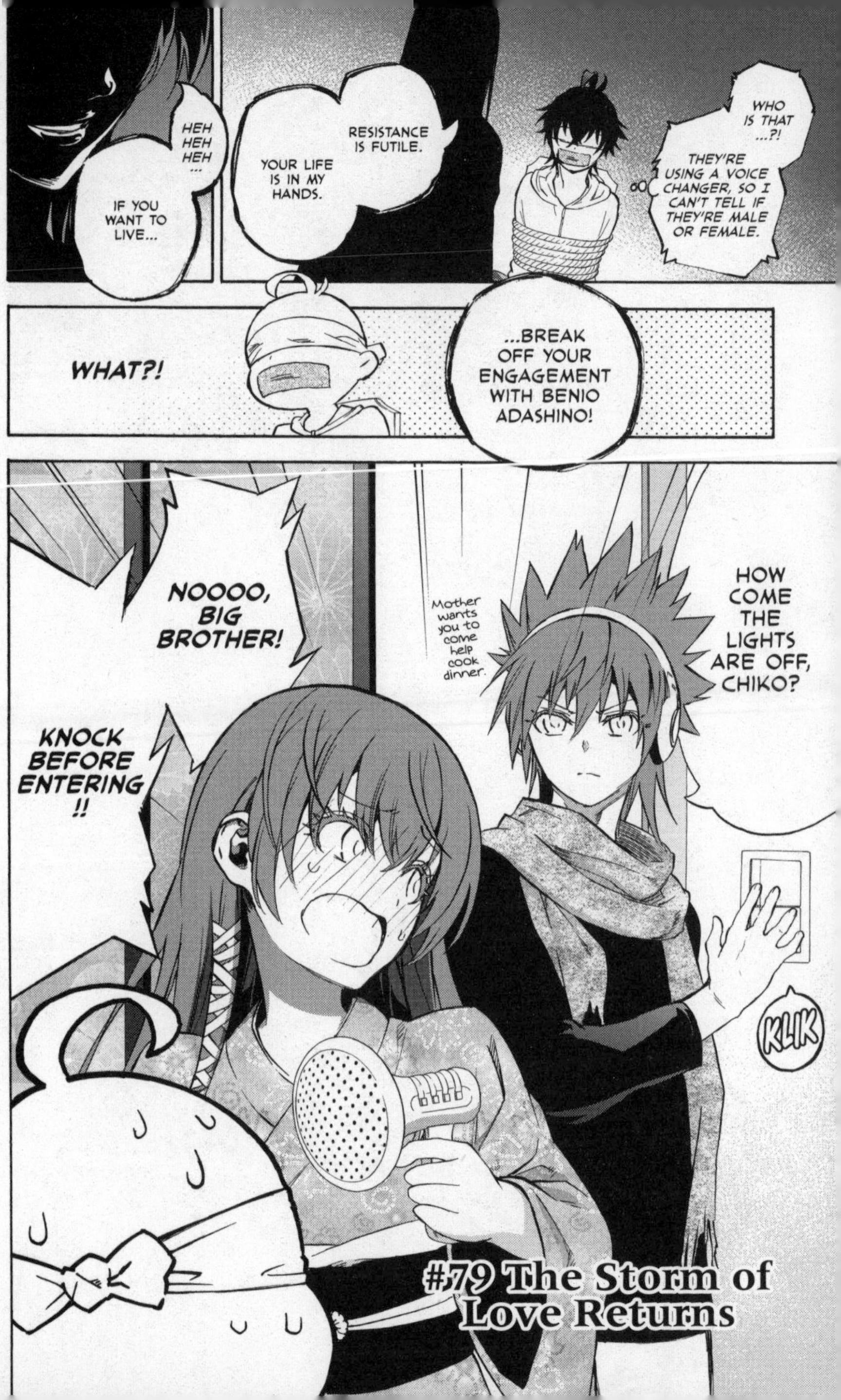
WHO IS THAT ...?!
THEY'RE USING A VOICE CHANGER, SO I CAN'T TELL IF THEY'RE MALE OR FEMALE.
RESISTANCE IS FUTILE.
YOUR LIFE IS IN MY HANDS.
HEH HEH HEH ...
IF YOU WANT TO LIVE...
...BREAK OFF YOUR ENGAGEMENT WITH BENIO ADASHINO!
WHAT?!
HOW COME THE LIGHTS ARE OFF, CHIKO?
Mother wants you to come help cook dinner.
KLIK
NOOOO, BIG BROTHER!
KNOCK BEFORE ENTERING !!
#79 The Storm of Love Returns

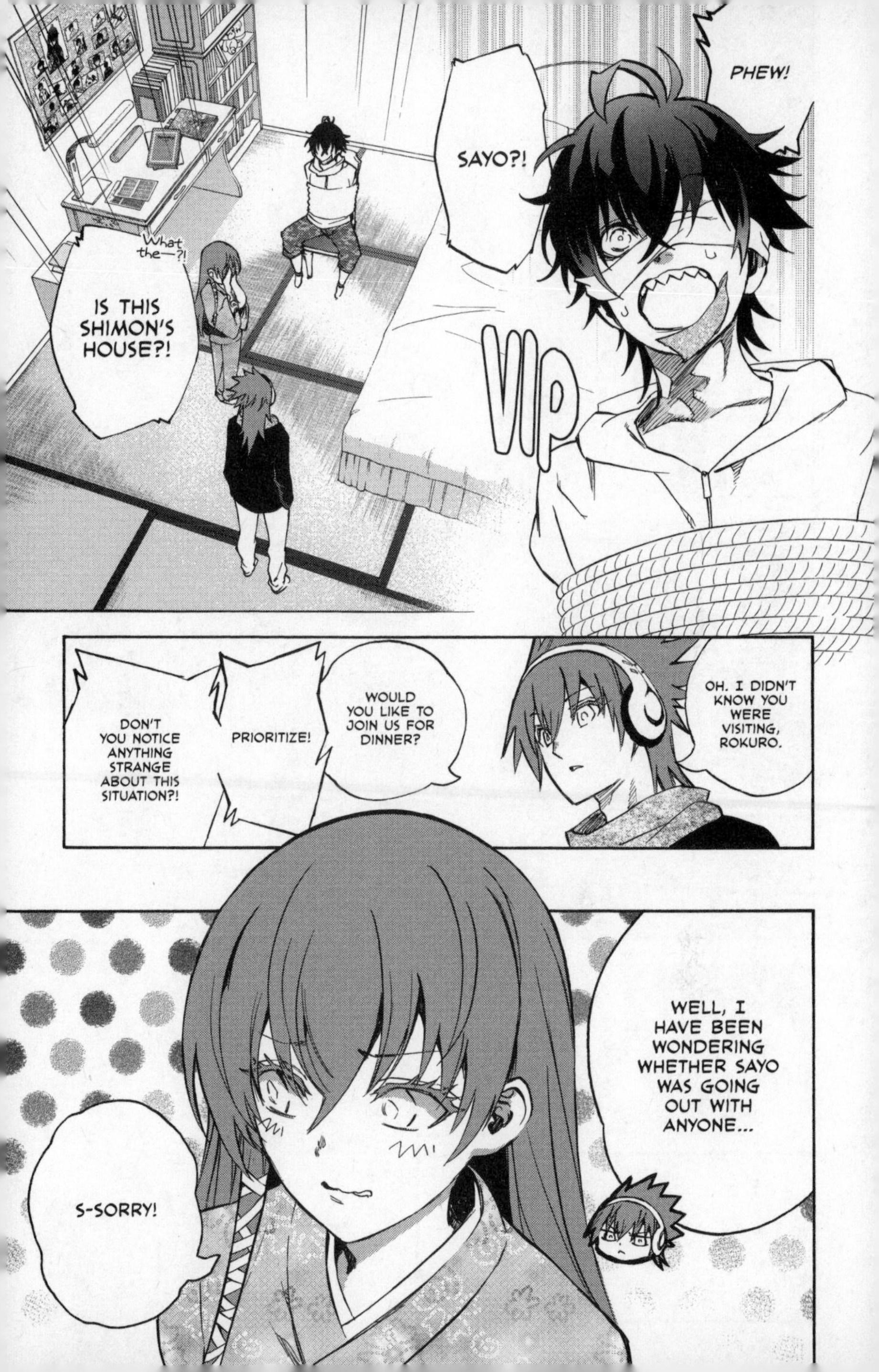
PHEW!
SAYO?!
VIP
What the—?!
IS THIS SHIMON'S HOUSE?!
OH. I DIDN'T KNOW YOU WERE VISITING, ROKURO.
WOULD YOU LIKE TO JOIN US FOR DINNER?
PRIORITIZE!
DON'T YOU NOTICE ANYTHING STRANGE ABOUT THIS SITUATION?!
WELL, I HAVE BEEN WONDERING WHETHER SAYO WAS GOING OUT WITH ANYONE...
S-SORRY!

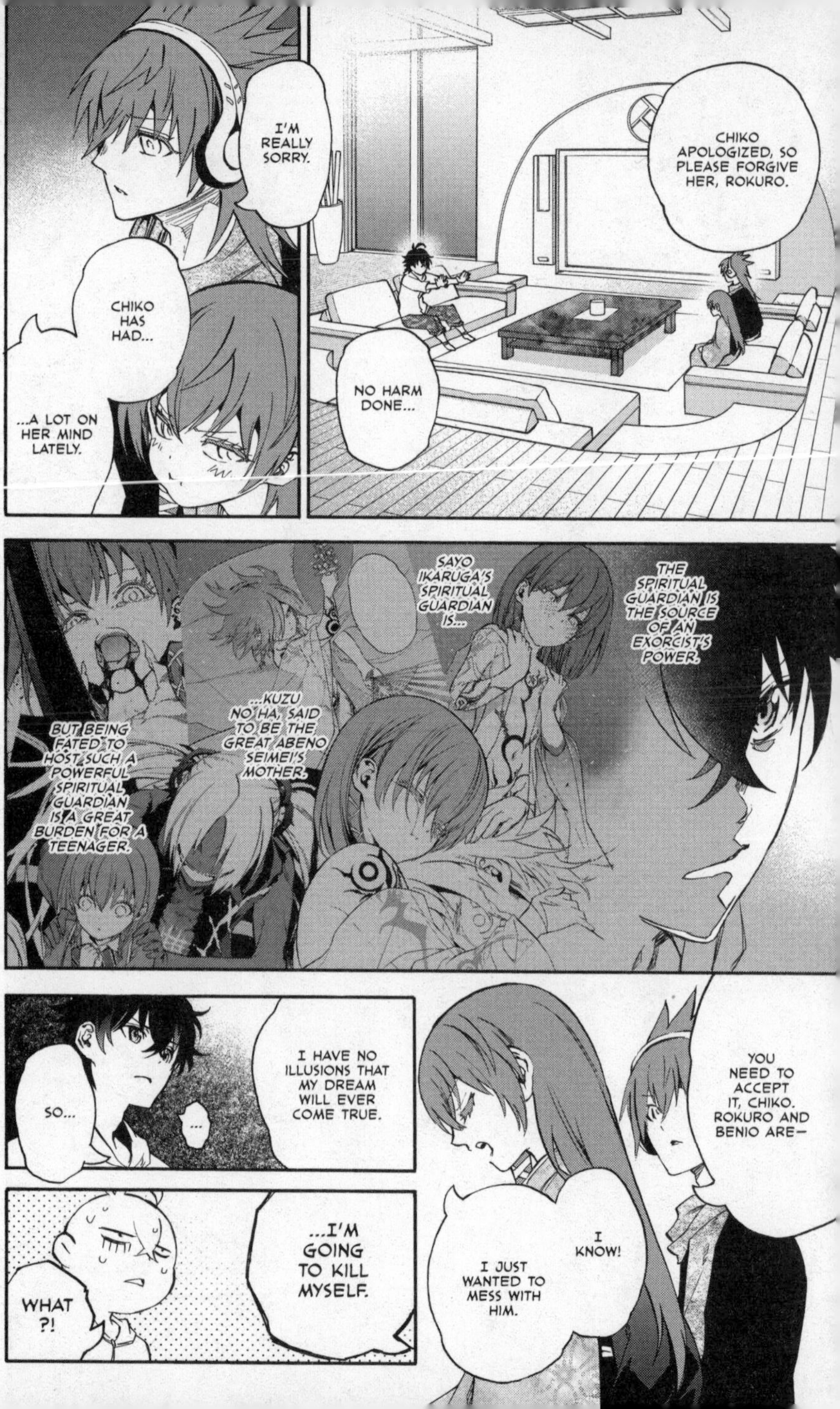
CHIKO APOLOGIZED, SO PLEASE FORGIVE HER, ROKURO.
NO HARM DONE...
I'M REALLY SORRY.
CHIKO HAS HAD...
...A LOT ON HER MIND LATELY.
THE SPIRITUAL GUARDIAN IS THE SOURCE OF AN EXORCIST'S POWER.
SAYO IKARUGA'S SPIRITUAL GUARDIAN IS...
...KUZU NO HA, SAID TO BE THE GREAT ABENO SEIMEI'S MOTHER.
BUT BEING FATED TO HOST SUCH A POWERFUL SPIRITUAL GUARDIAN IS A GREAT BURDEN FOR A TEENAGER.
YOU NEED TO ACCEPT IT, CHIKO. ROKURO AND BENIO ARE—
I KNOW!
I JUST WANTED TO MESS WITH HIM.
I HAVE NO ILLUSIONS THAT MY DREAM WILL EVER COME TRUE.
...
SO...
...I'M GOING TO KILL MYSELF.
WHAT ?!

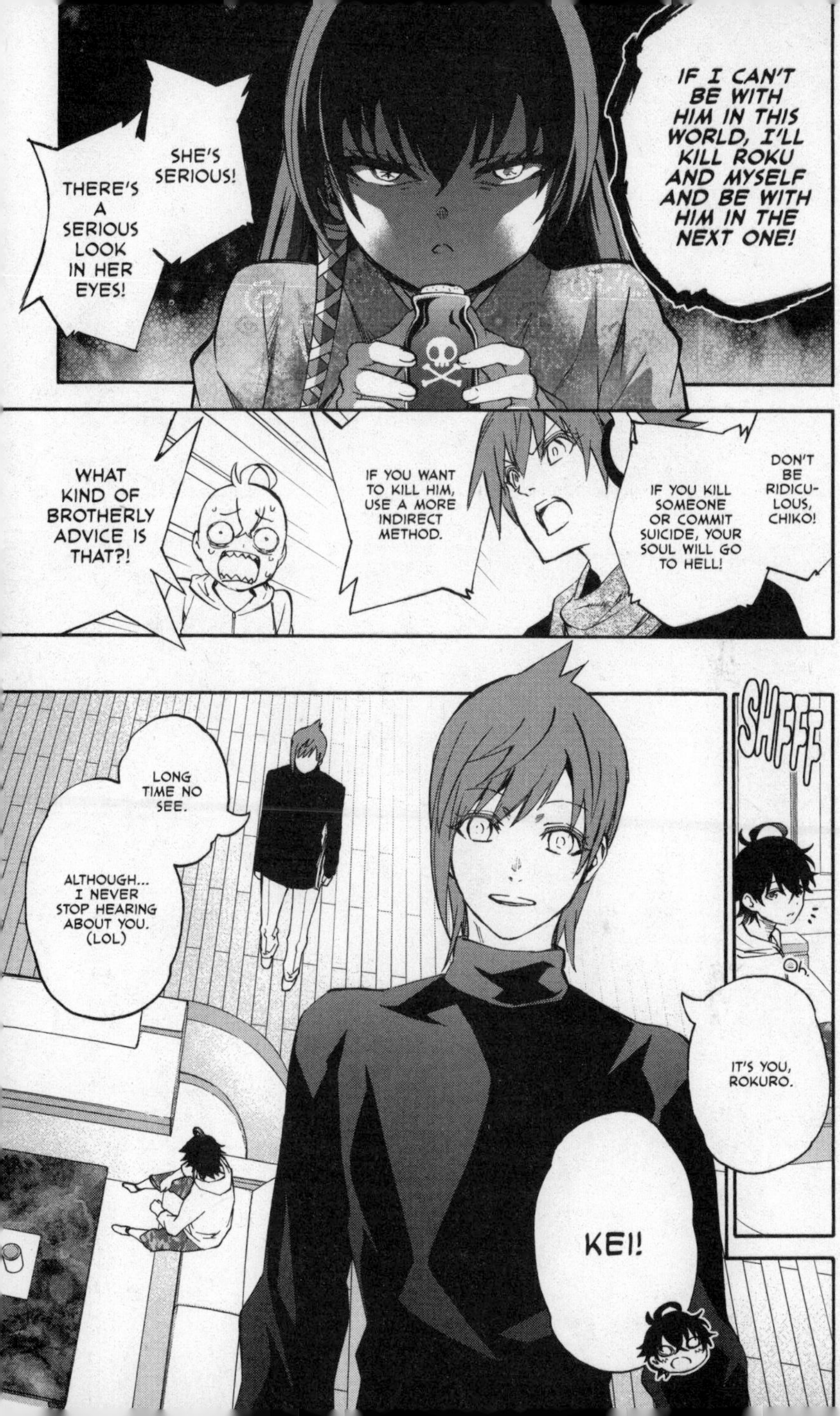
IF I CAN'T BE WITH HIM IN THIS WORLD, I'LL KILL ROKU AND MYSELF AND BE WITH HIM IN THE NEXT ONE!
SHE'S SERIOUS!
THERE'S A SERIOUS LOOK IN HER EYES!
DON'T BE RIDICULOUS, CHIKO!
IF YOU KILL SOMEONE OR COMMIT SUICIDE, YOUR SOUL WILL GO TO HELL!
IF YOU WANT TO KILL HIM, USE A MORE INDIRECT METHOD.
WHAT KIND OF BROTHERLY ADVICE IS THAT?!
SHFFF
Oh.
IT'S YOU, ROKURO.
LONG TIME NO SEE.
ALTHOUGH... I NEVER STOP HEARING ABOUT YOU. (LOL)
KEI!

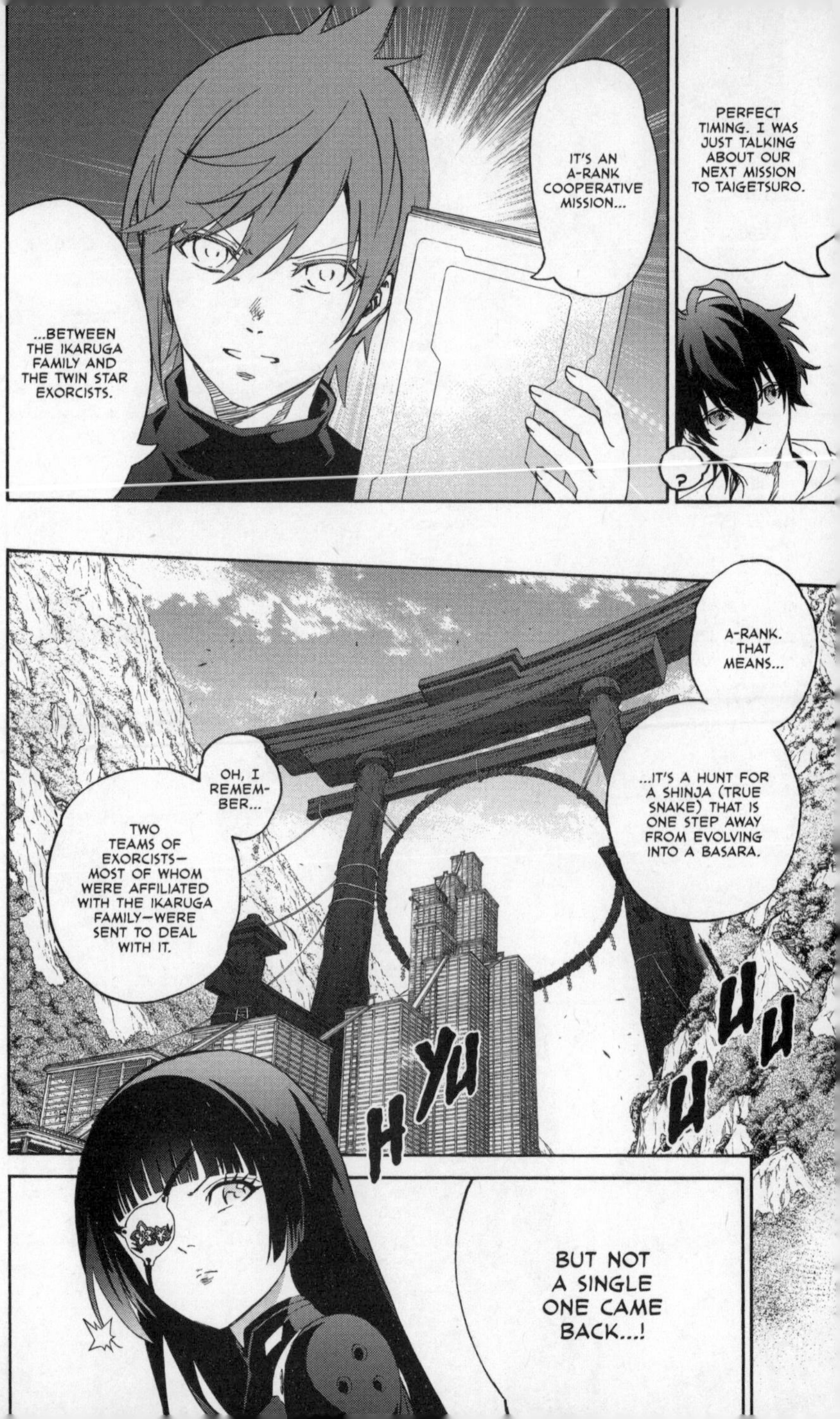
PERFECT TIMING. I WAS JUST TALKING ABOUT OUR NEXT MISSION TO TAIGETSURO.
?
IT'S AN A-RANK COOPERATIVE MISSION...
...BETWEEN THE IKARUGA FAMILY AND THE TWIN STAR EXORCISTS.
A-RANK. THAT MEANS...
...IT'S A HUNT FOR A SHINJA (TRUE SNAKE) THAT IS ONE STEP AWAY FROM EVOLVING INTO A BASARA.
OH, I REMEMBER...
TWO TEAMS OF EXORCISTS—MOST OF WHOM WERE AFFILIATED WITH THE IKARUGA FAMILY—WERE SENT TO DEAL WITH IT.
HYUUUU
BUT NOT A SINGLE ONE CAME BACK...!

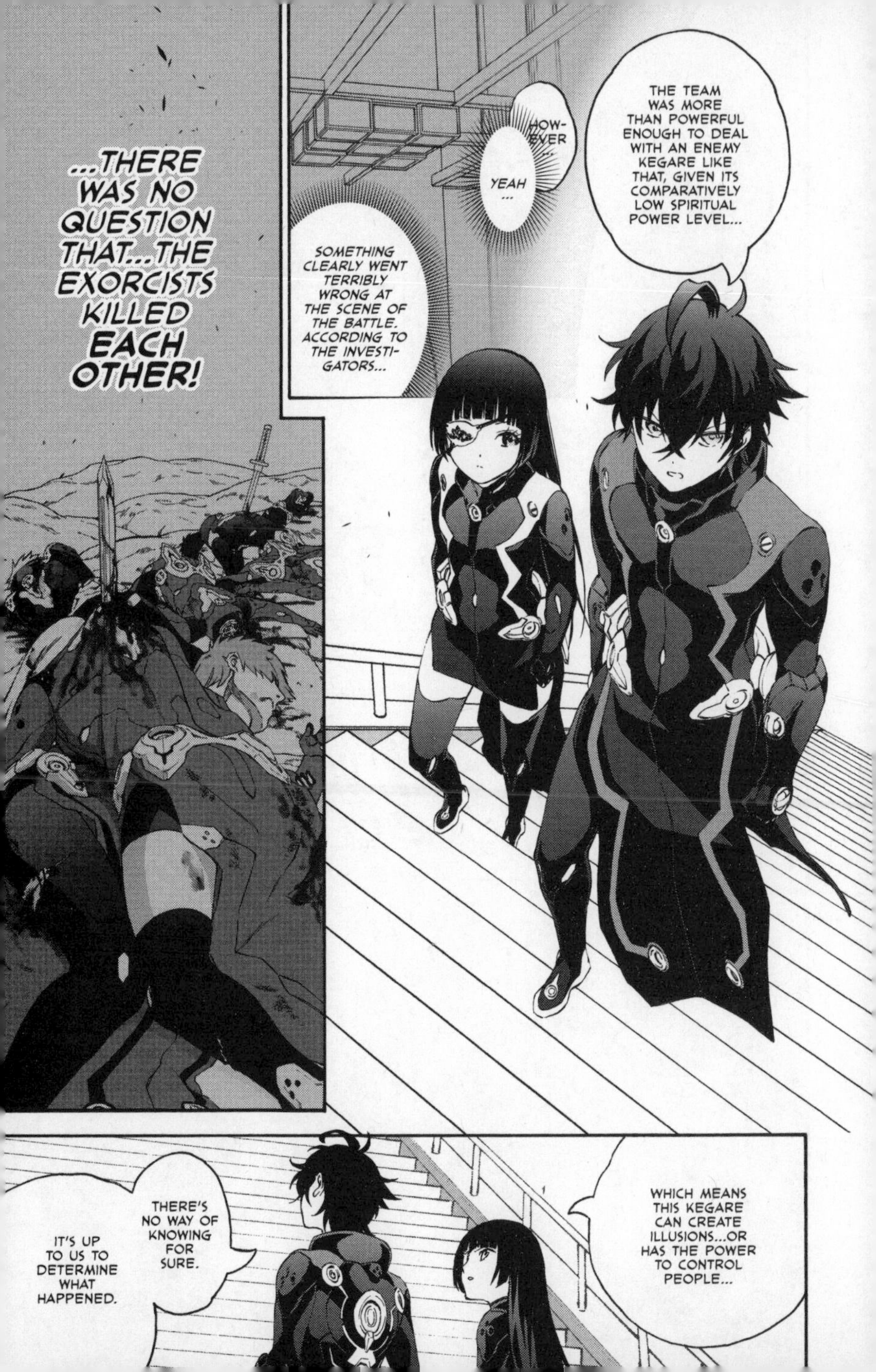
THE TEAM WAS MORE THAN POWERFUL ENOUGH TO DEAL WITH AN ENEMY KEGARE LIKE THAT, GIVEN ITS COMPARATIVELY LOW SPIRITUAL POWER LEVEL...
HOW-EVER...
YEAH...
SOMETHING CLEARLY WENT TERRIBLY WRONG AT THE SCENE OF THE BATTLE. ACCORDING TO THE INVESTI-GATORS...
...THERE WAS NO QUESTION THAT...THE EXORCISTS KILLED EACH OTHER!
WHICH MEANS THIS KEGARE CAN CREATE ILLUSIONS...OR HAS THE POWER TO CONTROL PEOPLE...
THERE'S NO WAY OF KNOWING FOR SURE.
IT'S UP TO US TO DETERMINE WHAT HAPPENED.

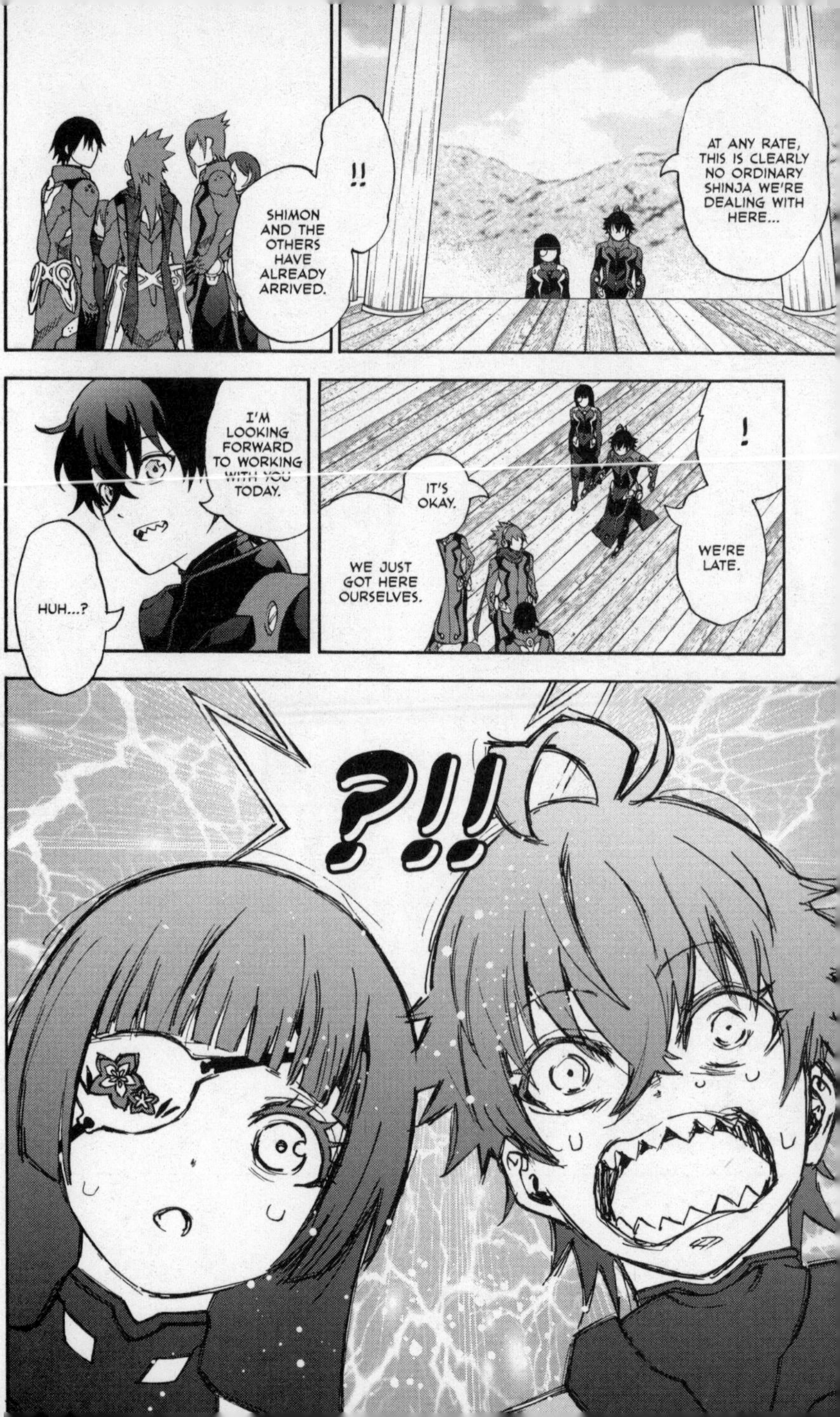
AT ANY RATE, THIS IS CLEARLY NO ORDINARY SHINJA WE'RE DEALING WITH HERE...
!!
SHIMON AND THE OTHERS HAVE ALREADY ARRIVED.
!
WE'RE LATE.
IT'S OKAY.
WE JUST GOT HERE OURSELVES.
I'M LOOKING FORWARD TO WORKING WITH YOU TODAY.
HUH...?
?!!

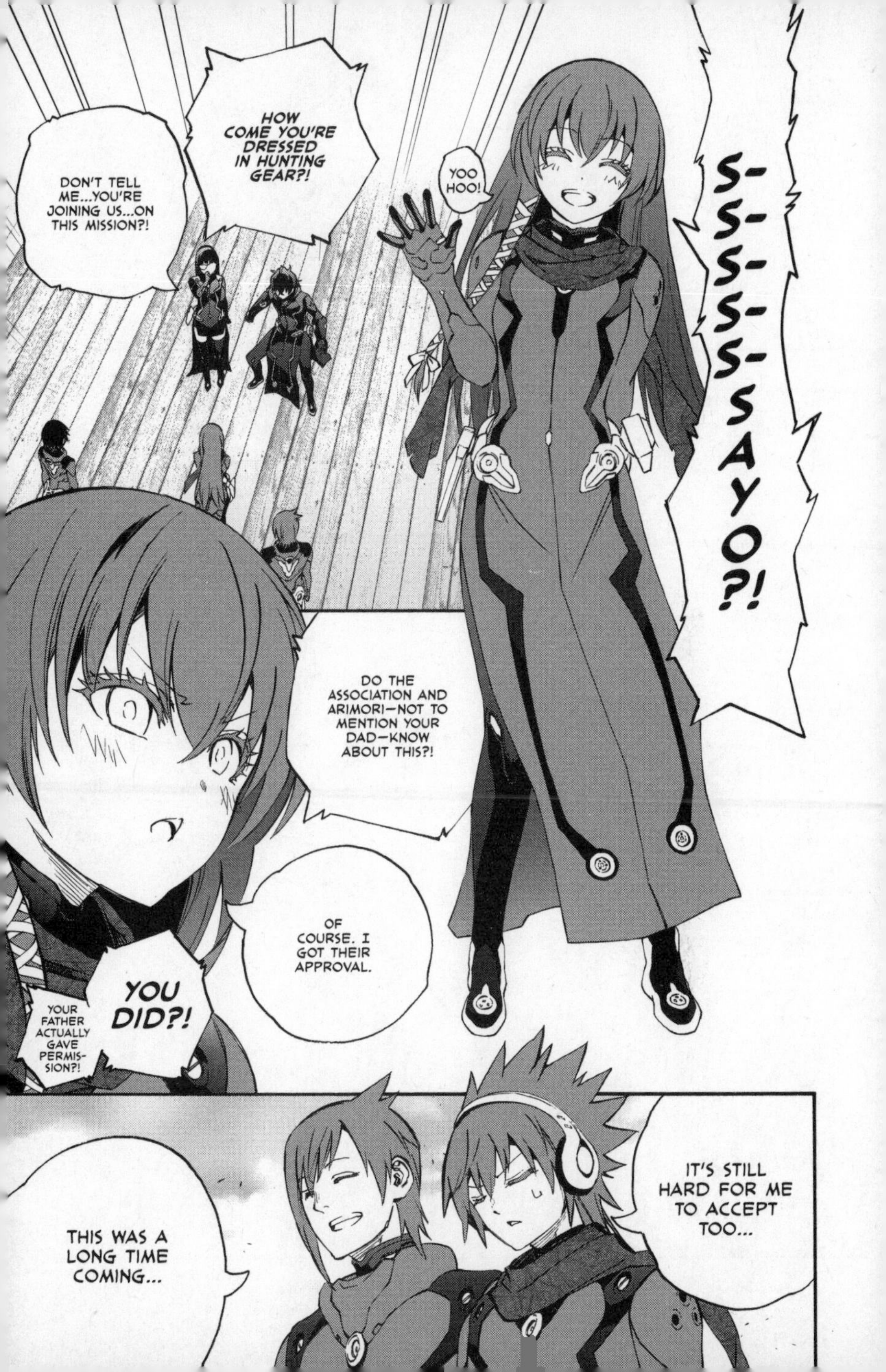
S-S-S-S-S-SAYO?!
YOO HOO!
HOW COME YOU'RE DRESSED IN HUNTING GEAR?!
DON'T TELL ME...YOU'RE JOINING US...ON THIS MISSION?!
DO THE ASSOCIATION AND ARIMORI—NOT TO MENTION YOUR DAD—KNOW ABOUT THIS?!
OF COURSE. I GOT THEIR APPROVAL.
YOU DID?!
YOUR FATHER ACTUALLY GAVE PERMIS-SION?!
IT'S STILL HARD FOR ME TO ACCEPT TOO...
THIS WAS A LONG TIME COMING...

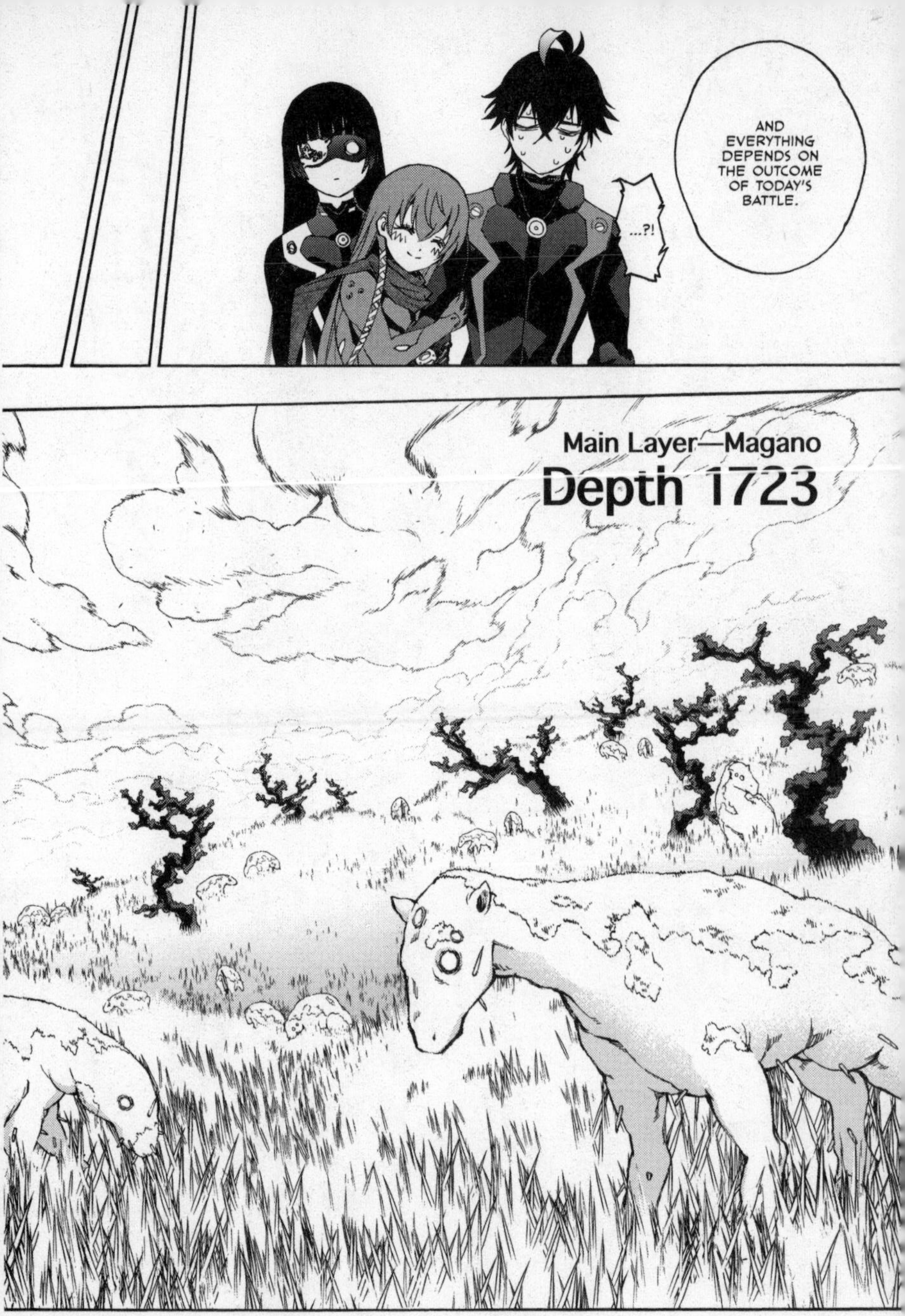
AND EVERYTHING DEPENDS ON THE OUTCOME OF TODAY'S BATTLE.
...?!
Main Layer—Magano
Depth 1723

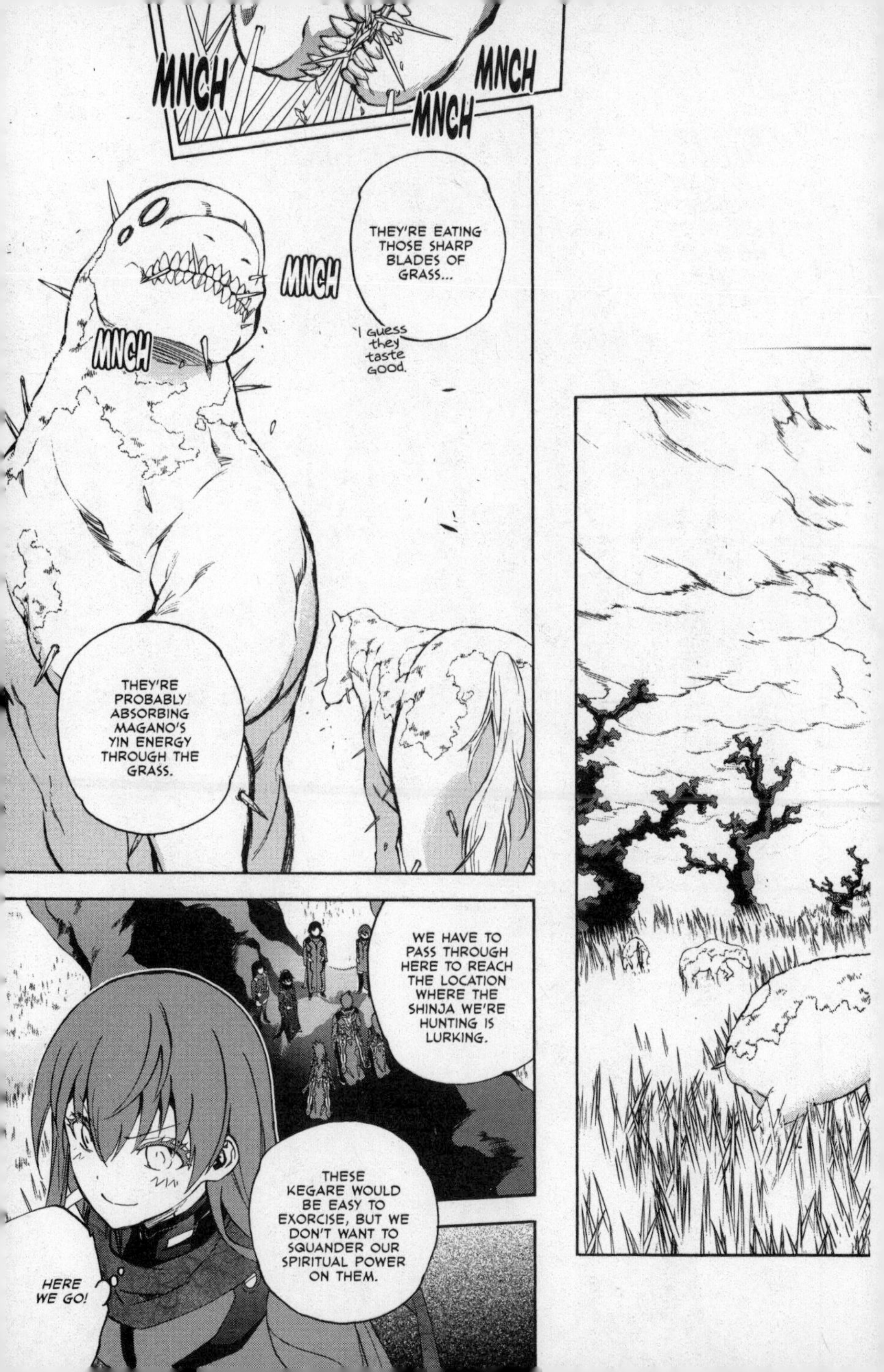
MNCH
MNCH
MNCH
THEY'RE EATING THOSE SHARP BLADES OF GRASS...
I guess they taste good.
MNCH
MNCH
THEY'RE PROBABLY ABSORBING MAGANO'S YIN ENERGY THROUGH THE GRASS.
WE HAVE TO PASS THROUGH HERE TO REACH THE LOCATION WHERE THE SHINJA WE'RE HUNTING IS LURKING.
THESE KEGARE WOULD BE EASY TO EXORCISE, BUT WE DON'T WANT TO SQUANDER OUR SPIRITUAL POWER ON THEM.
HERE WE GO!

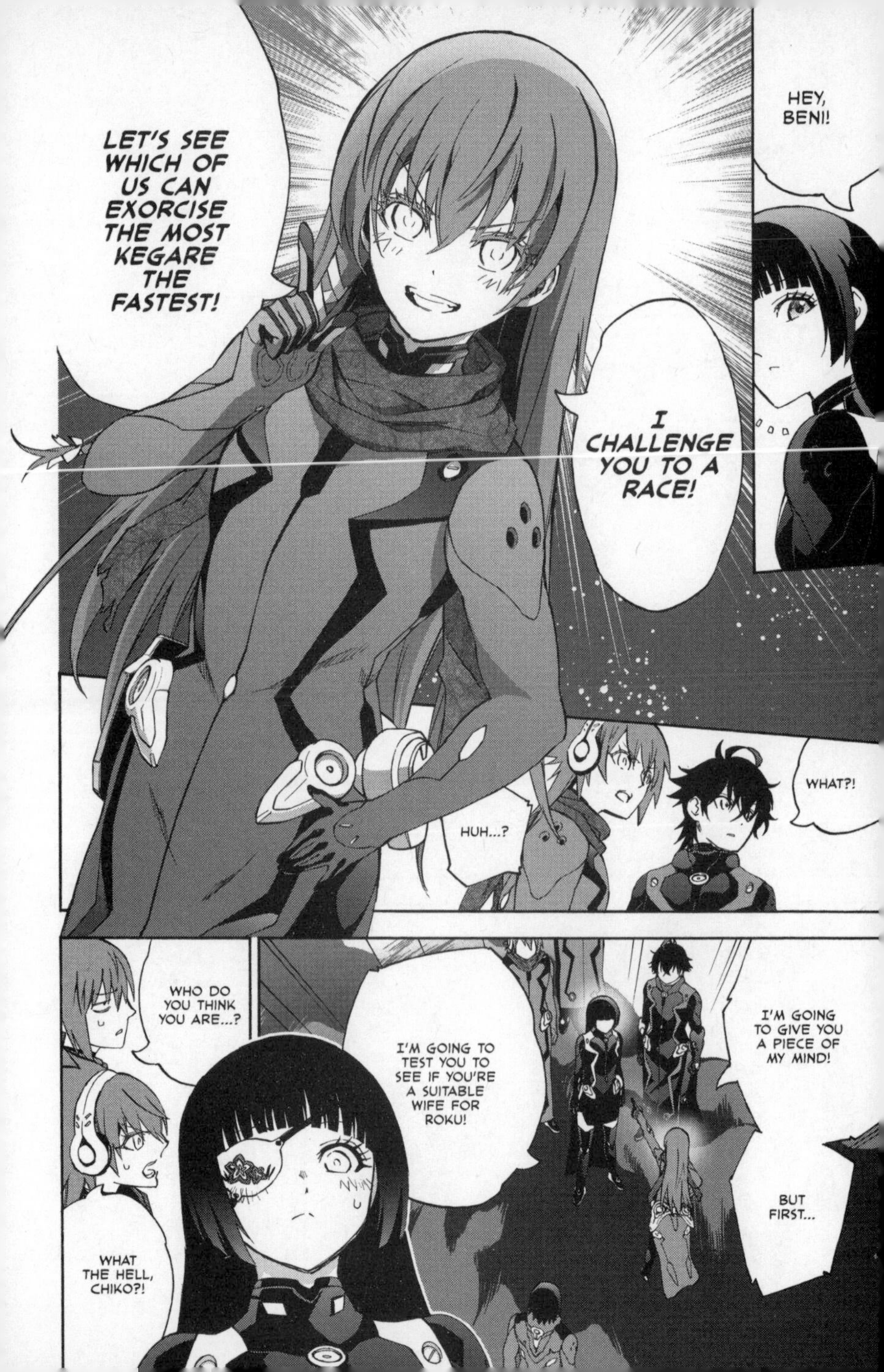
HEY, BENI!
I CHALLENGE YOU TO A RACE!
LET'S SEE WHICH OF US CAN EXORCISE THE MOST KEGARE THE FASTEST!
WHAT?!
HUH...?
I'M GOING TO GIVE YOU A PIECE OF MY MIND!
BUT FIRST...
I'M GOING TO TEST YOU TO SEE IF YOU'RE A SUITABLE WIFE FOR ROKU!
WHO DO YOU THINK YOU ARE...?
WHAT THE HELL, CHIKO?!

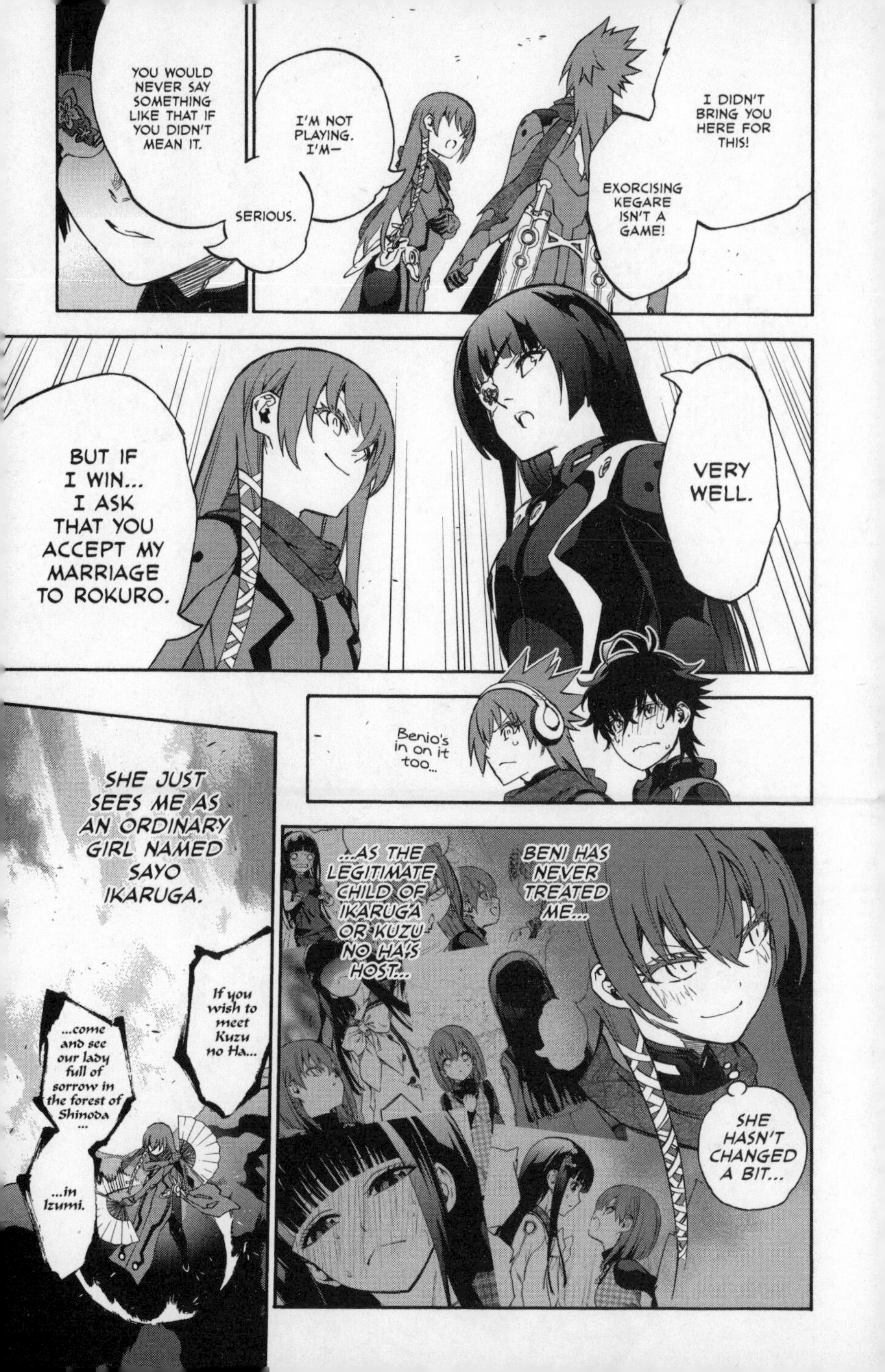

I DIDN'T BRING YOU HERE FOR THIS!
EXORCISING KEGARE ISN'T A GAME!
I'M NOT PLAYING. I'M—
SERIOUS.
YOU WOULD NEVER SAY SOMETHING LIKE THAT IF YOU DIDN'T MEAN IT.
VERY WELL.
BUT IF I WIN... I ASK THAT YOU ACCEPT MY MARRIAGE TO ROKURO.
Benio's in on it too...
BENI HAS NEVER TREATED ME...
...AS THE LEGITIMATE CHILD OF IKARUGA OR KUZU NO HA'S HOST...
SHE HASN'T CHANGED A BIT...
SHE JUST SEES ME AS AN ORDINARY GIRL NAMED SAYO IKARUGA.
If you wish to meet Kuzu no Ha...
...come and see our lady full of sorrow in the forest of Shinoda...
...in Izumi.

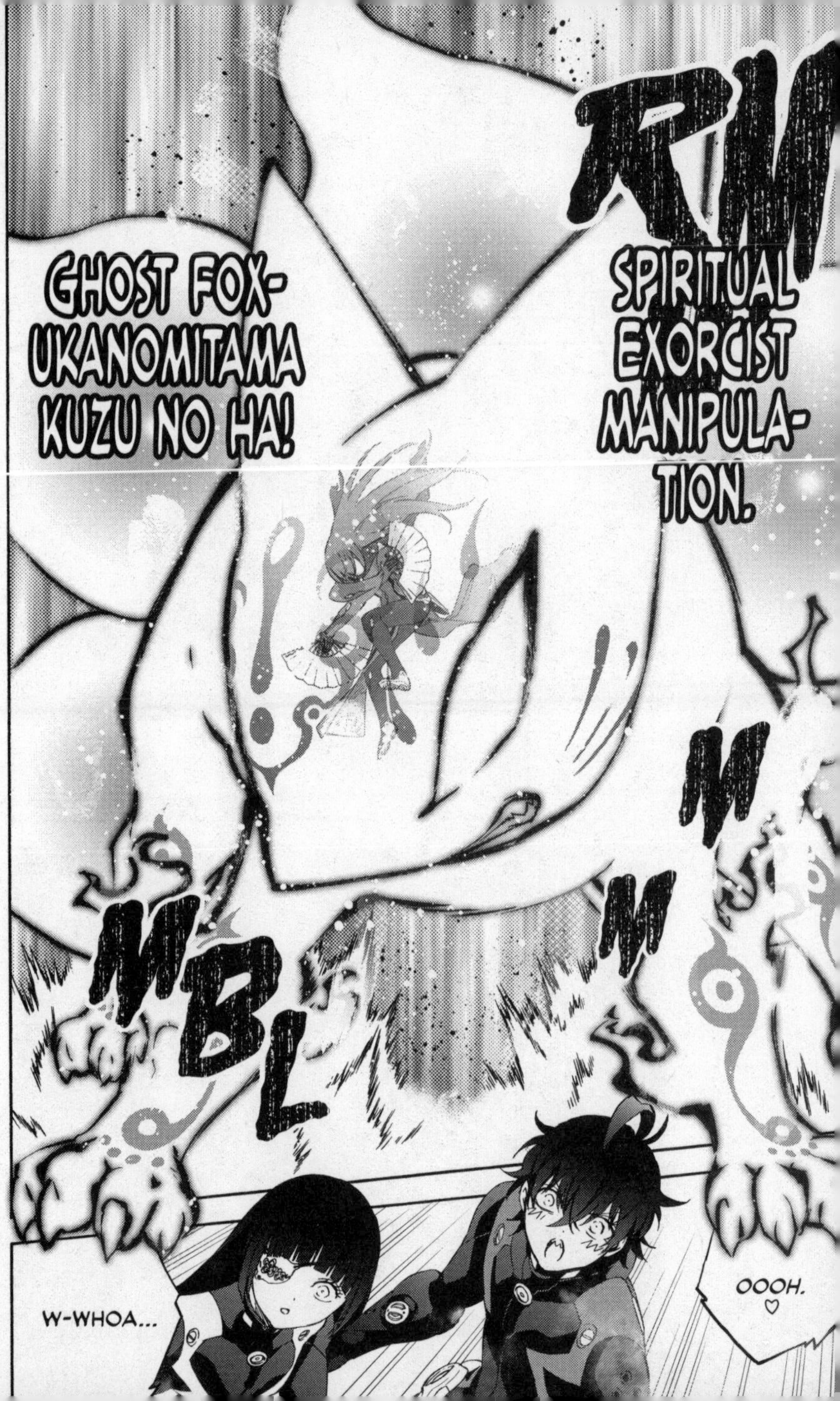
RM
SPIRITUAL EXORCIST MANIPULA-TION.
GHOST FOX-UKANOMITAMA KUZU NO HA!
M
M
MBL
OOOH. ♡
W-WHOA...

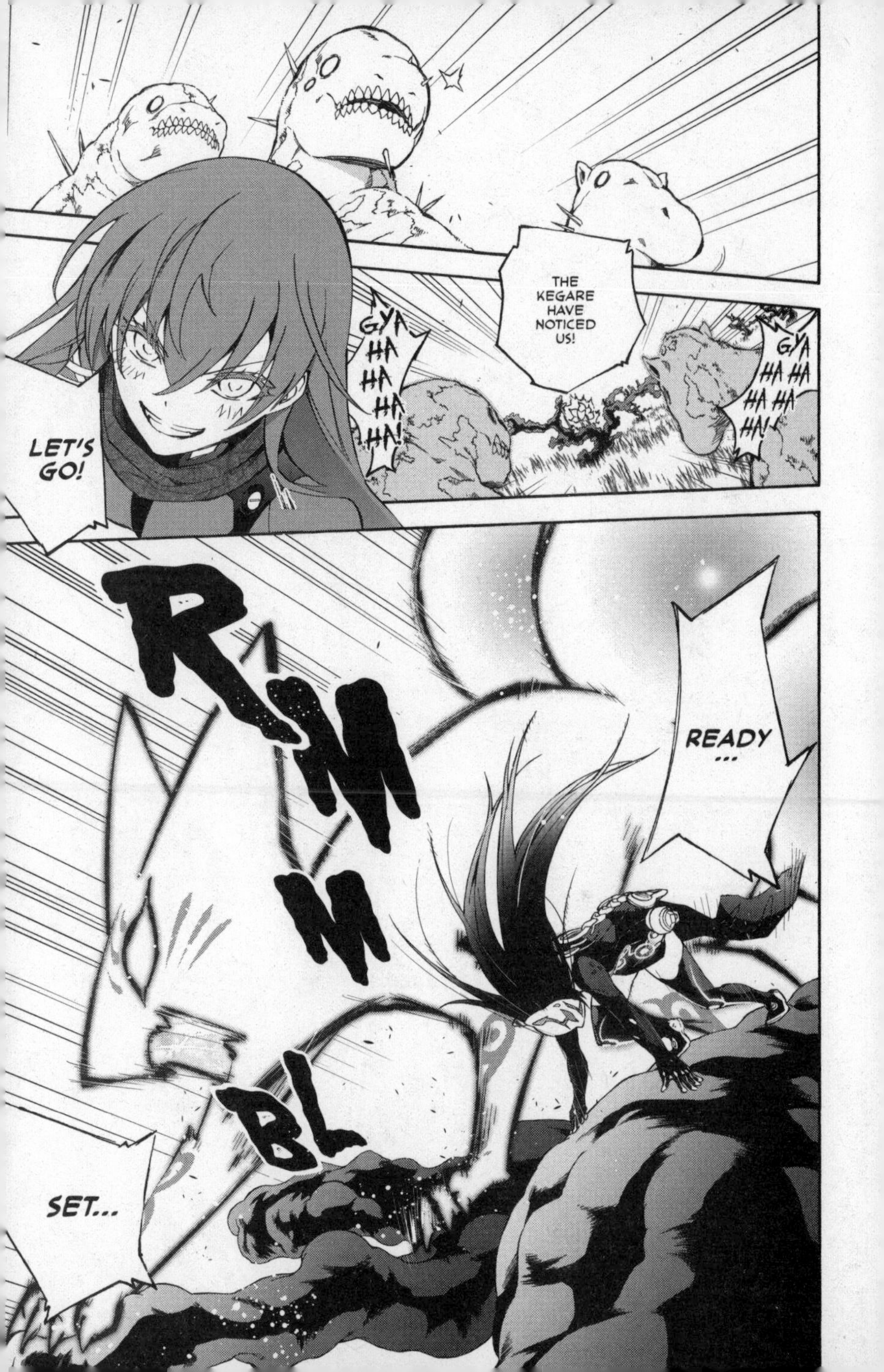
GYA HA HA HA HA HA!
THE KEGARE HAVE NOTICED US!
GYA HA HA HA HA HA!
LET'S GO!
READY...
RMMBL
SET...

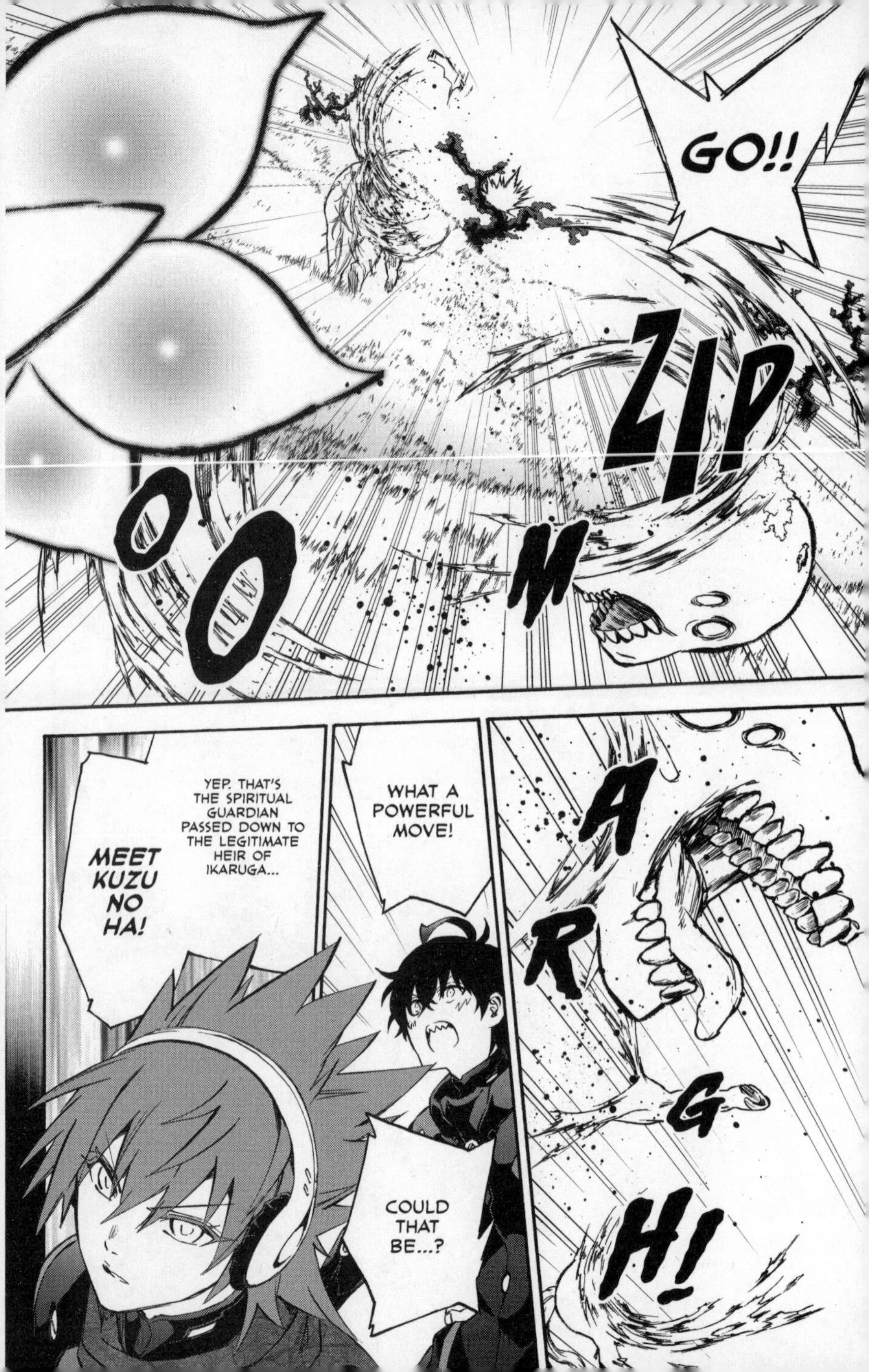
GO!!
ZIP
OOM
ARGH!
WHAT A POWERFUL MOVE!
COULD THAT BE...?
YEP. THAT'S THE SPIRITUAL GUARDIAN PASSED DOWN TO THE LEGITIMATE HEIR OF IKARUGA...
MEET KUZU NO HA!

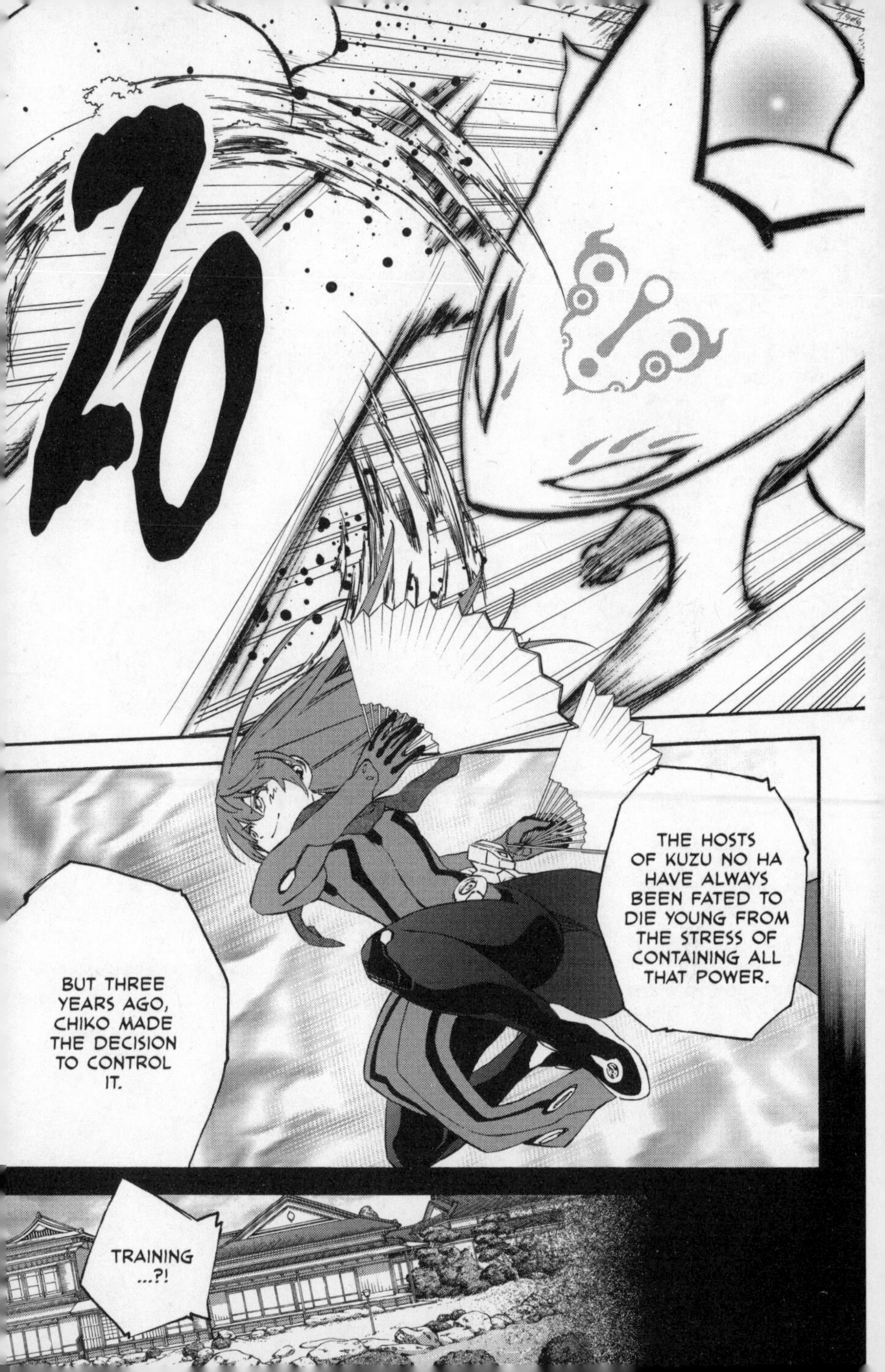
ZO
THE HOSTS OF KUZU NO HA HAVE ALWAYS BEEN FATED TO DIE YOUNG FROM THE STRESS OF CONTAINING ALL THAT POWER.
BUT THREE YEARS AGO, CHIKO MADE THE DECISION TO CONTROL IT.
TRAINING ...?!

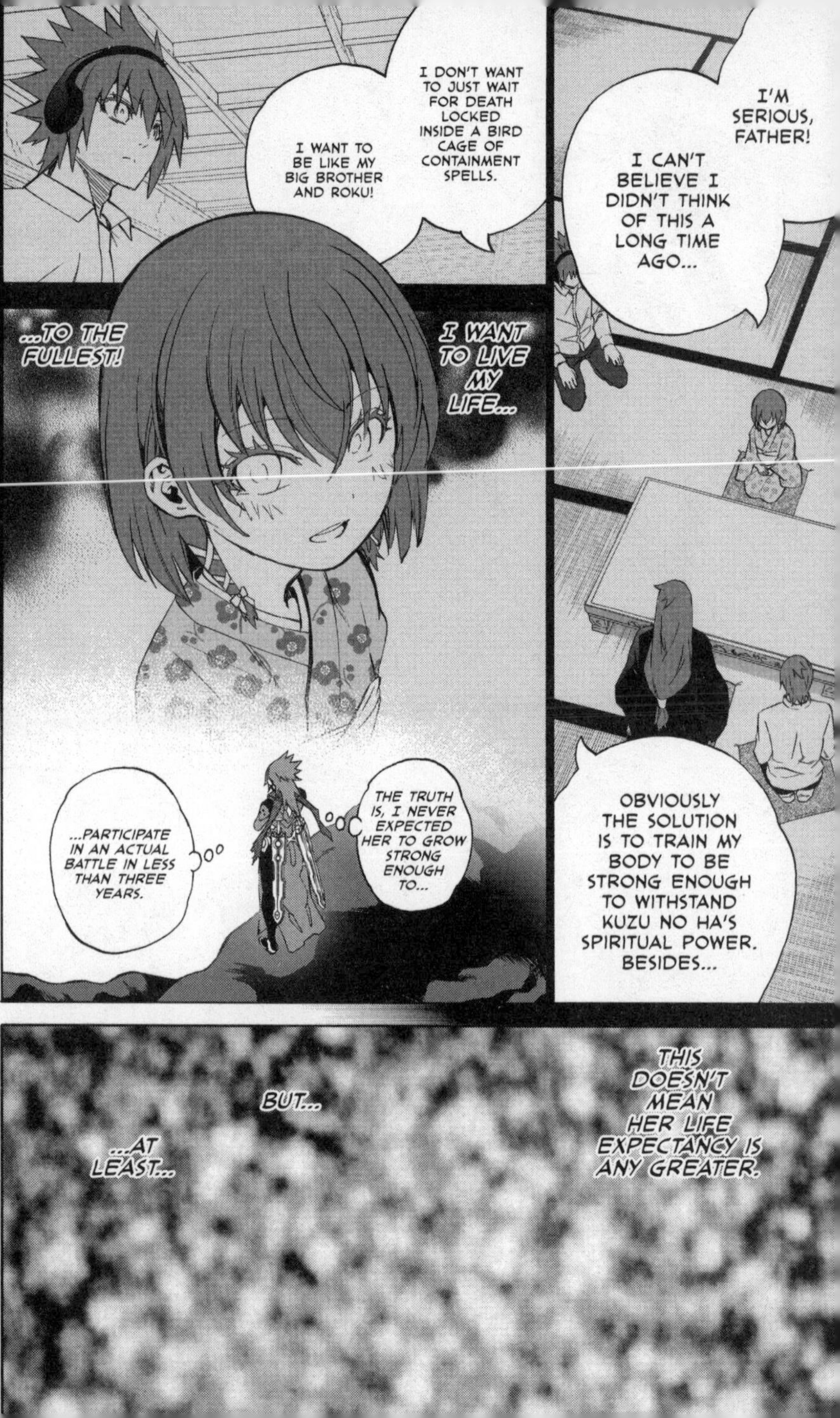
I'M SERIOUS, FATHER!
I CAN'T BELIEVE I DIDN'T THINK OF THIS A LONG TIME AGO...
OBVIOUSLY THE SOLUTION IS TO TRAIN MY BODY TO BE STRONG ENOUGH TO WITHSTAND KUZU NO HA'S SPIRITUAL POWER. BESIDES...
I DON'T WANT TO JUST WAIT FOR DEATH LOCKED INSIDE A BIRD CAGE OF CONTAINMENT SPELLS.
I WANT TO BE LIKE MY BIG BROTHER AND ROKU!
I WANT TO LIVE MY LIFE...
...TO THE FULLEST!
THE TRUTH IS, I NEVER EXPECTED HER TO GROW STRONG ENOUGH TO...
...PARTICIPATE IN AN ACTUAL BATTLE IN LESS THAN THREE YEARS.
THIS DOESN'T MEAN HER LIFE EXPECTANCY IS ANY GREATER.
BUT...
...AT LEAST...

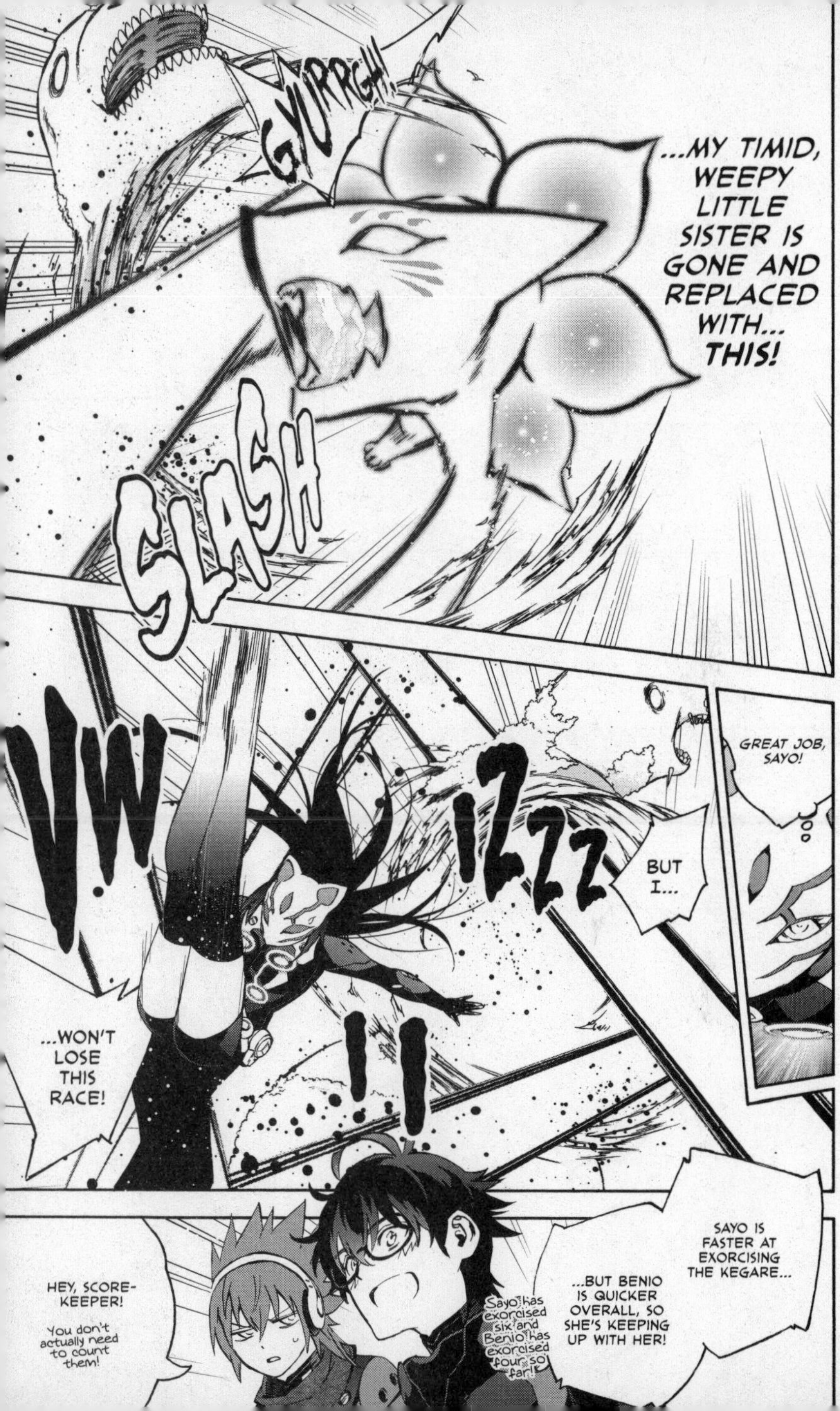
...MY TIMID, WEEPY LITTLE SISTER IS GONE AND REPLACED WITH... THIS!
GYURRGH!
SLASH
GREAT JOB, SAYO!
BUT I...
VWIZZZ
!!
...WON'T LOSE THIS RACE!
SAYO IS FASTER AT EXORCISING THE KEGARE...
...BUT BENIO IS QUICKER OVERALL, SO SHE'S KEEPING UP WITH HER!
Sayo has exorcised six and Benio has exorcised four so far!
HEY, SCORE-KEEPER!
You don't actually need to count them!

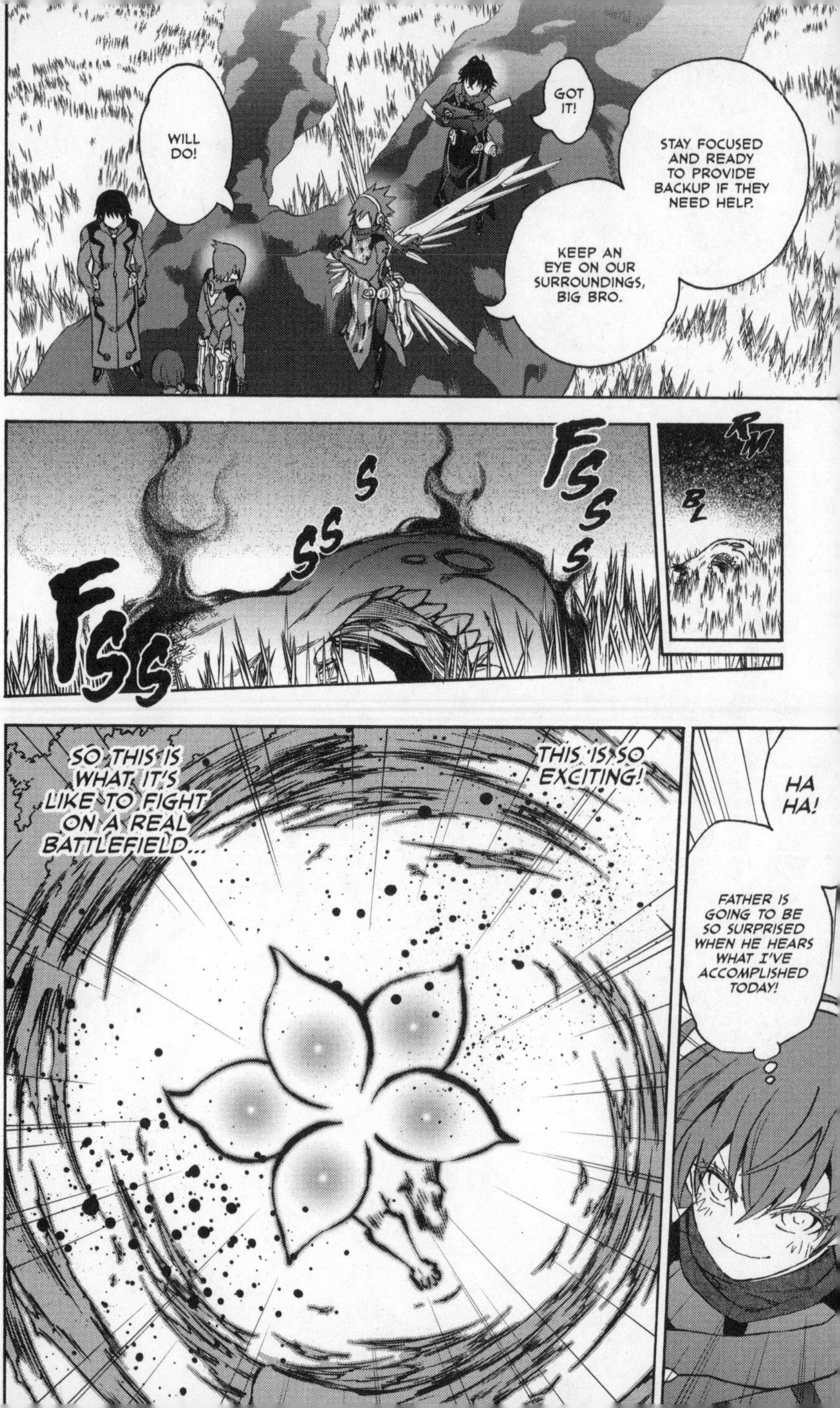
STAY FOCUSED AND READY TO PROVIDE BACKUP IF THEY NEED HELP.
KEEP AN EYE ON OUR SURROUNDINGS, BIG BRO.
GOT IT!
WILL DO!
RM
BL
FSSS
S
SS
FSS
HA HA!
FATHER IS GOING TO BE SO SURPRISED WHEN HE HEARS WHAT I'VE ACCOMPLISHED TODAY!
THIS IS SO EXCITING!
SO THIS IS WHAT IT'S LIKE TO FIGHT ON A REAL BATTLEFIELD...

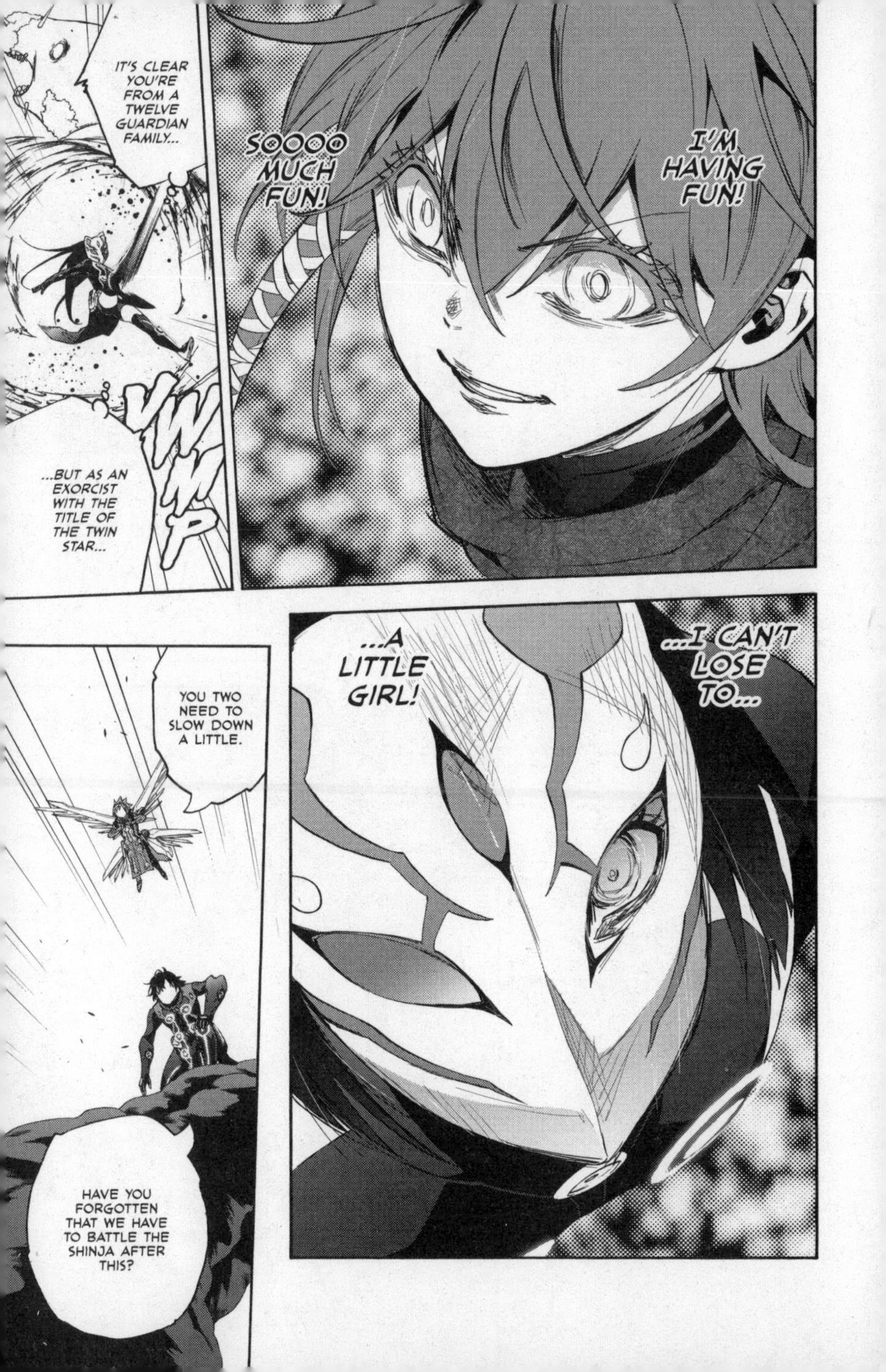
I'M HAVING FUN!
SOOOO MUCH FUN!
IT'S CLEAR YOU'RE FROM A TWELVE GUARDIAN FAMILY...
VWMP
...BUT AS AN EXORCIST WITH THE TITLE OF THE TWIN STAR...
...I CAN'T LOSE TO...
...A LITTLE GIRL!
YOU TWO NEED TO SLOW DOWN A LITTLE.
HAVE YOU FORGOTTEN THAT WE HAVE TO BATTLE THE SHINJA AFTER THIS?

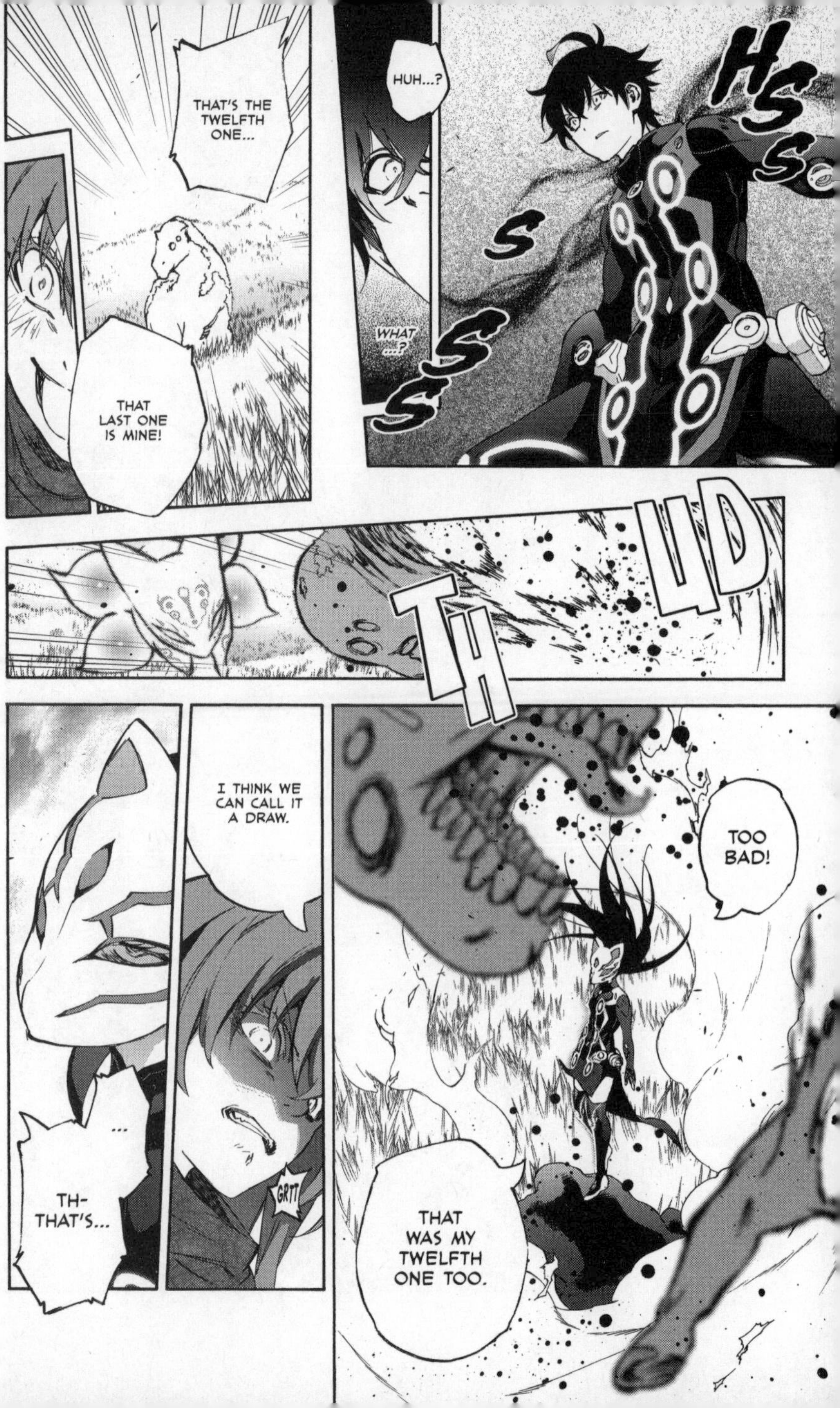
HSSSSSS
HUH...?
WHAT...?
THAT'S THE TWELFTH ONE...
THAT LAST ONE IS MINE!
THUD
TOO BAD!
THAT WAS MY TWELFTH ONE TOO.
I THINK WE CAN CALL IT A DRAW.
GRTT
...
TH- THAT'S...

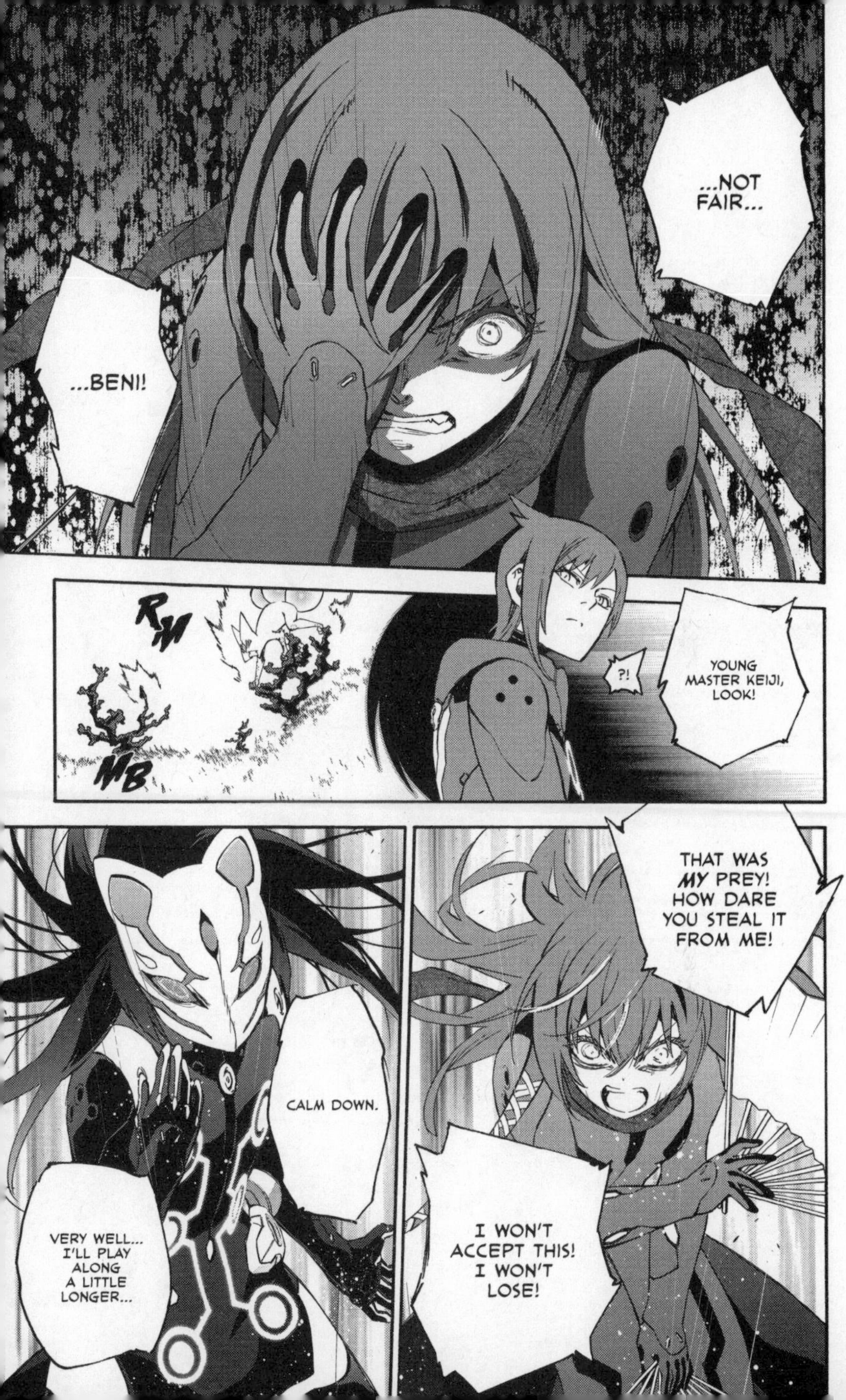
...NOT FAIR...
...BENI!
YOUNG MASTER KEIJI, LOOK!
?!
RM
MB
THAT WAS *MY* PREY! HOW DARE YOU STEAL IT FROM ME!
I WON'T ACCEPT THIS! I WON'T LOSE!
CALM DOWN.
VERY WELL... I'LL PLAY ALONG A LITTLE LONGER...

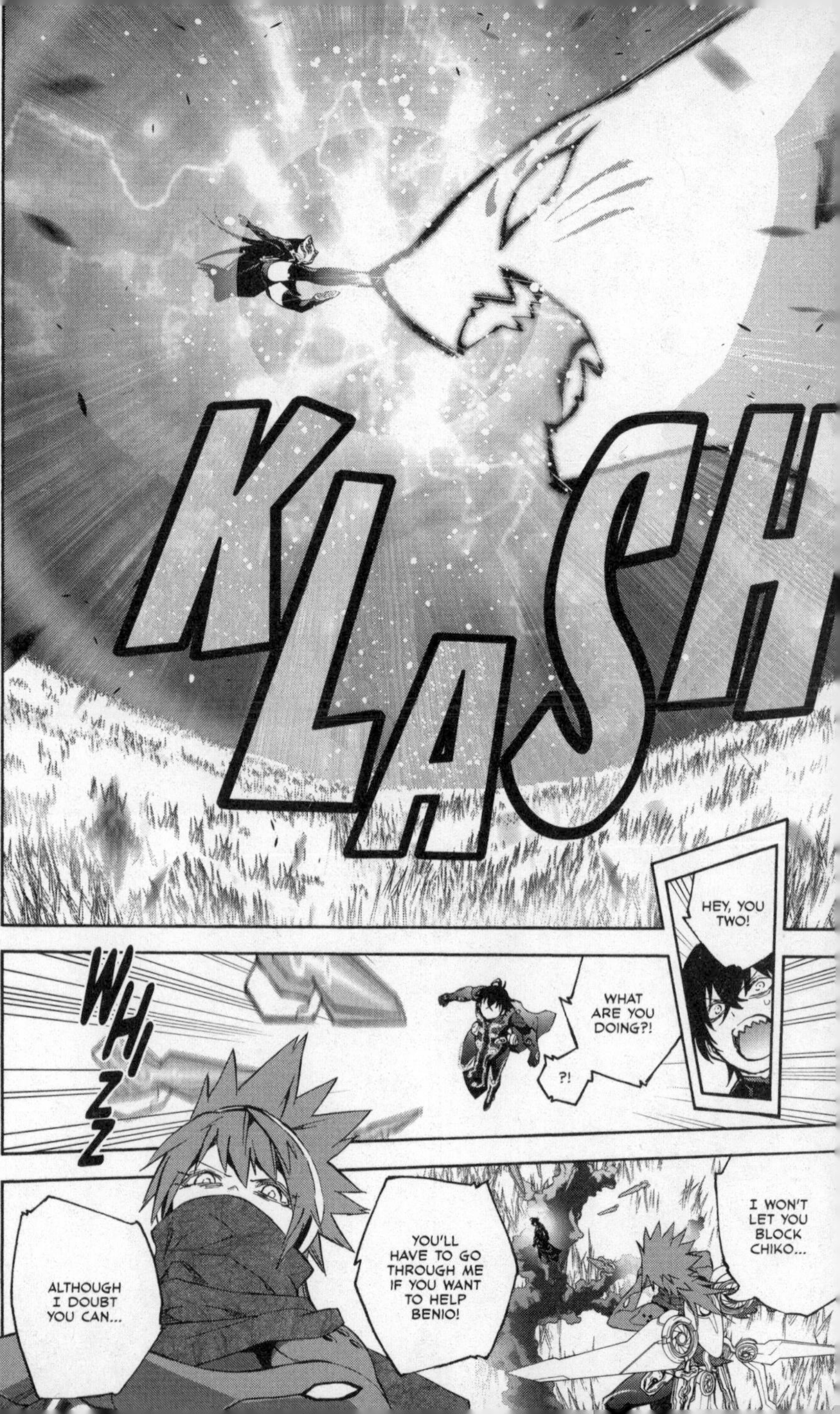
KLASH
HEY, YOU TWO!
WHAT ARE YOU DOING?!
?!
WHIZZZ
I WON'T LET YOU BLOCK CHIKO...
YOU'LL HAVE TO GO THROUGH ME IF YOU WANT TO HELP BENIO!
ALTHOUGH I DOUBT YOU CAN...

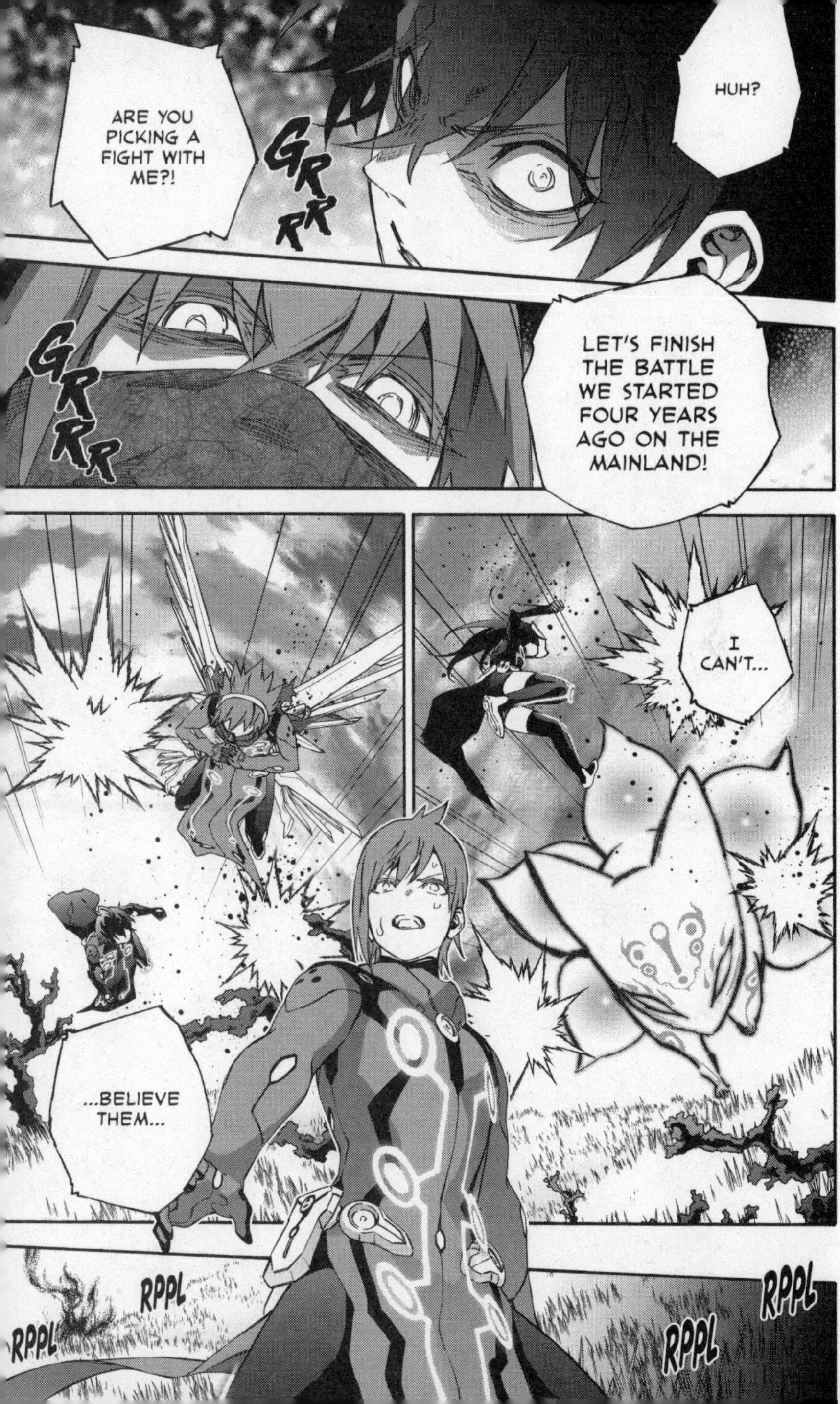
HUH?
ARE YOU PICKING A FIGHT WITH ME?!
GRRR
LET'S FINISH THE BATTLE WE STARTED FOUR YEARS AGO ON THE MAINLAND!
GRRR
I CAN'T...
...BELIEVE THEM...
RPPL
RPPL
RPPL
RPPL

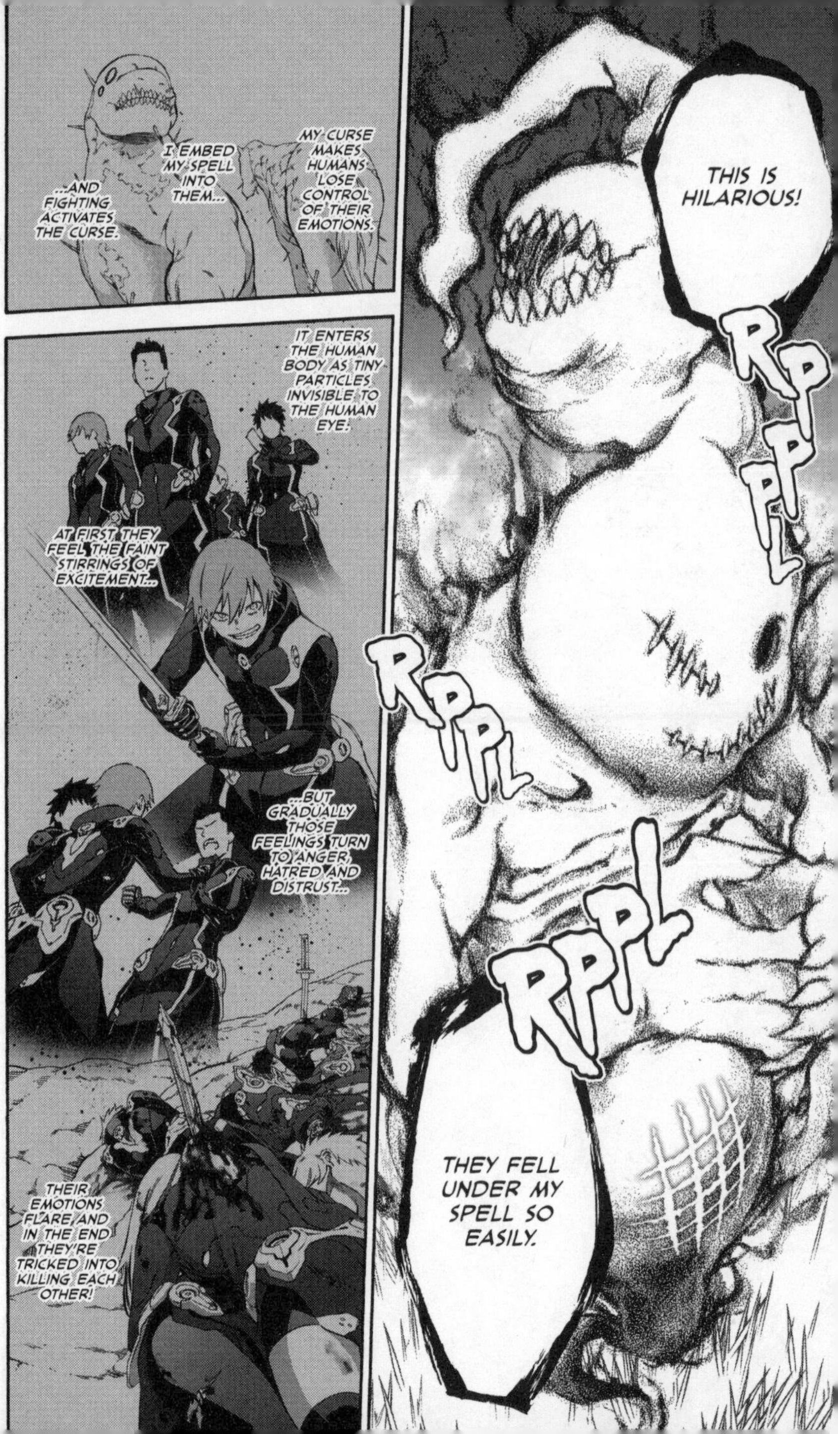
THIS IS HILARIOUS!
RPPPL
RPPL
RPPL
THEY FELL UNDER MY SPELL SO EASILY.
MY CURSE MAKES HUMANS LOSE CONTROL OF THEIR EMOTIONS.
I EMBED MY SPELL INTO THEM...
...AND FIGHTING ACTIVATES THE CURSE.
IT ENTERS THE HUMAN BODY AS TINY PARTICLES INVISIBLE TO THE HUMAN EYE.
AT FIRST THEY FEEL THE FAINT STIRRINGS OF EXCITEMENT...
...BUT GRADUALLY THOSE FEELINGS TURN TO ANGER, HATRED AND DISTRUST...
THEIR EMOTIONS FLARE AND IN THE END THEY'RE TRICKED INTO KILLING EACH OTHER!

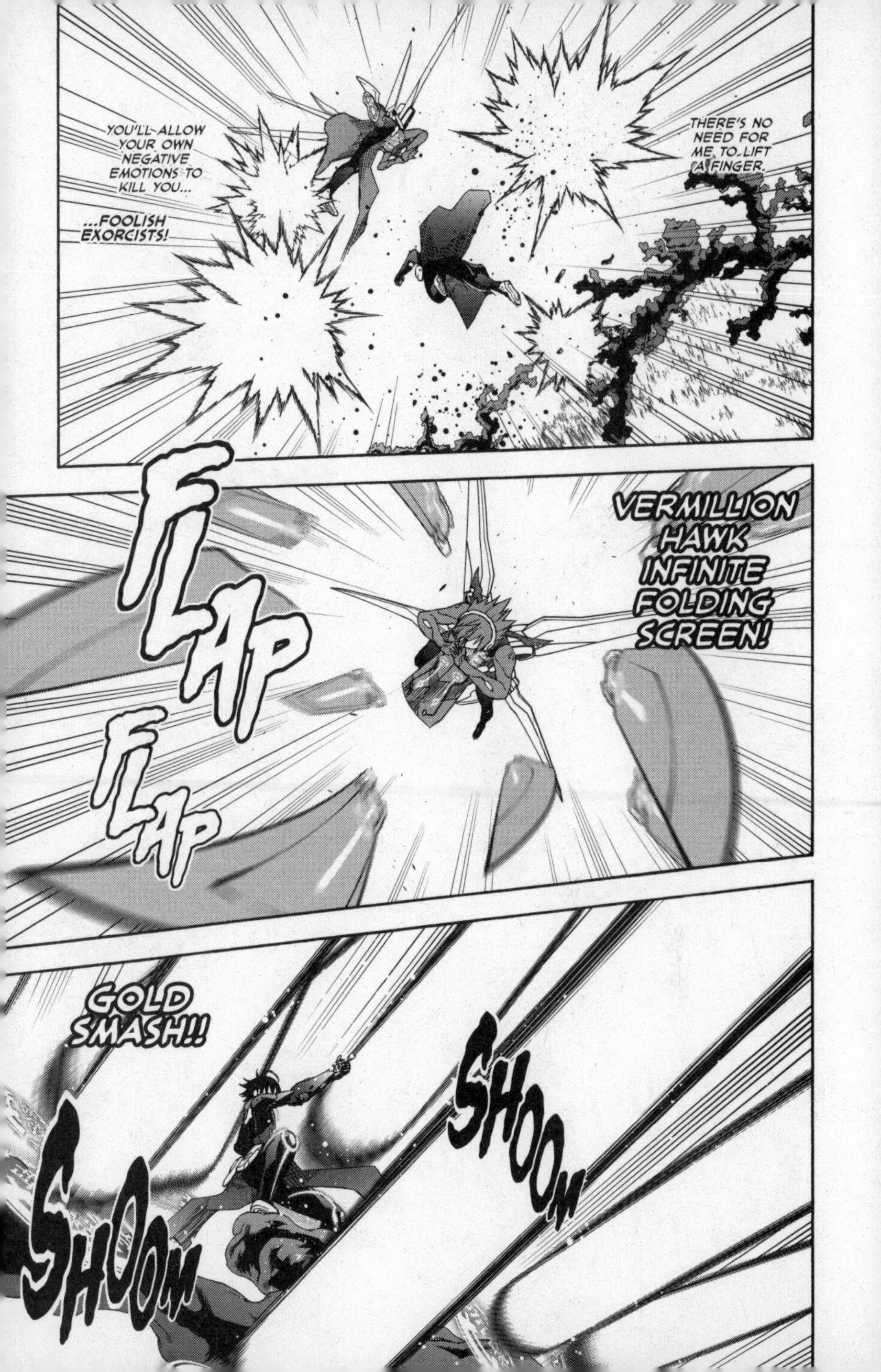
THERE'S NO NEED FOR ME TO LIFT A FINGER.
YOU'LL ALLOW YOUR OWN NEGATIVE EMOTIONS TO KILL YOU...
...FOOLISH EXORCISTS!
VERMILLION HAWK INFINITE FOLDING SCREEN!
FLAP
FLAP
SHOOM
GOLD SMASH!!
SHOOM

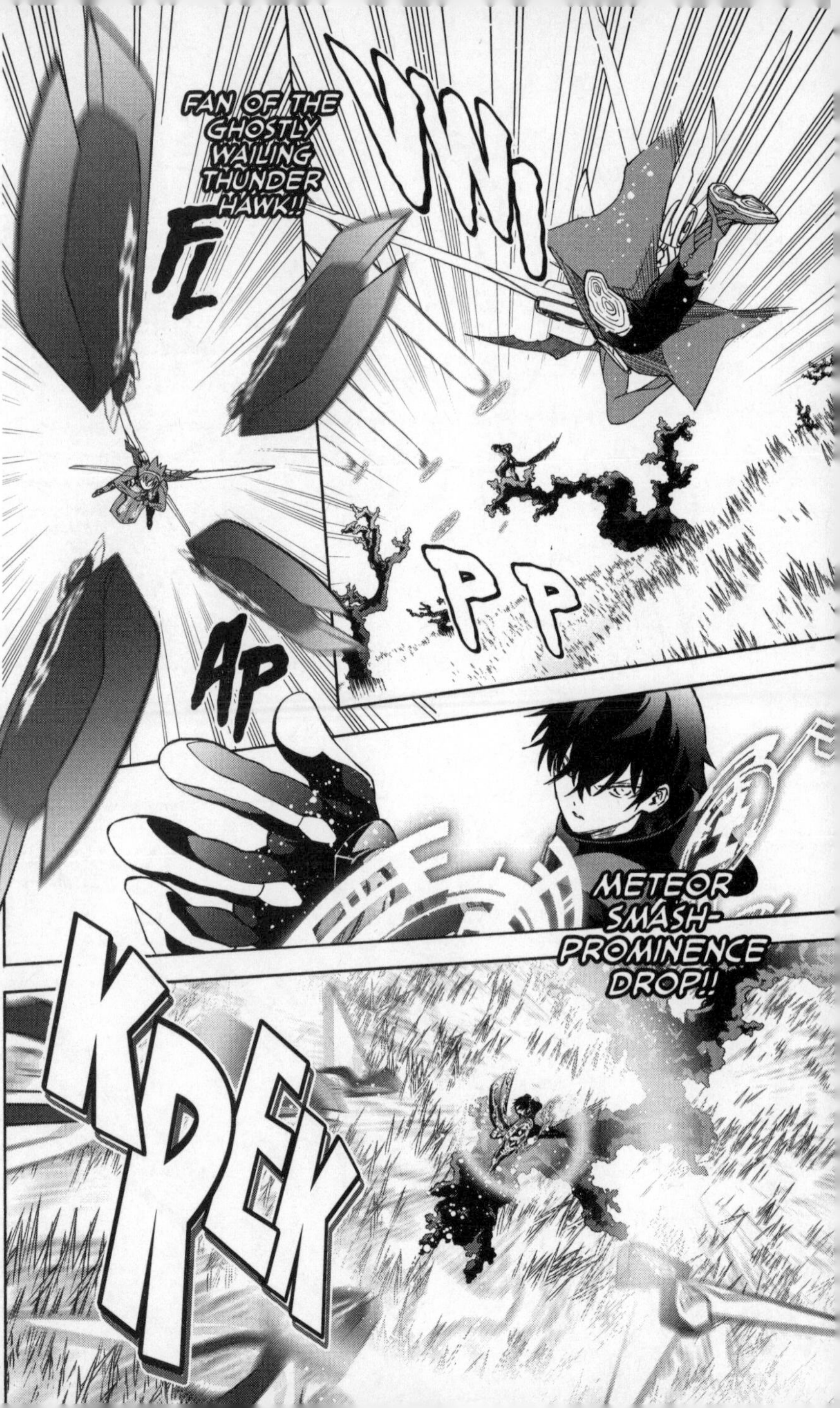
FAN OF THE GHOSTLY WAILING THUNDER HAWK!!
METEOR SMASH-PROMINENCE DROP!!

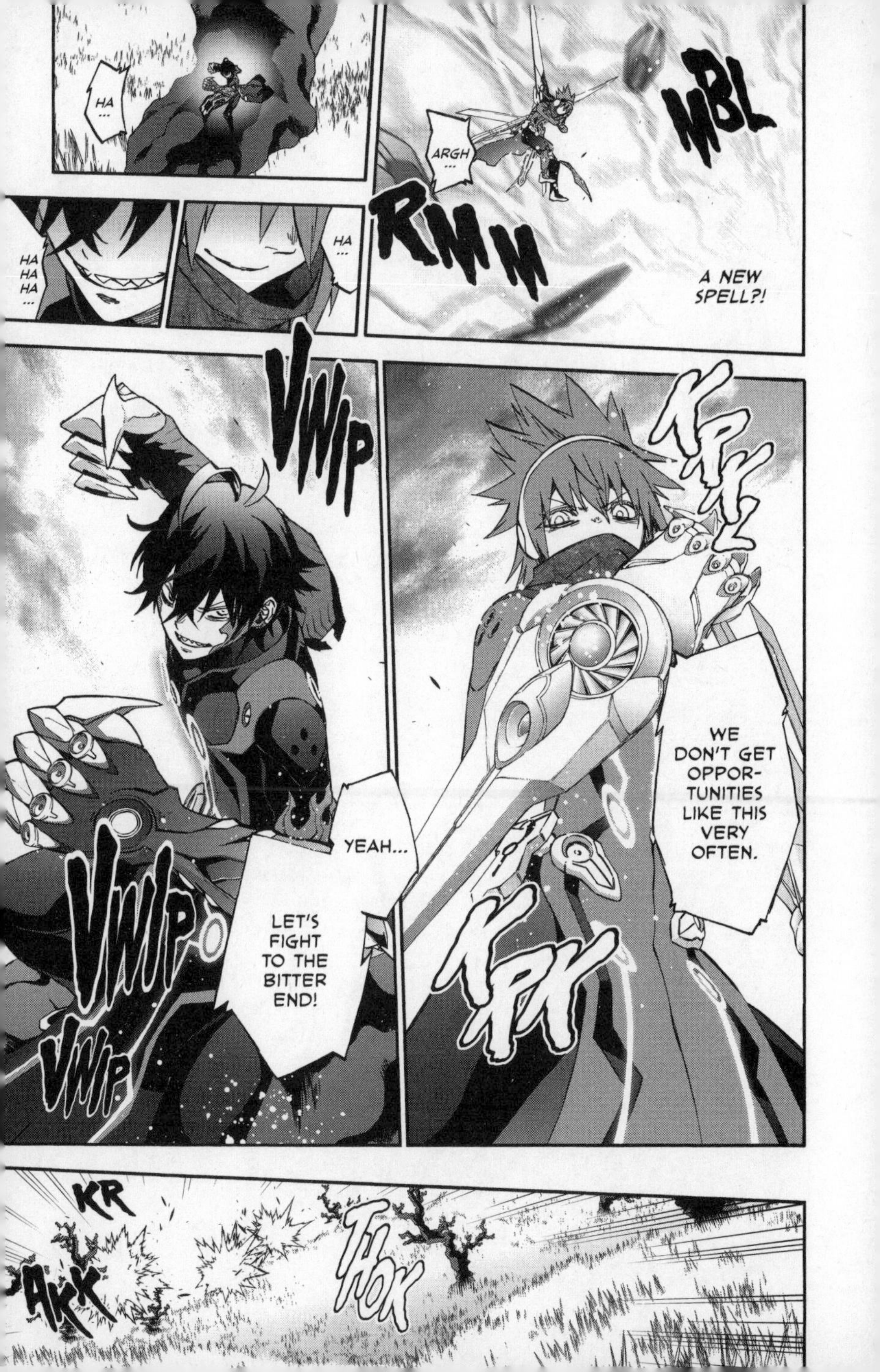
MBL
ARGH...
RMMM
A NEW SPELL?!
HA...
HA...
HA HA HA...
KPKL
WE DON'T GET OPPOR-TUNITIES LIKE THIS VERY OFTEN.
KPK
VWIP
YEAH...
LET'S FIGHT TO THE BITTER END!
VWIP
VWIP
THOK
KRAKK

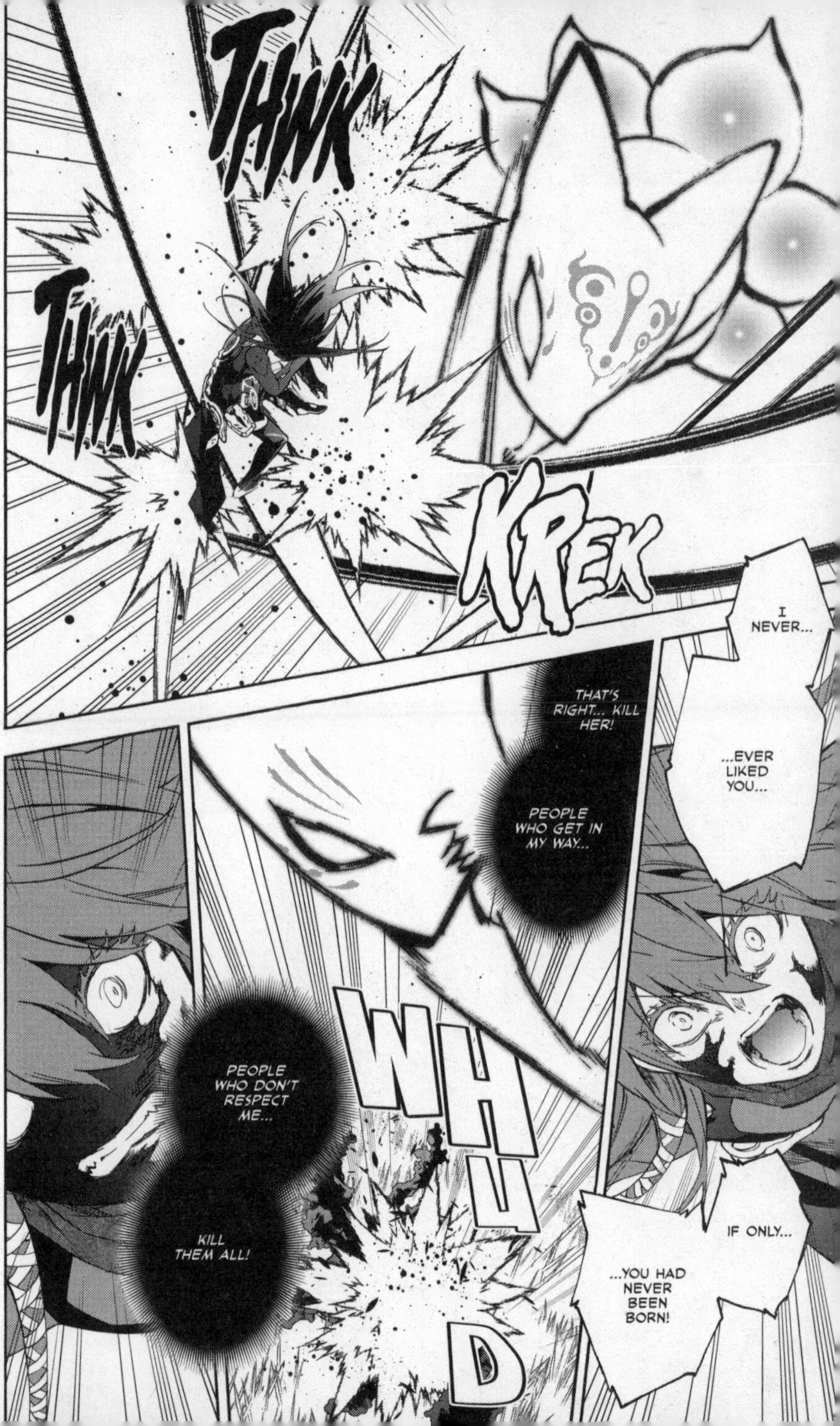
THWK
THWK
KREK
I NEVER...
...EVER LIKED YOU...
IF ONLY...
...YOU HAD NEVER BEEN BORN!
THAT'S RIGHT... KILL HER!
PEOPLE WHO GET IN MY WAY...
PEOPLE WHO DON'T RESPECT ME...
KILL THEM ALL!
WHUD

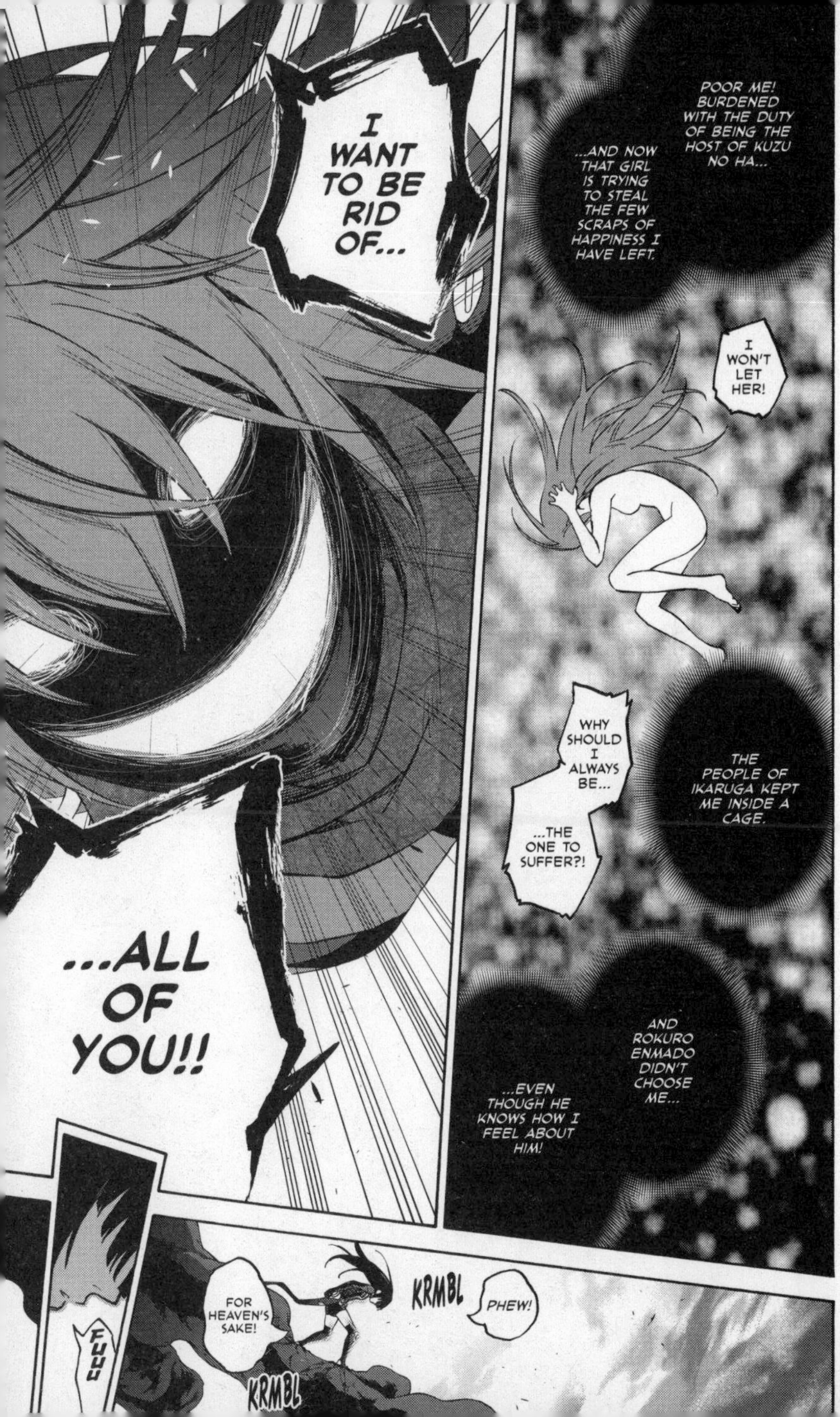
POOR ME! BURDENED WITH THE DUTY OF BEING THE HOST OF KUZU NO HA...
...AND NOW THAT GIRL IS TRYING TO STEAL THE FEW SCRAPS OF HAPPINESS I HAVE LEFT.
I WON'T LET HER!
THE PEOPLE OF IKARUGA KEPT ME INSIDE A CAGE.
WHY SHOULD I ALWAYS BE...
...THE ONE TO SUFFER?!
AND ROKURO ENMADO DIDN'T CHOOSE ME...
...EVEN THOUGH HE KNOWS HOW I FEEL ABOUT HIM!
I WANT TO BE RID OF...
...ALL OF YOU!!
PHEW!
KRMBL
FOR HEAVEN'S SAKE!
FUUU
KRMBL

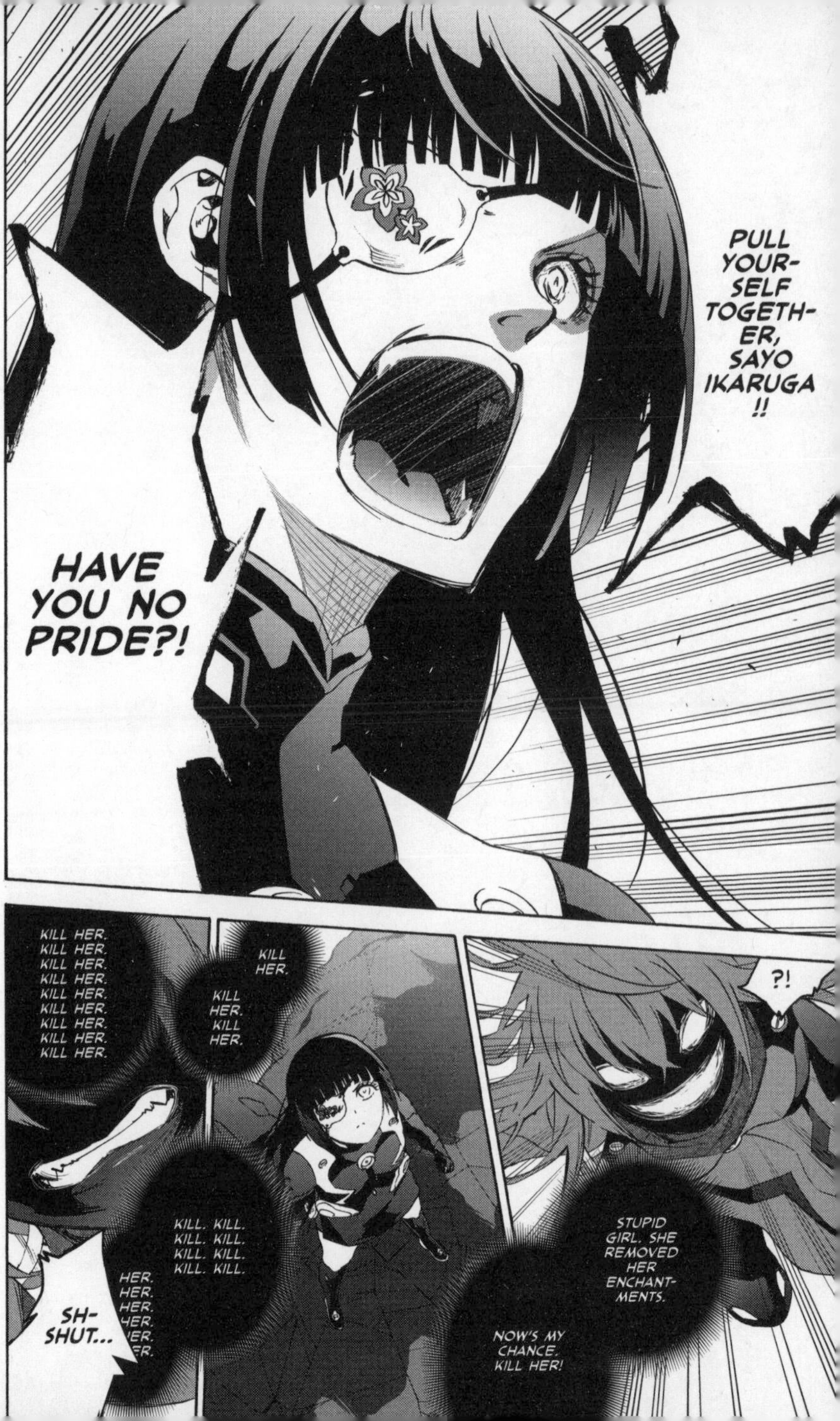
PULL YOURSELF TOGETHER, SAYO IKARUGA!!
HAVE YOU NO PRIDE?!
?!
STUPID GIRL. SHE REMOVED HER ENCHANTMENTS.
NOW'S MY CHANCE. KILL HER!
KILL HER.
KILL HER. KILL HER.
KILL HER. KILL HER. KILL HER. KILL HER. KILL HER. KILL HER. KILL HER. KILL HER. KILL HER.
KILL. KILL. KILL. KILL. KILL. KILL. KILL. KILL.
HER. HER. HER. HER.
SH-SHUT...

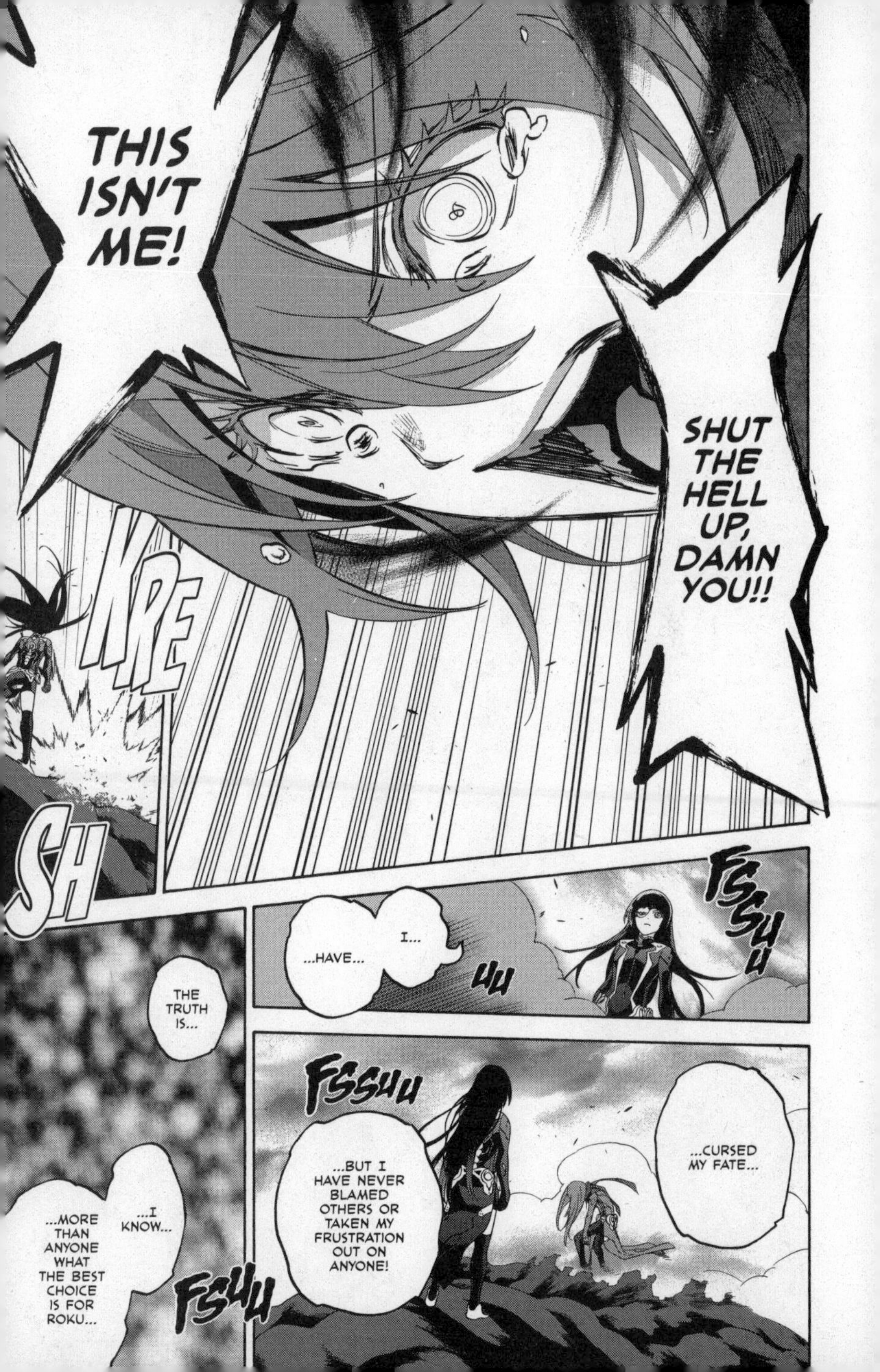
SHUT THE HELL UP, DAMN YOU!!
THIS ISN'T ME!
KRE
SH
FSSUU
I...
...HAVE...
UU
FSSUU
...CURSED MY FATE...
...BUT I HAVE NEVER BLAMED OTHERS OR TAKEN MY FRUSTRATION OUT ON ANYONE!
THE TRUTH IS...
...I KNOW...
...MORE THAN ANYONE WHAT THE BEST CHOICE IS FOR ROKU...
FSUU

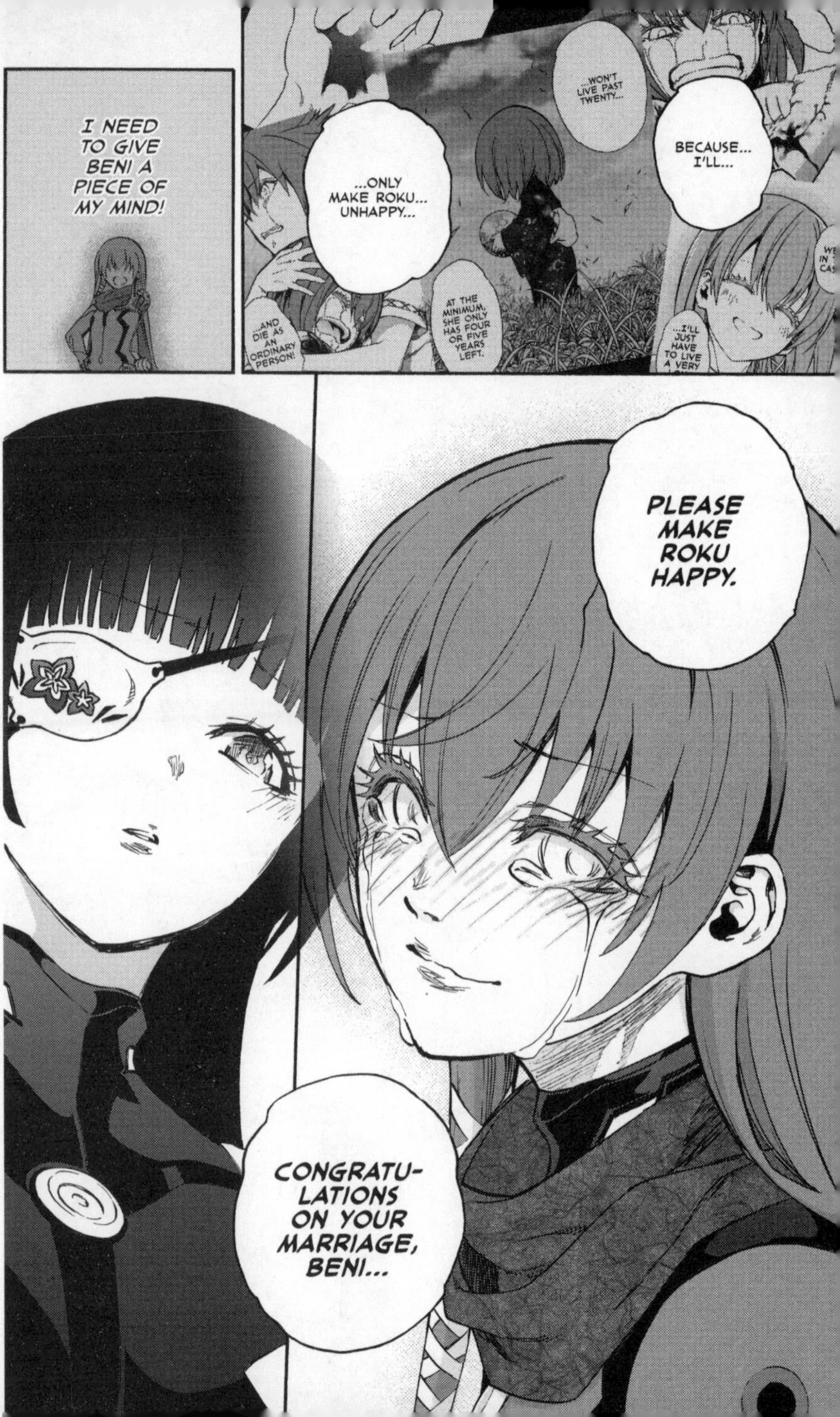
BECAUSE... I'LL...
...WON'T LIVE PAST TWENTY...
...I'LL JUST HAVE TO LIVE A VERY
...ONLY MAKE ROKU... UNHAPPY...
AT THE MINIMUM, SHE ONLY HAS FOUR OR FIVE YEARS LEFT.
...AND DIE AS AN ORDINARY PERSON!
I NEED TO GIVE BENI A PIECE OF MY MIND!
PLEASE MAKE ROKU HAPPY.
CONGRATULATIONS ON YOUR MARRIAGE, BENI...

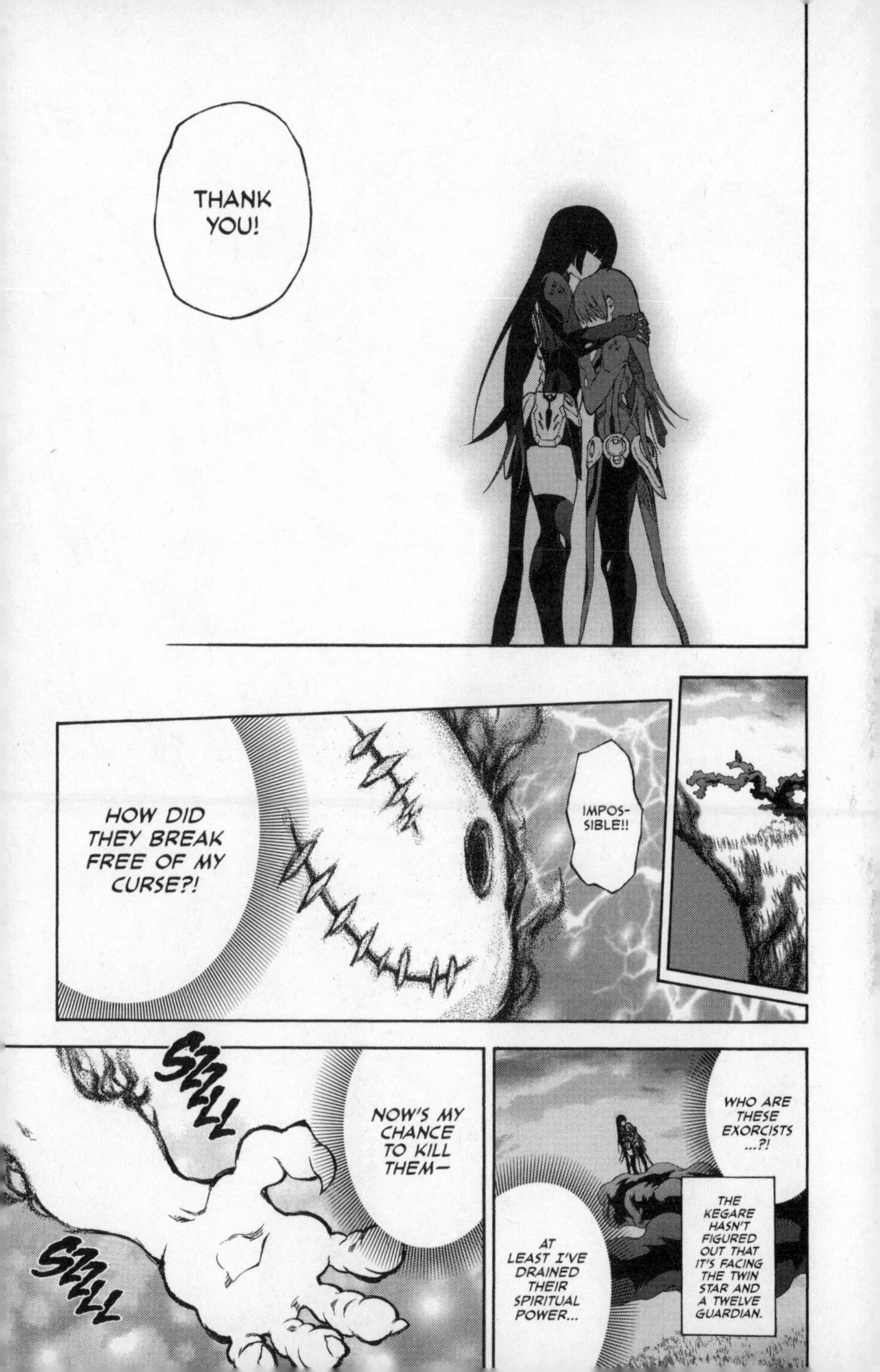
THANK YOU!
IMPOS-SIBLE!!
HOW DID THEY BREAK FREE OF MY CURSE?!
WHO ARE THESE EXORCISTS ...?!
THE KEGARE HASN'T FIGURED OUT THAT IT'S FACING THE TWIN STAR AND A TWELVE GUARDIAN.
AT LEAST I'VE DRAINED THEIR SPIRITUAL POWER...
NOW'S MY CHANCE TO KILL THEM—
SZZLL
SZZLL

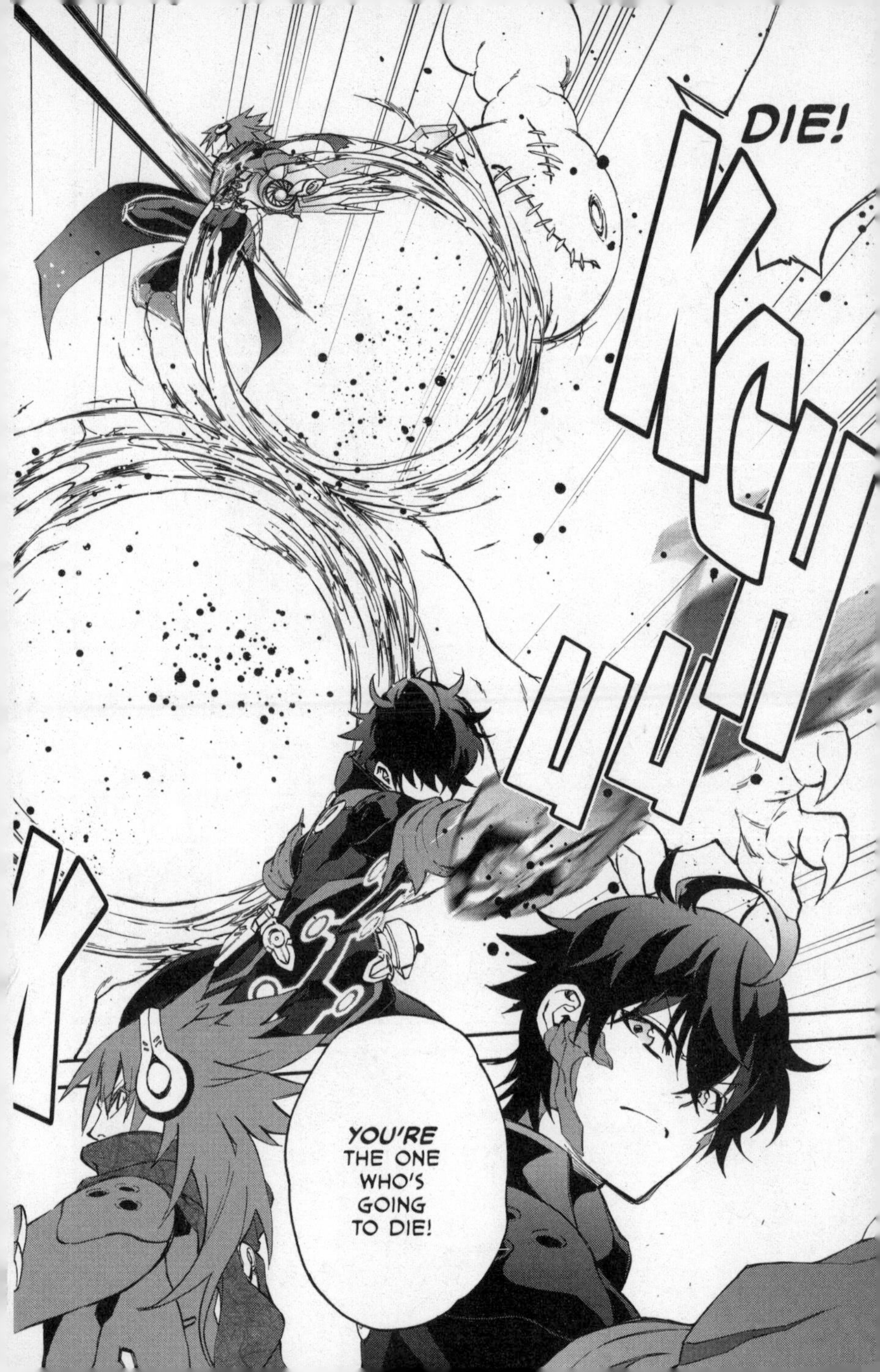
DIE!
YOU'RE THE ONE WHO'S GOING TO DIE!

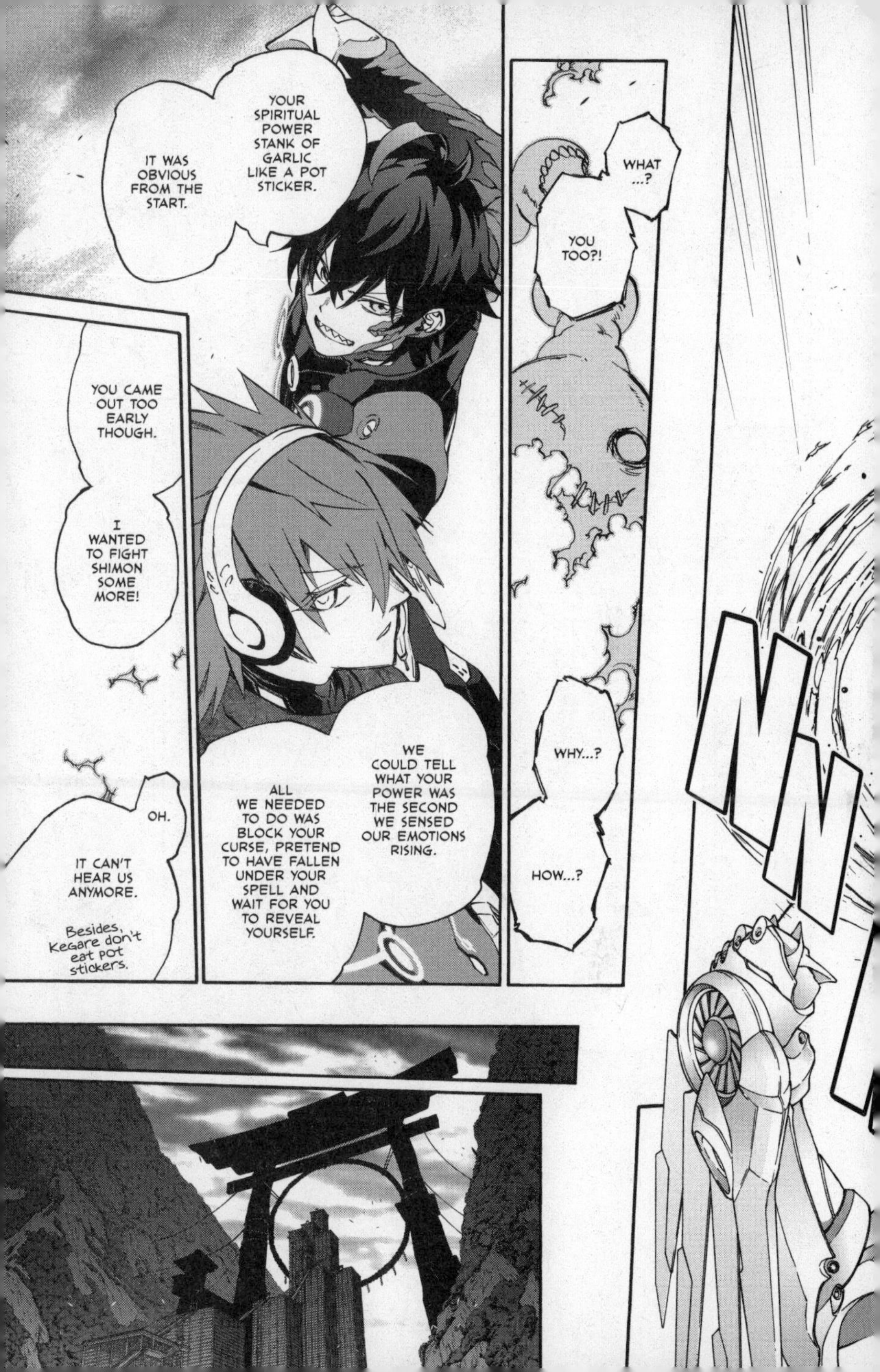
MN
WHAT ...?
YOU TOO?!
WHY...?
HOW...?
YOUR SPIRITUAL POWER STANK OF GARLIC LIKE A POT STICKER.
IT WAS OBVIOUS FROM THE START.
WE COULD TELL WHAT YOUR POWER WAS THE SECOND WE SENSED OUR EMOTIONS RISING.
ALL WE NEEDED TO DO WAS BLOCK YOUR CURSE, PRETEND TO HAVE FALLEN UNDER YOUR SPELL AND WAIT FOR YOU TO REVEAL YOURSELF.
YOU CAME OUT TOO EARLY THOUGH.
I WANTED TO FIGHT SHIMON SOME MORE!
OH.
IT CAN'T HEAR US ANYMORE.
Besides, Kegare don't eat pot stickers.

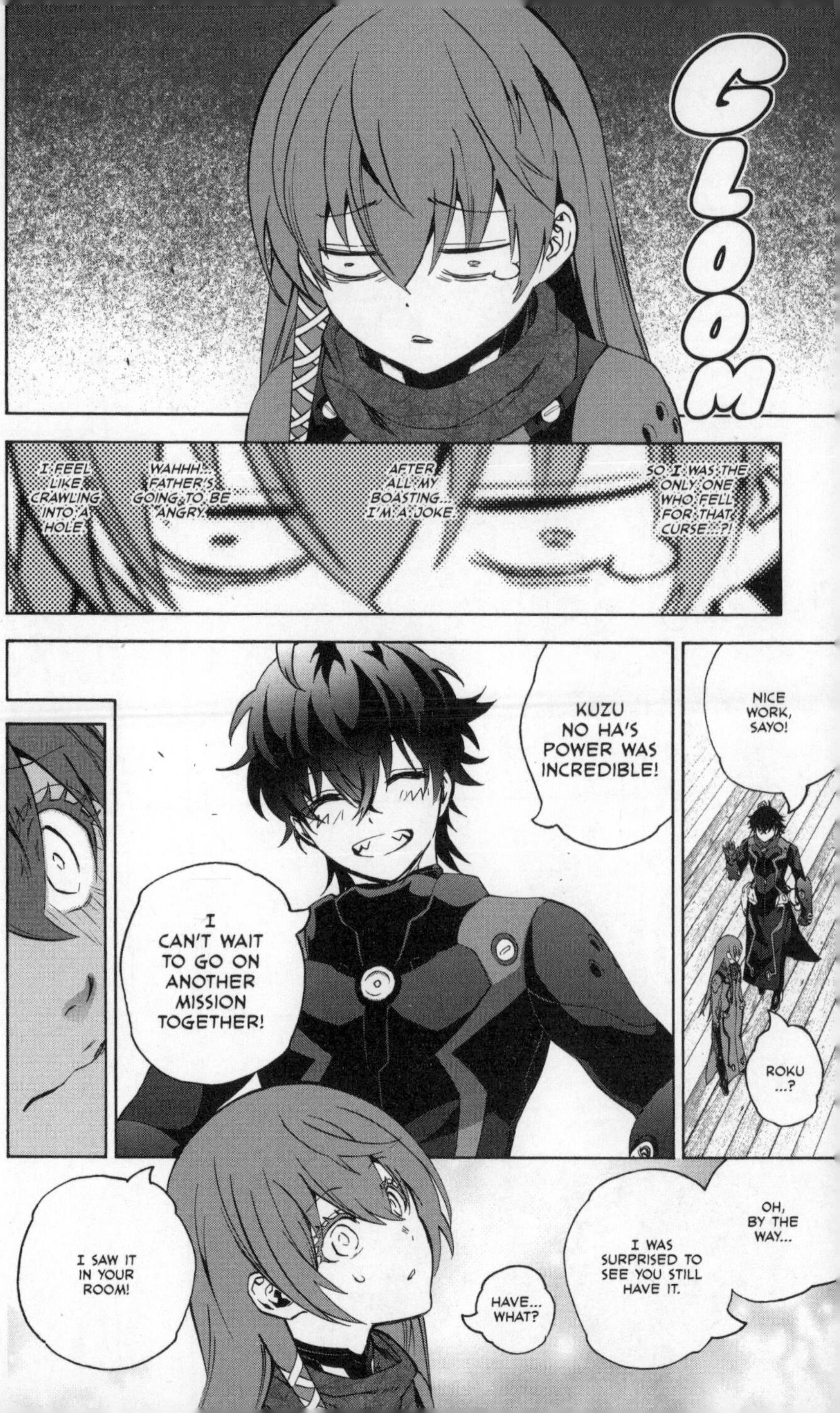
GLOOM
SO I WAS THE ONLY ONE WHO FELL FOR THAT CURSE...?!
AFTER ALL MY BOASTING... I'M A JOKE.
WAHHH... FATHER'S GOING TO BE ANGRY...
I FEEL LIKE CRAWLING INTO A HOLE.
NICE WORK, SAYO!
ROKU ...?
KUZU NO HA'S POWER WAS INCREDIBLE!
I CAN'T WAIT TO GO ON ANOTHER MISSION TOGETHER!
OH, BY THE WAY...
I WAS SURPRISED TO SEE YOU STILL HAVE IT.
HAVE... WHAT?
I SAW IT IN YOUR ROOM!

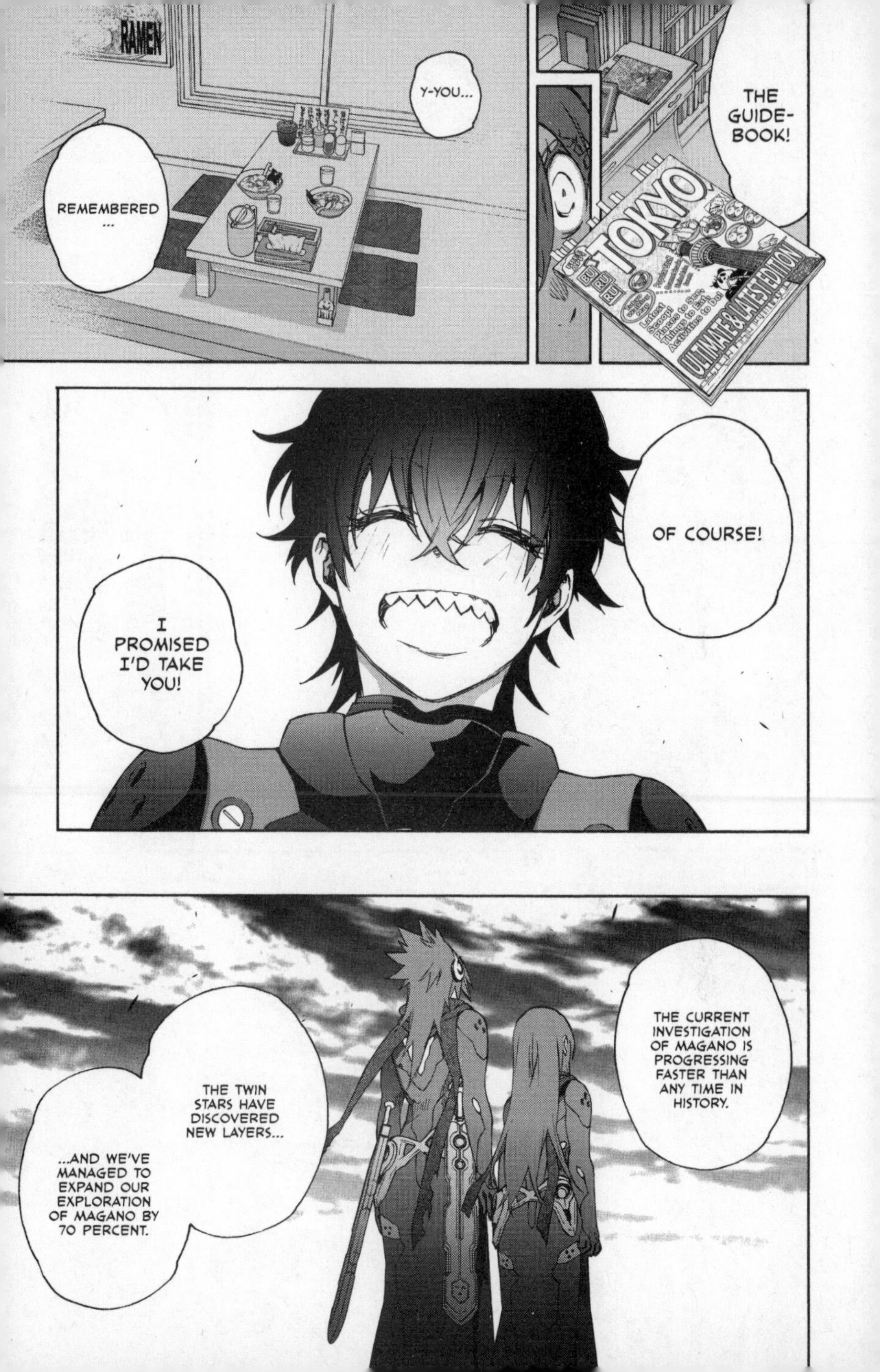
THE GUIDE-BOOK!
TOKYO
ULTIMATE & LATEST EDITION
Latest Scoop! Places to See, Things to Eat, Activities to Do!
RAMEN
Y-YOU...
REMEMBERED ...
OF COURSE!
I PROMISED I'D TAKE YOU!
THE CURRENT INVESTIGATION OF MAGANO IS PROGRESSING FASTER THAN ANY TIME IN HISTORY.
THE TWIN STARS HAVE DISCOVERED NEW LAYERS...
...AND WE'VE MANAGED TO EXPAND OUR EXPLORATION OF MAGANO BY 70 PERCENT.

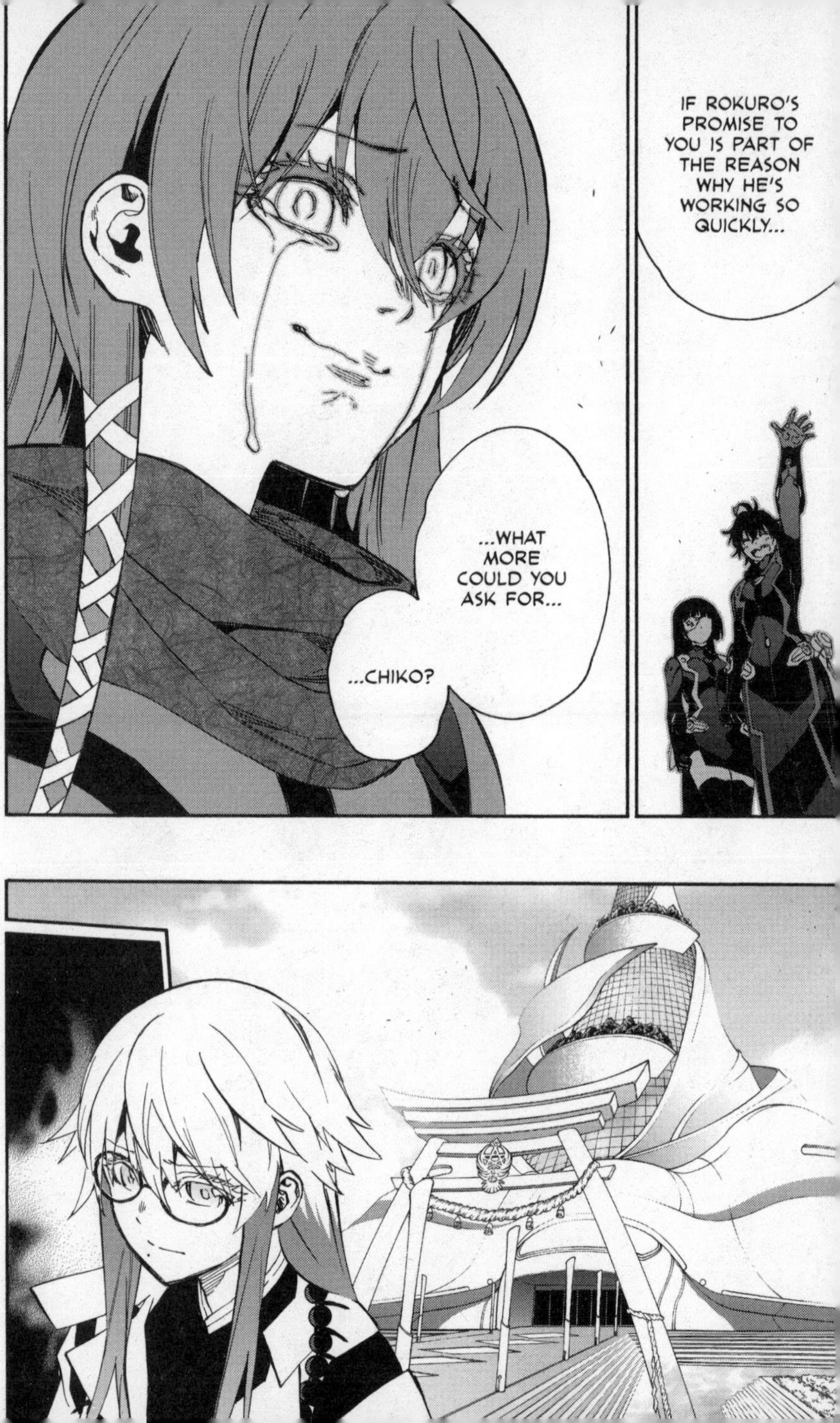
IF ROKURO'S PROMISE TO YOU IS PART OF THE REASON WHY HE'S WORKING SO QUICKLY...
...WHAT MORE COULD YOU ASK FOR...
...CHIKO?

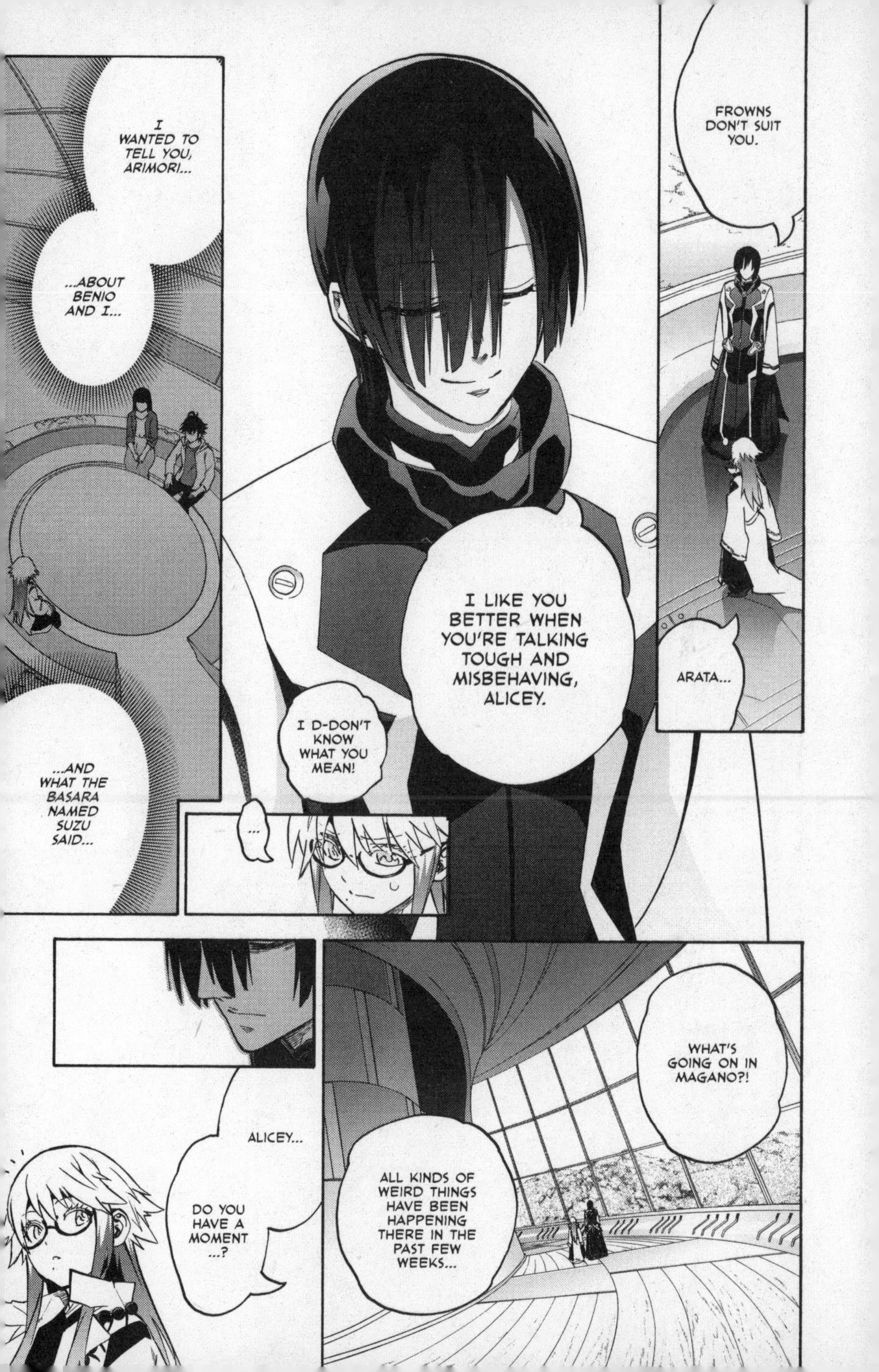

FROWNS DON'T SUIT YOU.
ARATA...
I LIKE YOU BETTER WHEN YOU'RE TALKING TOUGH AND MISBEHAVING, ALICEY.
I D-DON'T KNOW WHAT YOU MEAN!
...
I WANTED TO TELL YOU, ARIMORI...
...ABOUT BENIO AND I...
...AND WHAT THE BASARA NAMED SUZU SAID...
WHAT'S GOING ON IN MAGANO?!
ALL KINDS OF WEIRD THINGS HAVE BEEN HAPPENING THERE IN THE PAST FEW WEEKS...
ALICEY...
DO YOU HAVE A MOMENT ...?

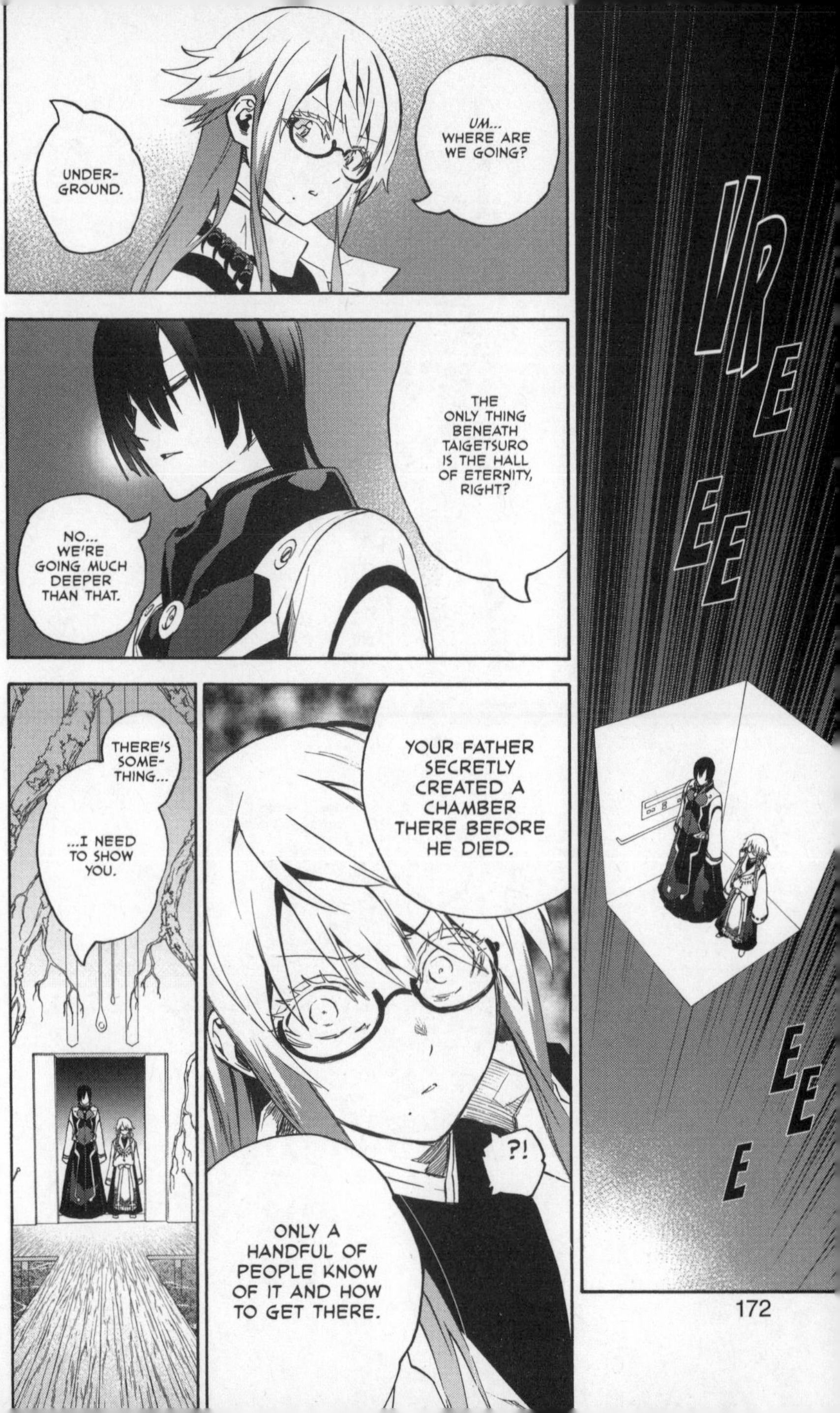
VREEE
EEEE
UM... WHERE ARE WE GOING?
UNDER-GROUND.
THE ONLY THING BENEATH TAIGETSURO IS THE HALL OF ETERNITY, RIGHT?
NO... WE'RE GOING MUCH DEEPER THAN THAT.
YOUR FATHER SECRETLY CREATED A CHAMBER THERE BEFORE HE DIED.
?!
ONLY A HANDFUL OF PEOPLE KNOW OF IT AND HOW TO GET THERE.
THERE'S SOME-THING...
...I NEED TO SHOW YOU.

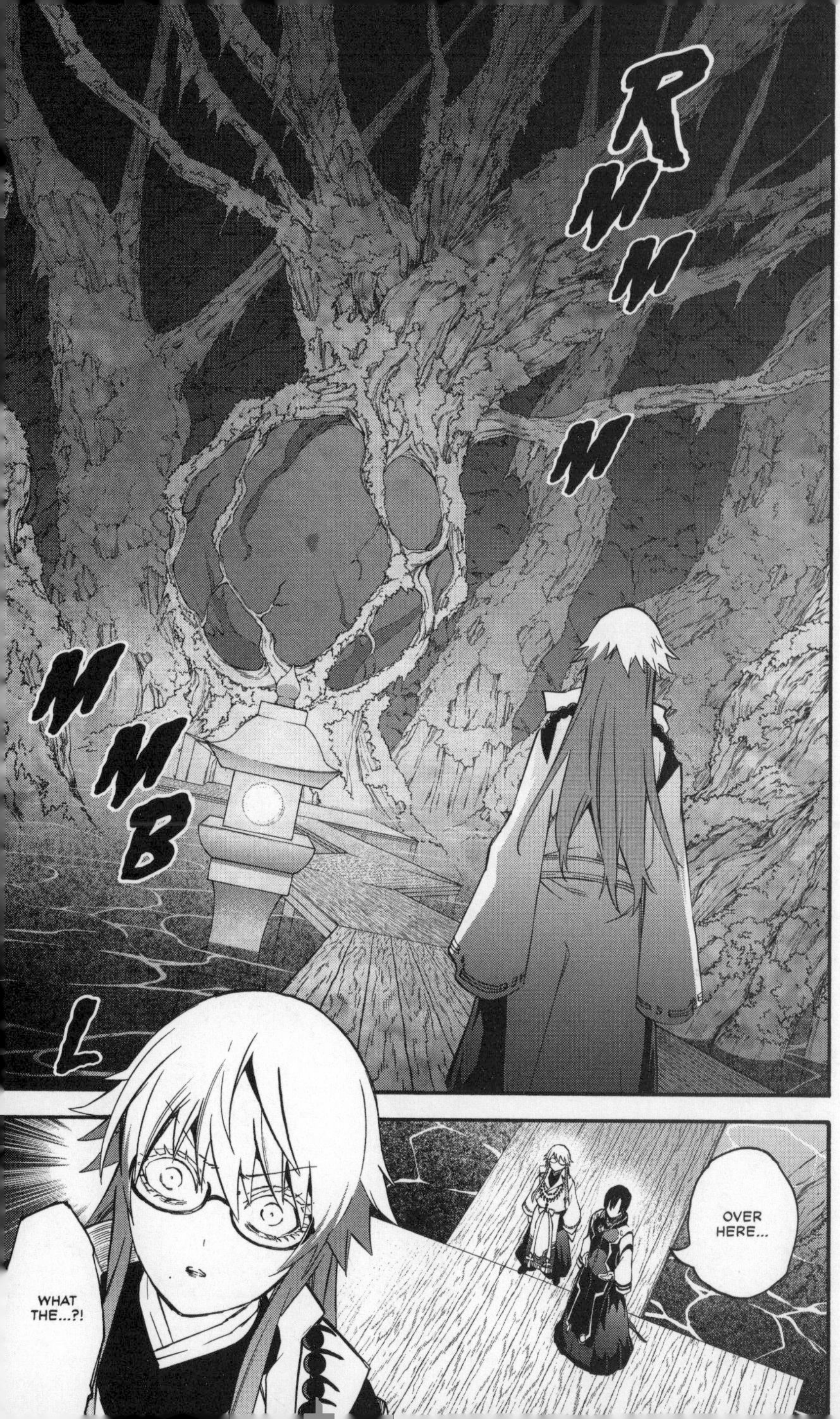
RMMMMMBL
OVER HERE...
WHAT THE...?!

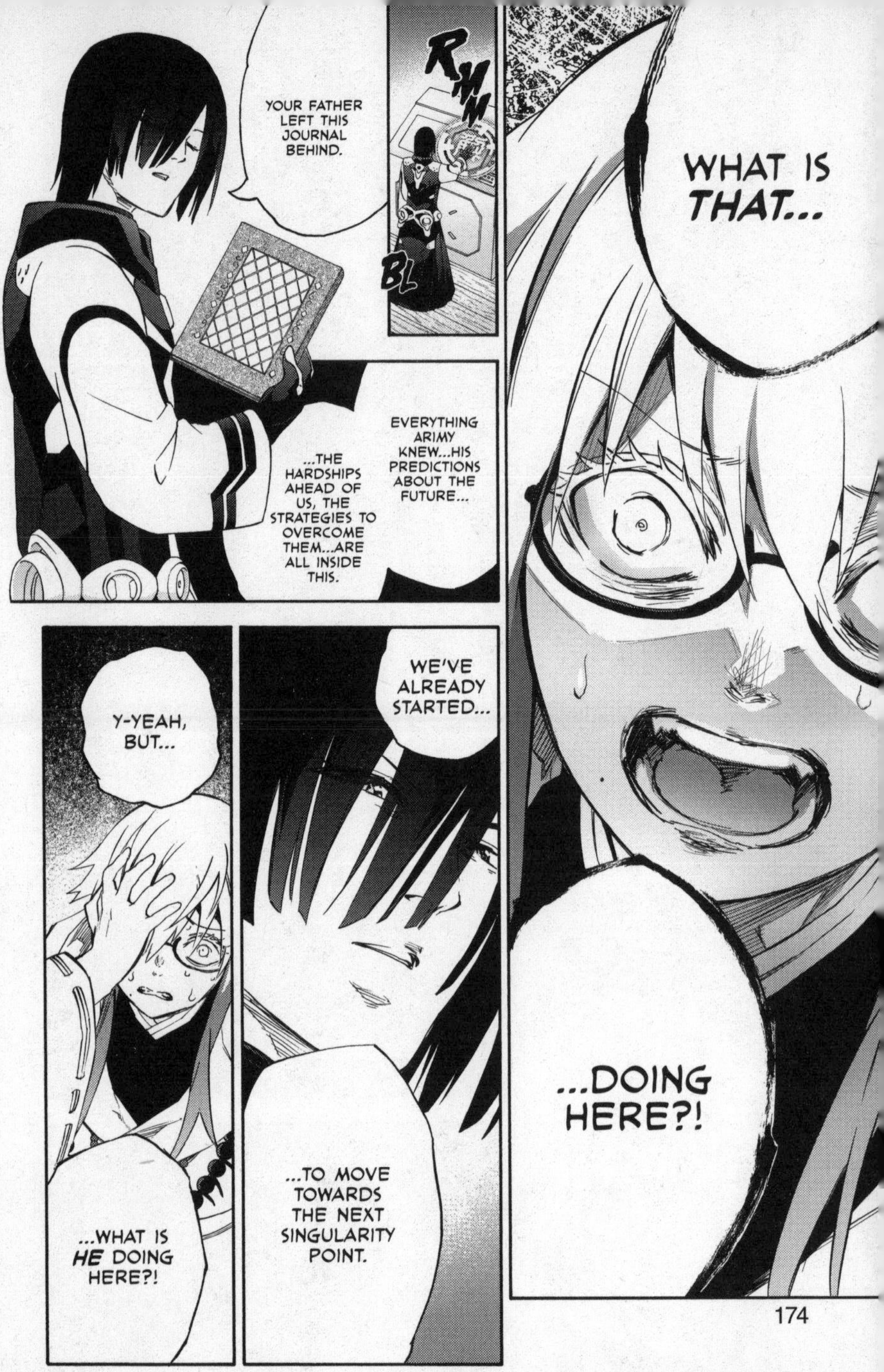
WHAT IS THAT...
...DOING HERE?!
RMM
BL
YOUR FATHER LEFT THIS JOURNAL BEHIND.
EVERYTHING ARIMY KNEW...HIS PREDICTIONS ABOUT THE FUTURE...
...THE HARDSHIPS AHEAD OF US, THE STRATEGIES TO OVERCOME THEM...ARE ALL INSIDE THIS.
WE'VE ALREADY STARTED...
...TO MOVE TOWARDS THE NEXT SINGULARITY POINT.
Y-YEAH, BUT...
...WHAT IS HE DOING HERE?!

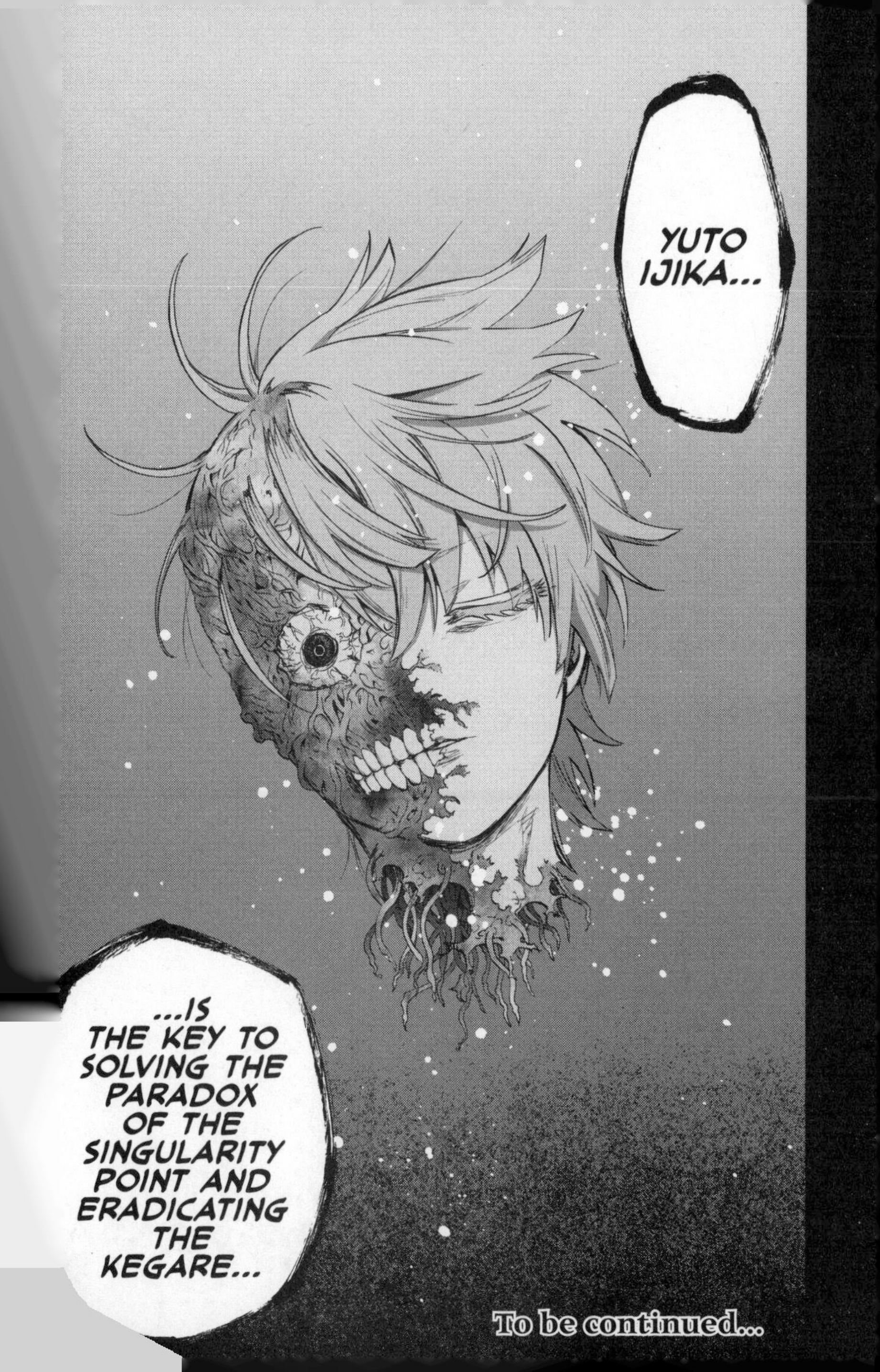
YUTO IJIKA...
...IS THE KEY TO SOLVING THE PARADOX OF THE SINGULARITY POINT AND ERADICATING THE KEGARE...
To be continued...

Twin Star Exorcists

ONMYOJI

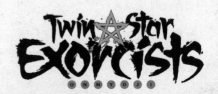

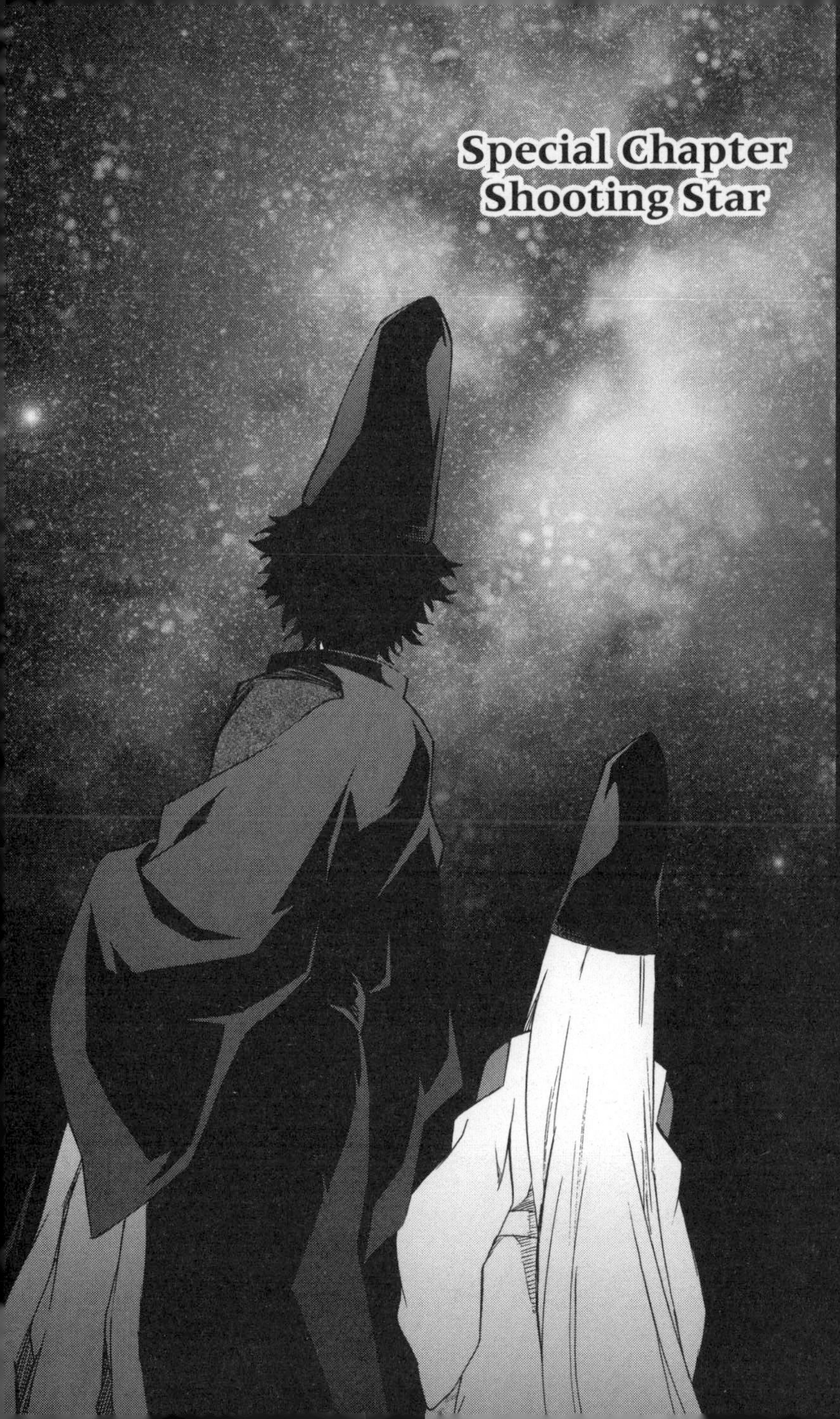
Special Chapter
Shooting Star

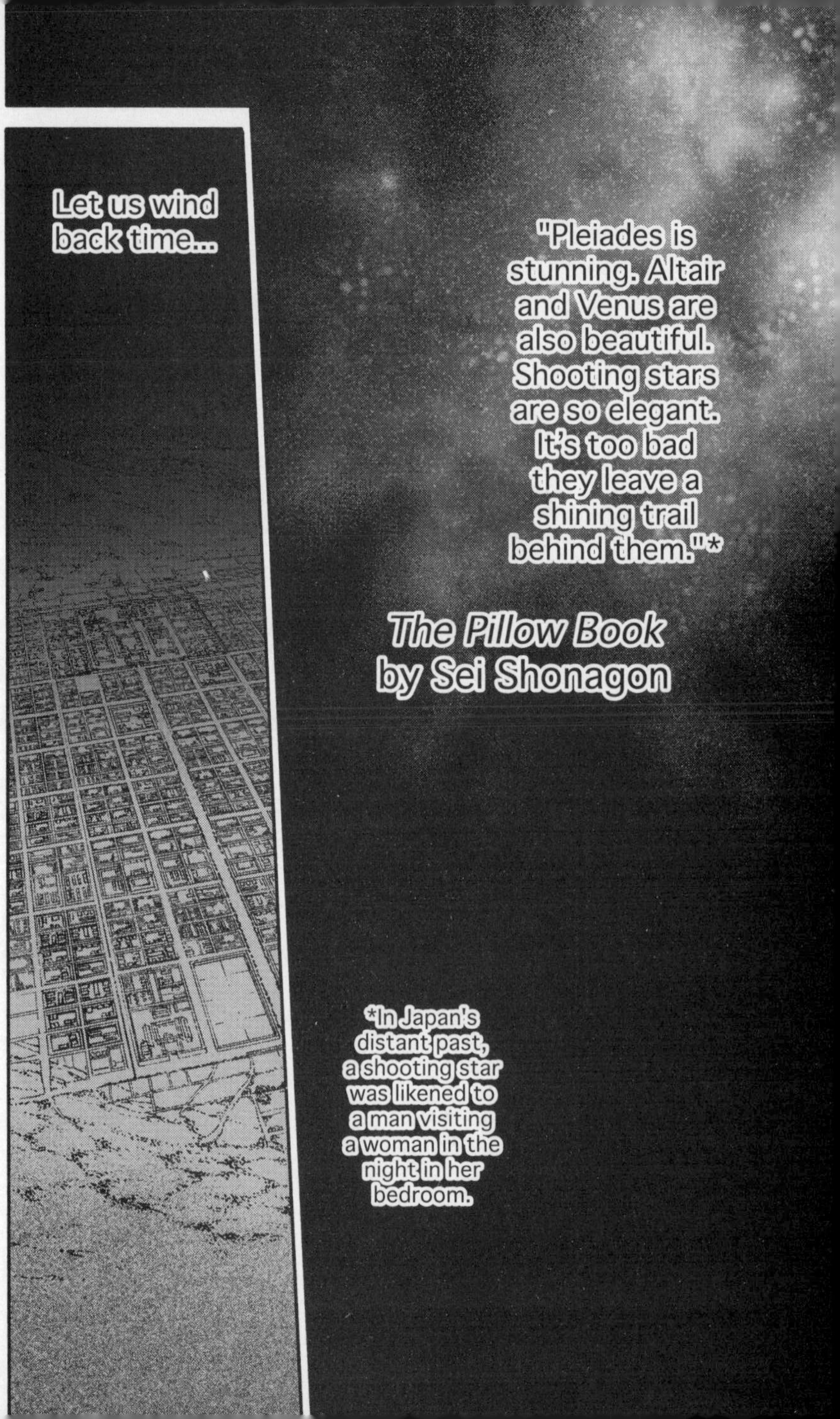
"Pleiades is stunning. Altair and Venus are also beautiful. Shooting stars are so elegant. It's too bad they leave a shining trail behind them."*
The Pillow Book
by Sei Shonagon
*In Japan's distant past, a shooting star was likened to a man visiting a woman in the night in her bedroom.
Let us wind back time...

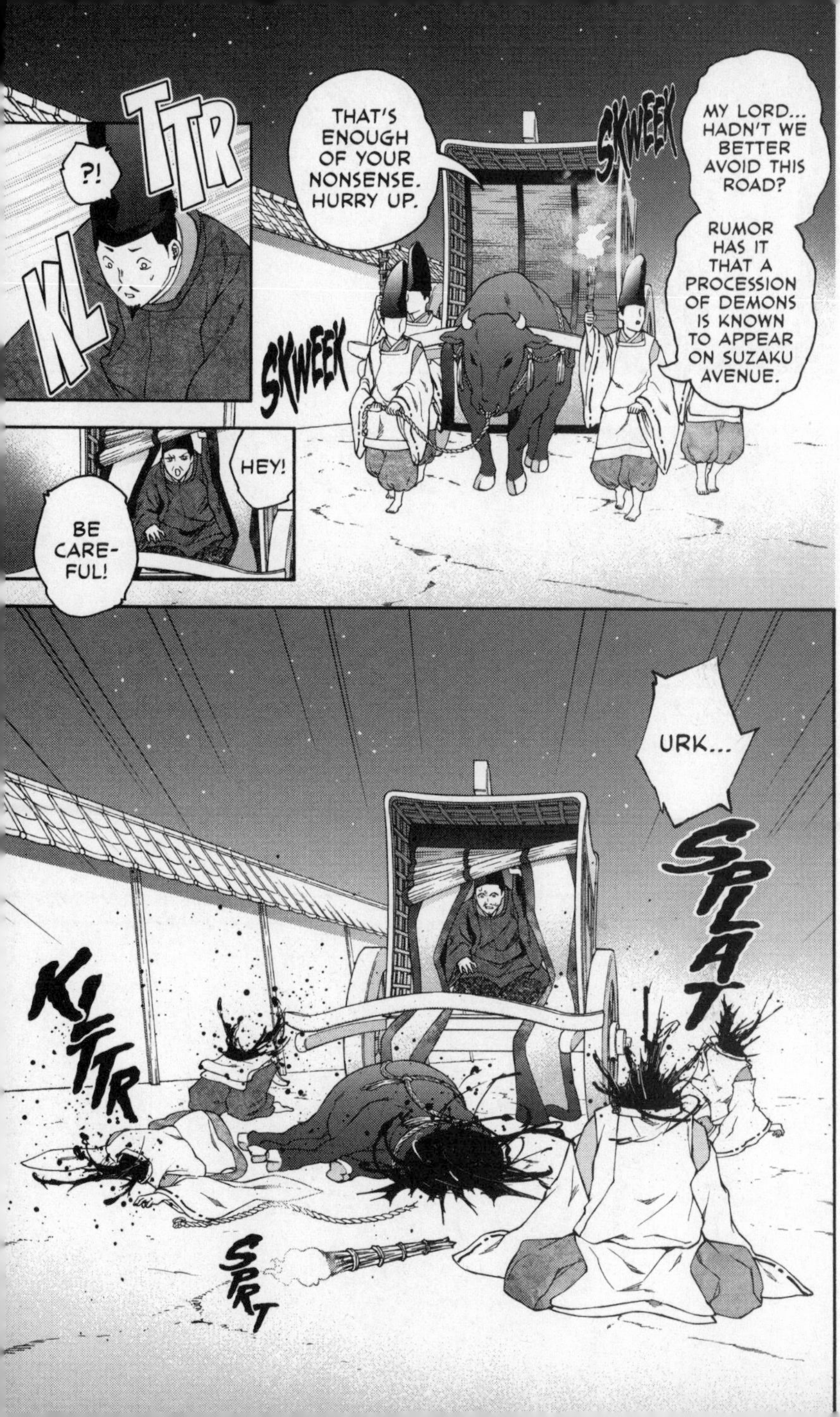
MY LORD... HADN'T WE BETTER AVOID THIS ROAD?
RUMOR HAS IT THAT A PROCESSION OF DEMONS IS KNOWN TO APPEAR ON SUZAKU AVENUE.
SKWEEK
THAT'S ENOUGH OF YOUR NONSENSE. HURRY UP.
SKWEEK
TTR
?!
KL
HEY!
BE CARE-FUL!
URK...
SPLAT
KITTR
SPRT

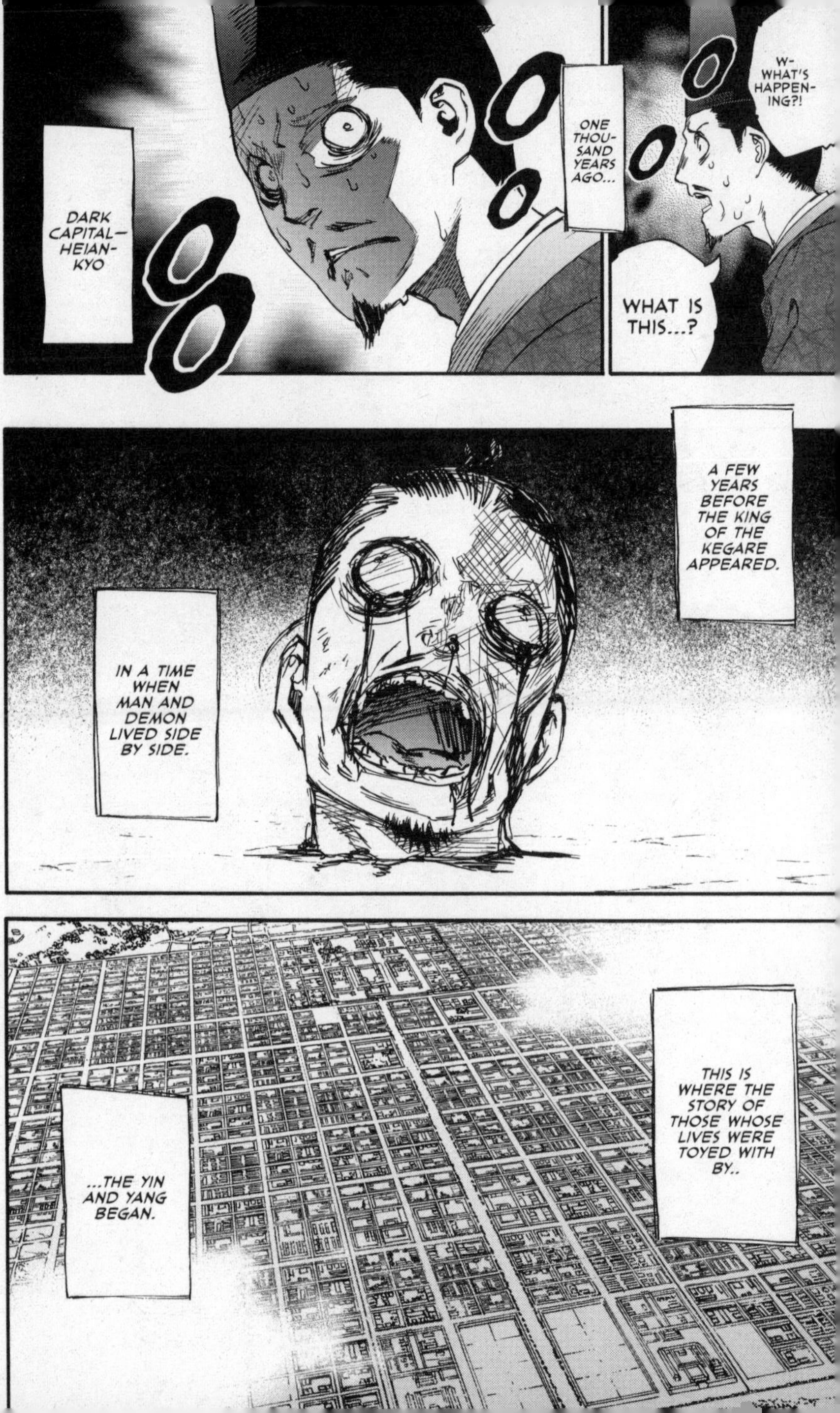
W-WHAT'S HAPPENING?!
WHAT IS THIS...?
ONE THOUSAND YEARS AGO...
DARK CAPITAL—HEIAN-KYO
A FEW YEARS BEFORE THE KING OF THE KEGARE APPEARED.
IN A TIME WHEN MAN AND DEMON LIVED SIDE BY SIDE.
THIS IS WHERE THE STORY OF THOSE WHOSE LIVES WERE TOYED WITH BY..
...THE YIN AND YANG BEGAN.

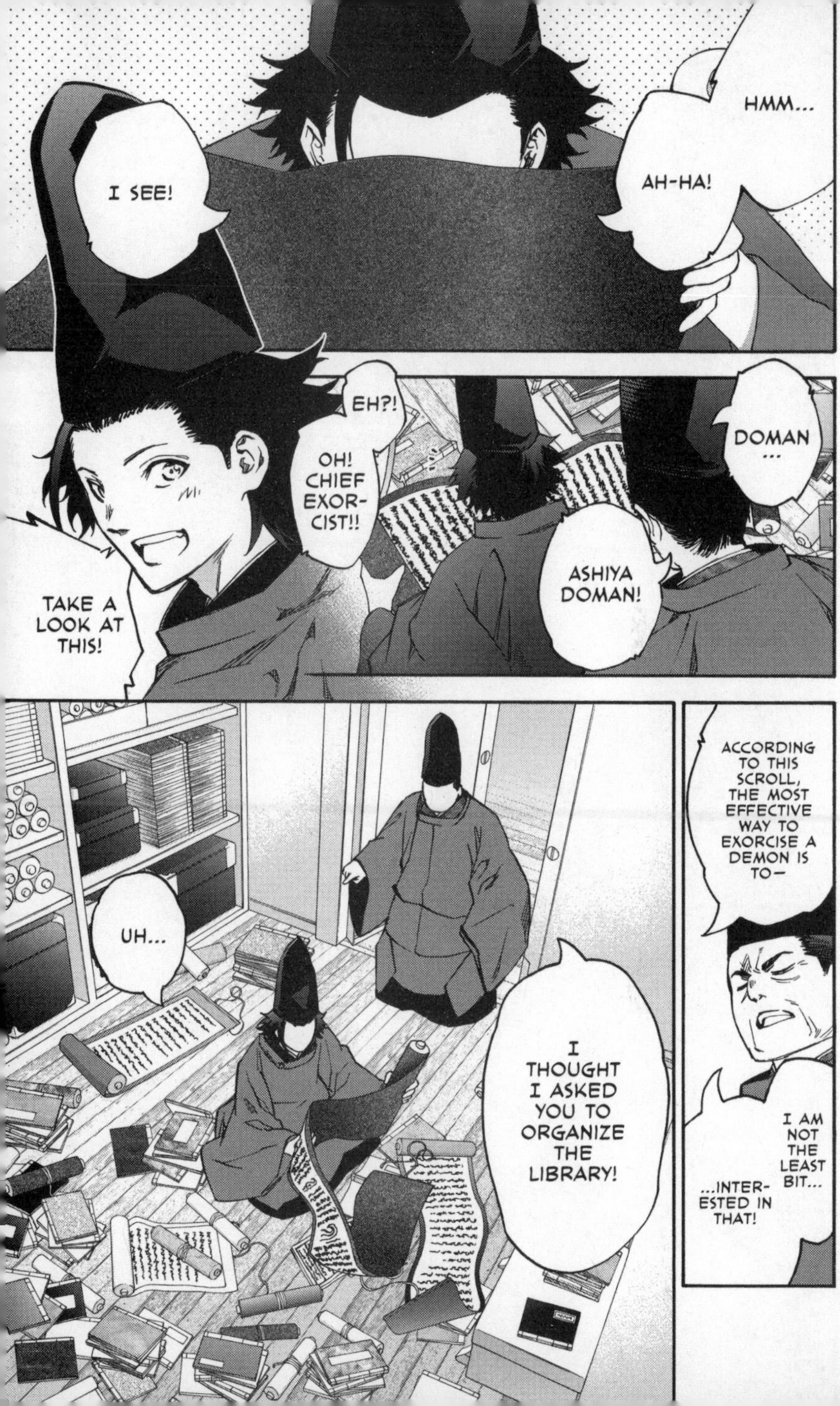
HMM...
AH-HA!
I SEE!
DOMAN...
ASHIYA DOMAN!
EH?!
OH! CHIEF EXORCIST!!
TAKE A LOOK AT THIS!
ACCORDING TO THIS SCROLL, THE MOST EFFECTIVE WAY TO EXORCISE A DEMON IS TO—
I AM NOT THE LEAST BIT...
...INTERESTED IN THAT!
I THOUGHT I ASKED YOU TO ORGANIZE THE LIBRARY!
UH...

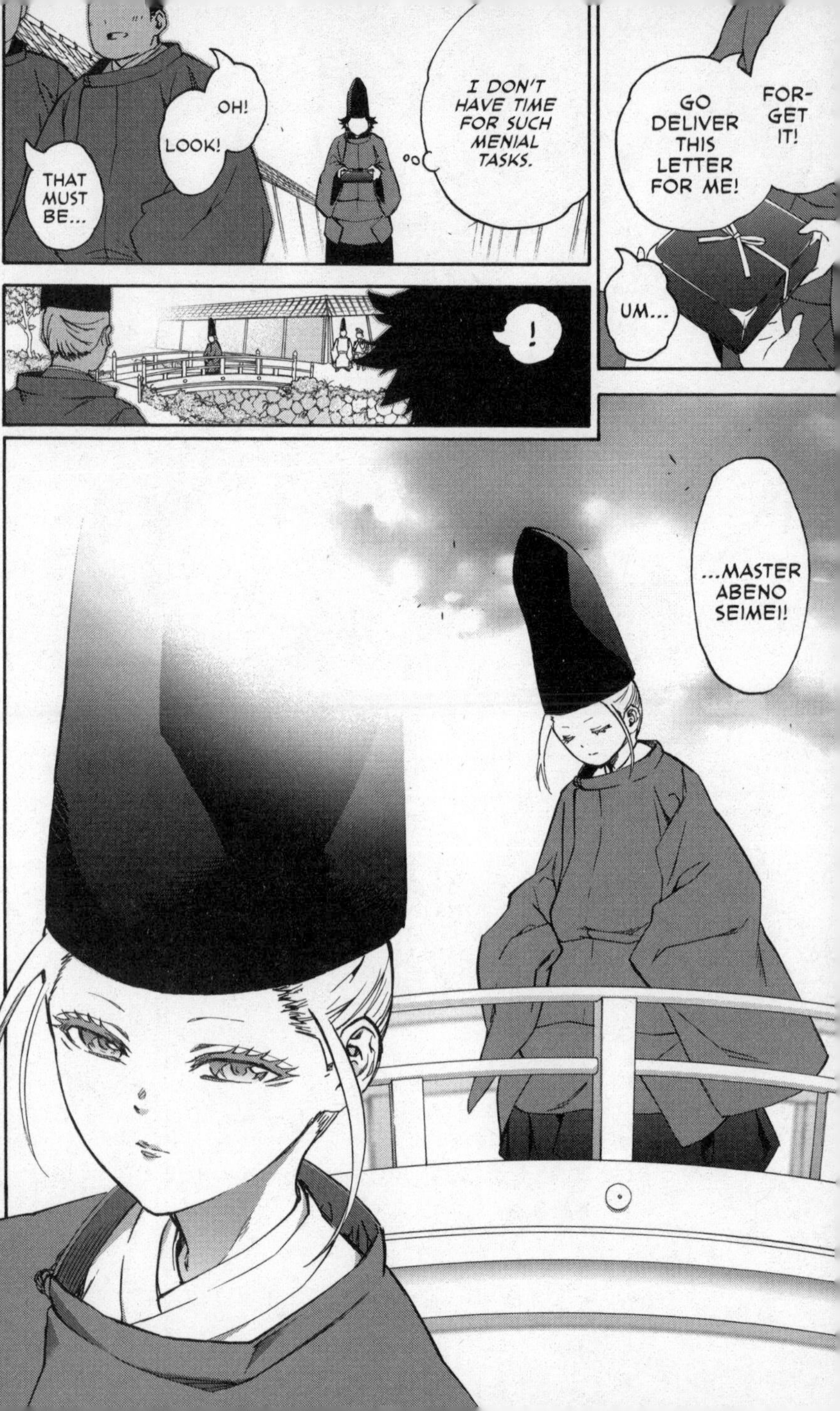
FOR-GET IT!
GO DELIVER THIS LETTER FOR ME!
UM...
I DON'T HAVE TIME FOR SUCH MENIAL TASKS.
OH!
LOOK!
THAT MUST BE...
!
...MASTER ABENO SEIMEI!

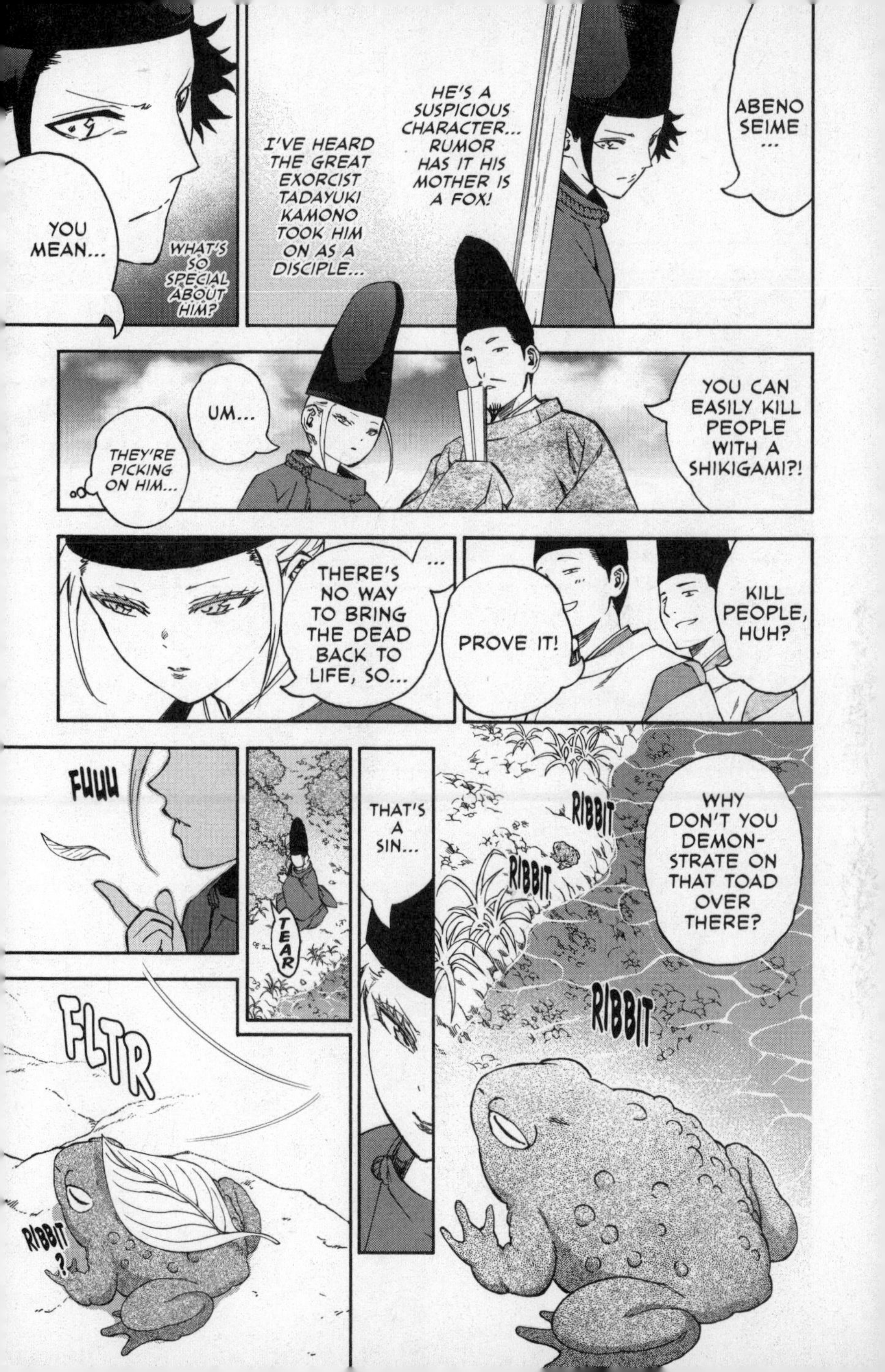
ABENO SEIME ...
HE'S A SUSPICIOUS CHARACTER... RUMOR HAS IT HIS MOTHER IS A FOX!
I'VE HEARD THE GREAT EXORCIST TADAYUKI KAMONO TOOK HIM ON AS A DISCIPLE...
WHAT'S SO SPECIAL ABOUT HIM?
YOU MEAN...
YOU CAN EASILY KILL PEOPLE WITH A SHIKIGAMI?!
UM...
THEY'RE PICKING ON HIM...
KILL PEOPLE, HUH?
PROVE IT!
...
THERE'S NO WAY TO BRING THE DEAD BACK TO LIFE, SO...
WHY DON'T YOU DEMON-STRATE ON THAT TOAD OVER THERE?
RIBBIT
RIBBIT
RIBBIT
THAT'S A SIN...
TEAR
FUUU
FLTR
RIBBIT ?

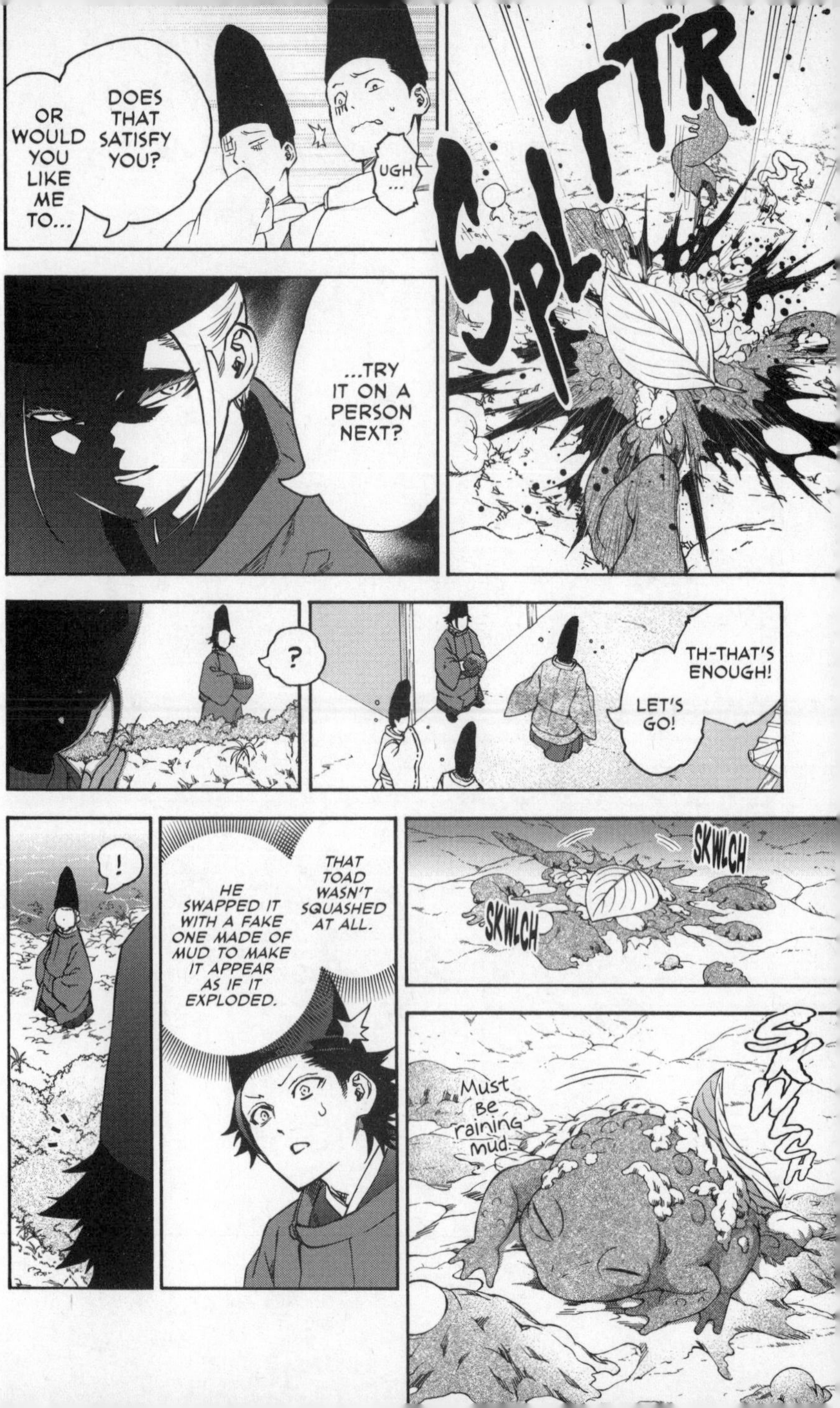
SPLTTR
DOES THAT SATISFY YOU?
OR WOULD YOU LIKE ME TO...
UGH...
...TRY IT ON A PERSON NEXT?
TH-THAT'S ENOUGH!
LET'S GO!
?
SKWLCH
SKWLCH
SKWLCH
Must be raining mud.
THAT TOAD WASN'T SQUASHED AT ALL.
HE SWAPPED IT WITH A FAKE ONE MADE OF MUD TO MAKE IT APPEAR AS IF IT EXPLODED.
!

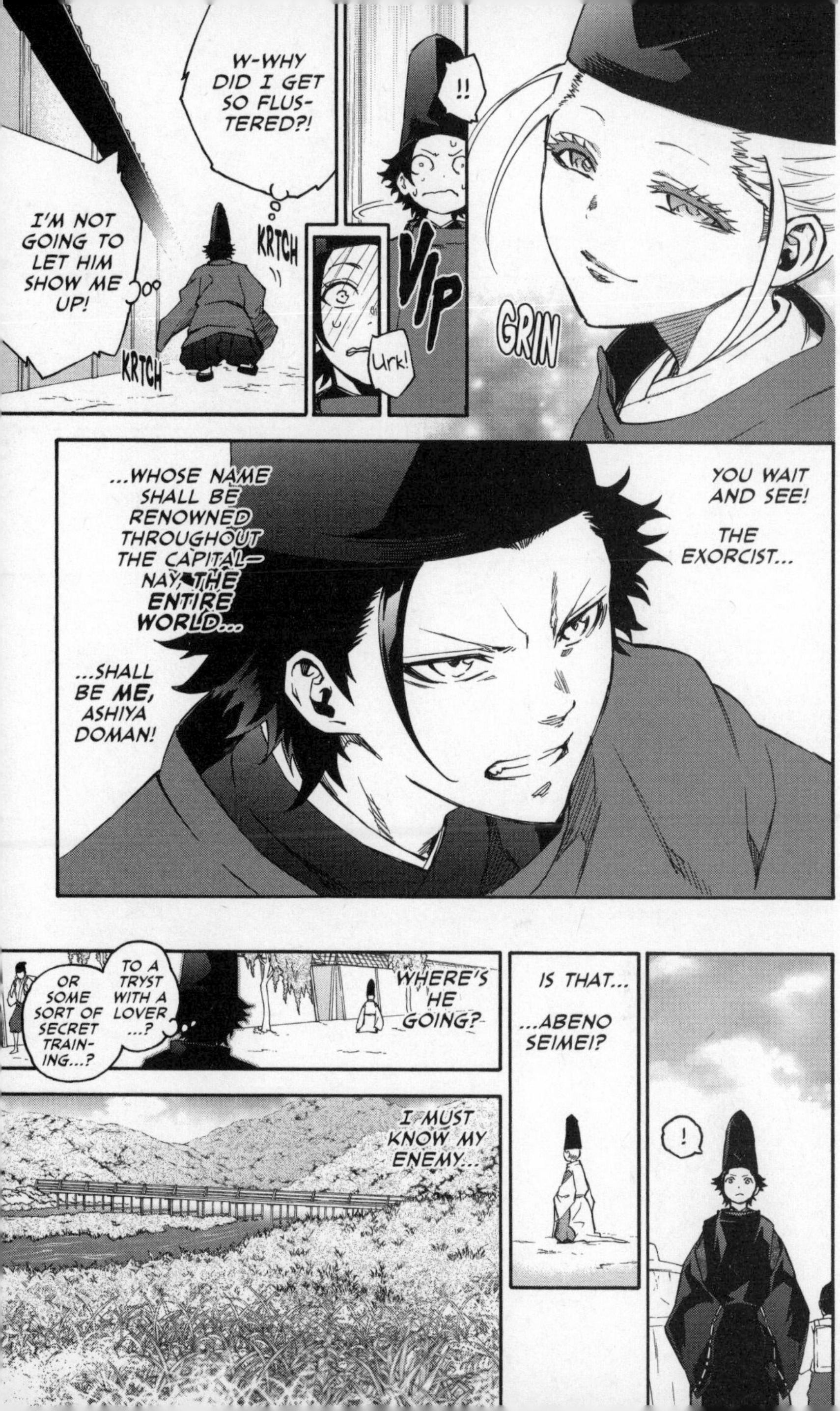
GRIN
!!
VIP
Urk!
W-WHY DID I GET SO FLUS-TERED?!
I'M NOT GOING TO LET HIM SHOW ME UP!
KRTCH
KRTCH
YOU WAIT AND SEE!
THE EXORCIST...
...WHOSE NAME SHALL BE RENOWNED THROUGHOUT THE CAPITAL—NAY, THE ENTIRE WORLD...
...SHALL BE ME, ASHIYA DOMAN!
!
IS THAT...
...ABENO SEIMEI?
WHERE'S HE GOING?
TO A TRYST WITH A LOVER...?
OR SOME SORT OF SECRET TRAIN-ING...?
I MUST KNOW MY ENEMY...

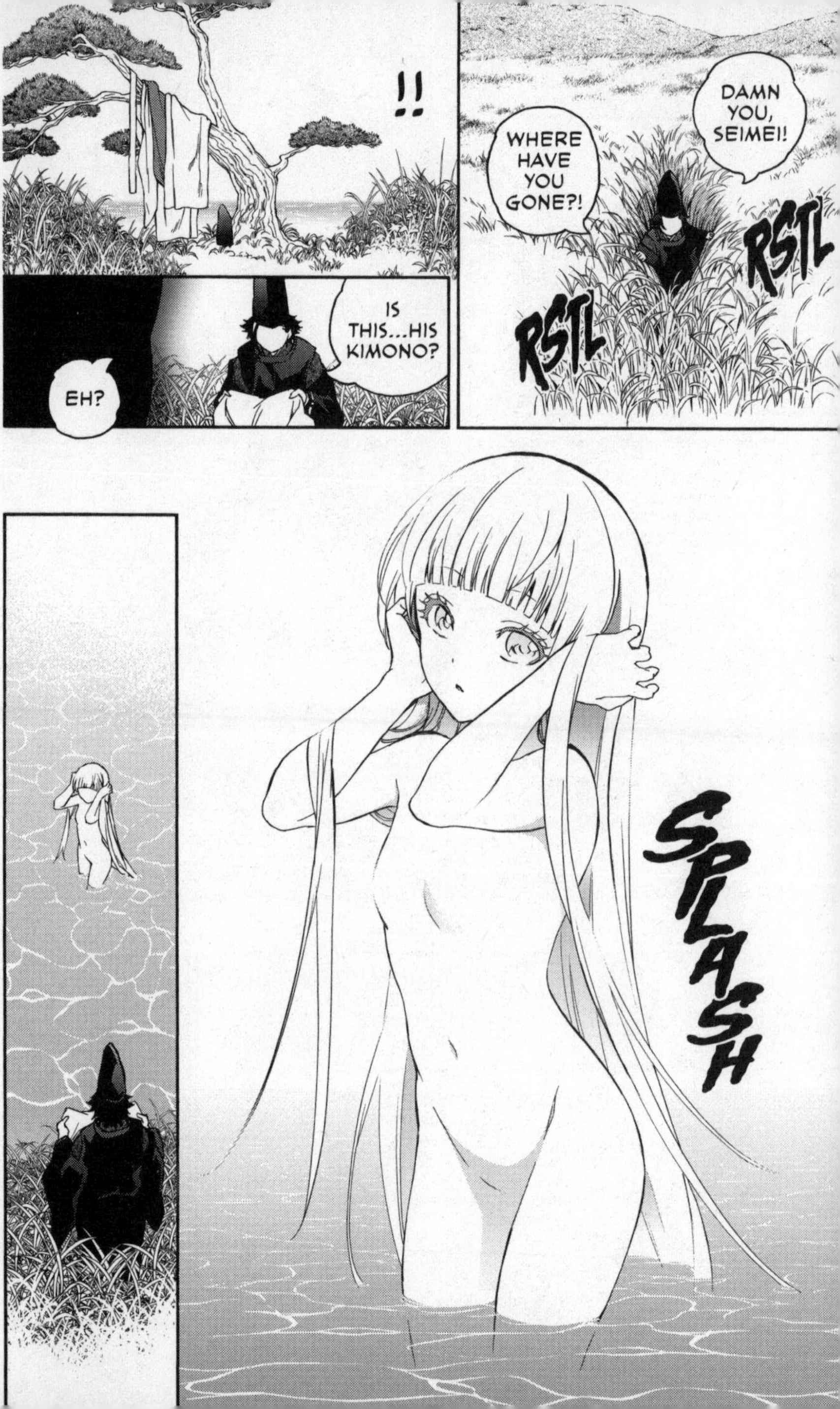
DAMN YOU, SEIMEI!
WHERE HAVE YOU GONE?!
RSTL
RSTL
!!
IS THIS...HIS KIMONO?
EH?
SPLASH

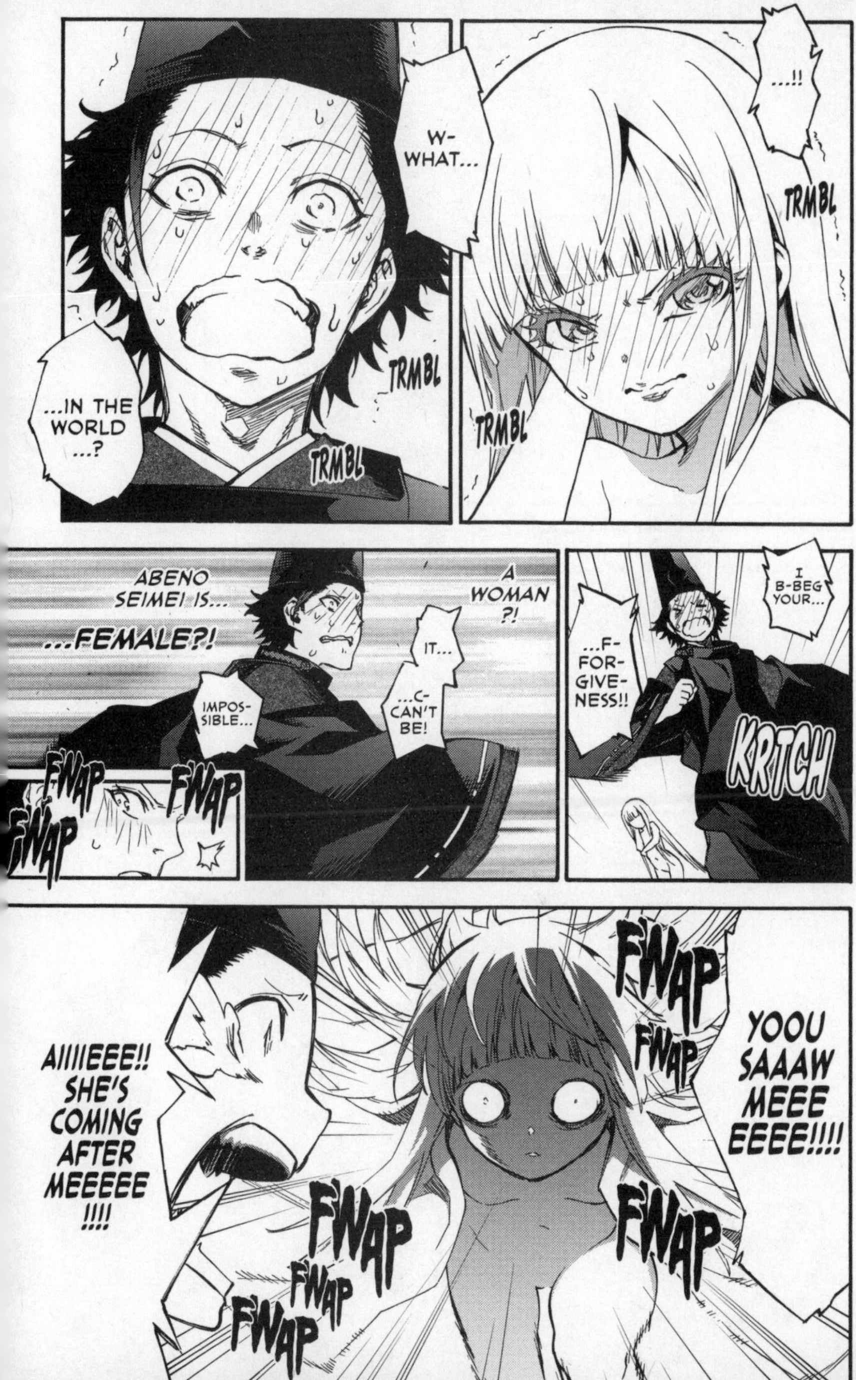
...!!
TRMBL
TRMBL
W-WHAT...
...IN THE WORLD ...?
TRMBL
TRMBL
I B-BEG YOUR...
...F-FORGIVENESS!!
KRTCH
A WOMAN ?!
IT...
...C-CAN'T BE!
ABENO SEIMEI IS...
...FEMALE?!
IMPOSSIBLE...
FWAP
FWAP
FWAP
FWAP
FWAP
YOOU SAAAW MEEE EEEE!!!!
AIIIIEEE!! SHE'S COMING AFTER MEEEEEE !!!!
FWAP
FWAP
FWAP
FWAP
FWAP

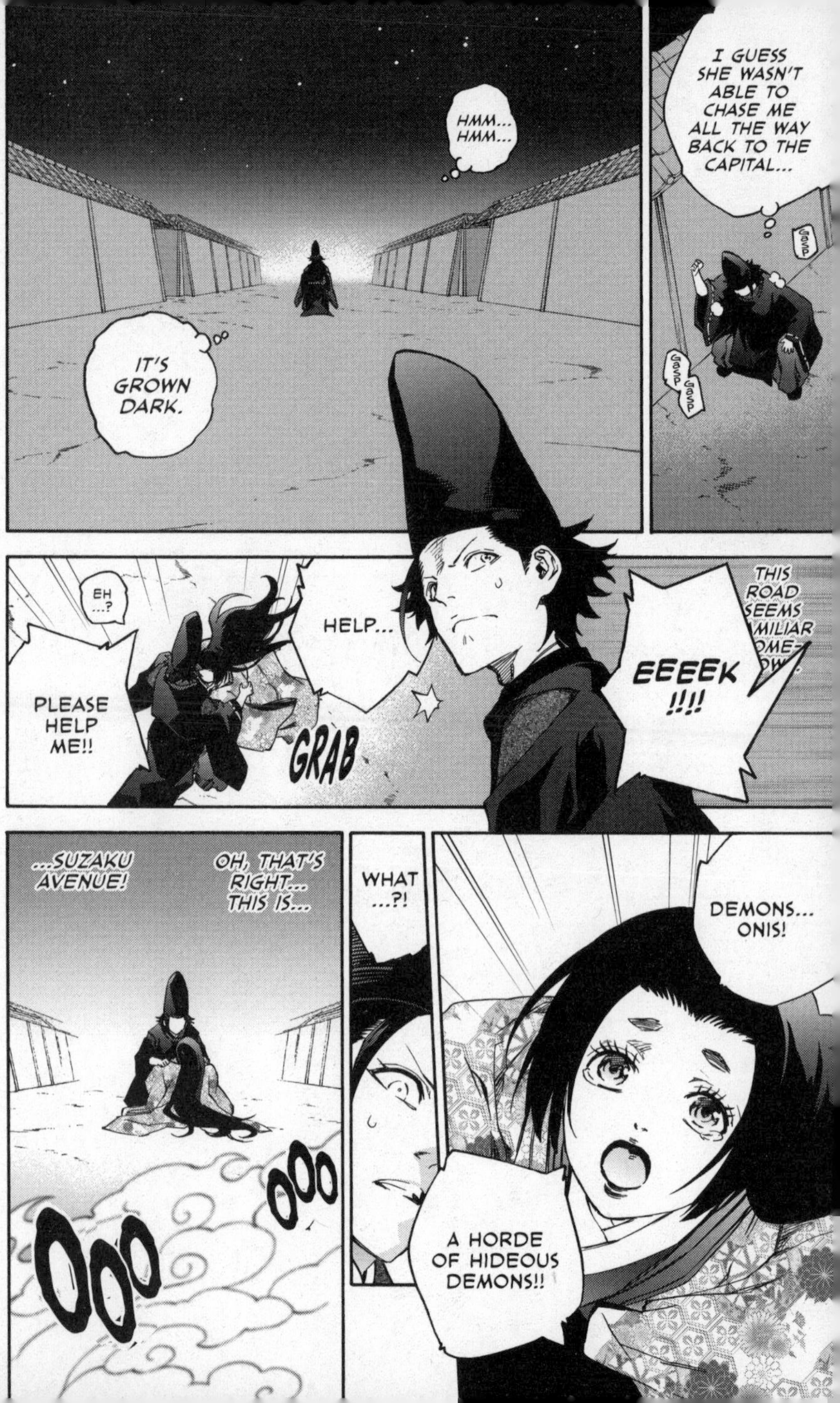

I GUESS SHE WASN'T ABLE TO CHASE ME ALL THE WAY BACK TO THE CAPITAL...
GASP
GASP GASP
HMM... HMM...
IT'S GROWN DARK.
THIS ROAD SEEMS
EEEEK!!!!
HELP...
EH...?
PLEASE HELP ME!!
GRAB
DEMONS... ONIS!
WHAT...?!
A HORDE OF HIDEOUS DEMONS!!
OH, THAT'S RIGHT... THIS IS...
...SUZAKU AVENUE!
OOO
OOO

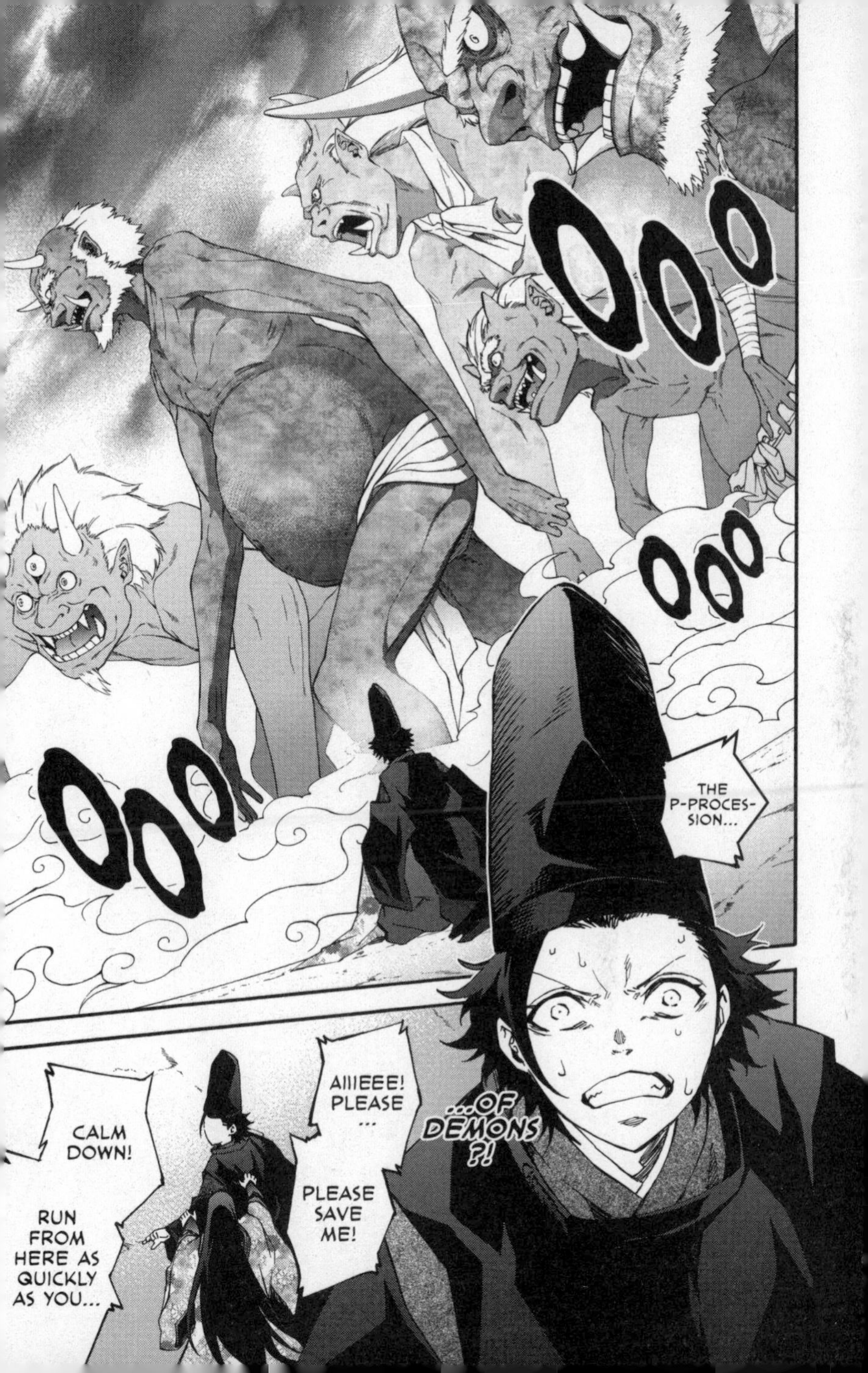
OOO
OOO
OOOO
THE P-PROCES-SION...
...OF DEMONS?!
AIIIEEE! PLEASE ...
PLEASE SAVE ME!
CALM DOWN!
RUN FROM HERE AS QUICKLY AS YOU...

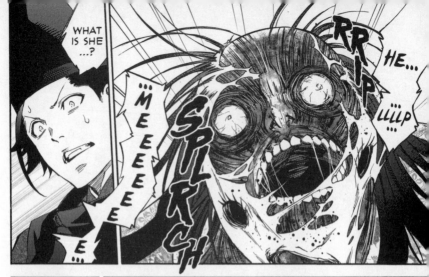

WHAT IS SHE ...?

R-RIP

HE... LLLP...

MEEEEEEE...

SPLRCH

N-NO...

AHHH...

AIIIEEE!

HEE HEE HEE HEE HEE HEE !

HEE HEE HEE HEE HI

HEE HEE HEE HEE HEE HEE!

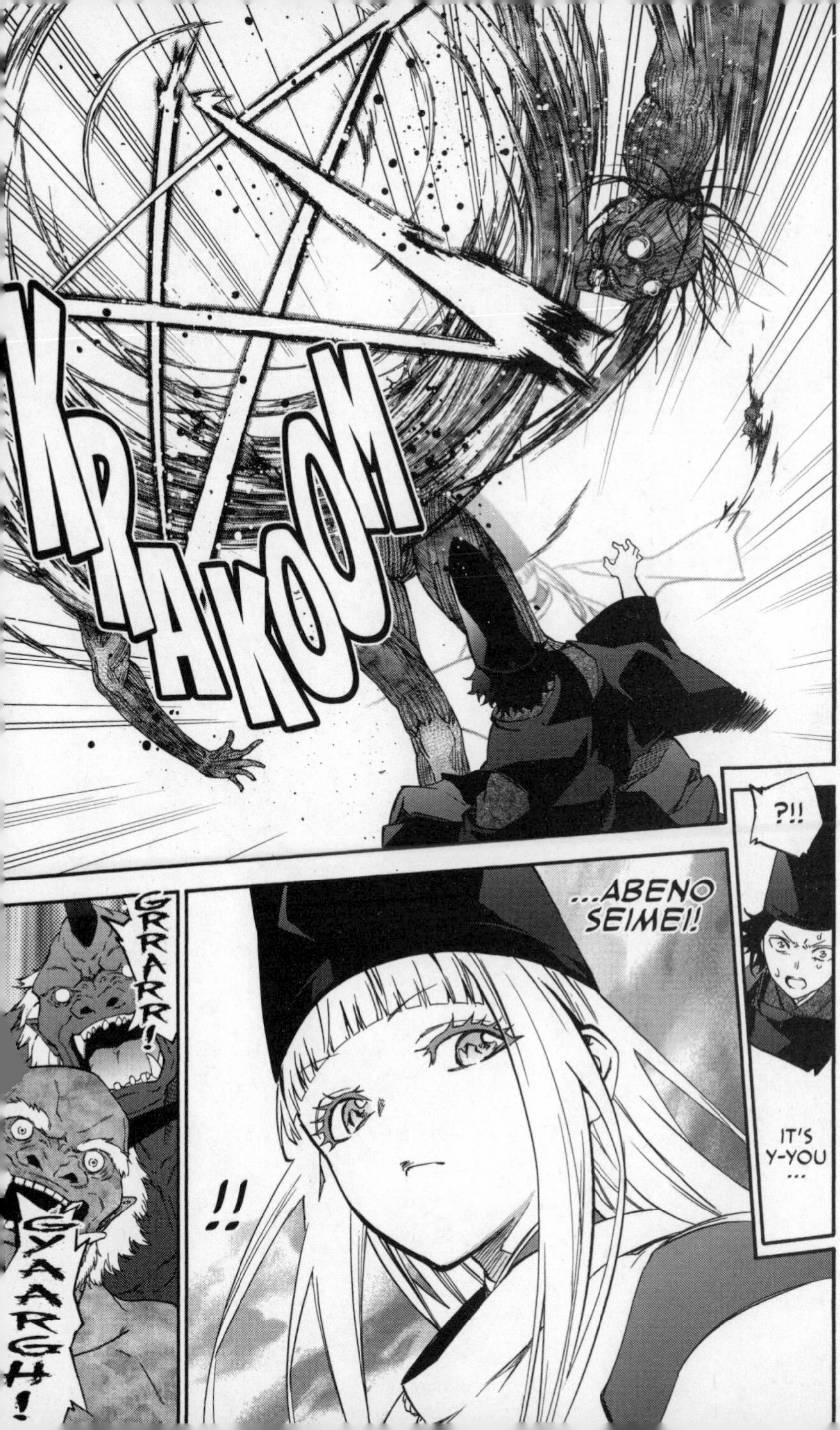
KRAKOOM
?!!
IT'S Y-YOU ...
...ABENO SEIMEI!
!!
GRRRARR!
GYAAARGH!

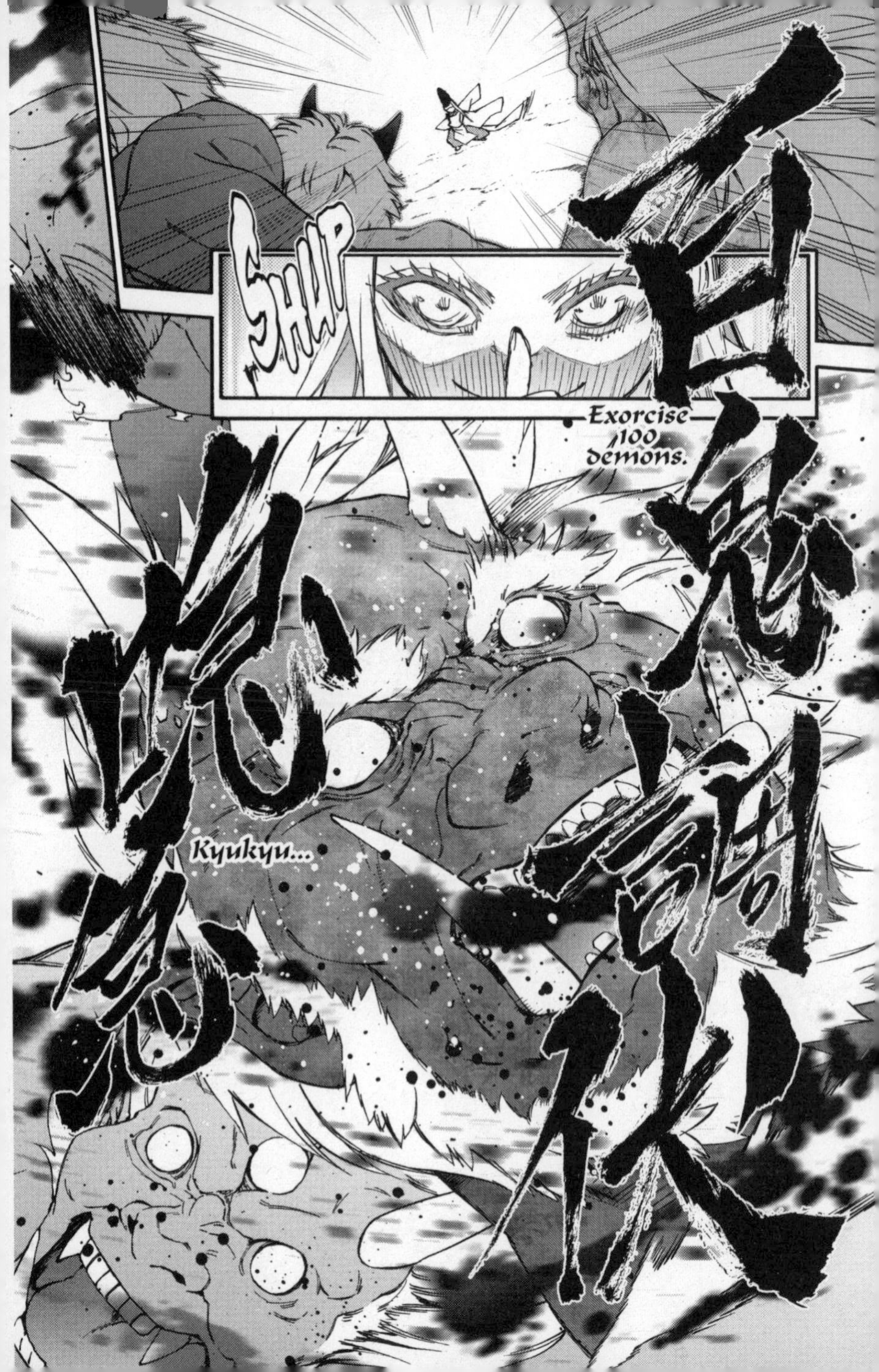
SHUP
Exorcise 100 demons.
Kyukyu...

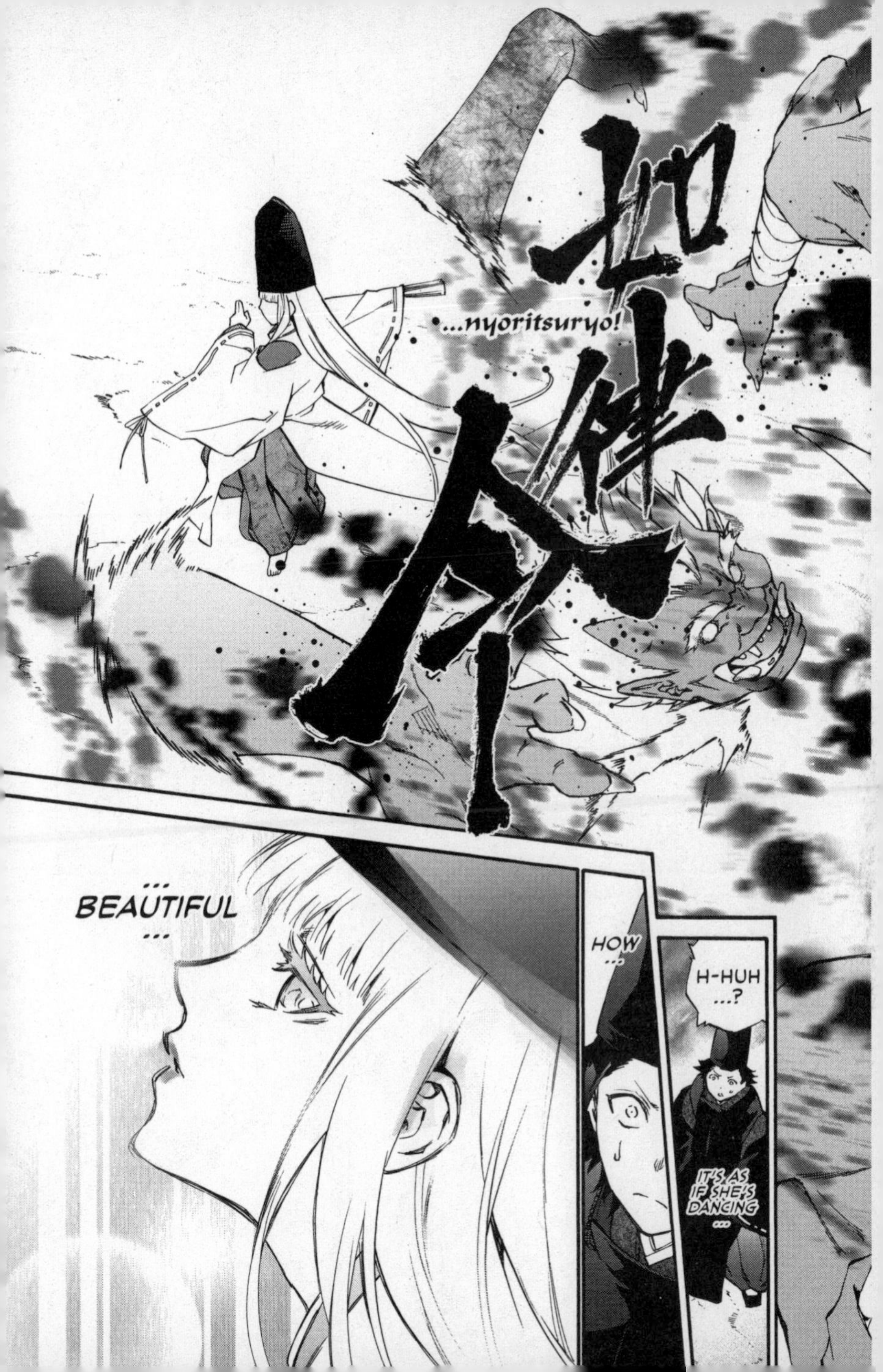
...nyoritsuryo!
H-HUH ...?
IT'S AS IF SHE'S DANCING ...
HOW ...
... BEAUTIFUL ...

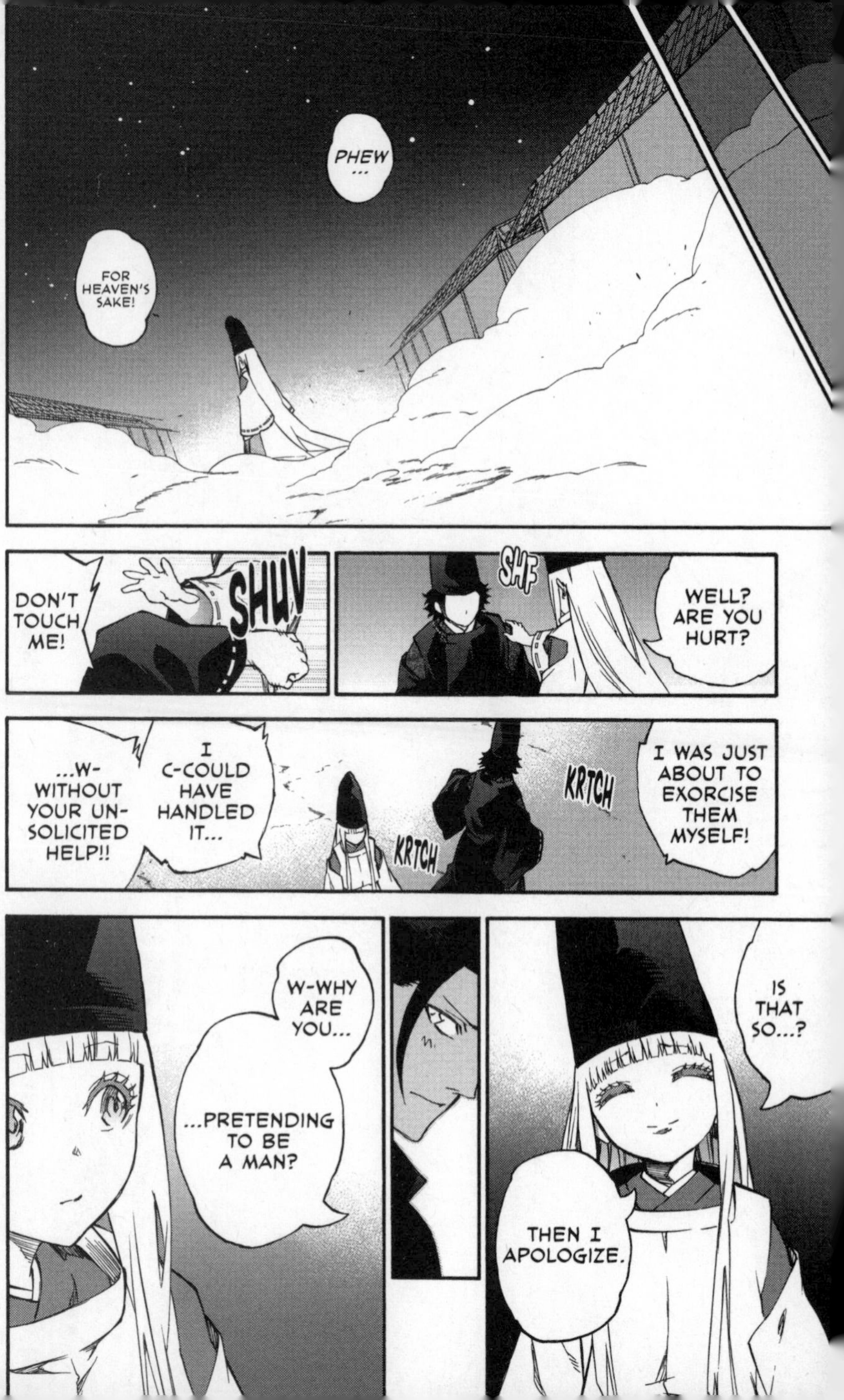
PHEW ...
FOR HEAVEN'S SAKE!
SHF
WELL? ARE YOU HURT?
DON'T TOUCH ME!
SHUV
I WAS JUST ABOUT TO EXORCISE THEM MYSELF!
KRTCH
KRTCH
I C-COULD HAVE HANDLED IT...
...W-WITHOUT YOUR UN-SOLICITED HELP!!
IS THAT SO...?
THEN I APOLOGIZE.
W-WHY ARE YOU...
...PRETENDING TO BE A MAN?

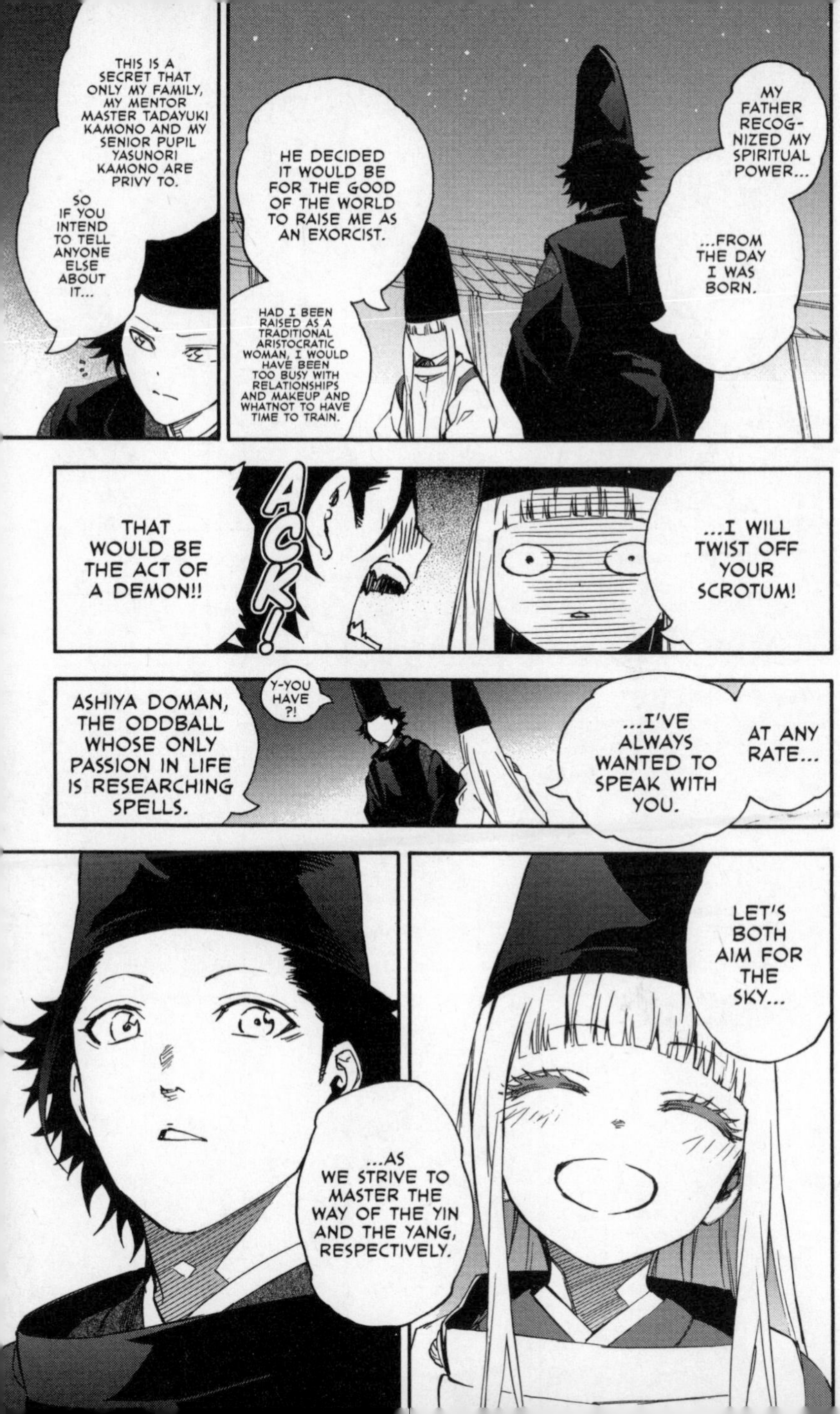
MY FATHER RECOGNIZED MY SPIRITUAL POWER...
...FROM THE DAY I WAS BORN.
HE DECIDED IT WOULD BE FOR THE GOOD OF THE WORLD TO RAISE ME AS AN EXORCIST.
HAD I BEEN RAISED AS A TRADITIONAL ARISTOCRATIC WOMAN, I WOULD HAVE BEEN TOO BUSY WITH RELATIONSHIPS AND MAKEUP AND WHATNOT TO HAVE TIME TO TRAIN.
THIS IS A SECRET THAT ONLY MY FAMILY, MY MENTOR MASTER TADAYUKI KAMONO AND MY SENIOR PUPIL YASUNORI KAMONO ARE PRIVY TO.
SO IF YOU INTEND TO TELL ANYONE ELSE ABOUT IT...
...I WILL TWIST OFF YOUR SCROTUM!
ACK!
THAT WOULD BE THE ACT OF A DEMON!!
AT ANY RATE...
...I'VE ALWAYS WANTED TO SPEAK WITH YOU.
Y-YOU HAVE ?!
ASHIYA DOMAN, THE ODDBALL WHOSE ONLY PASSION IN LIFE IS RESEARCHING SPELLS.
LET'S BOTH AIM FOR THE SKY...
...AS WE STRIVE TO MASTER THE WAY OF THE YIN AND THE YANG, RESPECTIVELY.

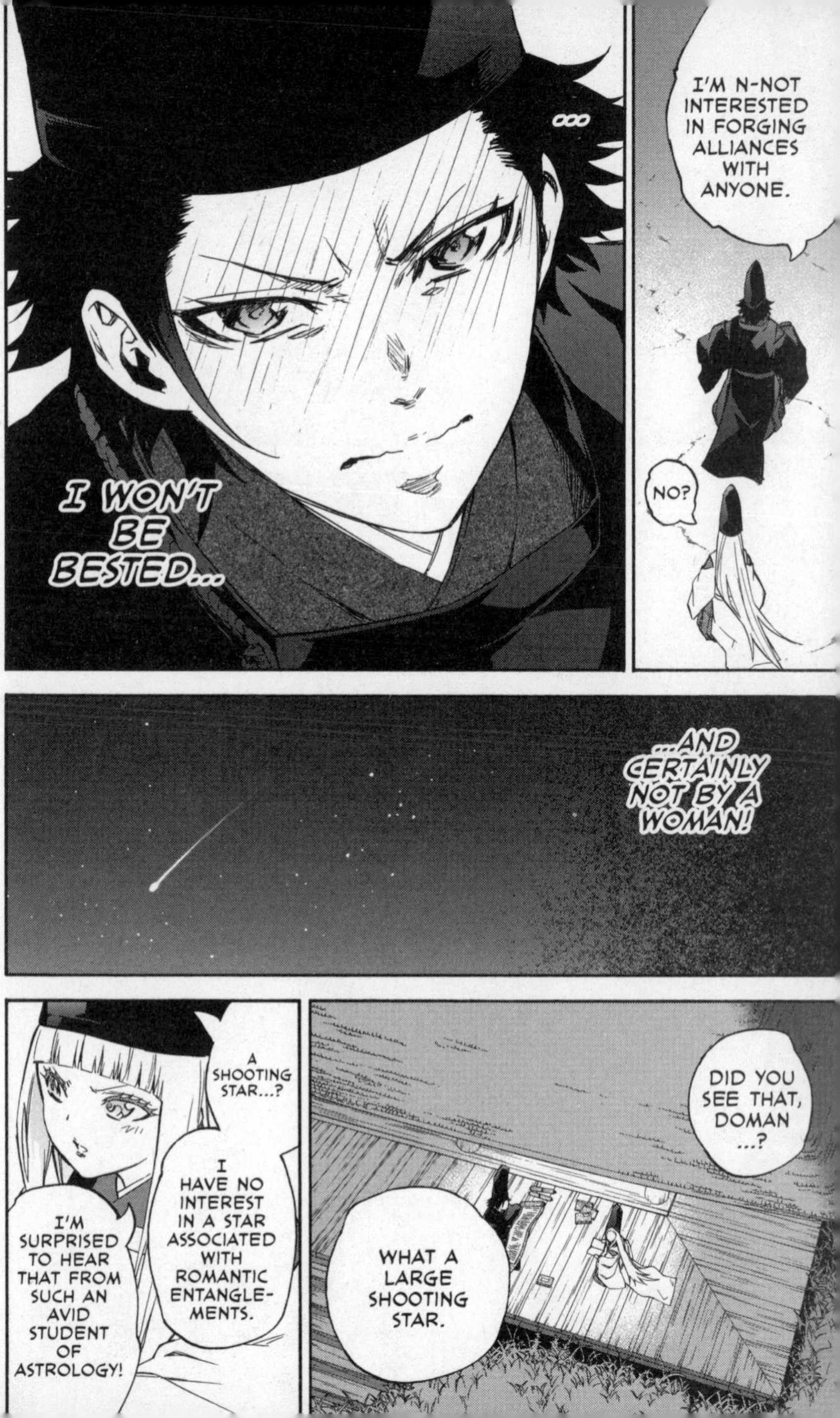
I'M N-NOT INTERESTED IN FORGING ALLIANCES WITH ANYONE.
NO?
...
I WON'T BE BESTED...
...AND CERTAINLY NOT BY A WOMAN!
DID YOU SEE THAT, DOMAN ...?
WHAT A LARGE SHOOTING STAR.
A SHOOTING STAR...?
I HAVE NO INTEREST IN A STAR ASSOCIATED WITH ROMANTIC ENTANGLE-MENTS.
I'M SURPRISED TO HEAR THAT FROM SUCH AN AVID STUDENT OF ASTROLOGY!

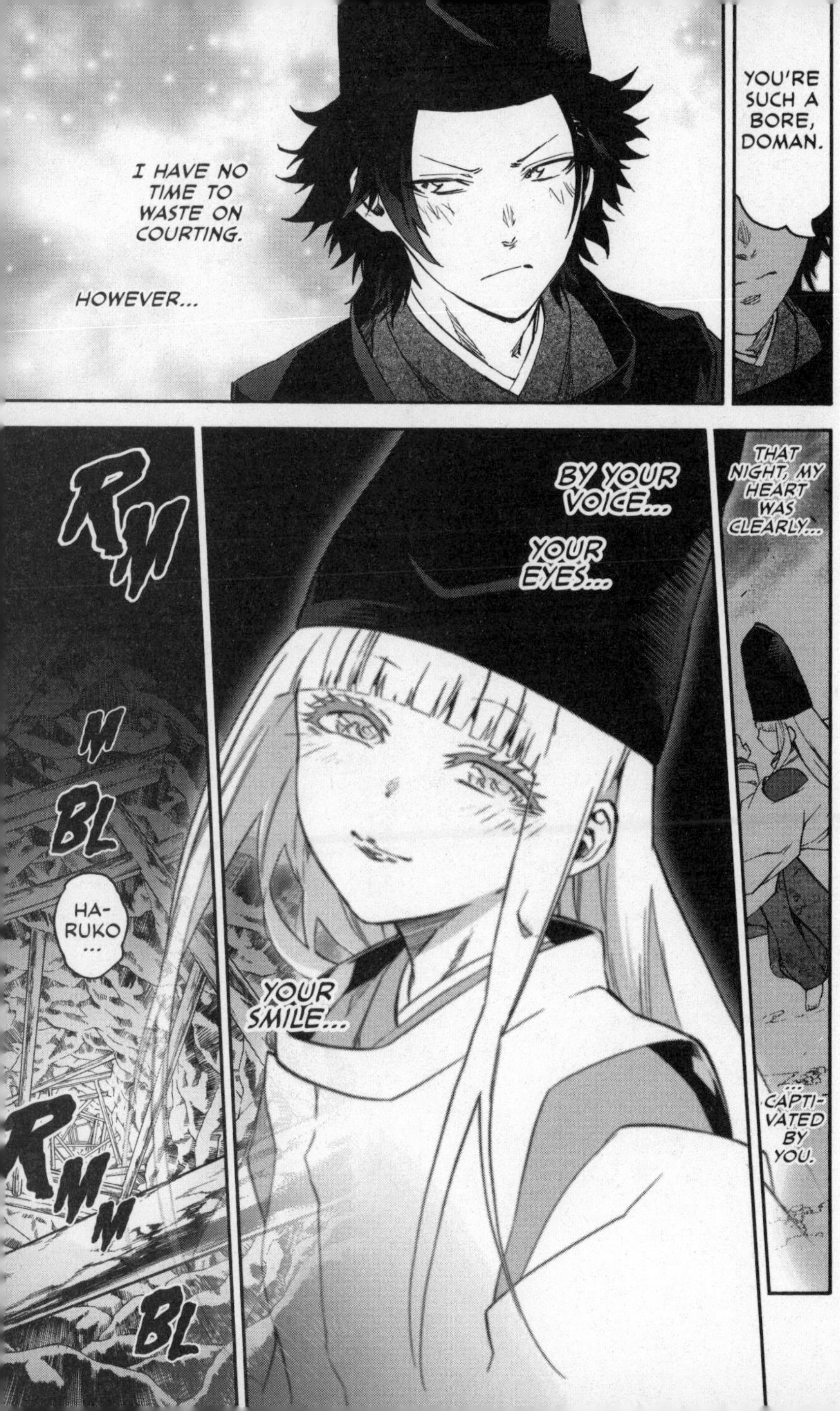
YOU'RE SUCH A BORE, DOMAN.
I HAVE NO TIME TO WASTE ON COURTING.
HOWEVER...
THAT NIGHT, MY HEART WAS CLEARLY...
...CAPTIVATED BY YOU.
BY YOUR VOICE...
YOUR EYES...
YOUR SMILE...
RMBL
HA-RUKO...
RMMBL

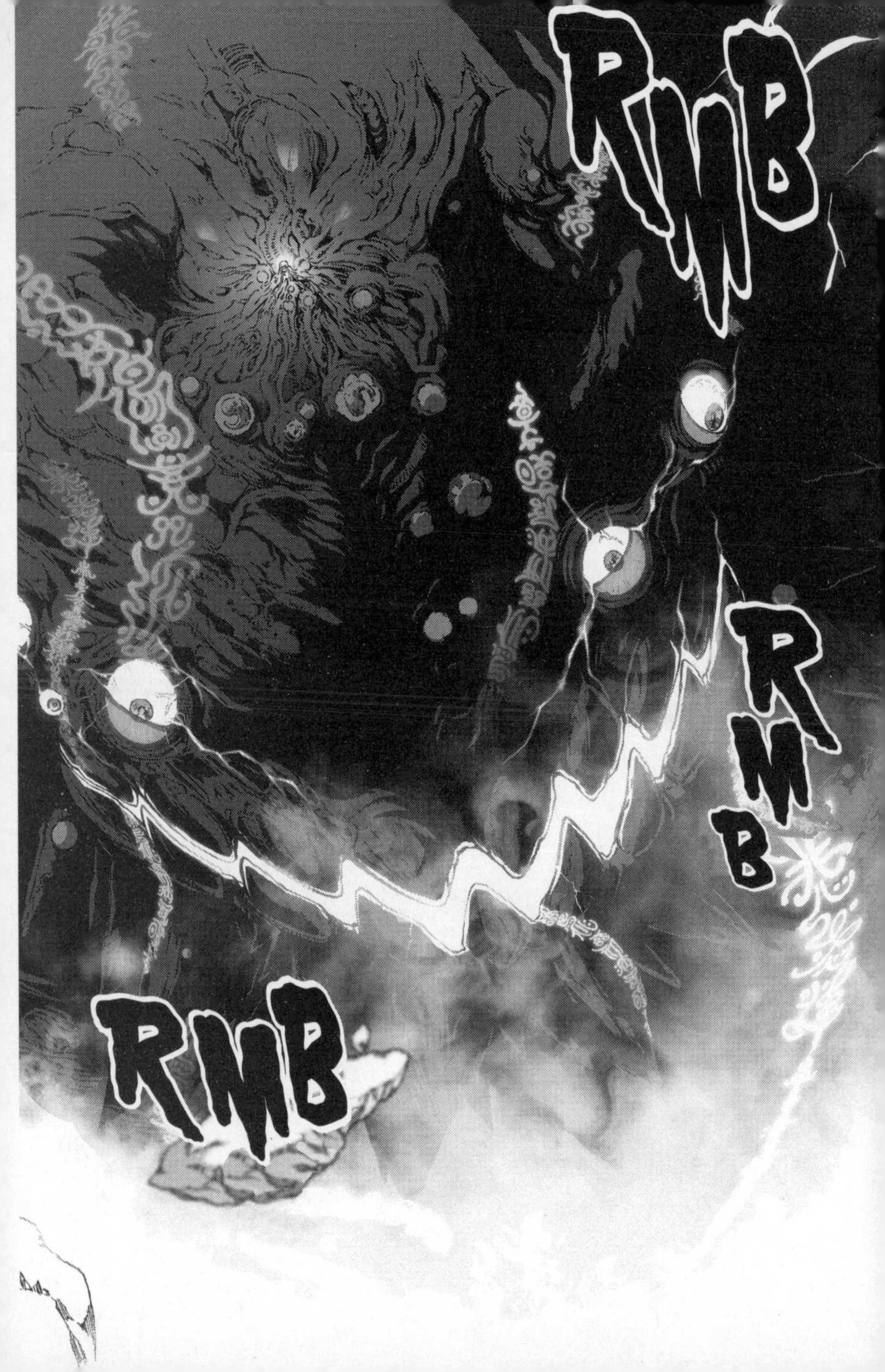
RMB
RMB
RMB

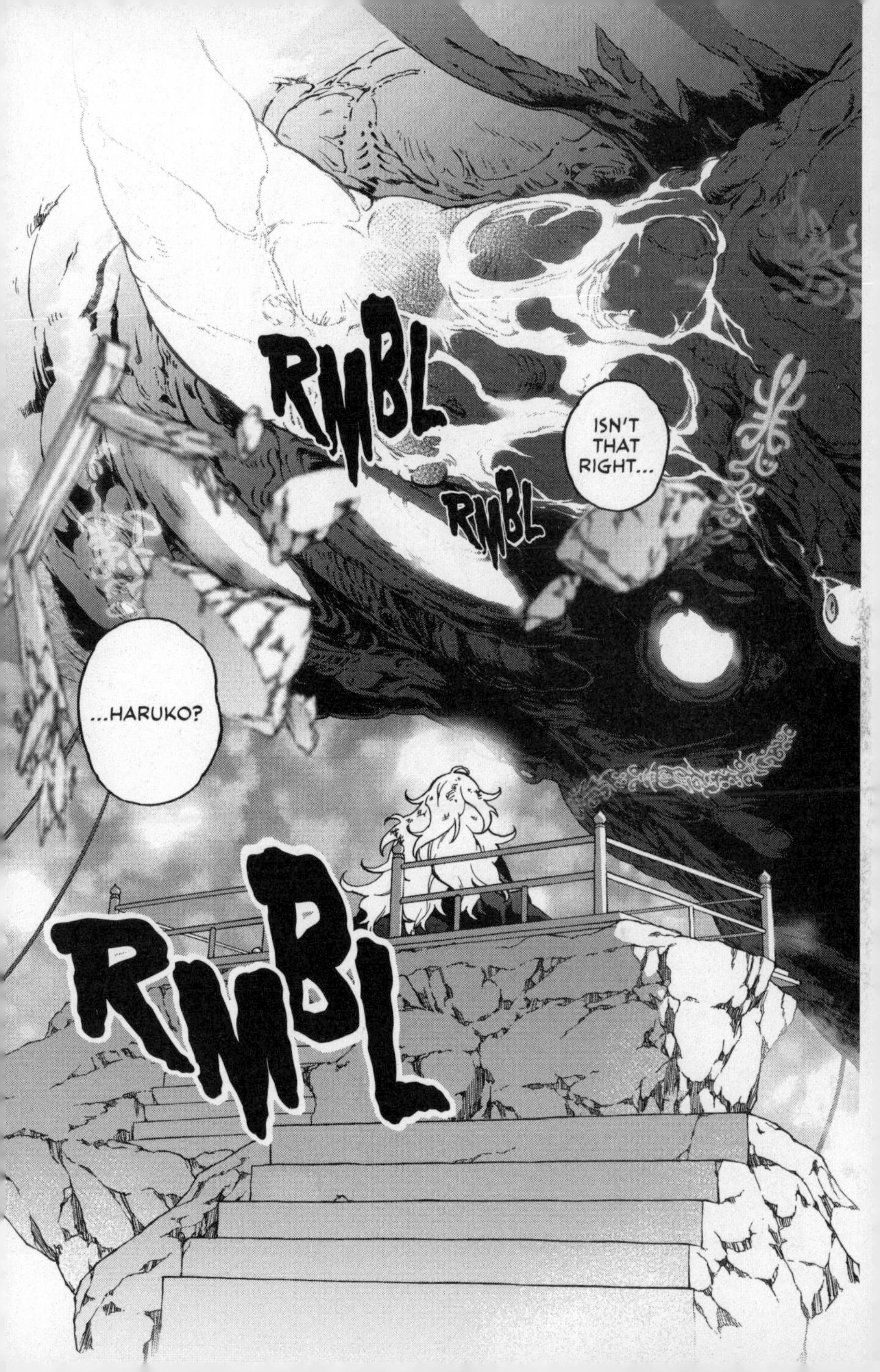
RMBL
ISN'T THAT RIGHT...
RMBL
...HARUKO?
RMBL

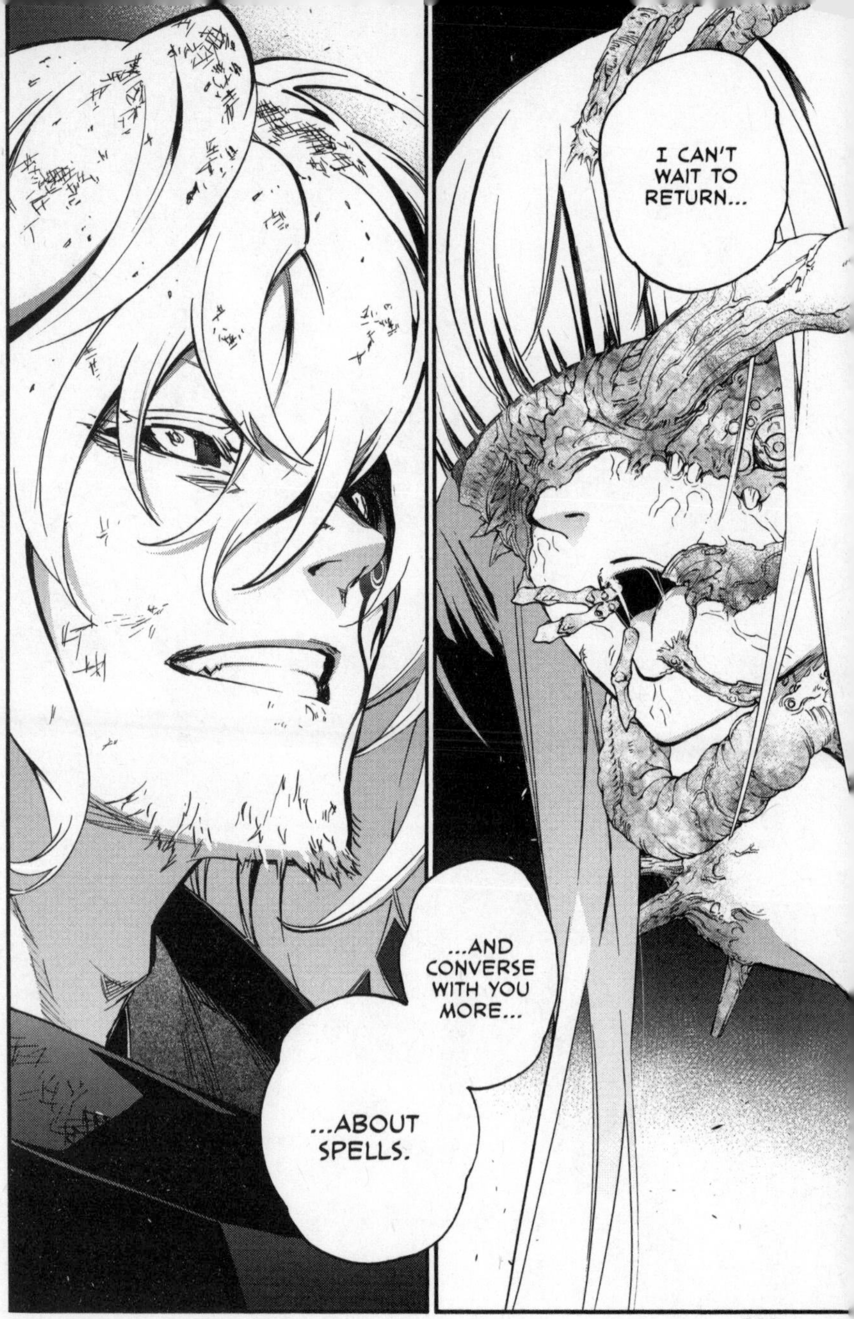
I CAN'T WAIT TO RETURN...
...AND CONVERSE WITH YOU MORE...
...ABOUT SPELLS.

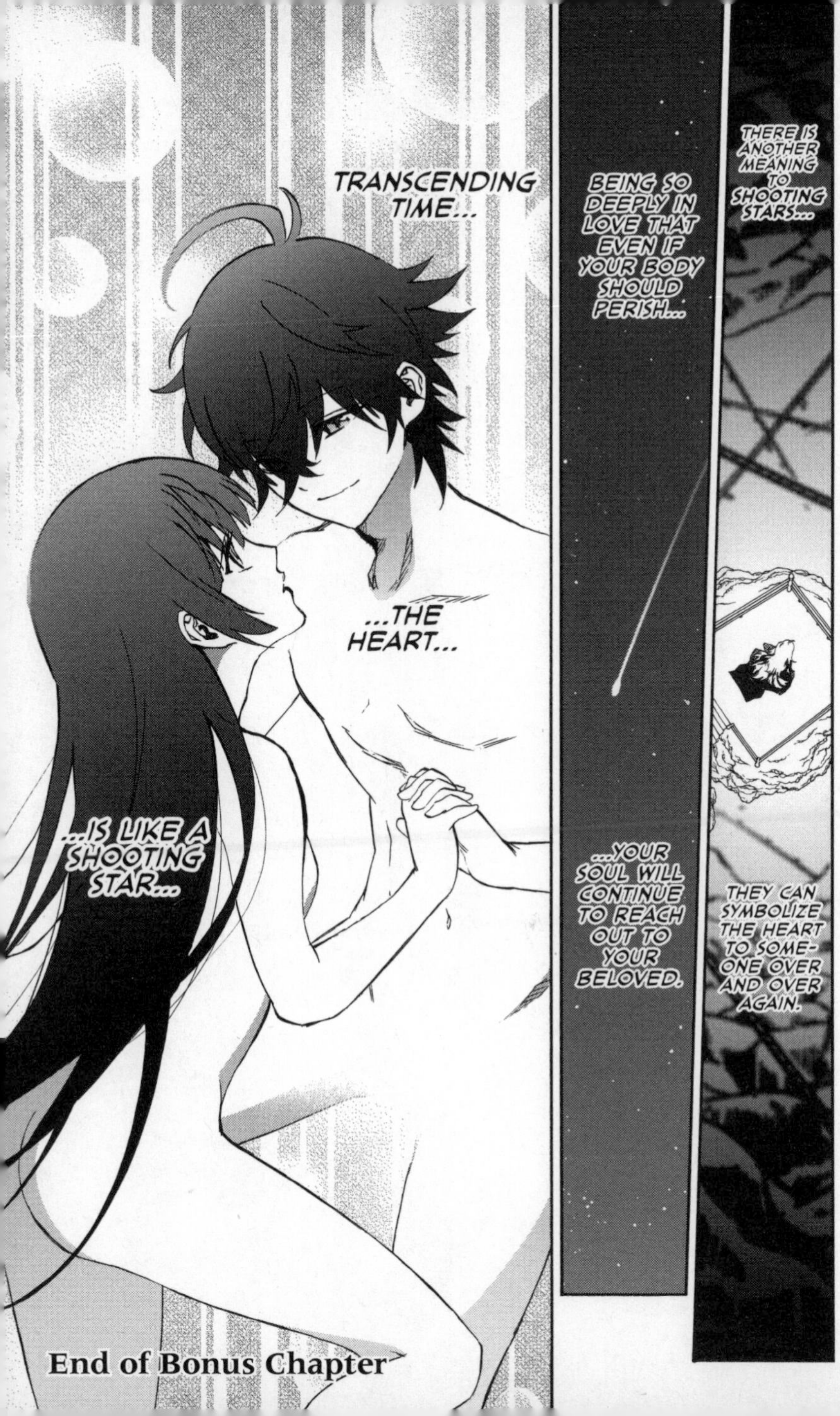
THERE IS ANOTHER MEANING TO SHOOTING STARS...
THEY CAN SYMBOLIZE THE HEART TO SOME-ONE OVER AND OVER AGAIN.
BEING SO DEEPLY IN LOVE THAT EVEN IF YOUR BODY SHOULD PERISH...
...YOUR SOUL WILL CONTINUE TO REACH OUT TO YOUR BELOVED.
TRANSCENDING TIME...
...THE HEART...
...IS LIKE A SHOOTING STAR...

End of Bonus Chapter

New Arc Costumes Prop Design

Hunting Gear (male)

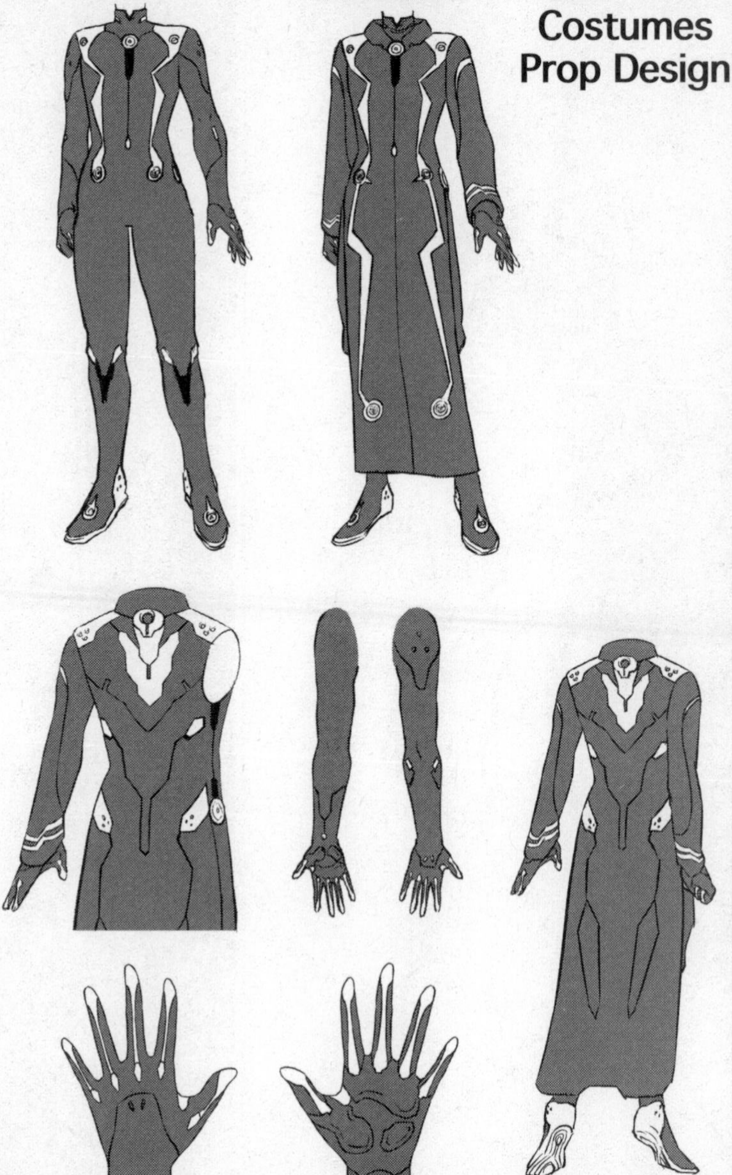

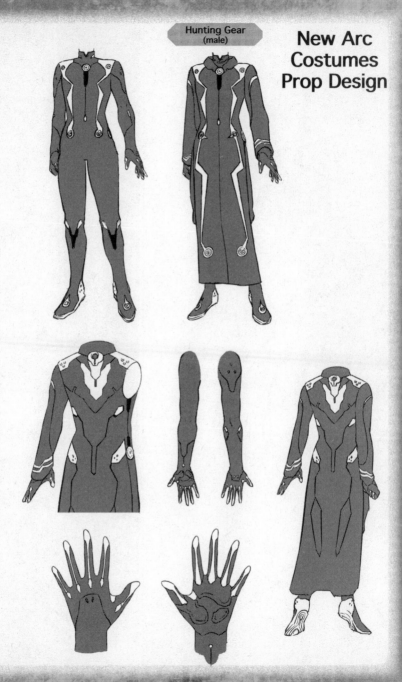

Hunting Gear (female)

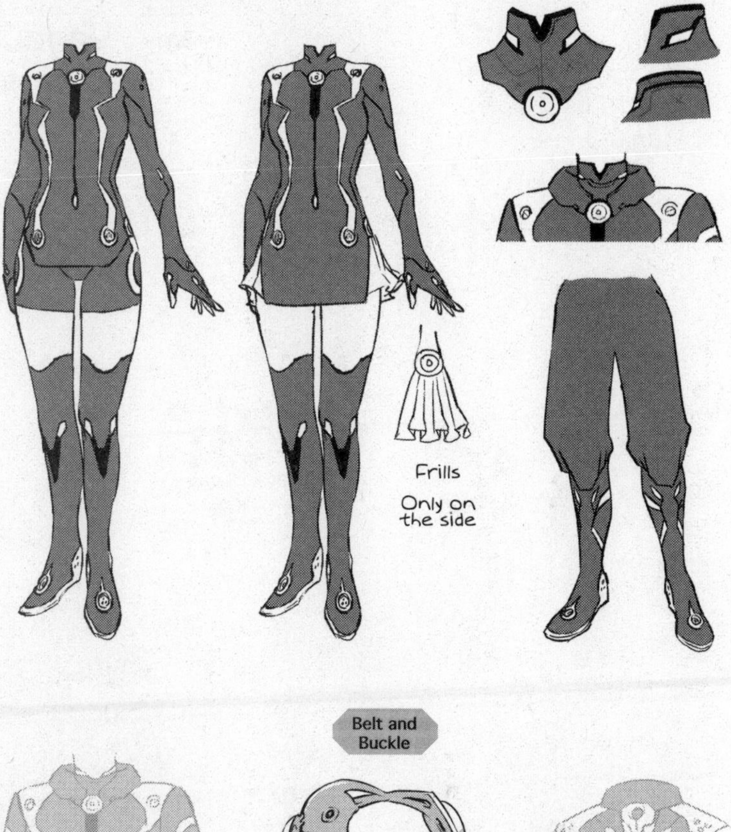
Frills
Only on the side

Belt and Buckle

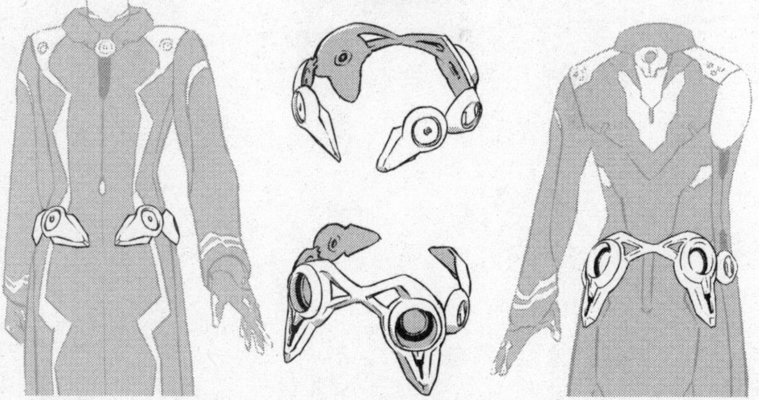

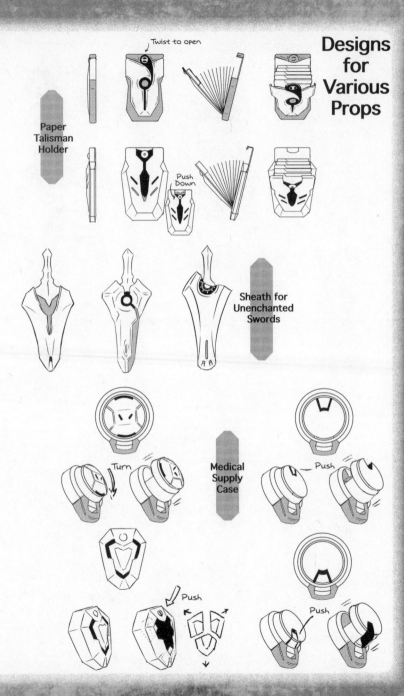

Designs for Various Props

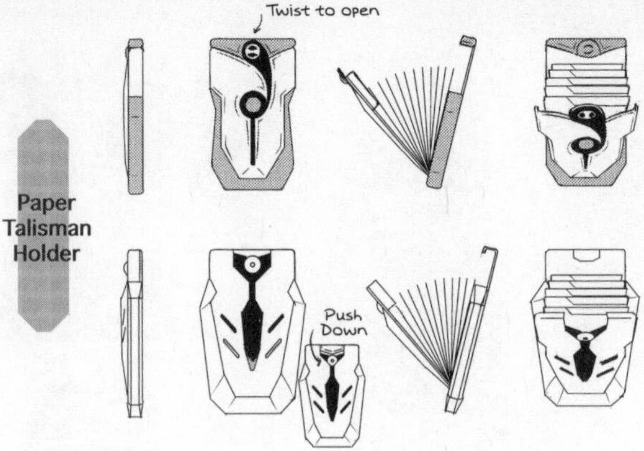
Twist to open
Paper Talisman Holder
Push Down

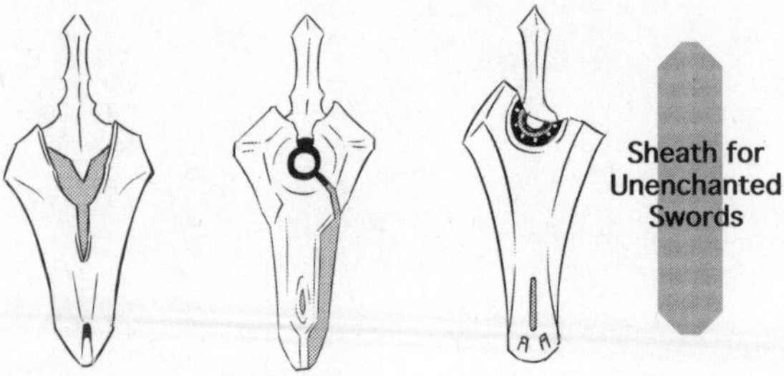
Sheath for Unenchanted Swords

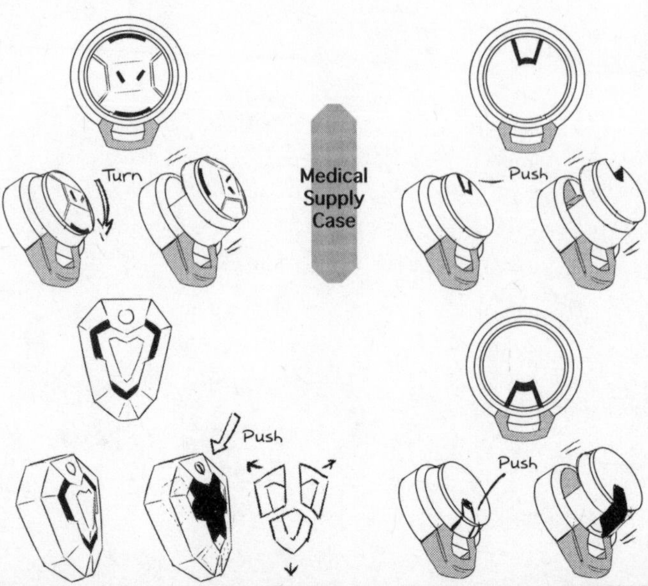
Medical Supply Case
Turn
Push
Push
Push

Rokuro and Benio's Back

Concepts for Benio's Eye Patch

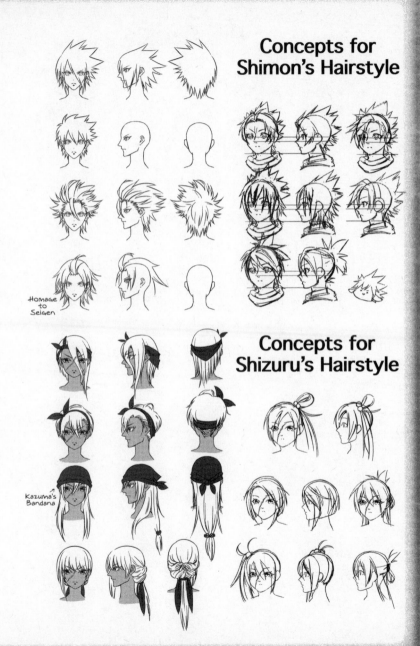

Concepts for Shimon's Hairstyle

Homage to Seigen

Concepts for Shizuru's Hairstyle

Kazuma's Bandana

Concepts for Mayura's Hairstyle

Too many...

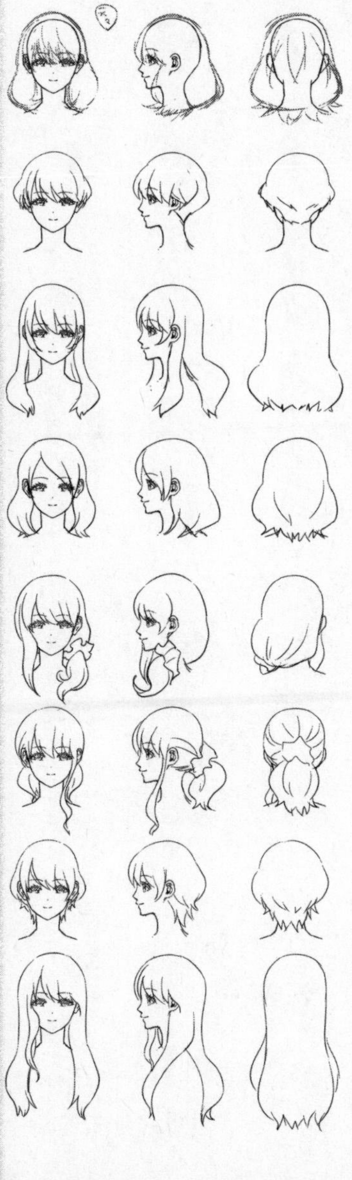

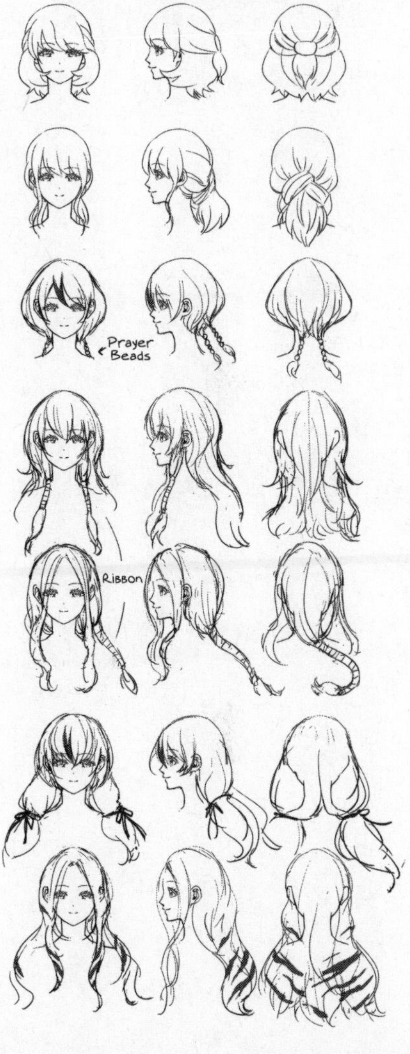
Prayer Beads
Ribbon

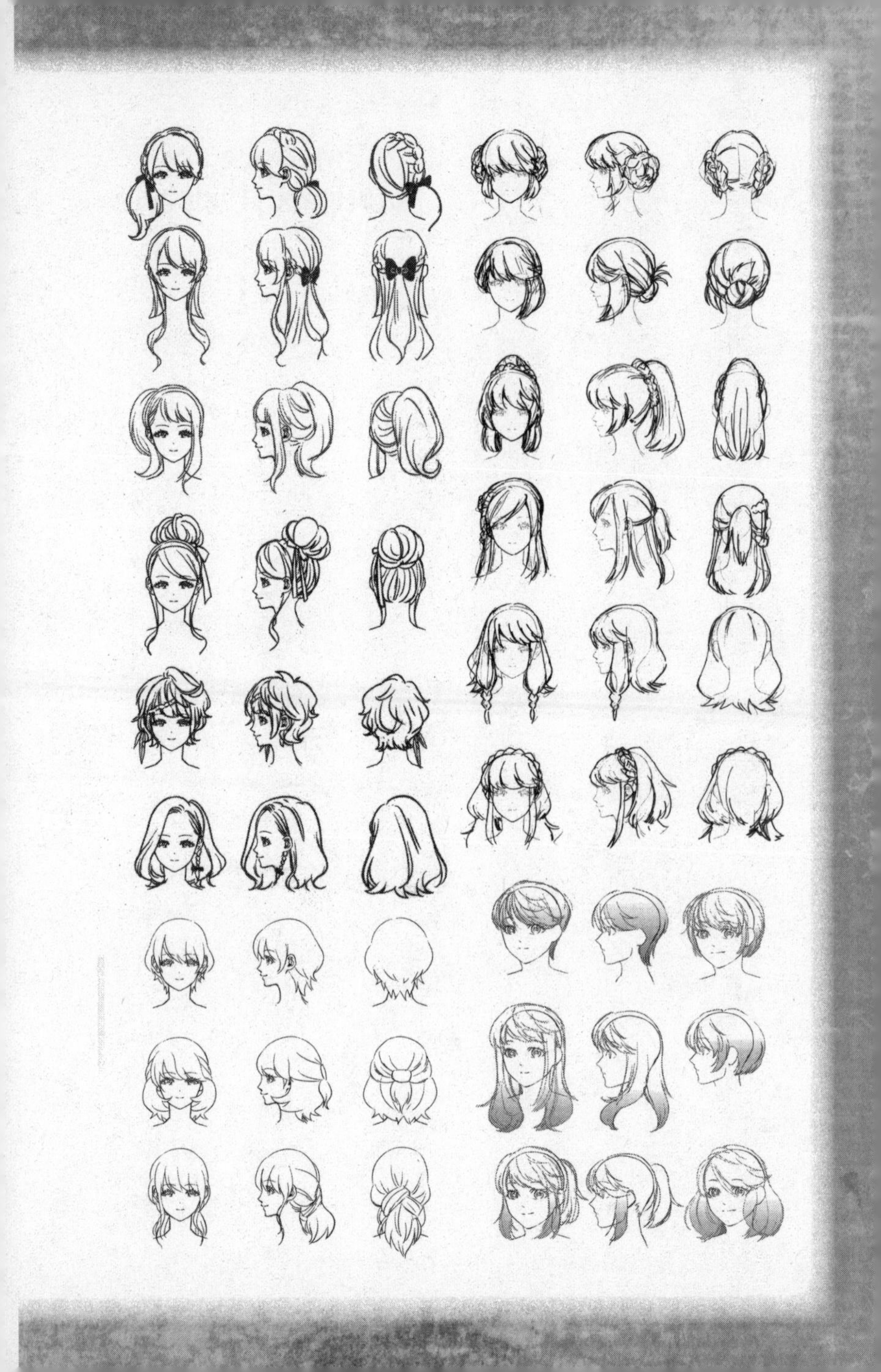

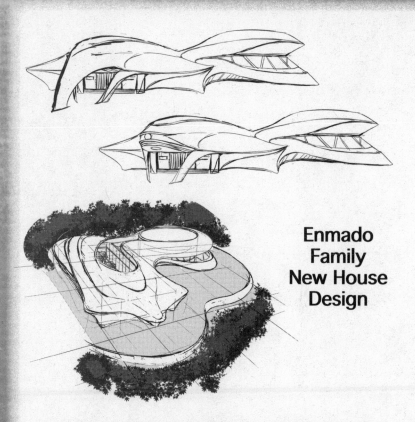

Enmado Family New House Design

STAFF

★ Artwork ★ Takumi Kikuta / koppy
　　　　　　Yukiya Yamazaki / Takumi Kaba /
　　　　　　Natsuki Ise
　　　　　　Yoshiaki Sukeno

★ Editor ★ Ryota Kasai
★ Graphic Novel Editor ★ Naomi Maehara
★ Graphic Novel Design ★ Tatsuo Ishino (Freiheit)

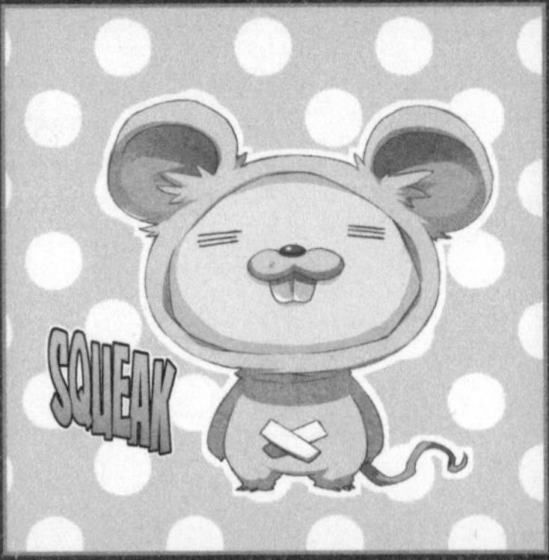
SQUEAK

Just as the first chapter of this new story arc was beginning, I started working on a short manga series for a different publisher's magazine. It was meant to be a comic relief series as a mood-stabilizing drug of sorts for me since the *Twin Star* series is quite intense...which means there's a possibility that *Twin Star* will become even more intense, I guess?

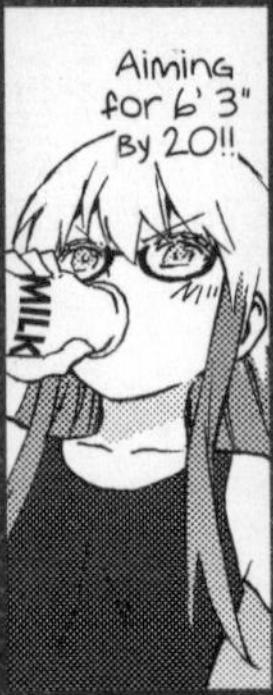
Aiming for 6' 3" By 20!!
MILK

YOSHIAKI SUKENO was born July 23, 1981, in Wakayama, Japan. He graduated from Kyoto Seika University, where he studied manga. In 2006, he won the Tezuka Award for Best Newcomer Shonen Manga Artist. In 2008, he began his previous work, the supernatural comedy *Binbougami ga!*, which was adapted into the anime *Good Luck Girl!* in 2012.

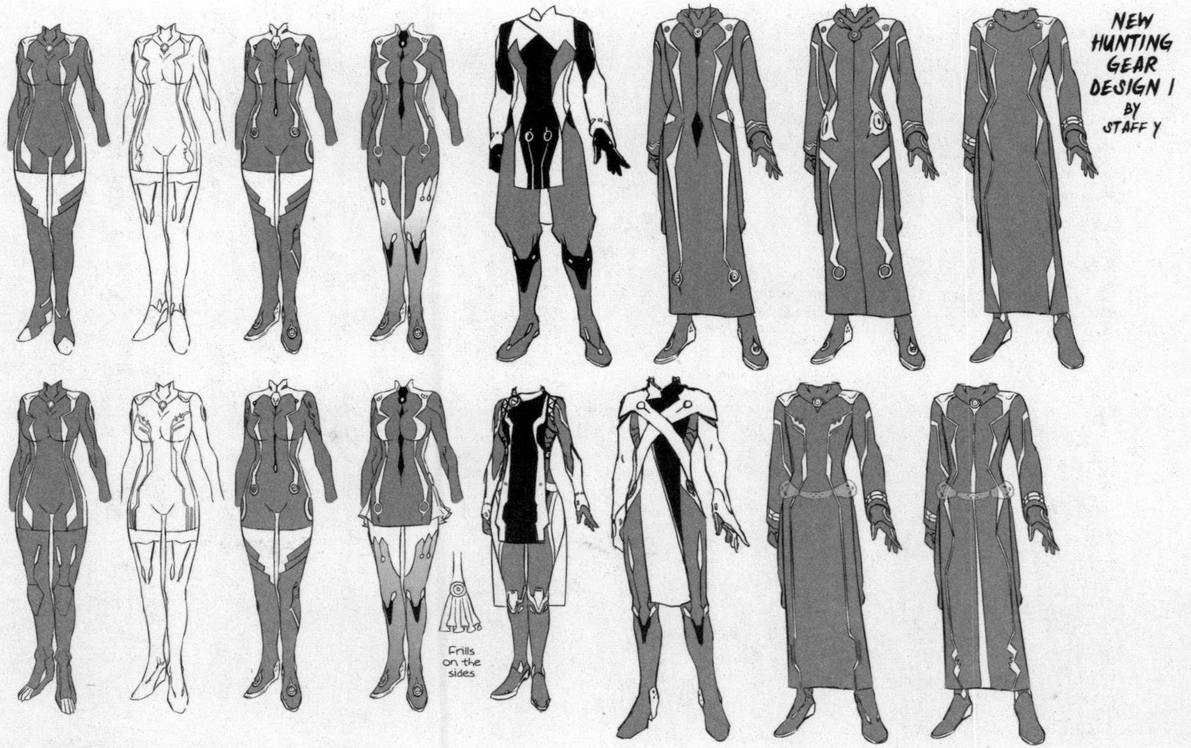
NEW HUNTING GEAR DESIGN 1 BY STAFF Y
Frills on the sides

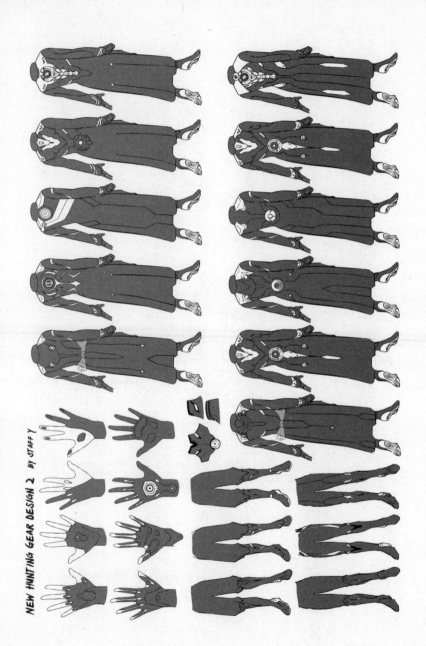

NEW HUNTING GEAR DESIGN 2 BY STAFF Y

—SHONEN JUMP Manga Edition—

STORY & ART **Yoshiaki Sukeno**

TRANSLATION · **Tetsuichiro Miyaki**
ENGLISH ADAPTATION **Annette Roman**
TOUCH-UP ART & LETTERING **Steve Dutro**
DESIGN **Shawn Carrico**
EDITOR **Annette Roman**

SOUSEI NO ONMYOJI © 2013 by Yoshiaki Sukeno
All rights reserved.
First published in Japan in 2013 by SHUEISHA Inc., Tokyo.
English translation rights arranged by SHUEISHA Inc.

The stories, characters and incidents mentioned in this
publication are entirely fictional.

Printed in the U.S.A.

Published by VIZ Media, LLC
P.O. Box 77010
San Francisco, CA 94107

10 9 8 7 6 5 4 3 2 1
First printing, March 2021

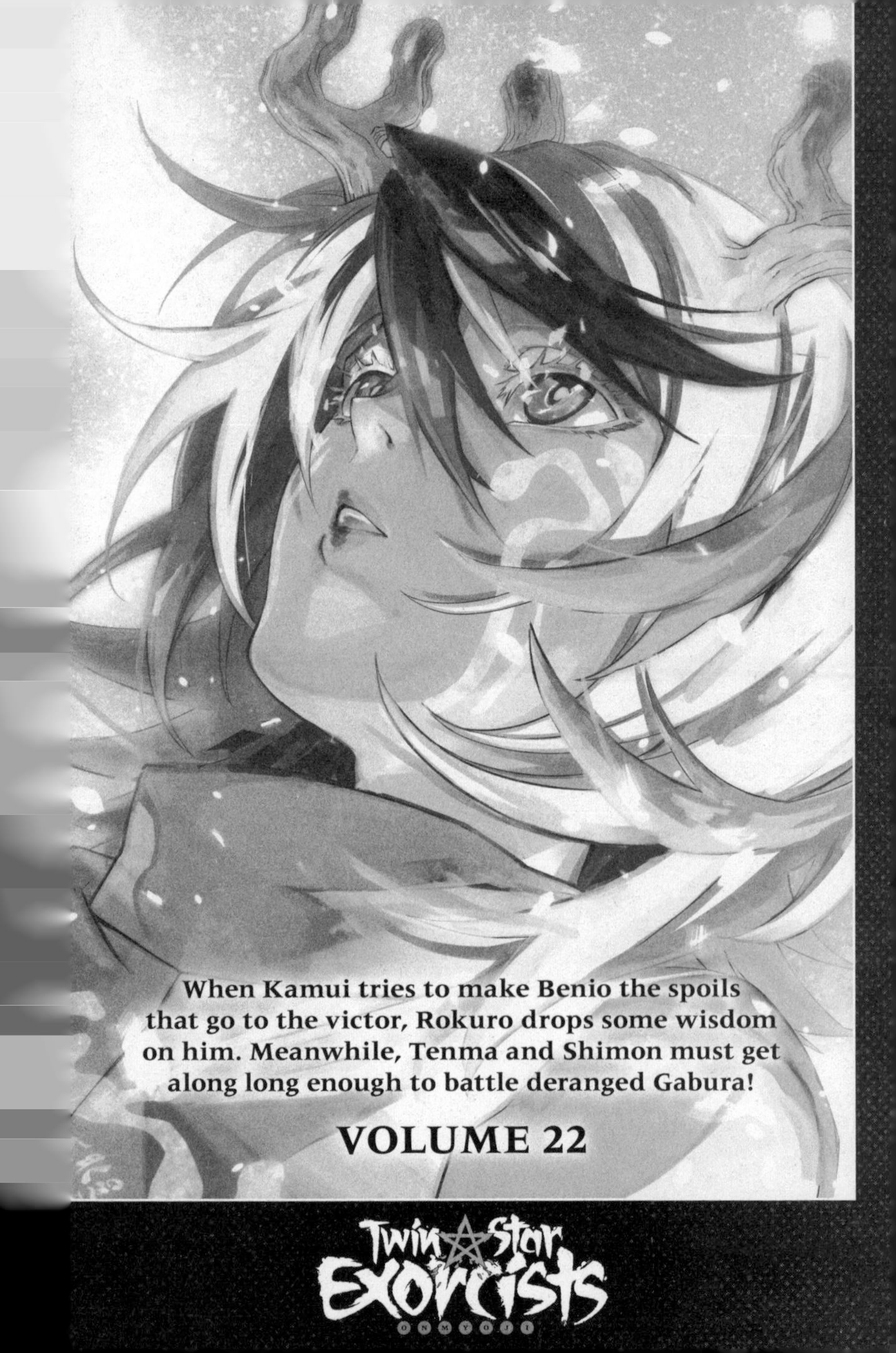
When Kamui tries to make Benio the spoils that go to the victor, Rokuro drops some wisdom on him. Meanwhile, Tenma and Shimon must get along long enough to battle deranged Gabura!
VOLUME 22

Twin Star Exorcists
ONMYOJI

ASSASSINATION
CLASSROOM

COMPLETE BOX SET

STORY AND ART BY YUSEI MATSUI

The complete bestselling *Assassination Classroom* series is now available in a boldly designed, value–priced box set!

- Includes all 21 volumes of this unique tale of a mysterious, smiley–faced, tentacled, superpowered teacher who guides a group of misfit students to find themselves—while doing their best to assassinate him.

- Also includes an exclusive, full–color, mini "yearbook" filled with images of favorite characters in different art styles and contexts (previously unreleased in the English editions).

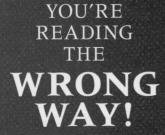

YOU'RE READING THE **WRONG WAY!**

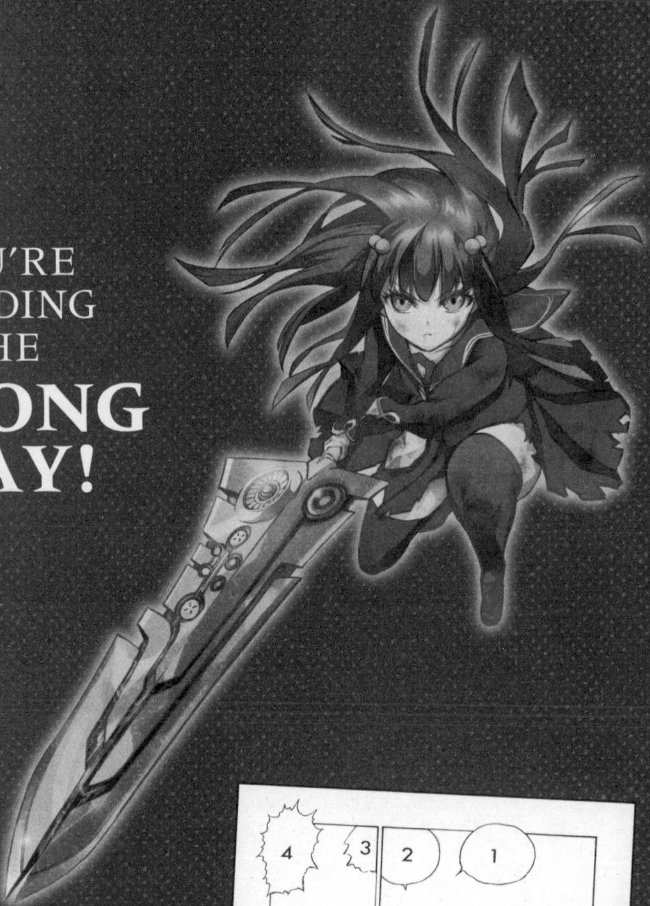

Twin Star Exorcists reads from right to left, starting in the upper-right corner. Japanese is read from right to left, meaning that action, sound effects and word-balloon order are completely reversed from English order.

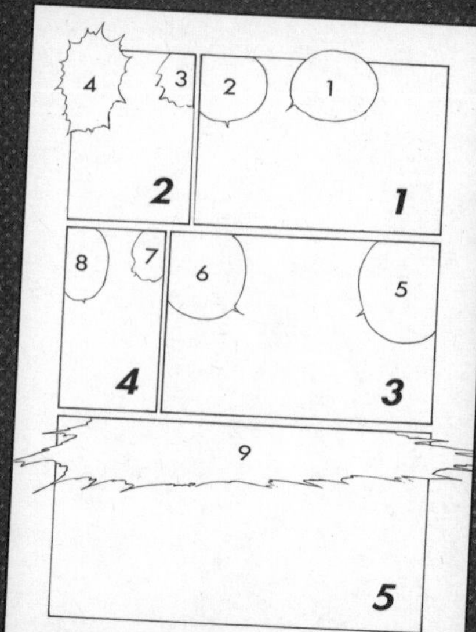

1
2
1
3
4
2
5
6
3
7
8
4
9
5
142